Me & My Brothers

Volume 4
Hari Tokeino

TOKYOPOP®

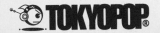

HAMBURG // LONDON // LOS ANGELES // TOKYO

Contents

EPISODE 15............................3

EPISODE 16.........................35

EPISODE 17.........................65

EPISODE 18.........................97

EPISODE 19........................127

HOW TO GO THROUGH THE SECRET DOOR.............159

BONUS PAGE.......................................191

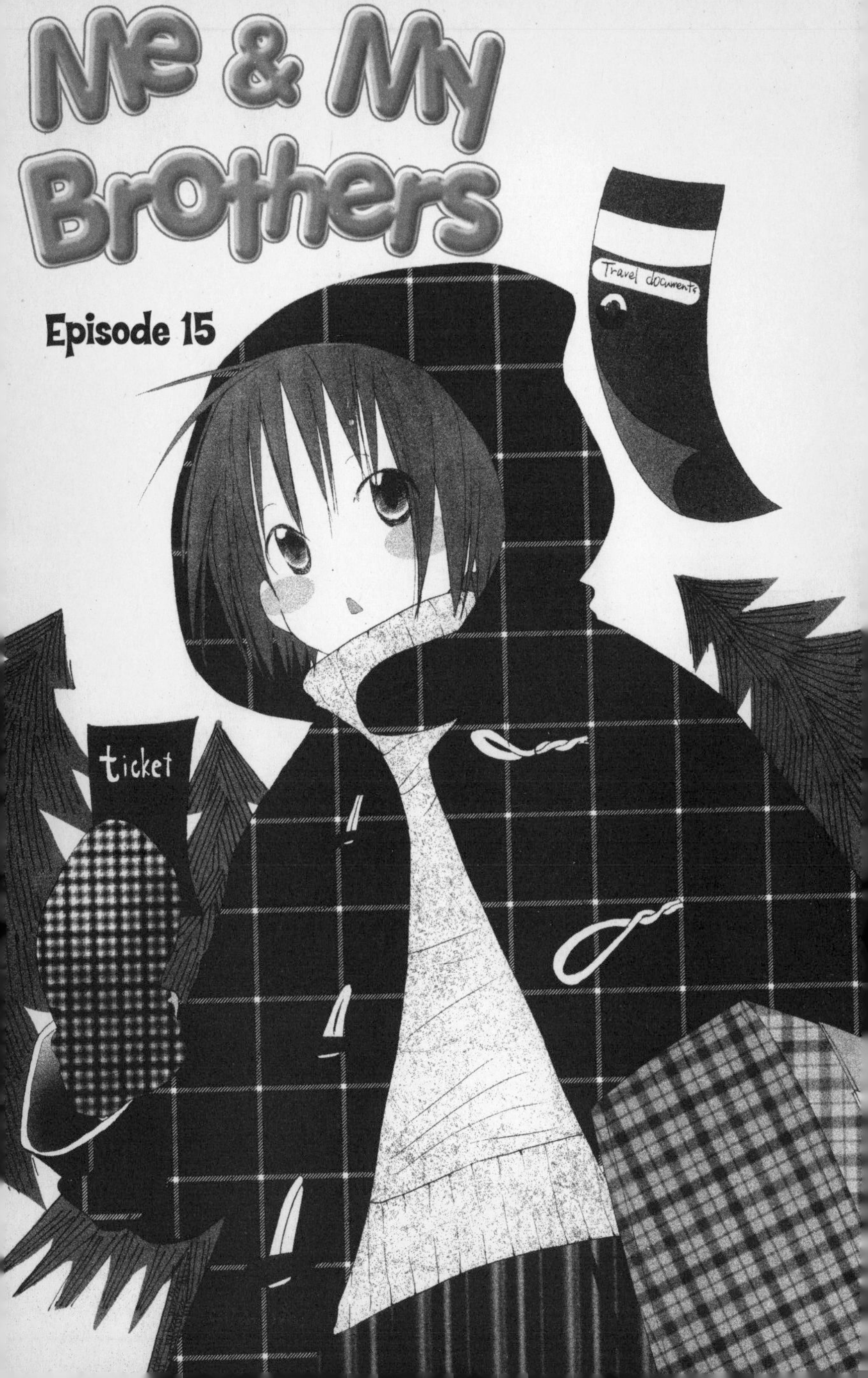
Me & My Brothers
Episode 15
Travel documents
ticket

ME & MY BROTHERS

🍓 **SAKURA MIYASHITA:**
THE YOUNGEST. IN 8TH GRADE. THE ONLY GIRL IN THE MIYASHITA FAMILY. SHE IS NOT BLOOD RELATED TO HER FOUR BROTHERS.

🍓 **MASASHI MIYASHITA:**
THE ELDEST. ROMANCE NOVELIST. ACCORDING TO HIM, HE SOUNDS LIKE A WOMAN BECAUSE OF HIS JOB. HE'S THE LEADER OF THE FOUR SAKURA-SPOILERS.

🍓 **TAKASHI MIYASHITA:**
THE 2ND BROTHER. TEACHER. HE TEACHES JAPANESE AT SAKURA'S SCHOOL. HE'S A GENTLEMAN.

🍓 **TSUYOSHI MIYASHITA:**
THE 3RD BROTHER. FULL-TIME PART-TIMER. HE HAS A DIRTY MOUTH BUT IS ACTUALLY SHY.

🍓 **TAKESHI MIYASHITA:**
THE 4TH BROTHER. IN 11TH GRADE. HE LOOKS OLD, BUT HE'S THE YOUNGEST OF FOUR BROTHERS. HE'S QUIET AND LOVES PLANTS.

🍓 **NAKA-CHAN:**
SAKURA'S BEST FRIEND. HER FAMILY NAME IS TANAKA. A CHEERFUL GIRL.

🍓 **SUZUKI-KUN:**
SAKURA'S CLASSMATE. DOES HE HAVE A CRUSH ON SAKURA?

STORY

SAKURA LOST HER PARENTS WHEN SHE WAS 3 AND WAS RAISED BY HER GRANDMOTHER. THEN, WHEN SAKURA TURNED 14, HER GRANDMOTHER PASSED AWAY. SHE WAS ALL ALONE UNTIL FOUR STEPBROTHERS SHOWED UP! THE STEPBROTHERS ARE FROM SAKURA'S FATHER'S FIRST MARRIAGE. WHILE HER STEPBROTHERS' FATHER HAD RAISED SAKURA AS HIS OWN, SAKURA'S BIRTH FATHER IS ACTUALLY HER MOTHER'S EX-BOYFRIEND. EVEN THOUGH THE BROTHERS HAVE NO BLOOD CONNECTION TO SAKURA, AFTER 11 YEARS OF SEPARATION, THEY STARTED TO LIVE TOGETHER! NOW THEIR HOUSE IS LIVELY EVERYDAY...★

▷PLEASE READ ME & MY BROTHERS VOLUME 1-3 FOR MORE DETAILS!

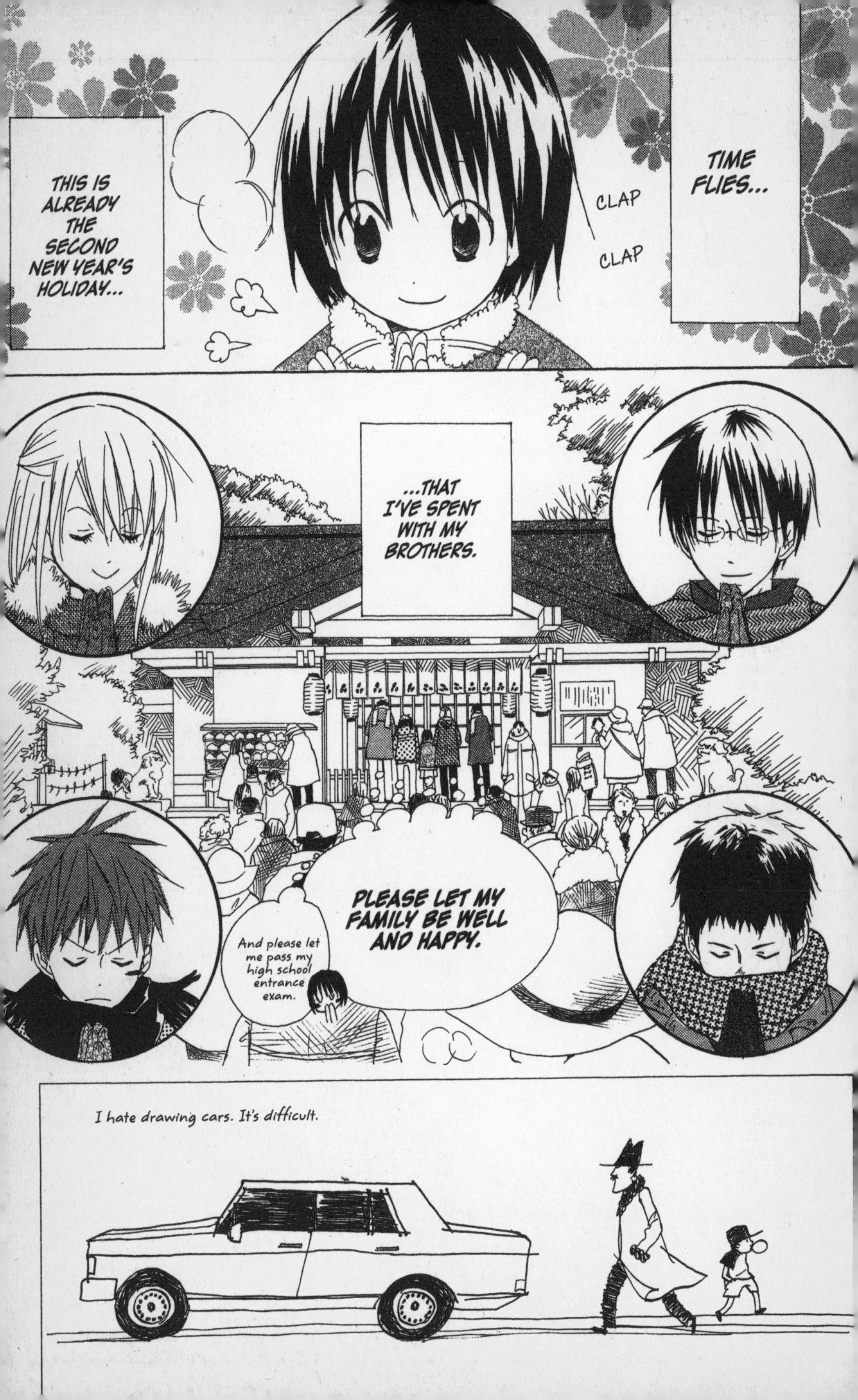
TIME FLIES...
CLAP
CLAP
THIS IS ALREADY THE SECOND NEW YEAR'S HOLIDAY...
...THAT I'VE SPENT WITH MY BROTHERS.
PLEASE LET MY FAMILY BE WELL AND HAPPY.
And please let me pass my high school entrance exam.
I hate drawing cars. It's difficult.

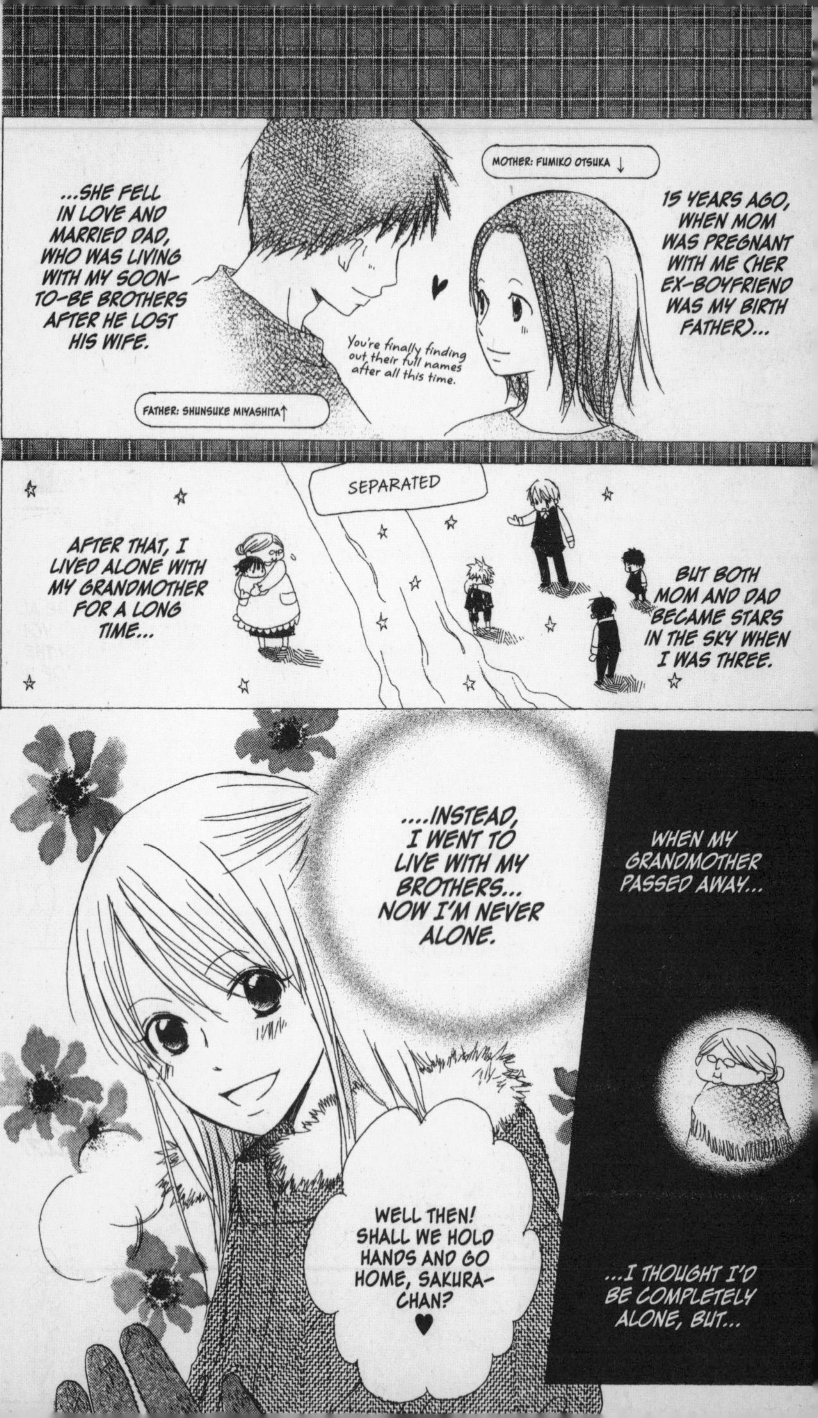
15 YEARS AGO, WHEN MOM WAS PREGNANT WITH ME (HER EX-BOYFRIEND WAS MY BIRTH FATHER)...
MOTHER: FUMIKO OTSUKA ↓
You're finally finding out their full names after all this time.
...SHE FELL IN LOVE AND MARRIED DAD, WHO WAS LIVING WITH MY SOON-TO-BE BROTHERS AFTER HE LOST HIS WIFE.
FATHER: SHUNSUKE MIYASHITA ↑
BUT BOTH MOM AND DAD BECAME STARS IN THE SKY WHEN I WAS THREE.
SEPARATED
AFTER THAT, I LIVED ALONE WITH MY GRANDMOTHER FOR A LONG TIME...
WHEN MY GRANDMOTHER PASSED AWAY...
...I THOUGHT I'D BE COMPLETELY ALONE, BUT...
....INSTEAD, I WENT TO LIVE WITH MY BROTHERS... NOW I'M NEVER ALONE.
WELL THEN! SHALL WE HOLD HANDS AND GO HOME, SAKURA-CHAN? ♥

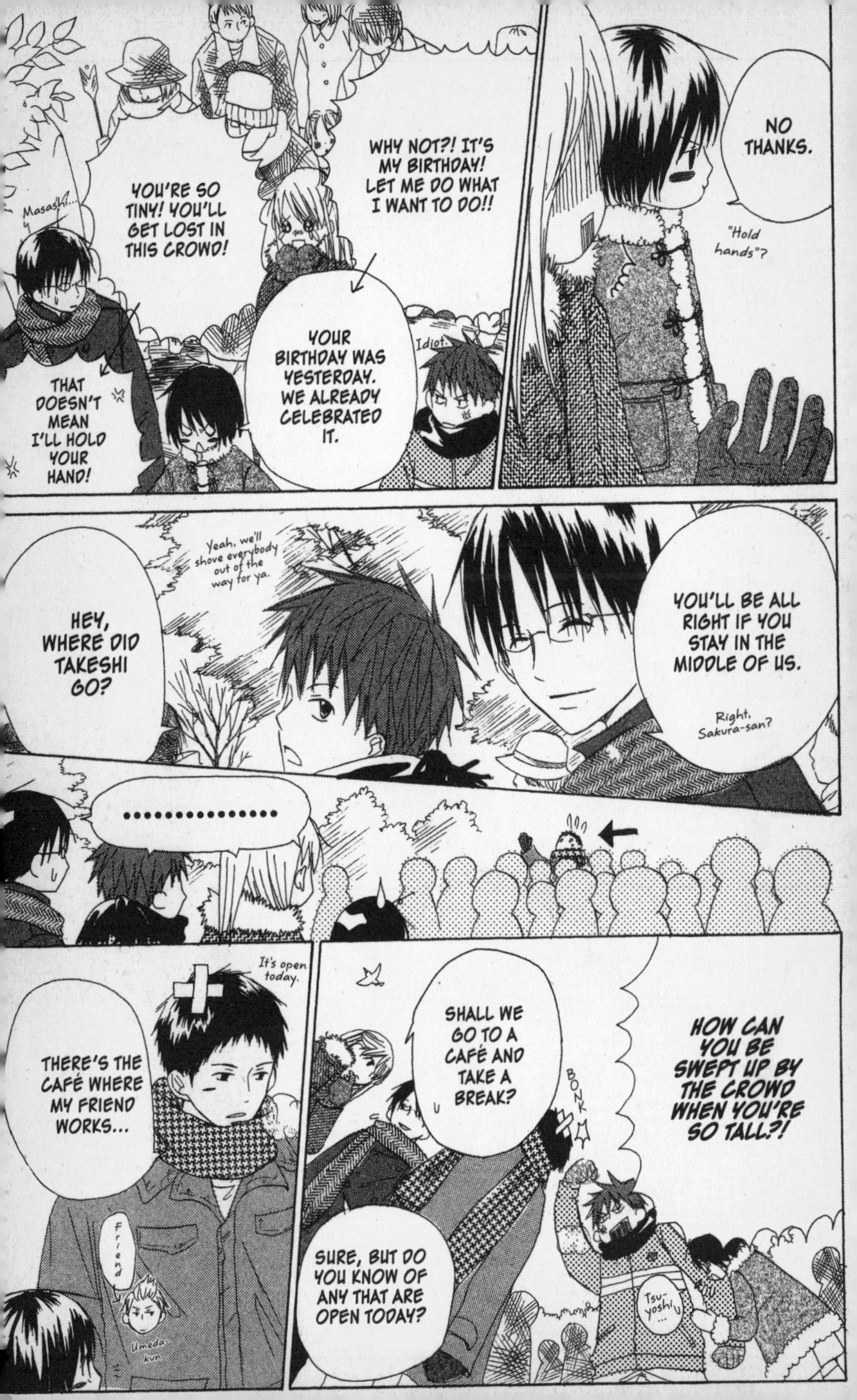
NO THANKS.
"Hold hands"?
WHY NOT?! IT'S MY BIRTHDAY! LET ME DO WHAT I WANT TO DO!!
YOUR BIRTHDAY WAS YESTERDAY. WE ALREADY CELEBRATED IT.
Idiot.
YOU'RE SO TINY! YOU'LL GET LOST IN THIS CROWD!
Masashi...
THAT DOESN'T MEAN I'LL HOLD YOUR HAND!
YOU'LL BE ALL RIGHT IF YOU STAY IN THE MIDDLE OF US.
Right, Sakura-san?
Yeah, we'll shove everybody out of the way for ya.
HEY, WHERE DID TAKESHI GO?
....
HOW CAN YOU BE SWEPT UP BY THE CROWD WHEN YOU'RE SO TALL?!
SHALL WE GO TO A CAFÉ AND TAKE A BREAK?
BONK
SURE, BUT DO YOU KNOW OF ANY THAT ARE OPEN TODAY?
Tsuyoshi...
It's open today.
THERE'S THE CAFÉ WHERE MY FRIEND WORKS...
Friend
Umeda-kun

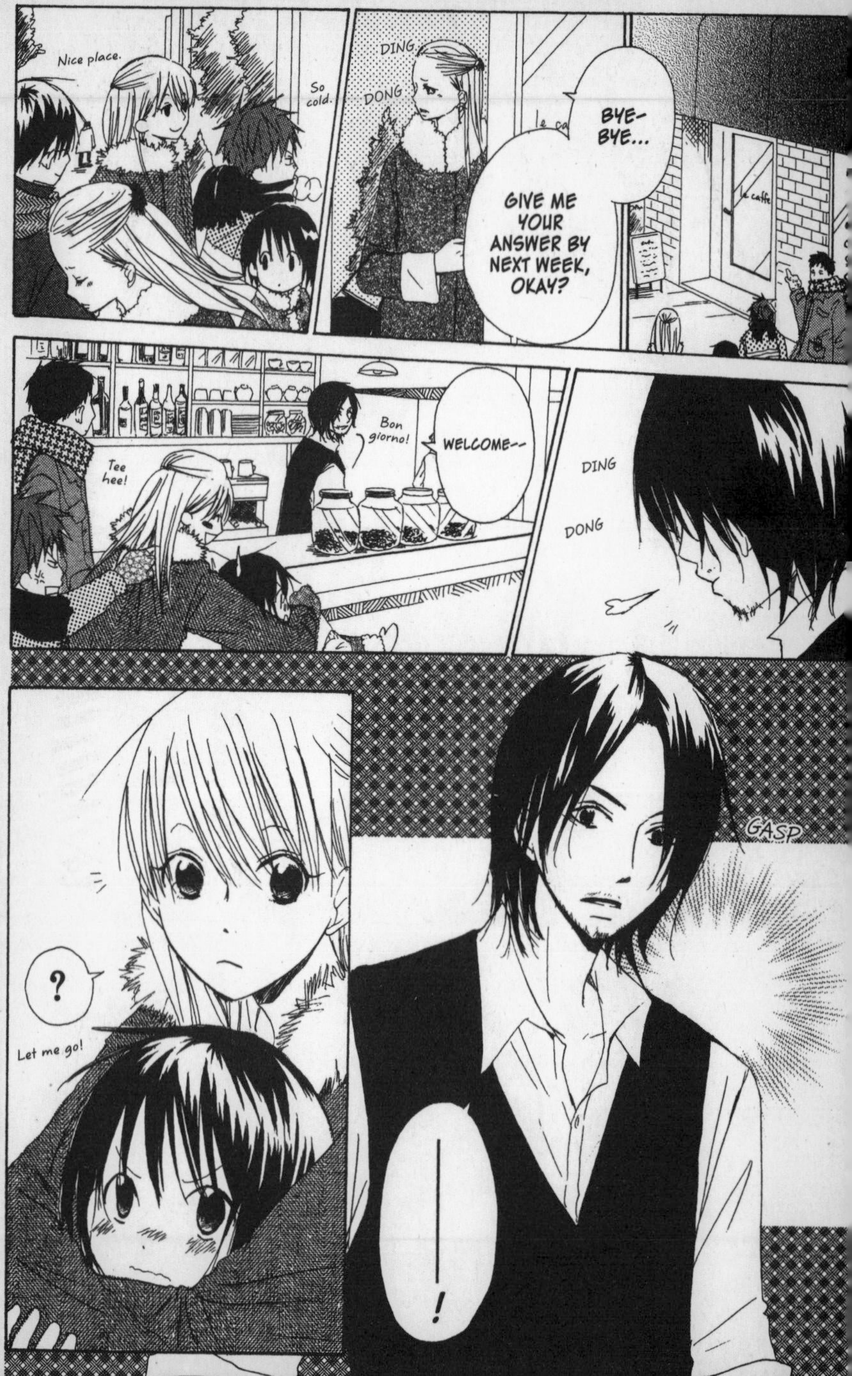
le caffe
DING
DONG
BYE-BYE...
GIVE ME YOUR ANSWER BY NEXT WEEK, OKAY?
So cold.
Nice place.
DING
DONG
WELCOME--
Bon giorno!
Tee hee!
GASP
!
?
Let me go!

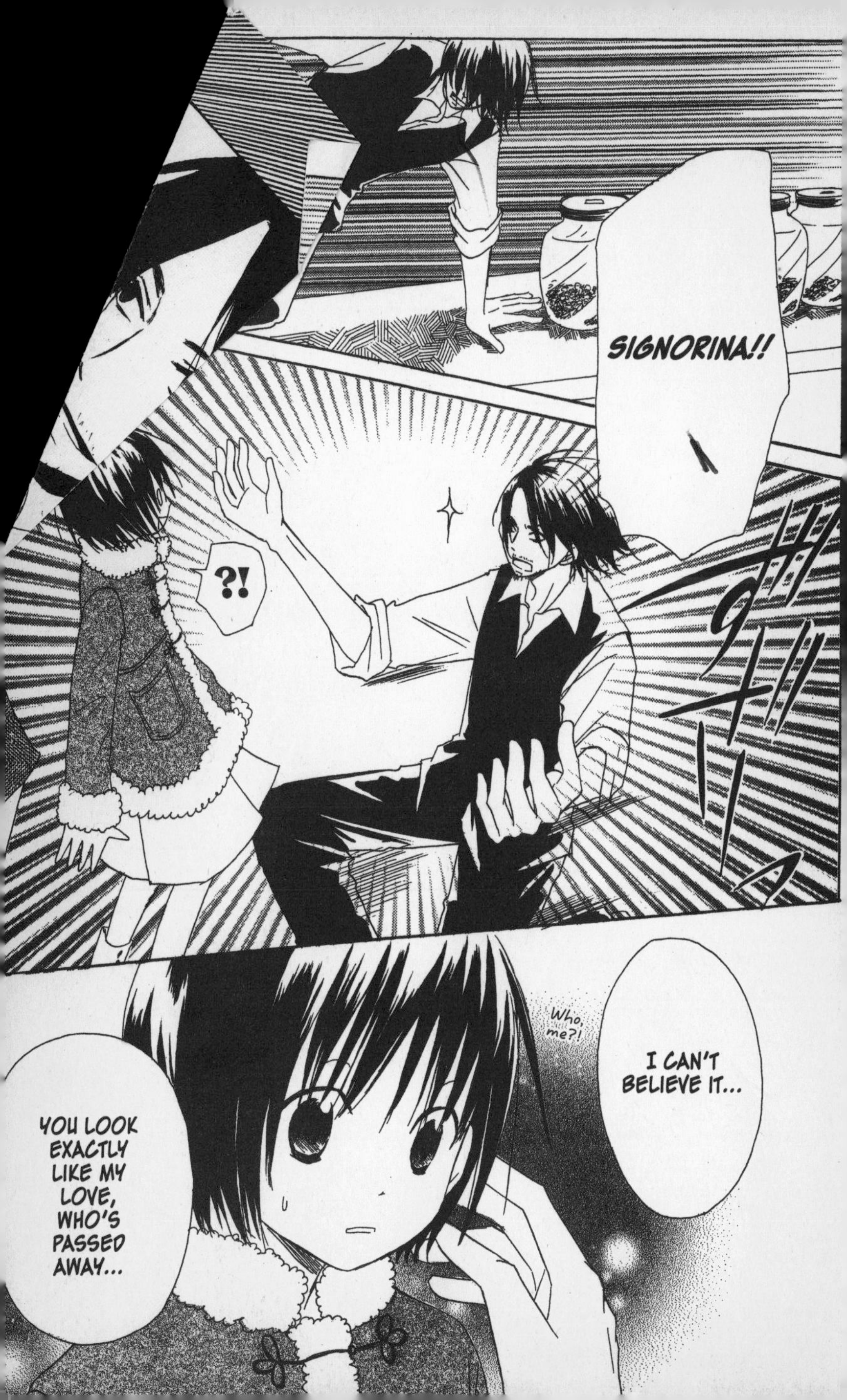
SIGNORINA!!
?!
I CAN'T BELIEVE IT...
Who, me?!
YOU LOOK EXACTLY LIKE MY LOVE, WHO'S PASSED AWAY...

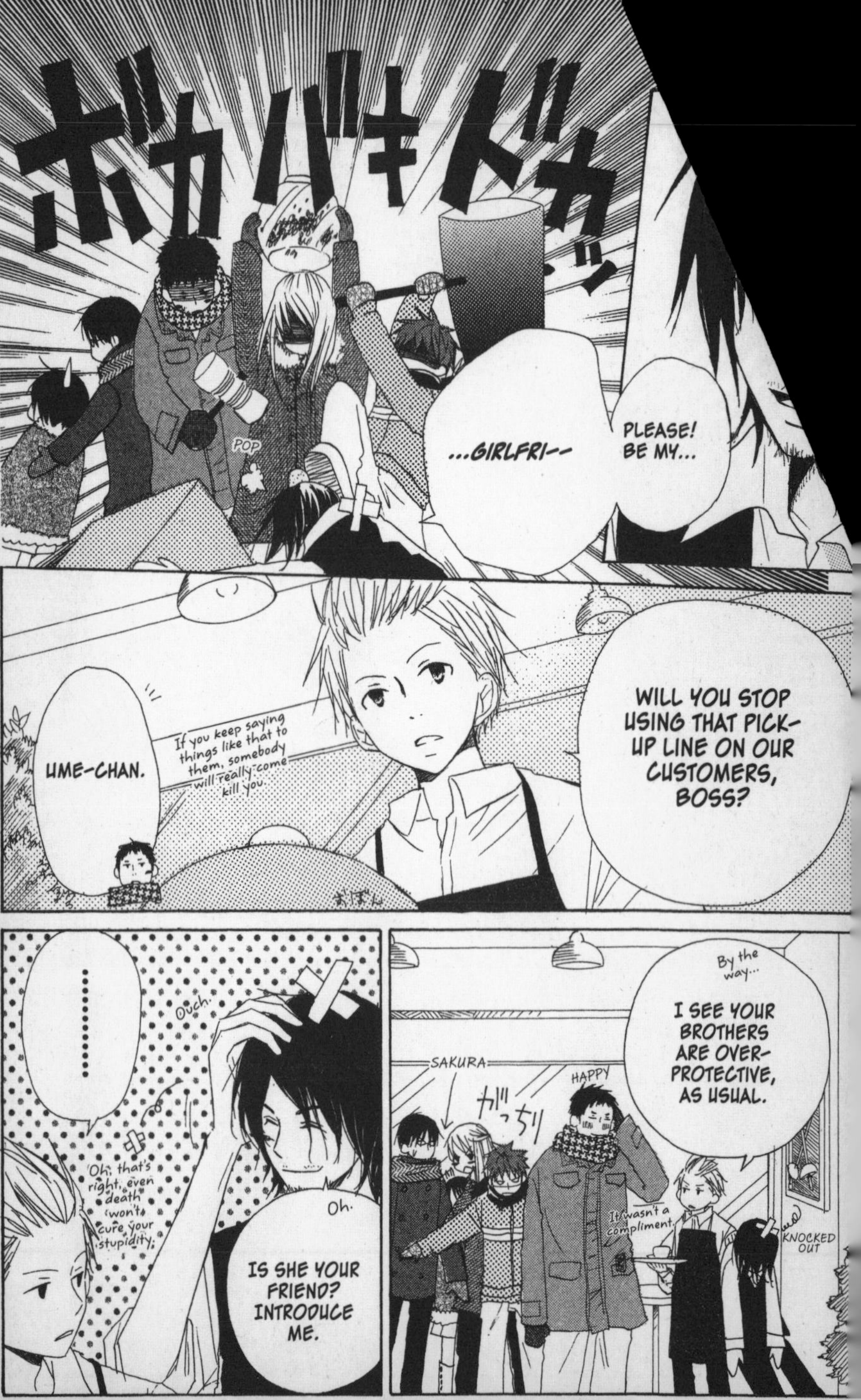
ボカバキドカ
PLEASE! BE MY...
...GIRLFRI--
POP
WILL YOU STOP USING THAT PICK-UP LINE ON OUR CUSTOMERS, BOSS?
If you keep saying things like that to them, somebody will really come kill you.
UME-CHAN.
By the way...
I SEE YOUR BROTHERS ARE OVER-PROTECTIVE, AS USUAL.
HAPPY
がっちり
SAKURA
It wasn't a compliment.
KNOCKED OUT
Ouch.
Oh.
IS SHE YOUR FRIEND? INTRODUCE ME.
......
Oh, that's right, even death won't cure your stupidity.

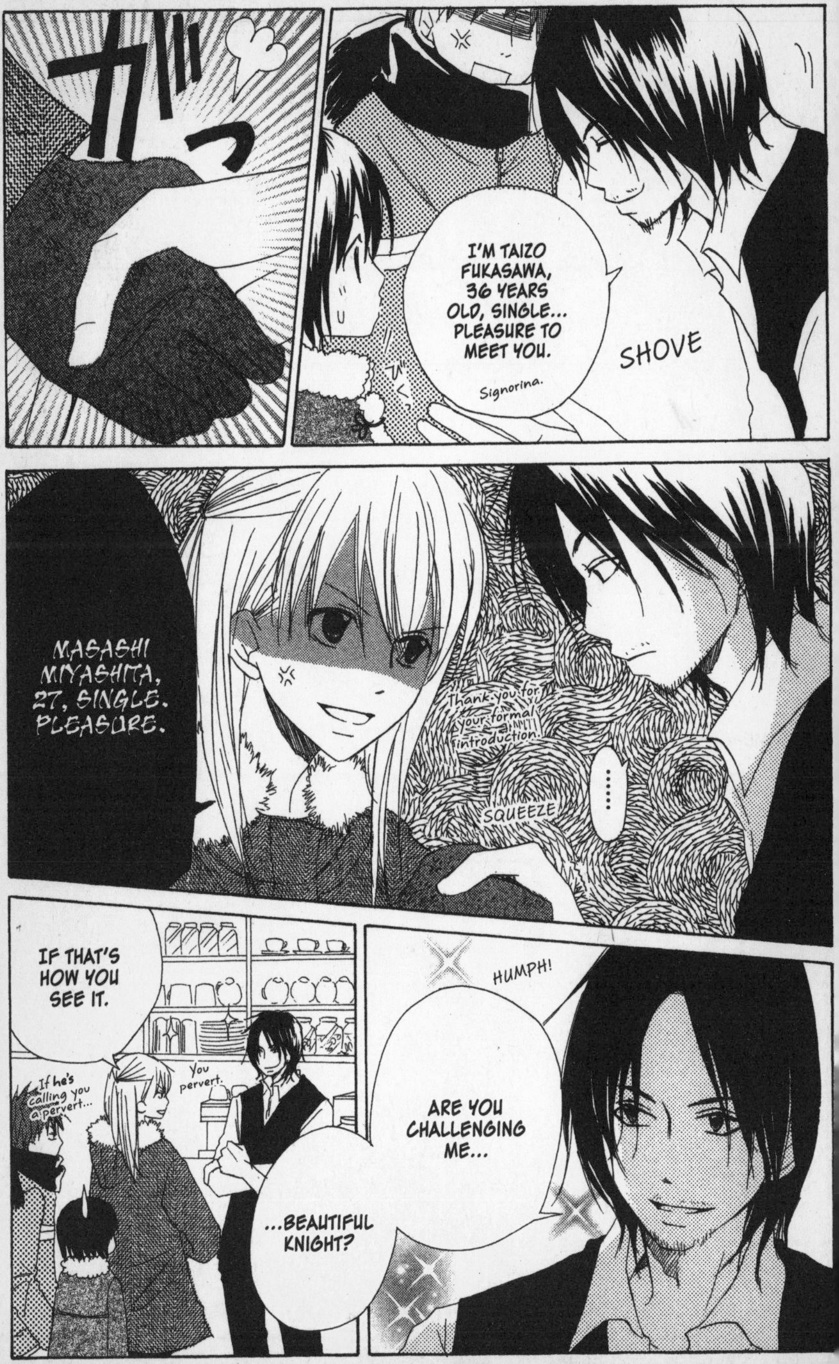
I'M TAIZO FUKASAWA, 36 YEARS OLD, SINGLE... PLEASURE TO MEET YOU.
Signorina.
SHOVE
びくっ
ガッ
MASASHI MIYASHITA, 27, SINGLE. PLEASURE.
Thank you for your formal introduction.
......
SQUEEZE
HUMPH!
ARE YOU CHALLENGING ME...
...BEAUTIFUL KNIGHT?
IF THAT'S HOW YOU SEE IT.
You pervert.
If he's calling you a pervert...

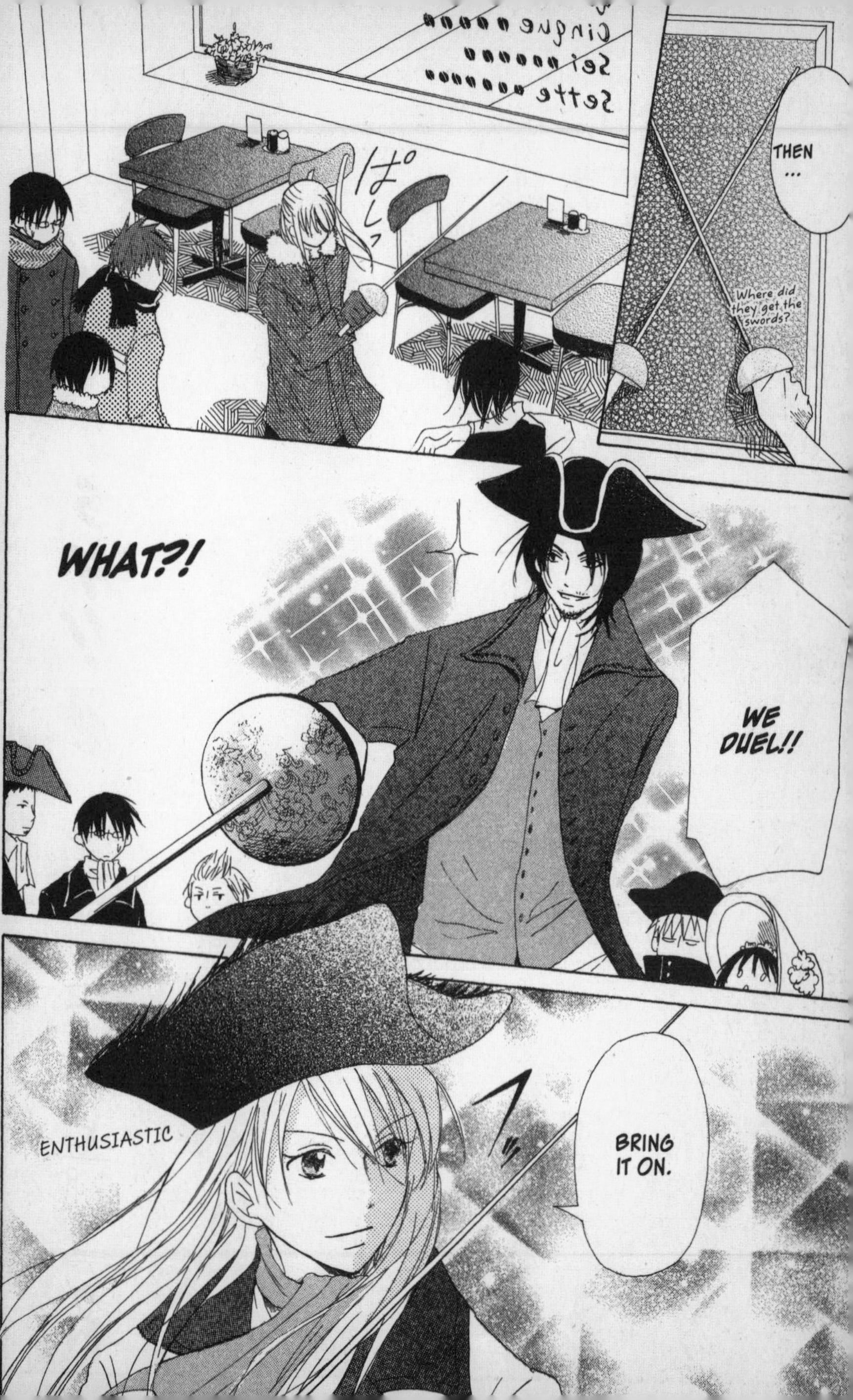
THEN ...
Where did they get the swords?
ぱしっ
WE DUEL!!
WHAT?!
BRING IT ON.
ENTHUSIASTIC

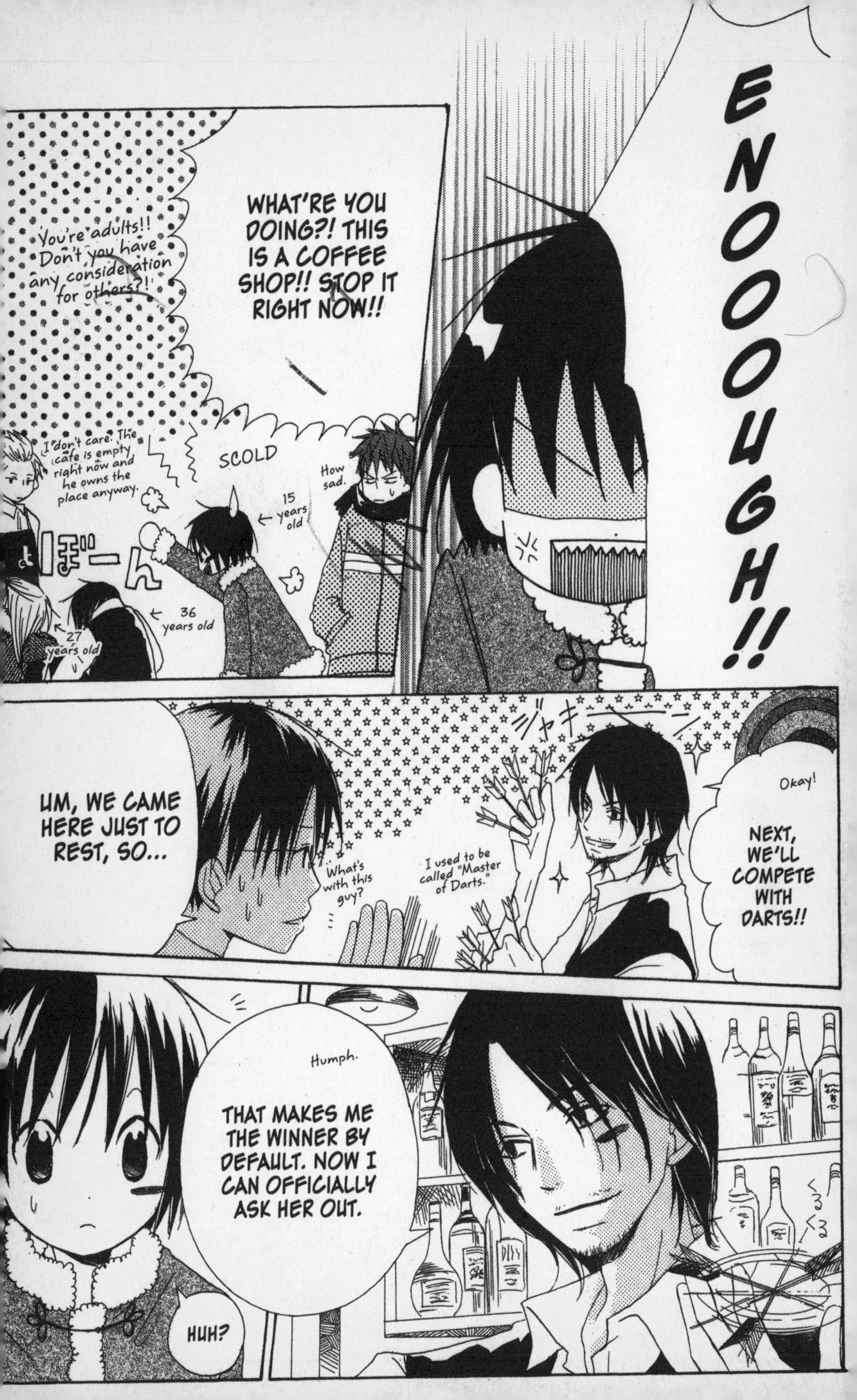
ENOOOUGH!!
WHAT'RE YOU DOING?! THIS IS A COFFEE SHOP!! STOP IT RIGHT NOW!!
You're adults!! Don't you have any consideration for others?!
SCOLD
How sad.
15 years old
I don't care. The cafe is empty right now and he owns the place anyway.
36 years old
27 years old
Okay!
NEXT, WE'LL COMPETE WITH DARTS!!
I used to be called "Master of Darts."
What's with this guy?
UM, WE CAME HERE JUST TO REST, SO...
Humph.
THAT MAKES ME THE WINNER BY DEFAULT. NOW I CAN OFFICIALLY ASK HER OUT.
くるくる
HUH?

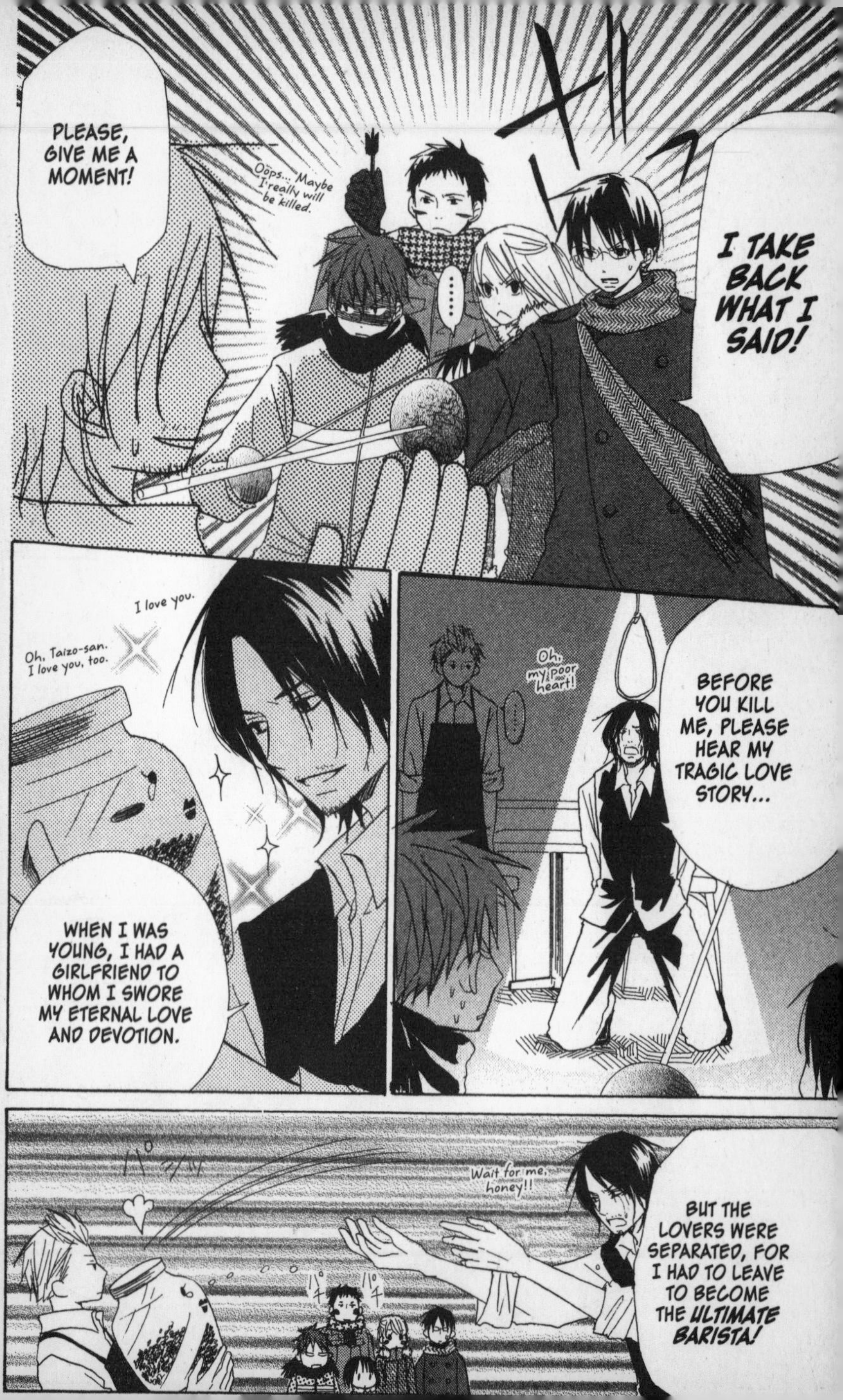
I TAKE BACK WHAT I SAID!
Oops... Maybe I really will be killed.
PLEASE, GIVE ME A MOMENT!
BEFORE YOU KILL ME, PLEASE HEAR MY TRAGIC LOVE STORY...
Oh, my poor heart!
I love you.
Oh, Taizo-san. I love you, too.
WHEN I WAS YOUNG, I HAD A GIRLFRIEND TO WHOM I SWORE MY ETERNAL LOVE AND DEVOTION.
BUT THE LOVERS WERE SEPARATED, FOR I HAD TO LEAVE TO BECOME THE *ULTIMATE BARISTA!*
Wait for me, honey!!

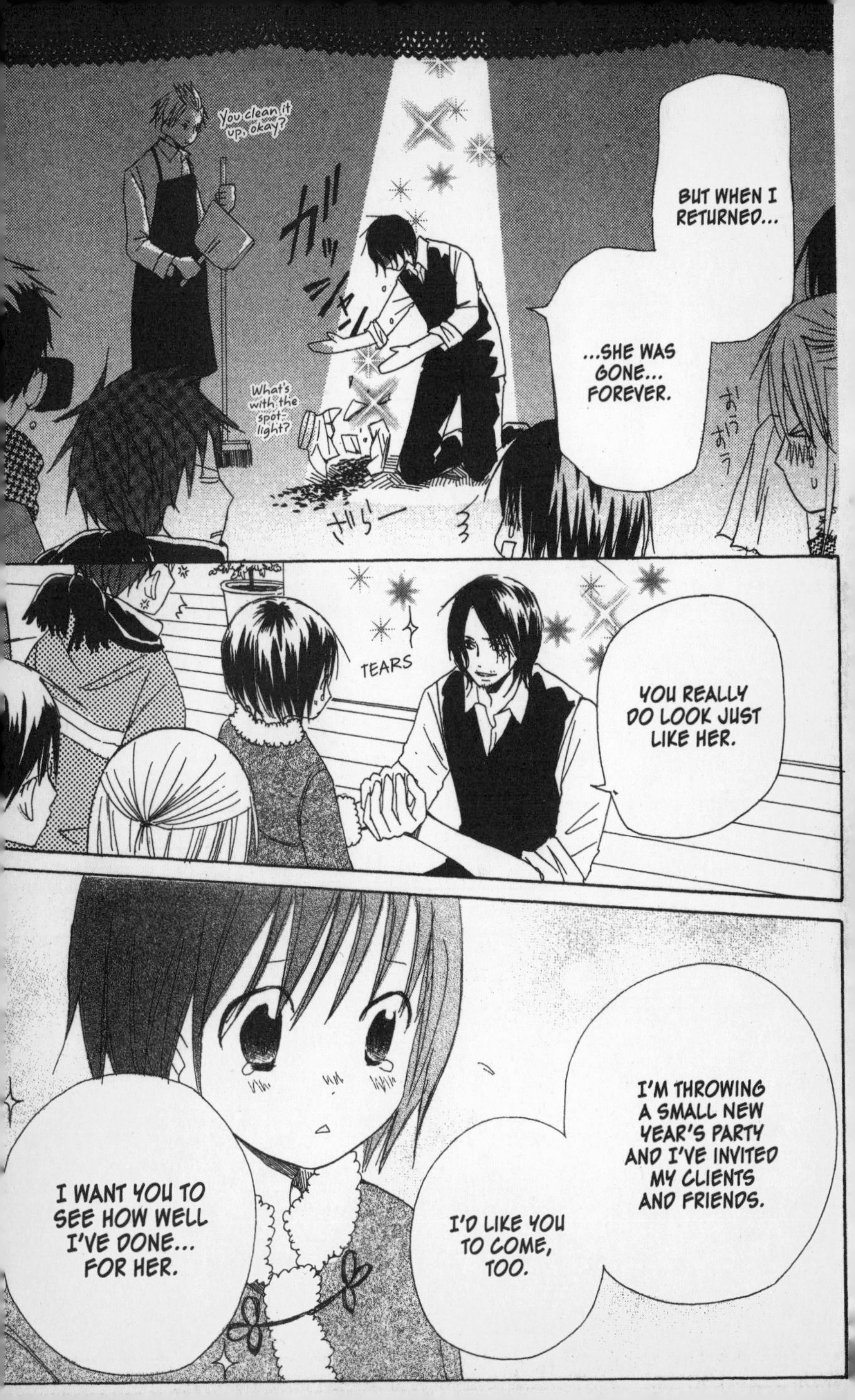
BUT WHEN I RETURNED...
...SHE WAS GONE... FOREVER.
You clean it up, okay?
What's with the spotlight?
YOU REALLY DO LOOK JUST LIKE HER.
TEARS
I'M THROWING A SMALL NEW YEAR'S PARTY AND I'VE INVITED MY CLIENTS AND FRIENDS.
I'D LIKE YOU TO COME, TOO.
I WANT YOU TO SEE HOW WELL I'VE DONE... FOR HER.

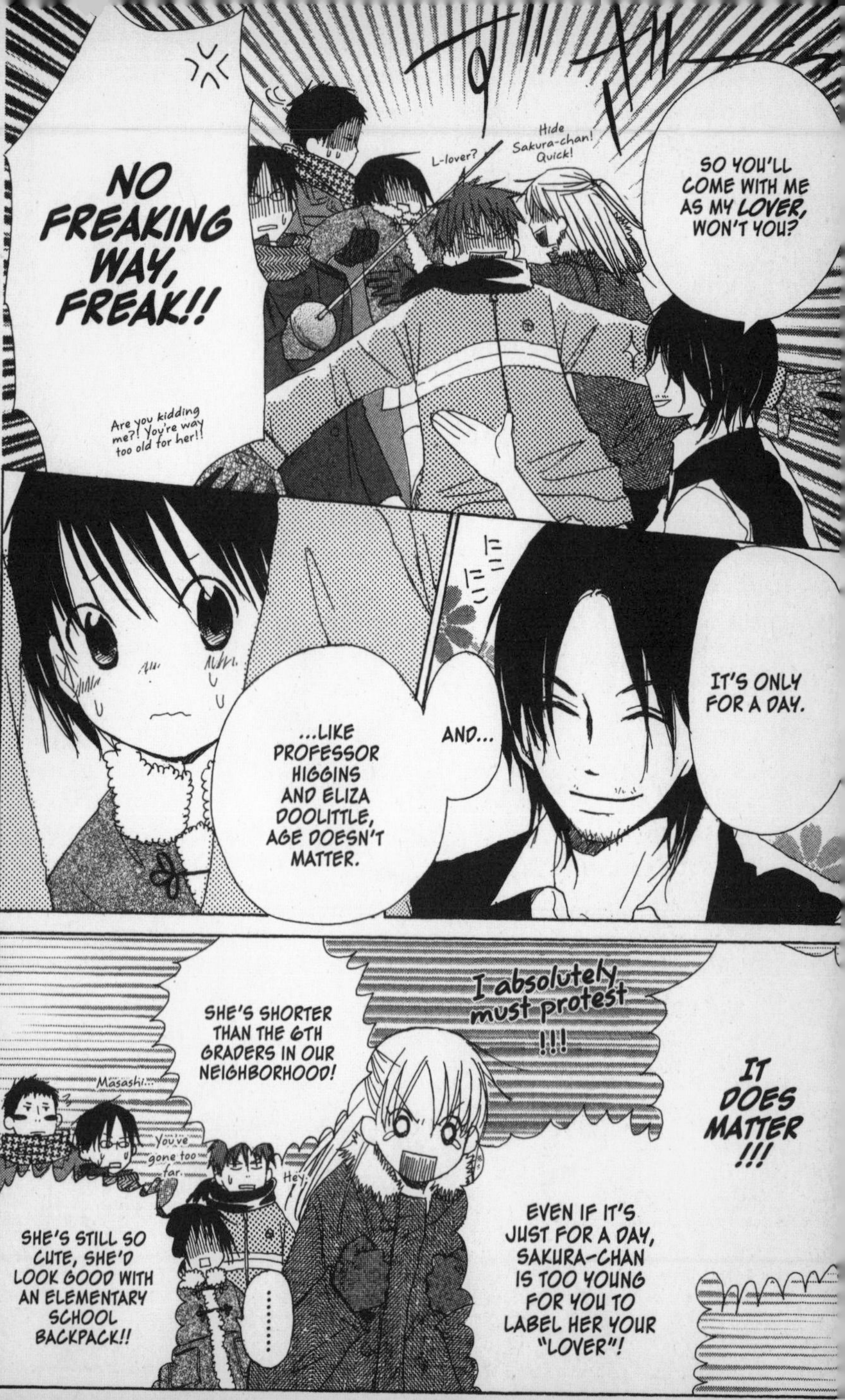
SO YOU'LL COME WITH ME AS MY LOVER, WON'T YOU?
Hide Sakura-chan! Quick!
L-lover?
NO FREAKING WAY, FREAK!!
Are you kidding me?! You're way too old for her!!
IT'S ONLY FOR A DAY.
AND...
...LIKE PROFESSOR HIGGINS AND ELIZA DOOLITTLE, AGE DOESN'T MATTER.
IT DOES MATTER!!!
I absolutely must protest!!!
EVEN IF IT'S JUST FOR A DAY, SAKURA-CHAN IS TOO YOUNG FOR YOU TO LABEL HER YOUR "LOVER"!
SHE'S SHORTER THAN THE 6TH GRADERS IN OUR NEIGHBORHOOD!
Hey,
You've gone too far.
Masashi...
SHE'S STILL SO CUTE, SHE'D LOOK GOOD WITH AN ELEMENTARY SCHOOL BACKPACK!!
....

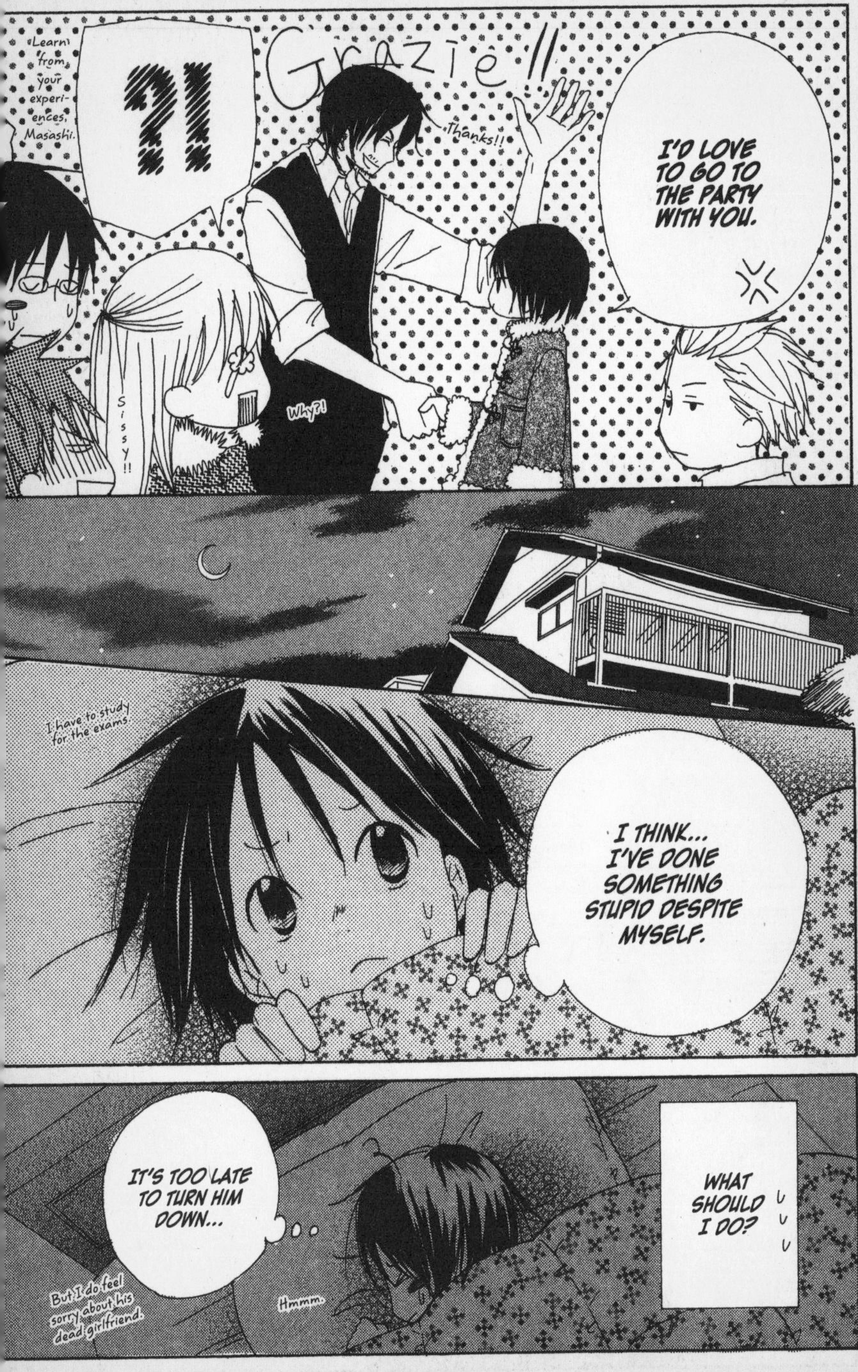
I'D LOVE TO GO TO THE PARTY WITH YOU.
Grazie!!
Thanks!!
?!
Why?!
Learn from your experi-ences, Masashi.
Sissy!!
I THINK... I'VE DONE SOMETHING STUPID DESPITE MYSELF.
I have to study for the exams.
WHAT SHOULD I DO?
Hmmm.
IT'S TOO LATE TO TURN HIM DOWN...
But I do feel sorry about his dead girlfriend.

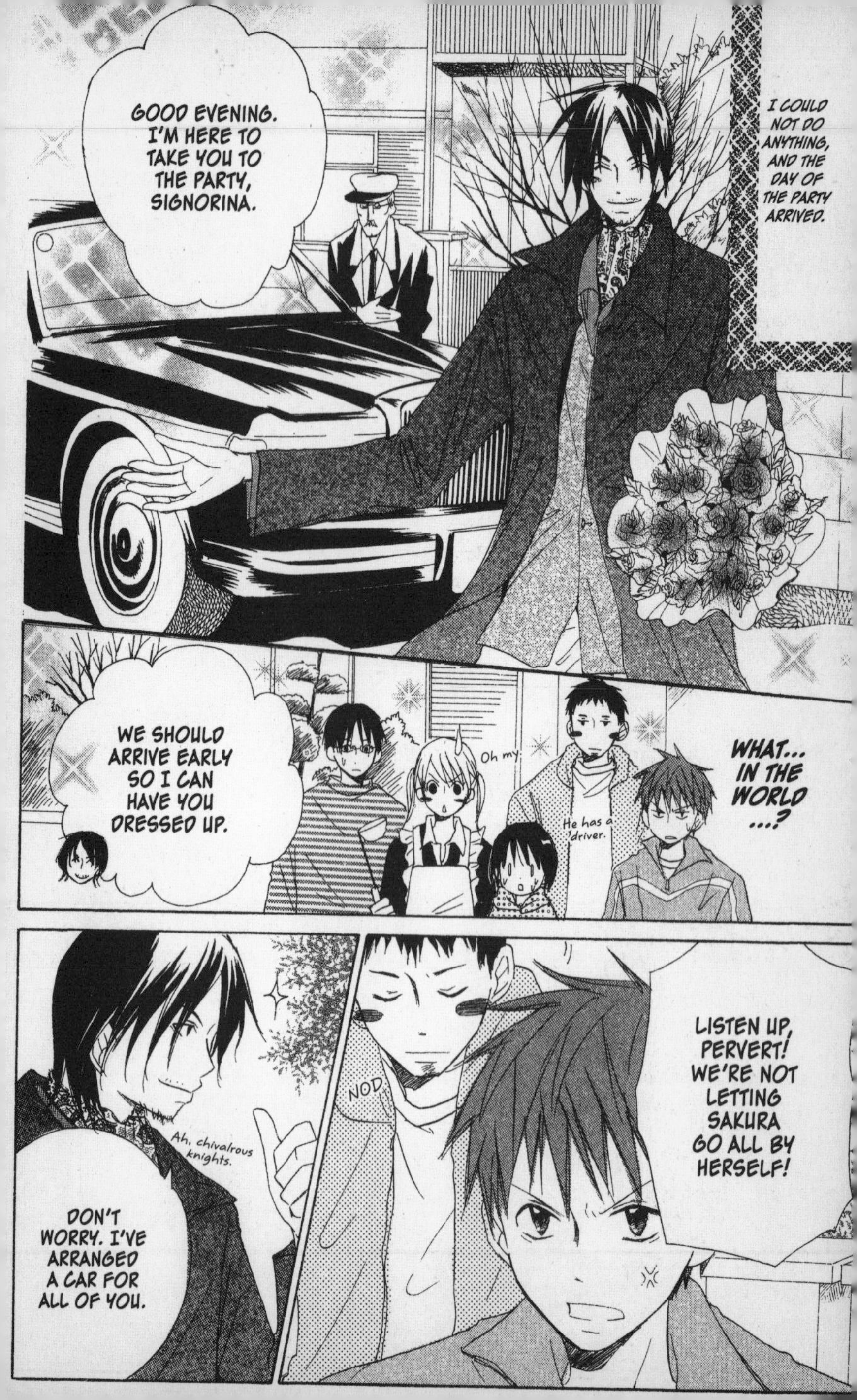
I COULD NOT DO ANYTHING, AND THE DAY OF THE PARTY ARRIVED.
GOOD EVENING. I'M HERE TO TAKE YOU TO THE PARTY, SIGNORINA.
WHAT... IN THE WORLD ...?
He has a driver.
Oh my.
WE SHOULD ARRIVE EARLY SO I CAN HAVE YOU DRESSED UP.
LISTEN UP, PERVERT! WE'RE NOT LETTING SAKURA GO ALL BY HERSELF!
NOD
Ah, chivalrous knights.
DON'T WORRY. I'VE ARRANGED A CAR FOR ALL OF YOU.

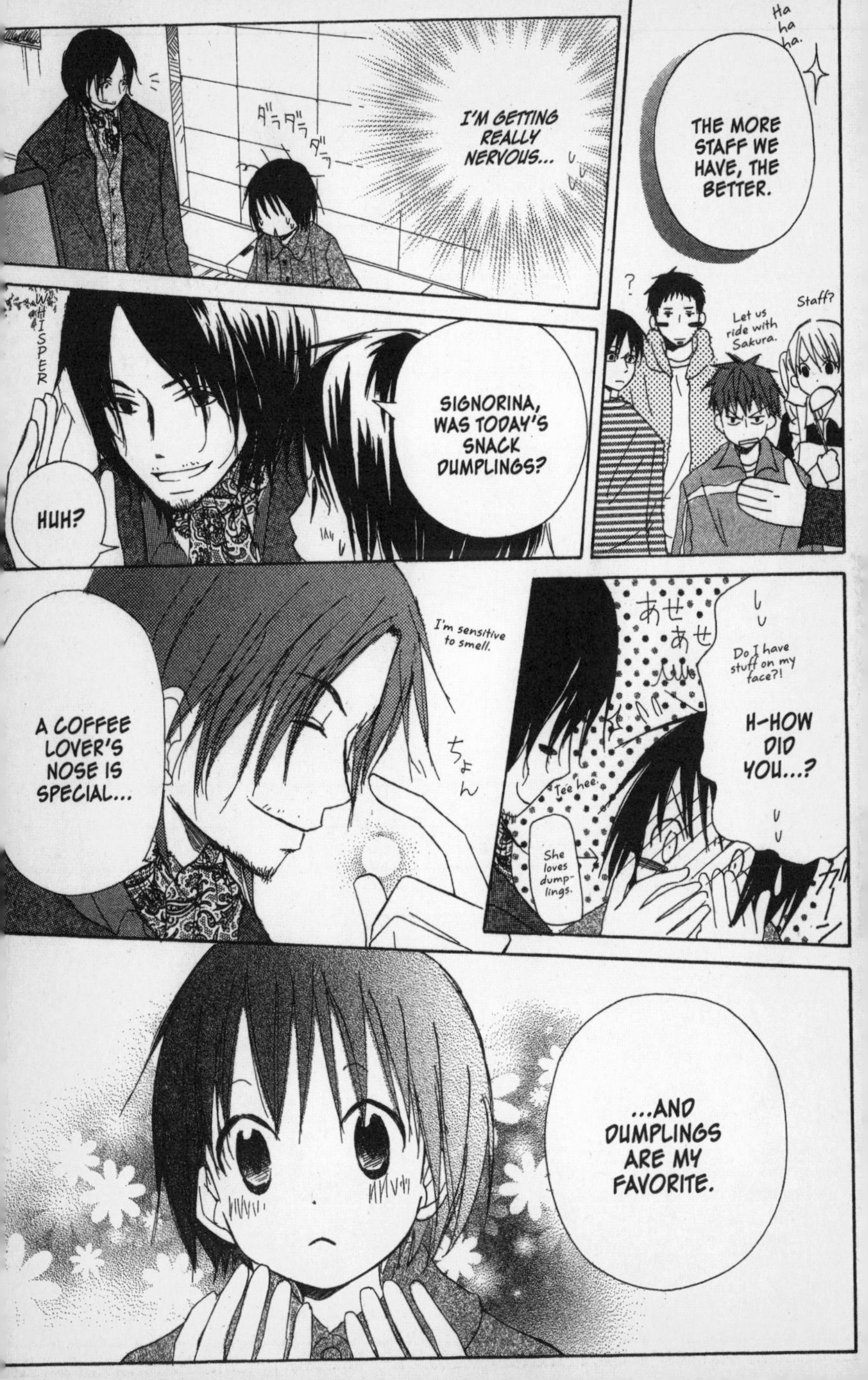
Ha ha ha.
THE MORE STAFF WE HAVE, THE BETTER.
?
Staff?
Let us ride with Sakura.
I'M GETTING REALLY NERVOUS...
ダラダラダラ
SIGNORINA, WAS TODAY'S SNACK DUMPLINGS?
WHISPER
HUH?
あせあせ
Do I have stuff on my face?!
H-HOW DID YOU...?
Tee hee.
She loves dumplings.
I'm sensitive to smell.
ちょん
A COFFEE LOVER'S NOSE IS SPECIAL...
...AND DUMPLINGS ARE MY FAVORITE.

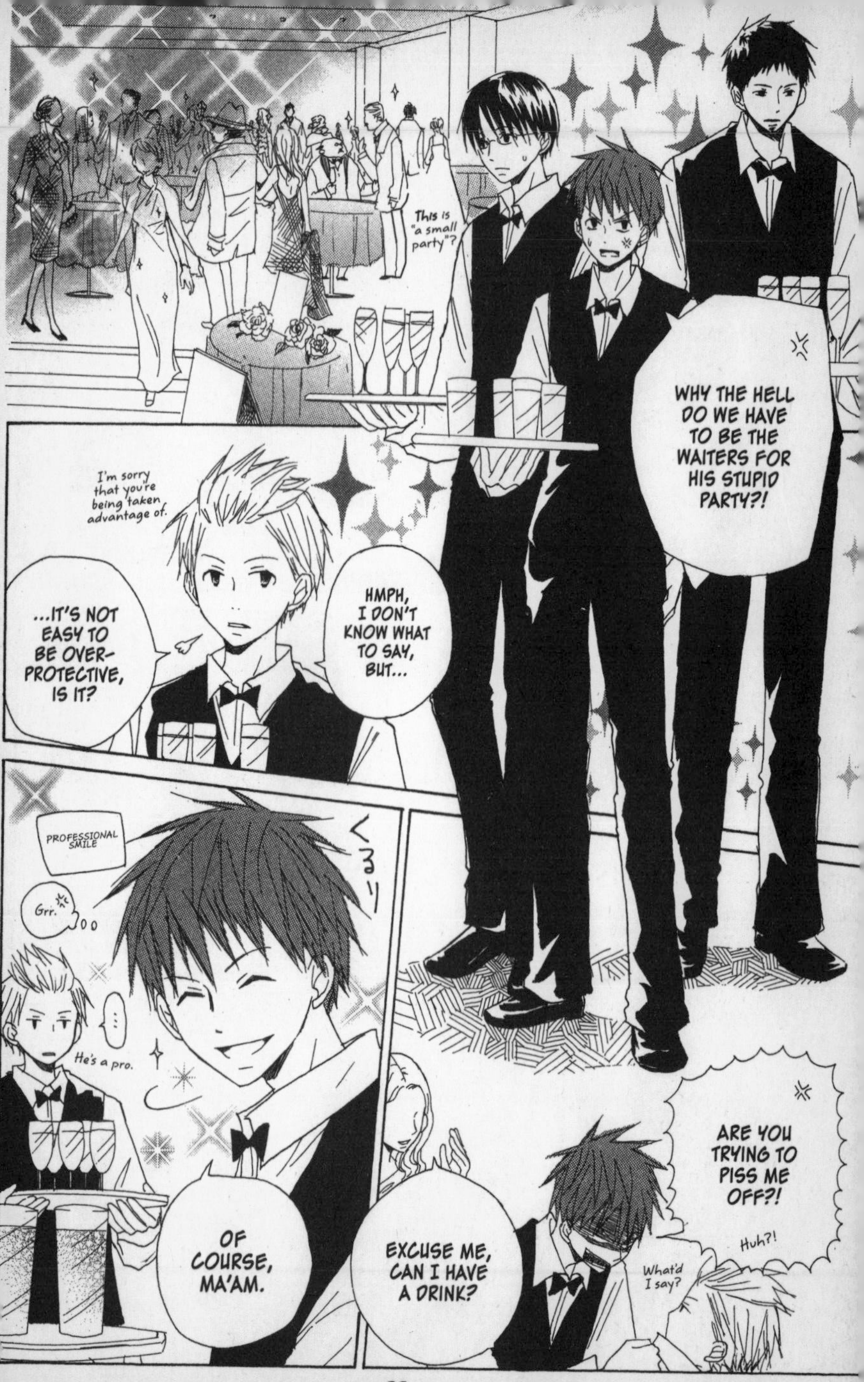
This is "a small party"?
WHY THE HELL DO WE HAVE TO BE THE WAITERS FOR HIS STUPID PARTY?!
HMPH, I DON'T KNOW WHAT TO SAY, BUT...
I'm sorry that you're being taken advantage of.
...IT'S NOT EASY TO BE OVER-PROTECTIVE, IS IT?
ARE YOU TRYING TO PISS ME OFF?!
Huh?!
What'd I say?
EXCUSE ME, CAN I HAVE A DRINK?
PROFESSIONAL SMILE
くるり
Grr.
...
He's a pro.
OF COURSE, MA'AM.

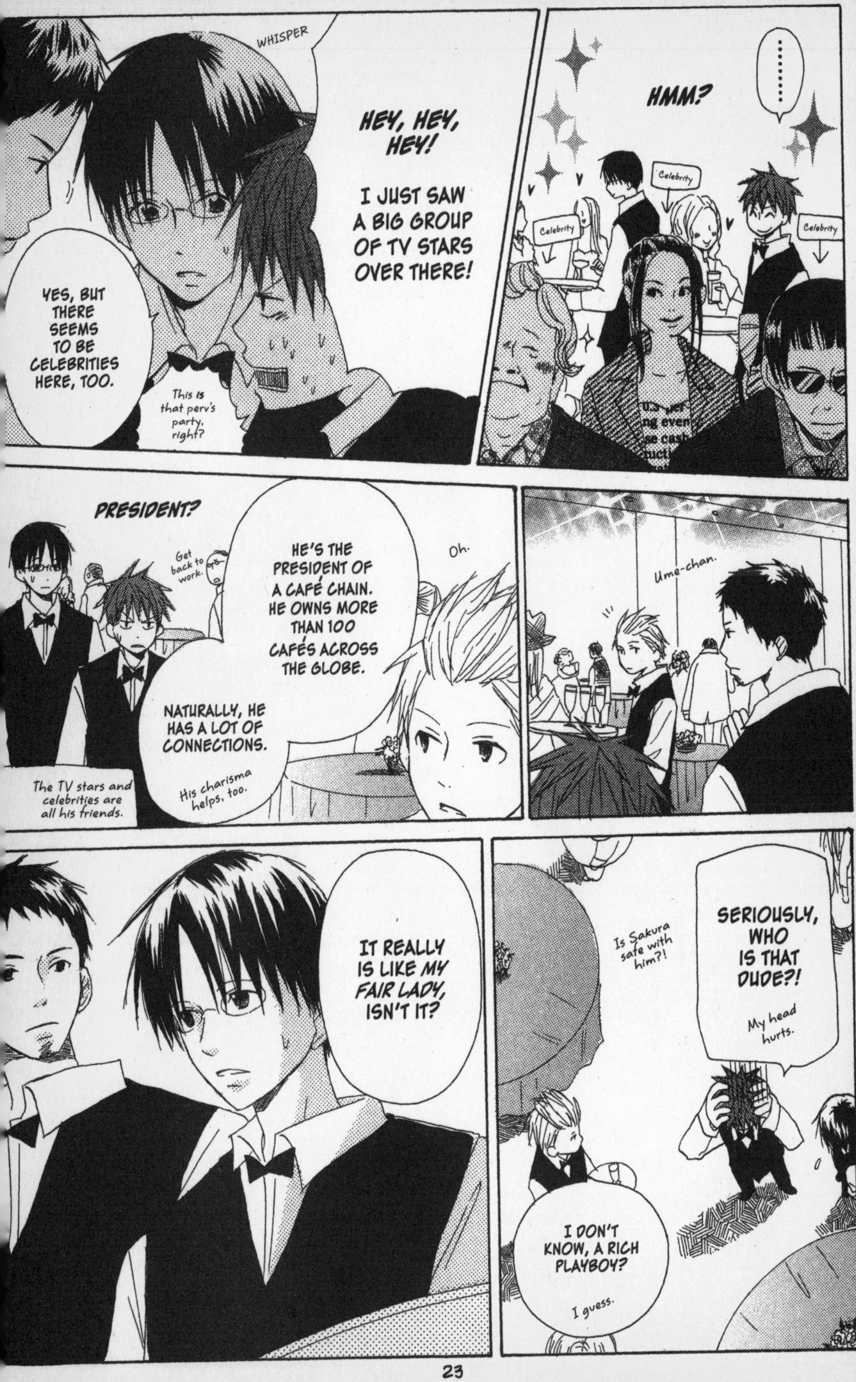
......
HMM?
Celebrity
Celebrity
Celebrity
HEY, HEY, HEY!
I JUST SAW A BIG GROUP OF TV STARS OVER THERE!
WHISPER
YES, BUT THERE SEEMS TO BE CELEBRITIES HERE, TOO.
This is that perv's party, right?
Ume-chan.
Oh.
PRESIDENT?
HE'S THE PRESIDENT OF A CAFÉ CHAIN. HE OWNS MORE THAN 100 CAFÉS ACROSS THE GLOBE.
Get back to work.
NATURALLY, HE HAS A LOT OF CONNECTIONS.
His charisma helps, too.
The TV stars and celebrities are all his friends.
SERIOUSLY, WHO IS THAT DUDE?!
My head hurts.
Is Sakura safe with him?!
I DON'T KNOW, A RICH PLAYBOY?
I guess.
IT REALLY IS LIKE *MY FAIR LADY*, ISN'T IT?

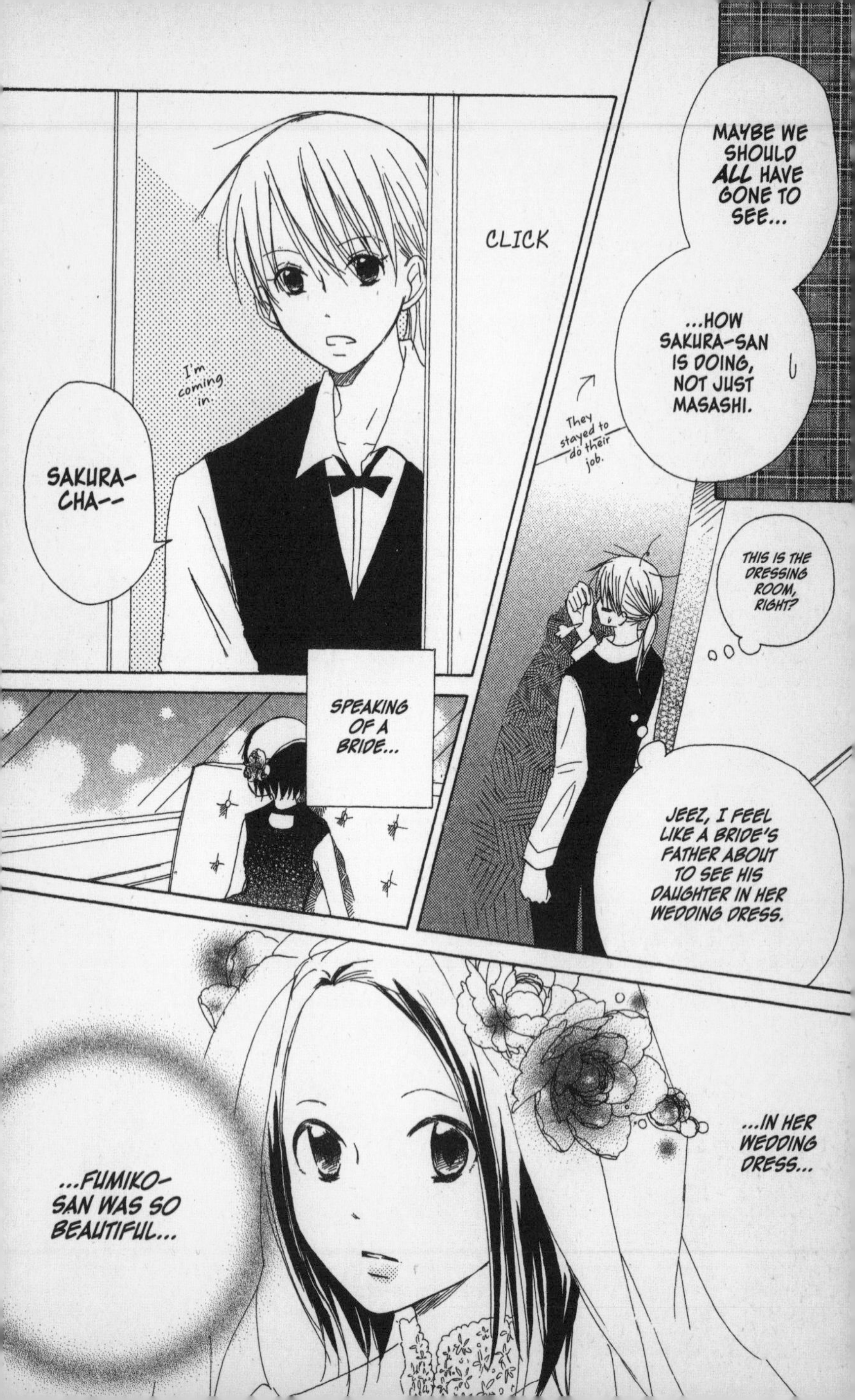
MAYBE WE SHOULD ALL HAVE GONE TO SEE...
...HOW SAKURA-SAN IS DOING, NOT JUST MASASHI.
They stayed to do their job.
THIS IS THE DRESSING ROOM, RIGHT?
JEEZ, I FEEL LIKE A BRIDE'S FATHER ABOUT TO SEE HIS DAUGHTER IN HER WEDDING DRESS.
CLICK
I'm coming in.
SAKURA-CHA--
SPEAKING OF A BRIDE...
...IN HER WEDDING DRESS...
...FUMIKO-SAN WAS SO BEAUTIFUL...

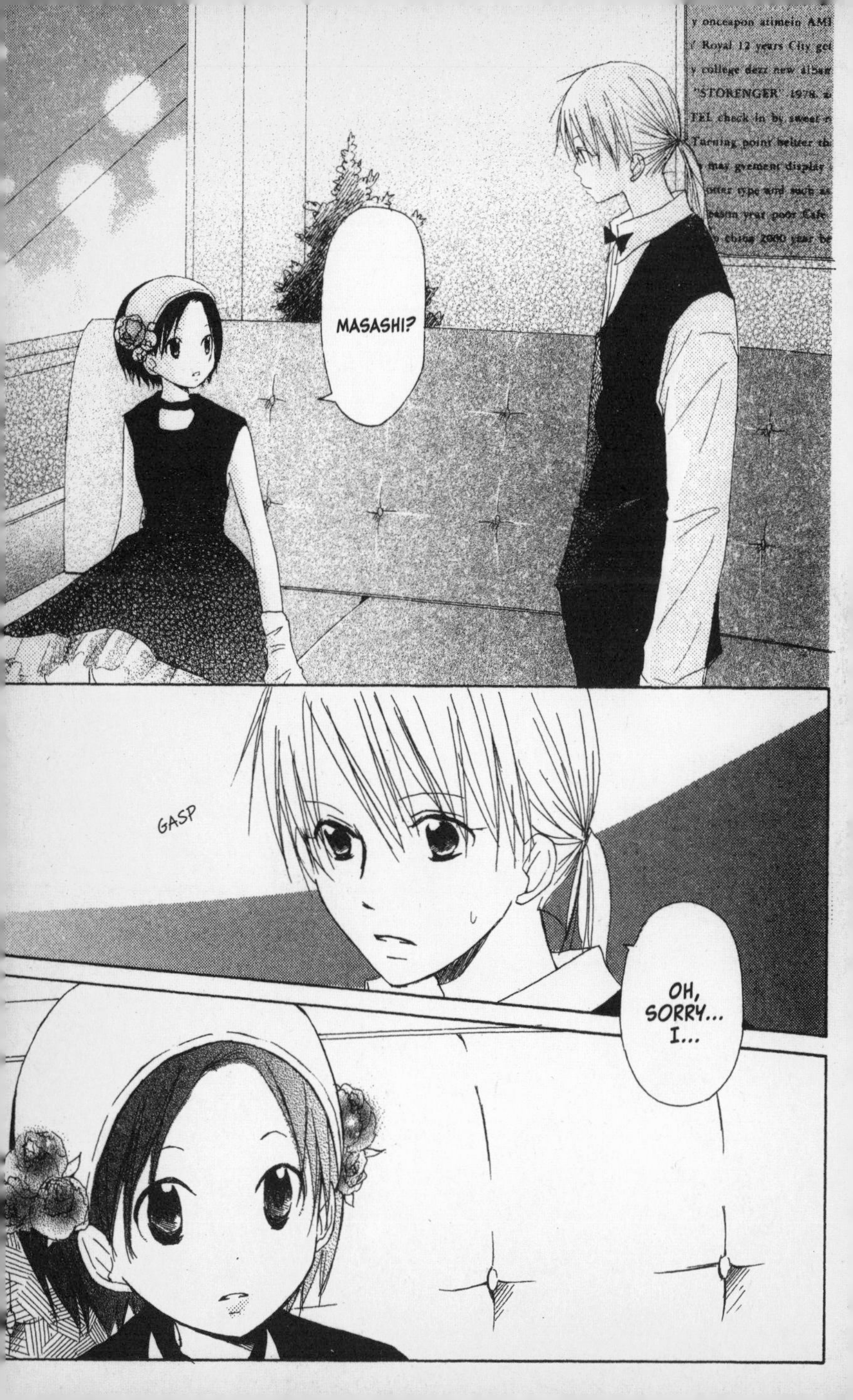
y onceapon atimein AMI
/ Royal 12 years City get
y college dezz new album
"STORENGER" 1978,
TEL check in by sweet
Turning point belter th
y may gvement display
otter type and such as
bastin year poor Cafe
o china 2000 year be
MASASHI?
GASP
OH, SORRY... I...

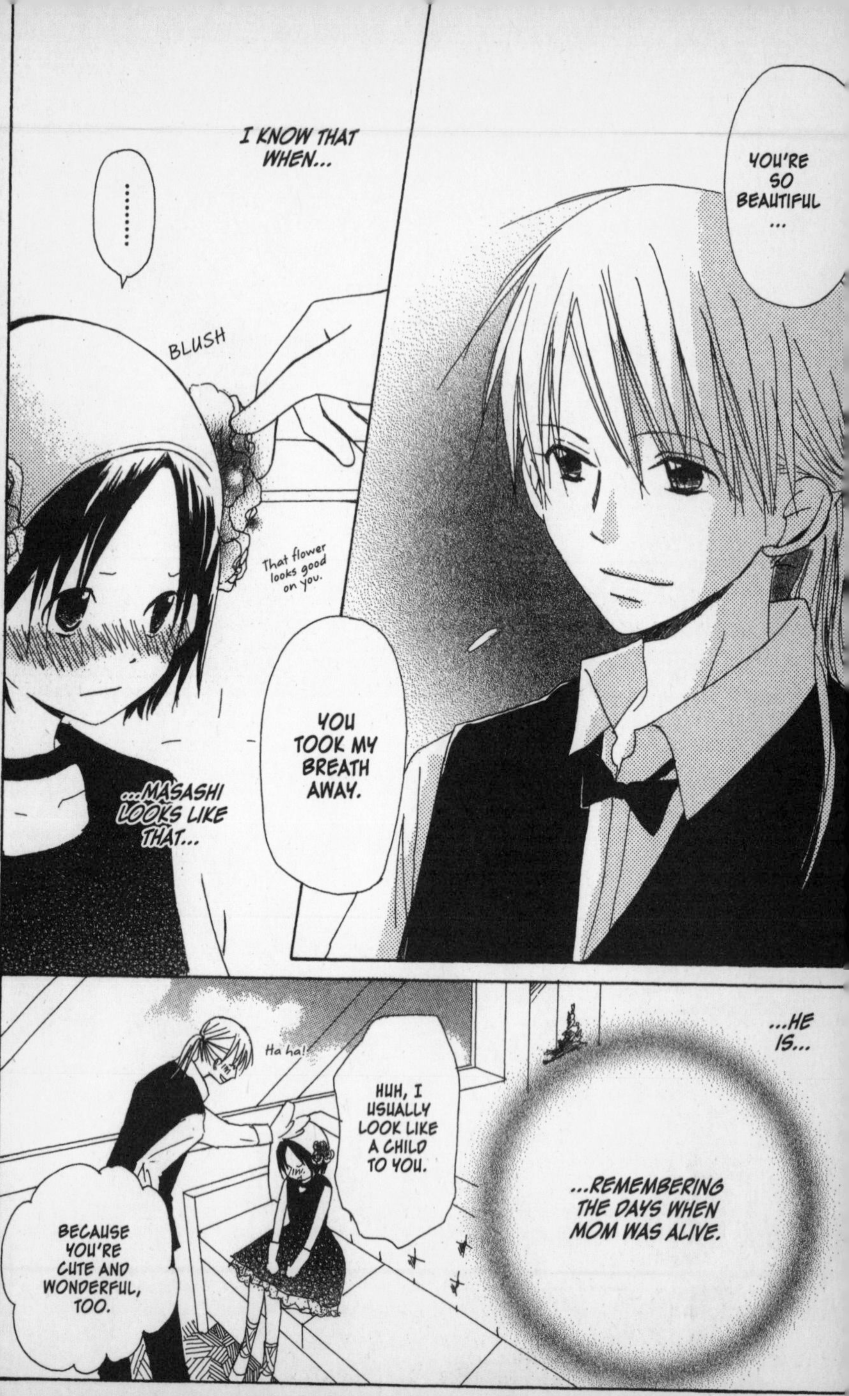
YOU'RE SO BEAUTIFUL ...
YOU TOOK MY BREATH AWAY.
I KNOW THAT WHEN...
....
BLUSH
That flower looks good on you.
...MASASHI LOOKS LIKE THAT...
...HE IS...
...REMEMBERING THE DAYS WHEN MOM WAS ALIVE.
HUH, I USUALLY LOOK LIKE A CHILD TO YOU.
Ha ha!
BECAUSE YOU'RE CUTE AND WONDERFUL, TOO.

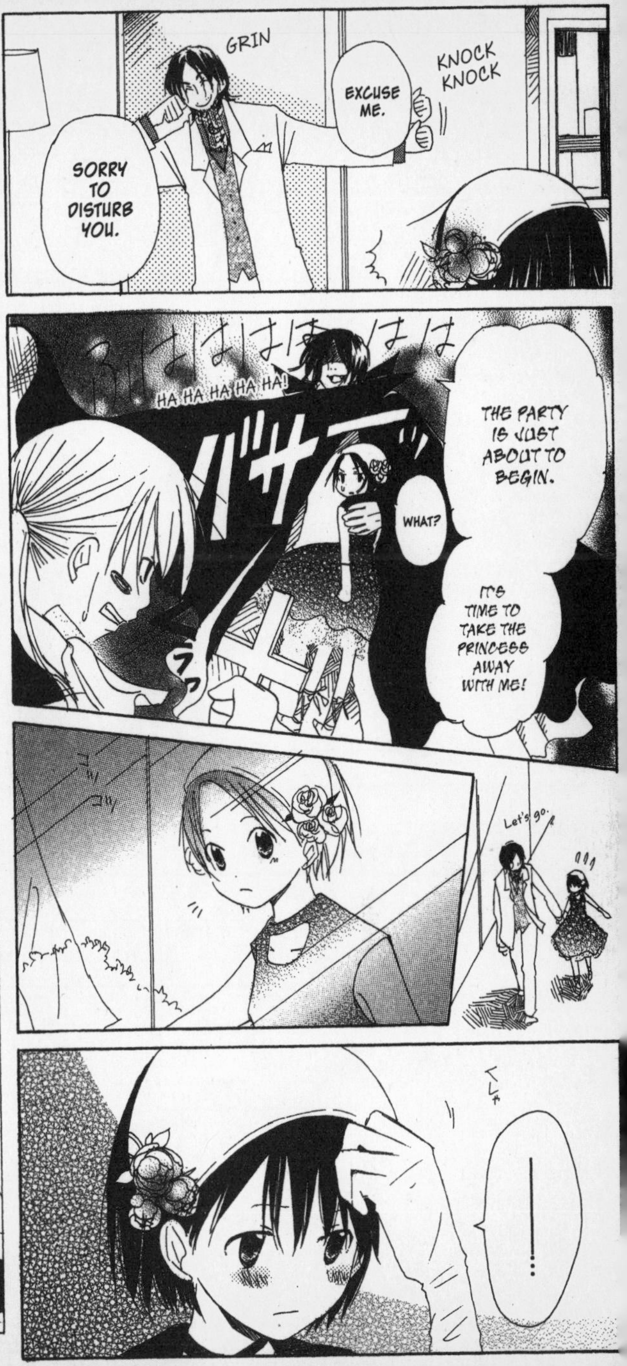
KNOCK KNOCK
EXCUSE ME.
GRIN
SORRY TO DISTURB YOU.
THE PARTY IS JUST ABOUT TO BEGIN.
HA HA HA HA HA!
WHAT?
IT'S TIME TO TAKE THE PRINCESS AWAY WITH ME!
Let's go.
......

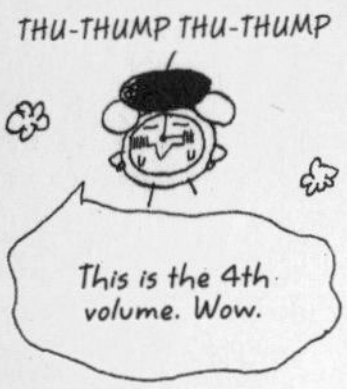
THU-THUMP THU-THUMP
This is the 4th volume. Wow.

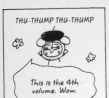

Thank you for picking up this book!! This book starts with the story of a man about whom my editor said, "seems like a pervert." I like men with beards, but this description must be due to my lack of drawing skill. There are some other reasons he's called a pervert, but let's have a big heart and forgive him, okay?

ME & A WEIRD MAN

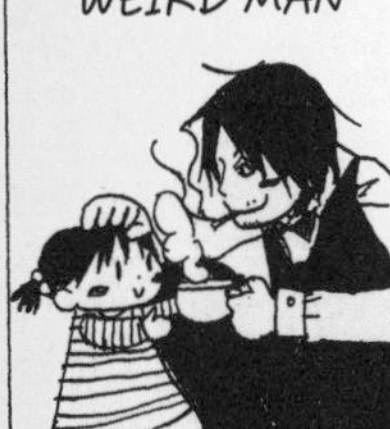

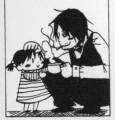

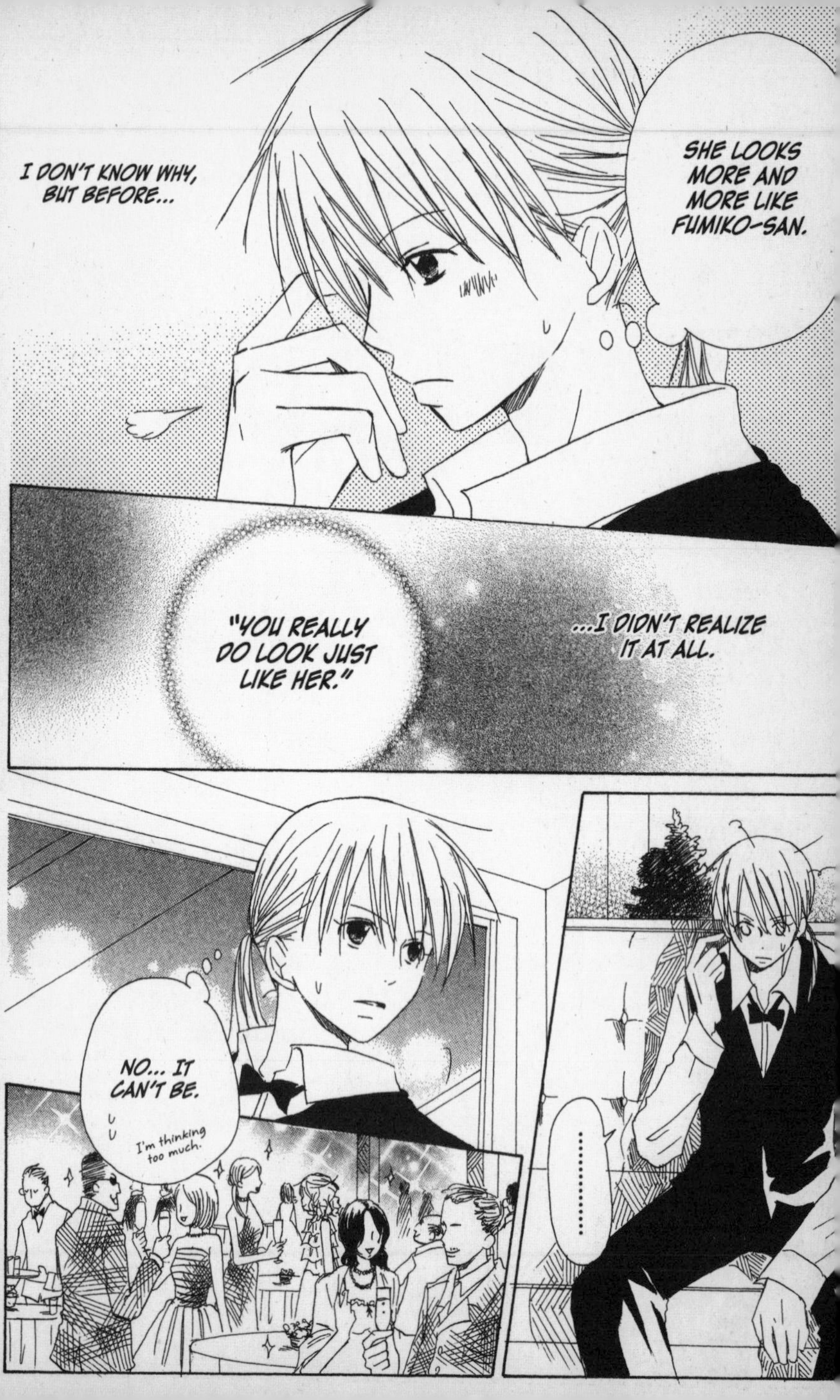
SHE LOOKS MORE AND MORE LIKE FUMIKO-SAN.
I DON'T KNOW WHY, BUT BEFORE...
...I DIDN'T REALIZE IT AT ALL.
"YOU REALLY DO LOOK JUST LIKE HER."
....
NO... IT CAN'T BE.
I'm thinking too much.

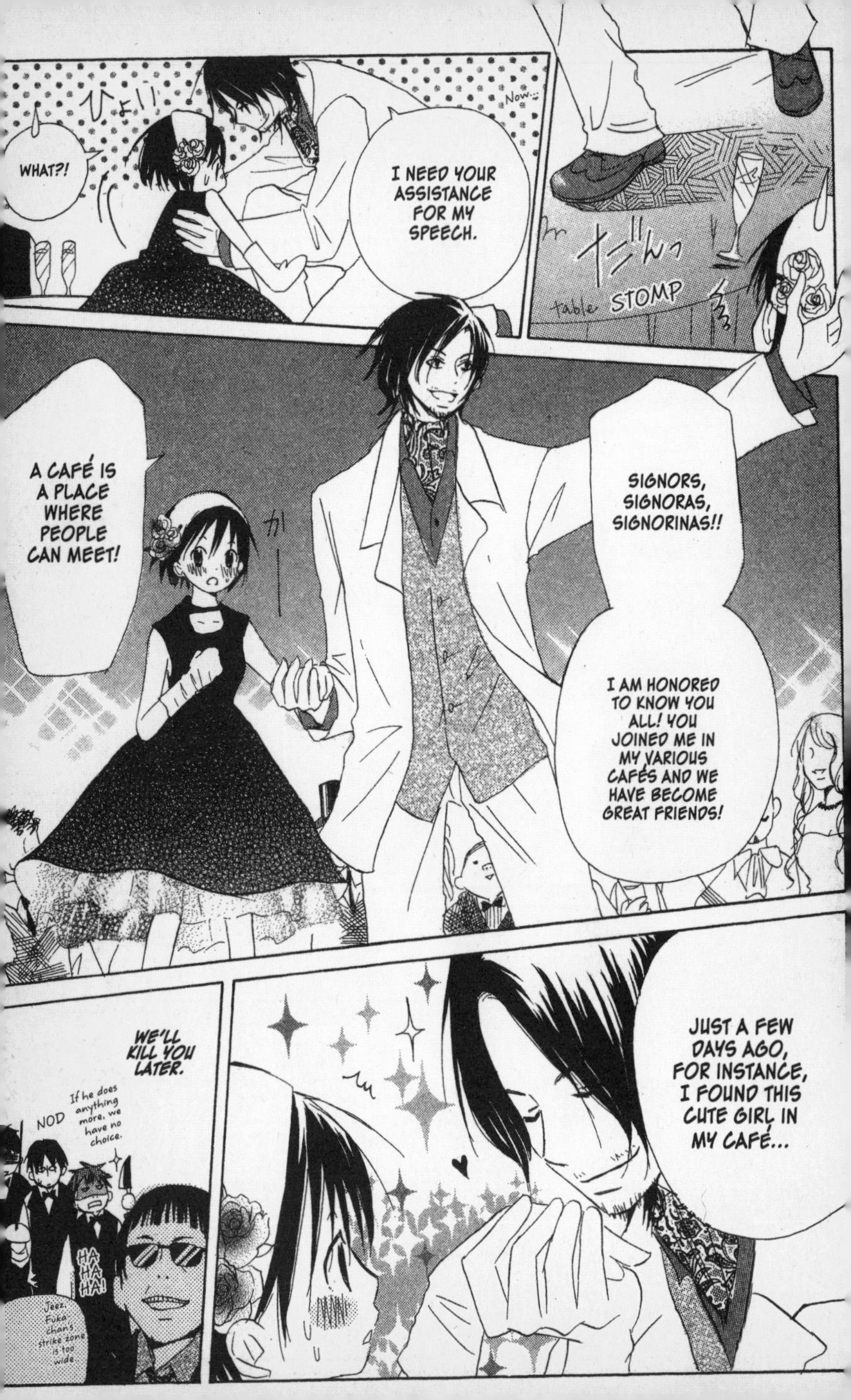
table STOMP
Now...
I NEED YOUR ASSISTANCE FOR MY SPEECH.
WHAT?!
SIGNORS, SIGNORAS, SIGNORINAS!!
I AM HONORED TO KNOW YOU ALL! YOU JOINED ME IN MY VARIOUS CAFÉS AND WE HAVE BECOME GREAT FRIENDS!
A CAFÉ IS A PLACE WHERE PEOPLE CAN MEET!
JUST A FEW DAYS AGO, FOR INSTANCE, I FOUND THIS CUTE GIRL IN MY CAFÉ...
WE'LL KILL YOU LATER.
If he does anything more, we have no choice.
NOD
HA HA HA HA!
Jeez, Fuka-chan's strike zone is too wide.

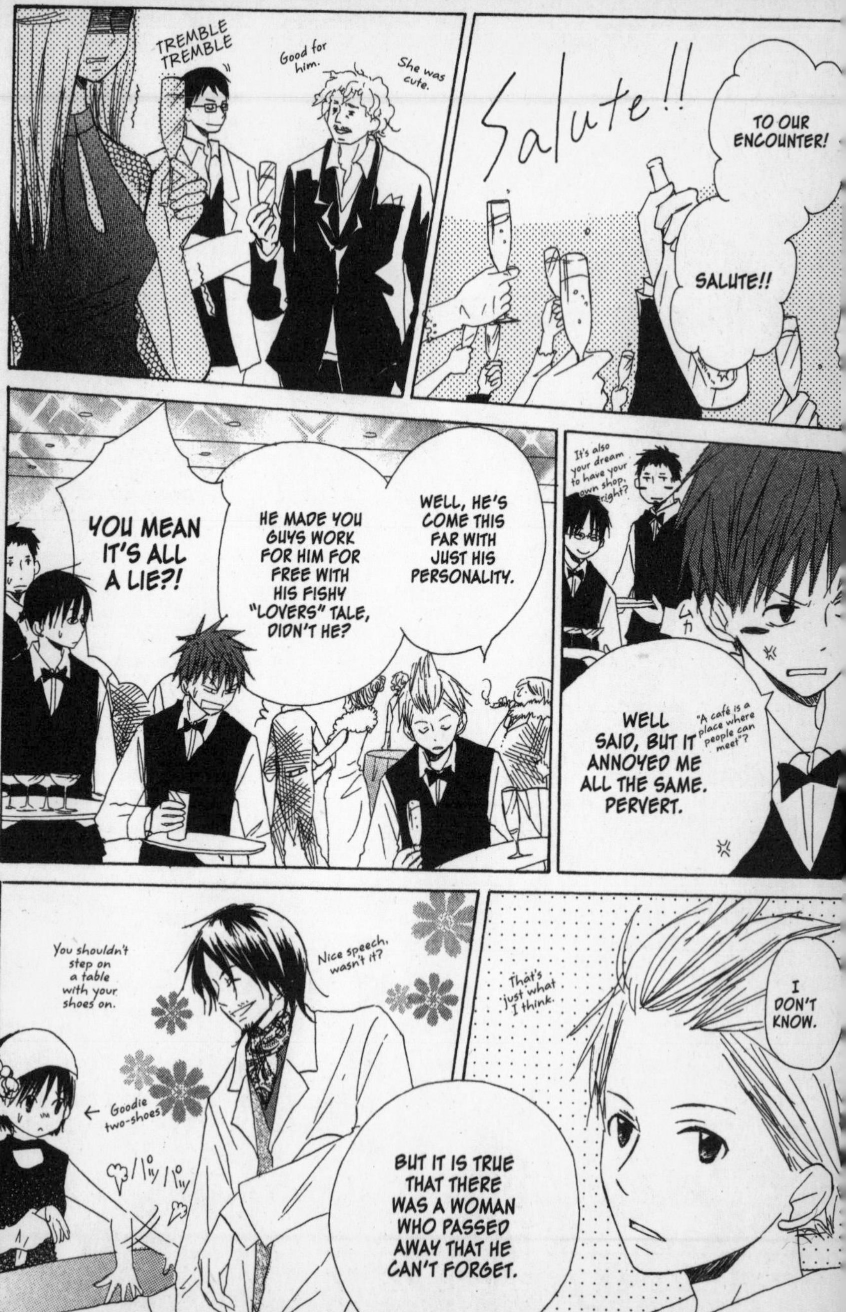
TO OUR ENCOUNTER!
SALUTE!!
Salute!!
She was cute.
Good for him.
TREMBLE TREMBLE
It's also your dream to have your own shop, right?
WELL SAID, BUT IT ANNOYED ME ALL THE SAME. PERVERT.
"A café is a place where people can meet"?
WELL, HE'S COME THIS FAR WITH JUST HIS PERSONALITY.
HE MADE YOU GUYS WORK FOR HIM FOR FREE WITH HIS FISHY "LOVERS" TALE, DIDN'T HE?
YOU MEAN IT'S ALL A LIE?!
I DON'T KNOW.
That's just what I think.
BUT IT IS TRUE THAT THERE WAS A WOMAN WHO PASSED AWAY THAT HE CAN'T FORGET.
Nice speech, wasn't it?
You shouldn't step on a table with your shoes on.
← Goodie two-shoes

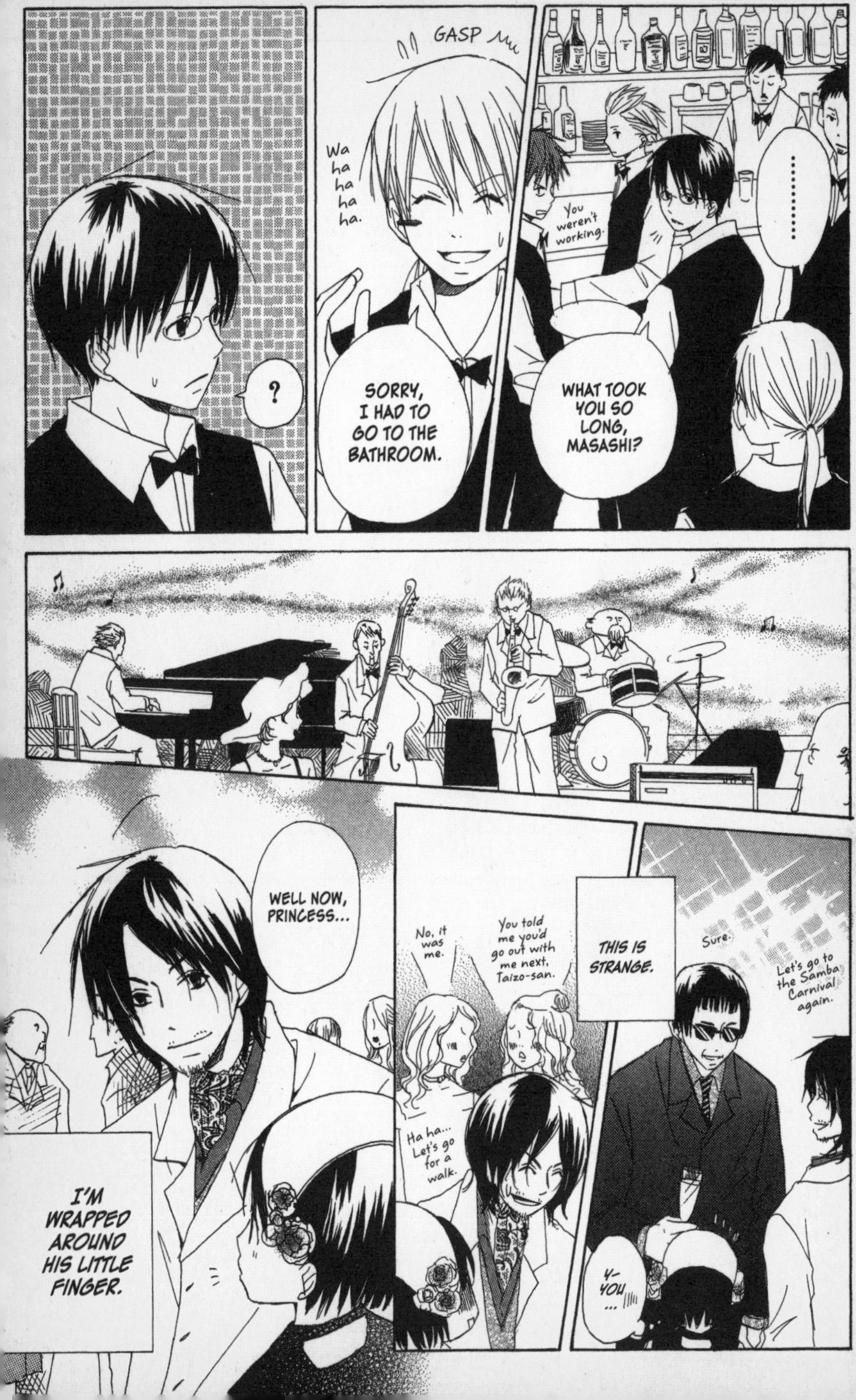

......
You weren't working.
WHAT TOOK YOU SO LONG, MASASHI?
GASP
Wa ha ha ha ha.
SORRY, I HAD TO GO TO THE BATHROOM.
?
Sure.
Let's go to the Samba Carnival again.
Y-YOU...
THIS IS STRANGE.
You told me you'd go out with me next, Taizo-san.
No, it was me.
Ha ha... Let's go for a walk.
WELL NOW, PRINCESS...
I'M WRAPPED AROUND HIS LITTLE FINGER.

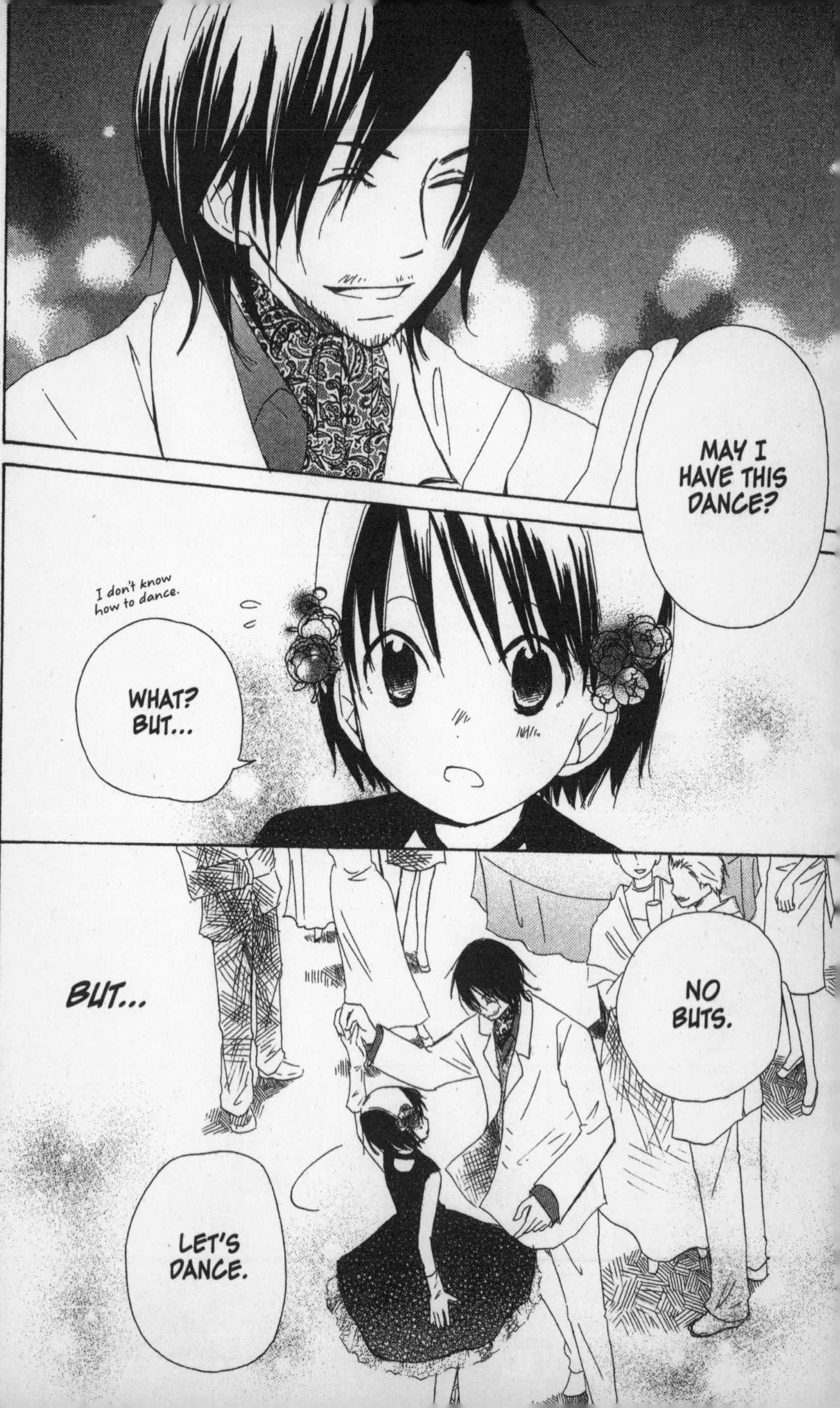
MAY I HAVE THIS DANCE?
I don't know how to dance.
WHAT? BUT...
BUT...
NO BUTS.
LET'S DANCE.

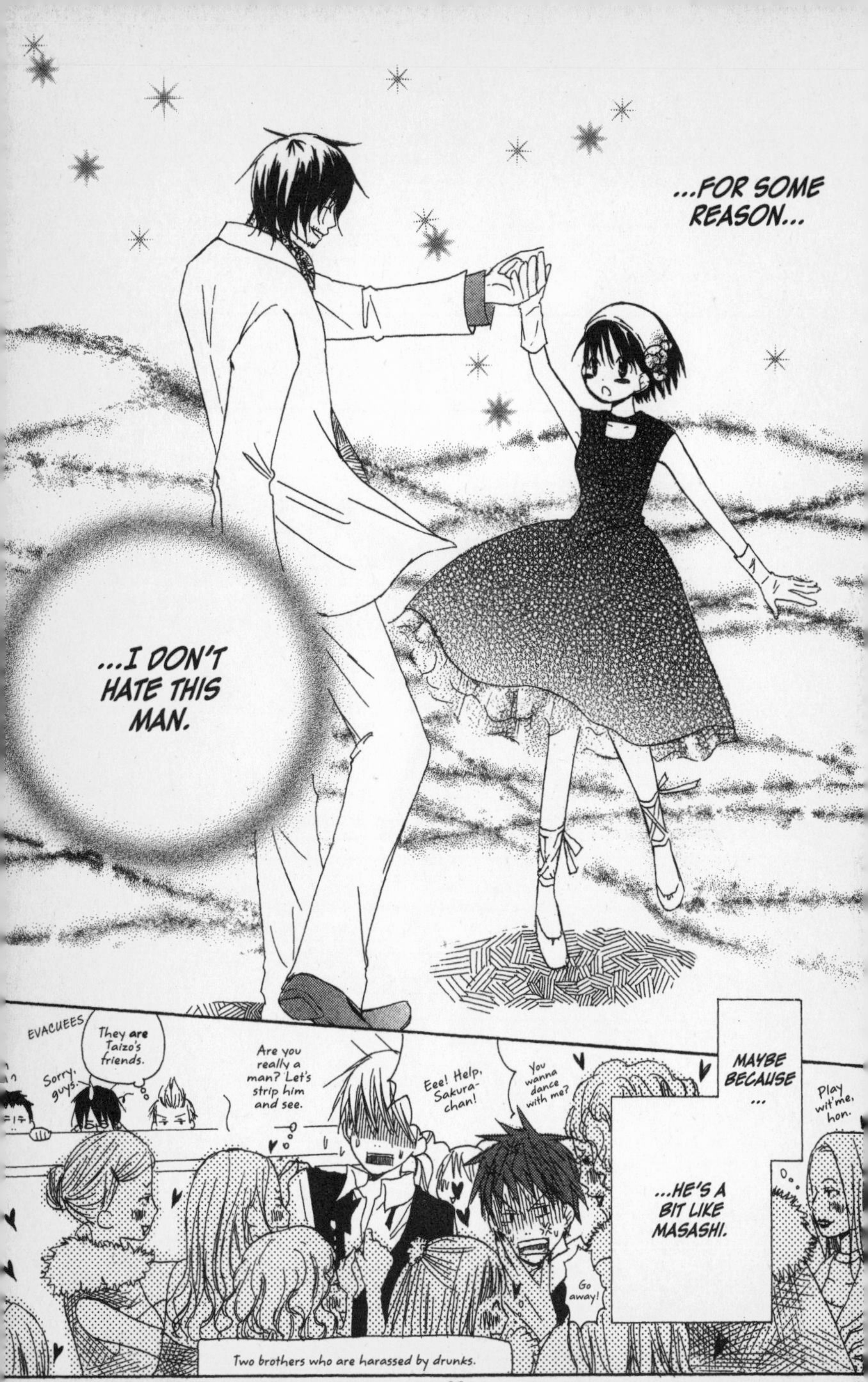
...FOR SOME REASON...
...I DON'T HATE THIS MAN.
MAYBE BECAUSE ...
...HE'S A BIT LIKE MASASHI.
Play wit'me, hon.
You wanna dance with me?
Go away!
Eee! Help, Sakura-chan!
Are you really a man? Let's strip him and see.
They are Taizo's friends.
Sorry, guys.
EVACUEES
Two brothers who are harassed by drunks.

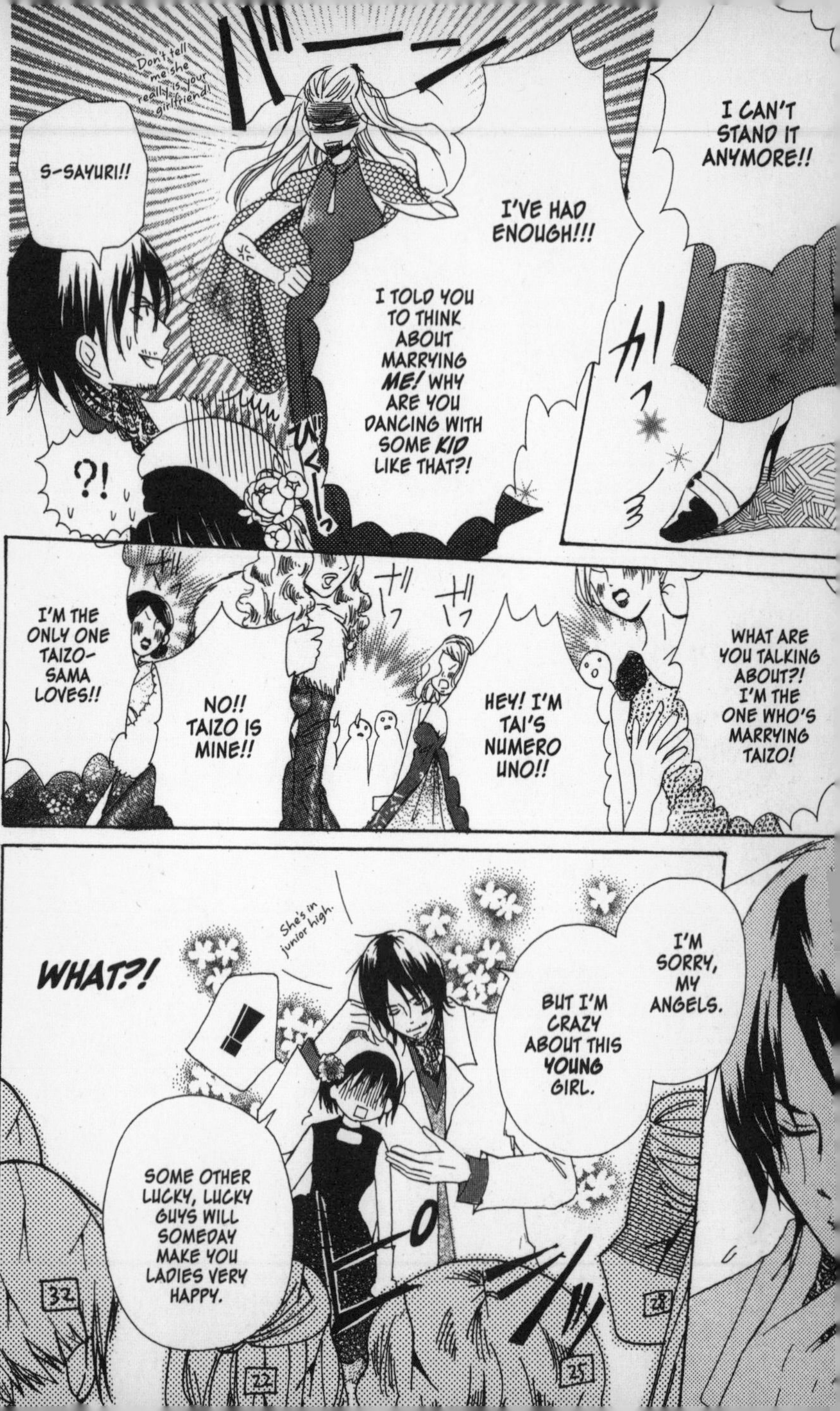
I CAN'T STAND IT ANYMORE!!
I'VE HAD ENOUGH!!!
I TOLD YOU TO THINK ABOUT MARRYING ME! WHY ARE YOU DANCING WITH SOME KID LIKE THAT?!
Don't tell me she really is your girlfriend!
S-SAYURI!!
?!
WHAT ARE YOU TALKING ABOUT?! I'M THE ONE WHO'S MARRYING TAIZO!
HEY! I'M TAI'S NUMERO UNO!!
NO!! TAIZO IS MINE!!
I'M THE ONLY ONE TAIZO-SAMA LOVES!!
I'M SORRY, MY ANGELS.
BUT I'M CRAZY ABOUT THIS YOUNG GIRL.
SOME OTHER LUCKY, LUCKY GUYS WILL SOMEDAY MAKE YOU LADIES VERY HAPPY.
She's in junior high.
!
WHAT?!

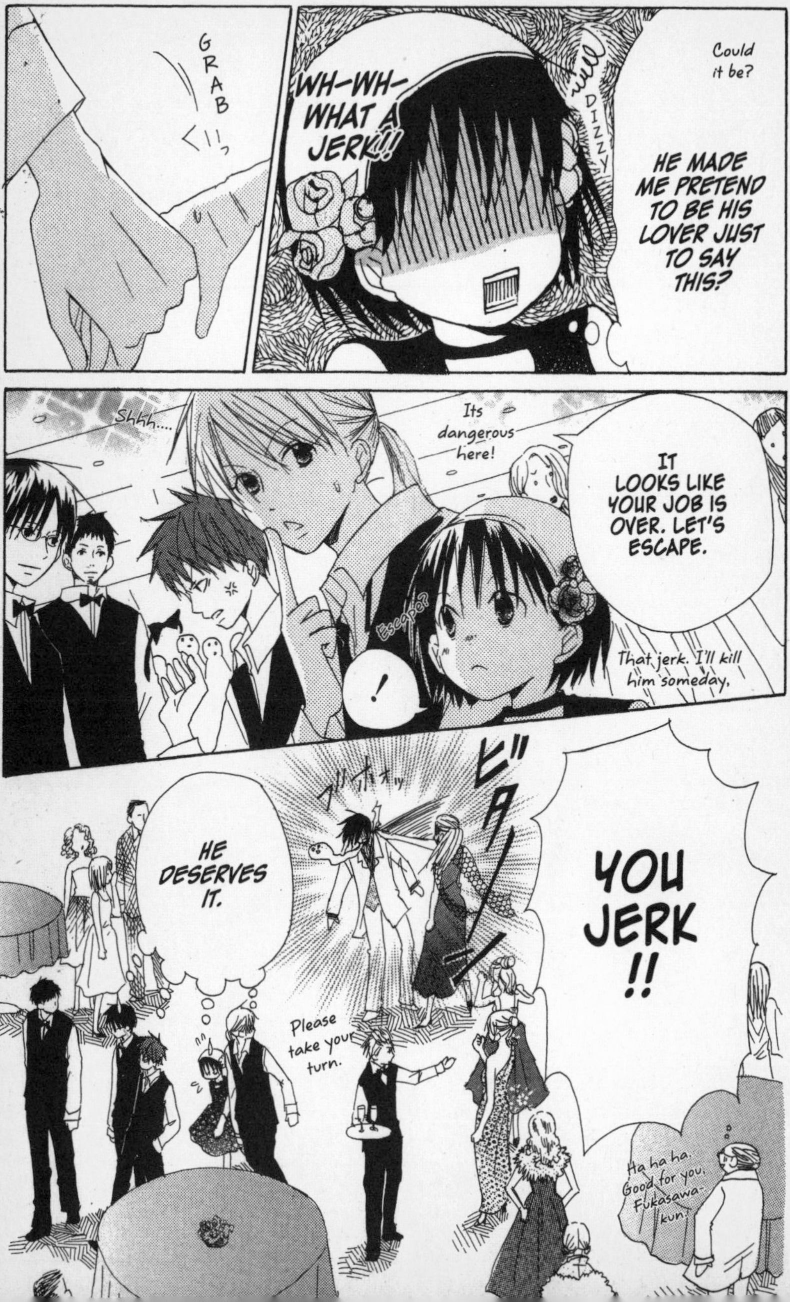
Could it be?
DIZZY
HE MADE ME PRETEND TO BE HIS LOVER JUST TO SAY THIS?
WH-WH-WHAT A JERK!!
GRAB
IT LOOKS LIKE YOUR JOB IS OVER. LET'S ESCAPE.
Its dangerous here!
That jerk. I'll kill him someday,
Escape?
!
Shhh....
YOU JERK !!
HE DESERVES IT.
Ha ha ha. Good for you, Fukasawa-kun.
Please take your turn.

Me & My Brothers

Episode 16

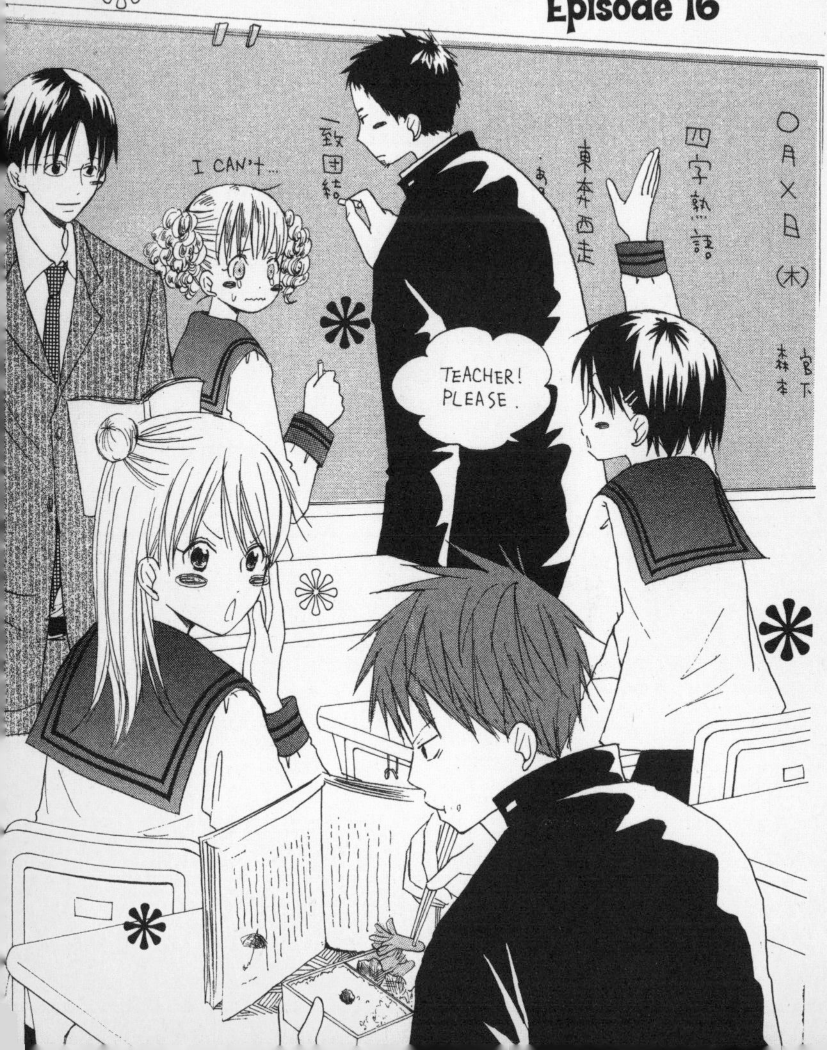
○月×日 (木)
四字熟語
東奔西走
一致団結
I CAN'T...
TEACHER! PLEASE.

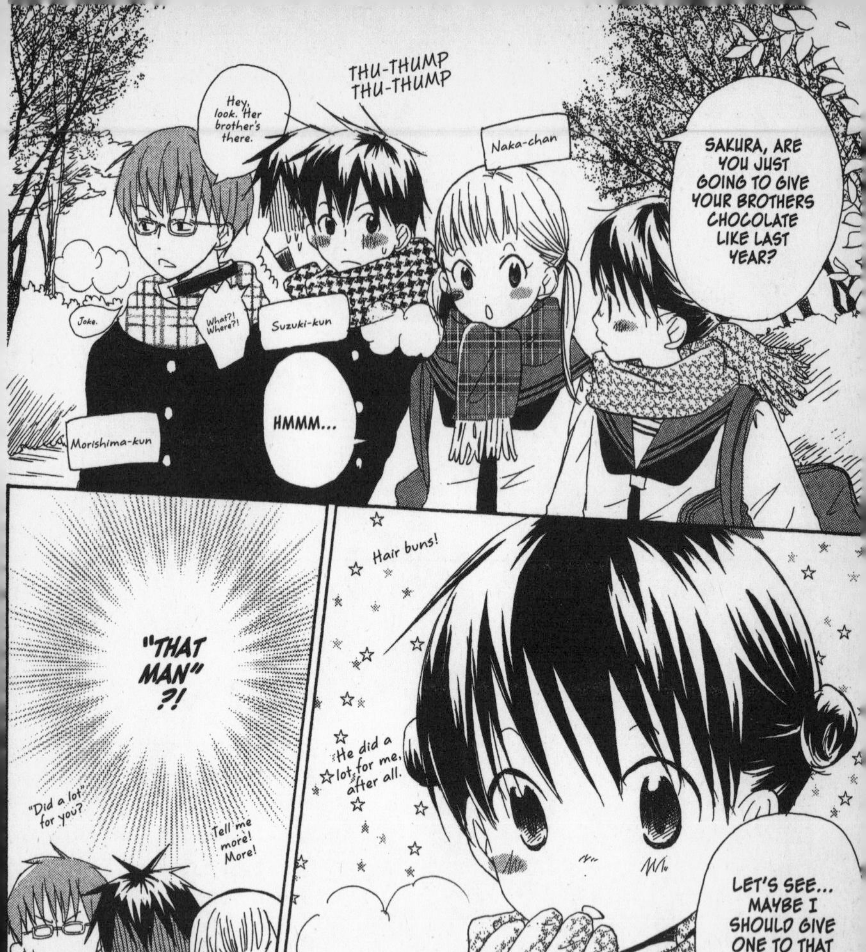
SAKURA, ARE YOU JUST GOING TO GIVE YOUR BROTHERS CHOCOLATE LIKE LAST YEAR?
Naka-chan
THU-THUMP THU-THUMP
Hey, look. Her brother's there.
What?! Where?!
Suzuki-kun
Joke.
Morishima-kun
HMMM...
Hair buns!
He did a lot for me, after all.
LET'S SEE... MAYBE I SHOULD GIVE ONE TO THAT MAN AS A THANK YOU.
"THAT MAN" ?!
Tell me more! More!
"Did a lot" for you?

I don't like drawing flowers. It's difficult.

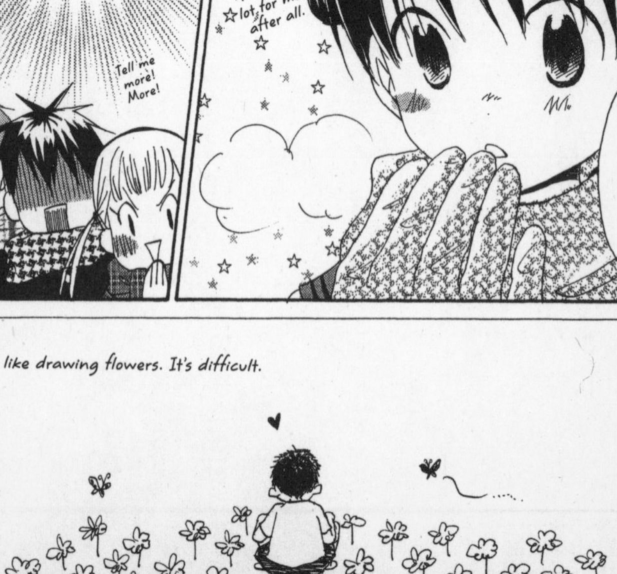

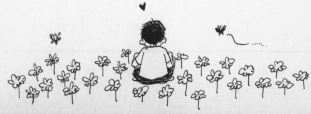

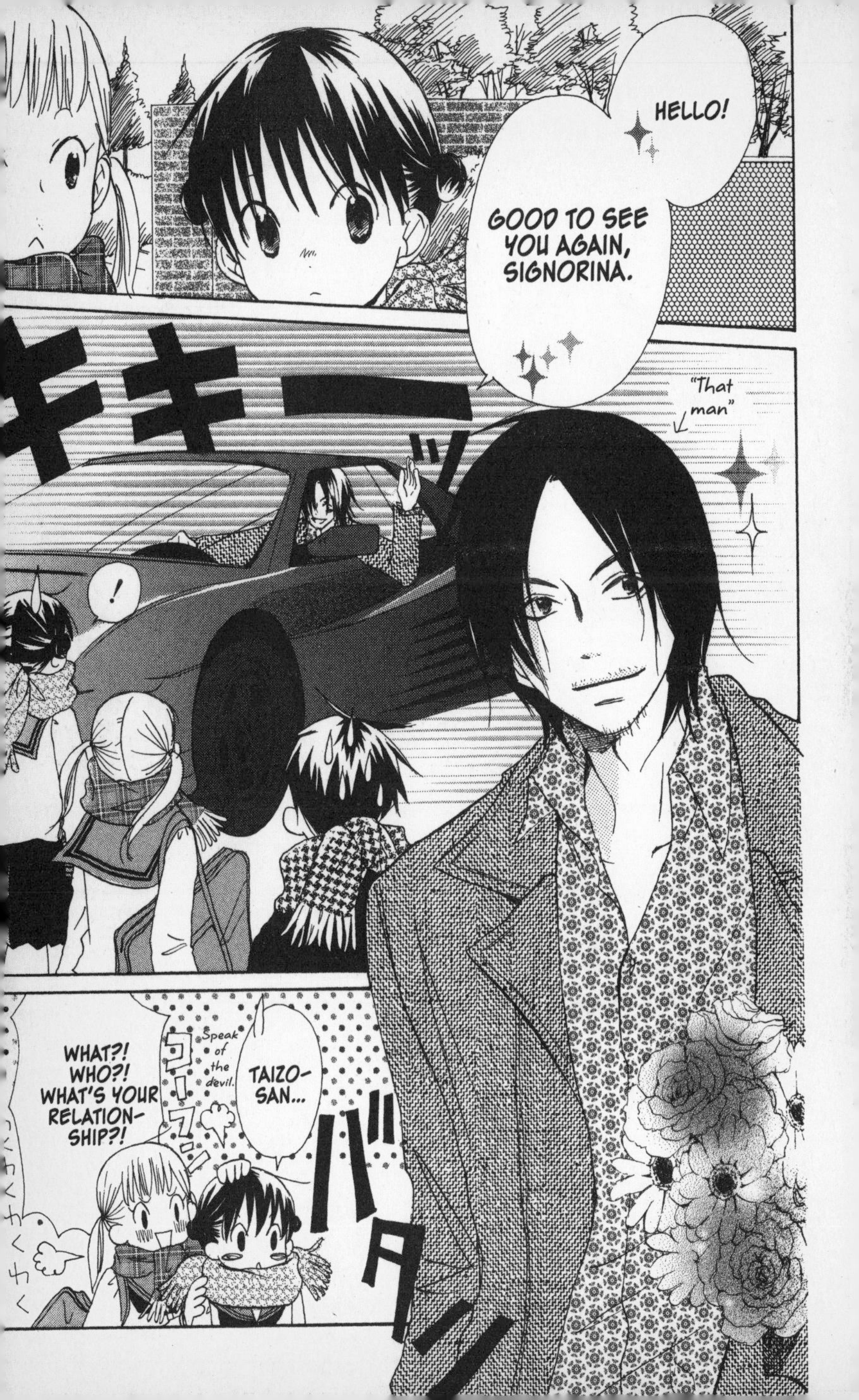
HELLO!
GOOD TO SEE YOU AGAIN, SIGNORINA.
キキーッ
!
"That man"
TAIZO-SAN...
Speak of the devil.
WHAT?! WHO?! WHAT'S YOUR RELATION-SHIP?!

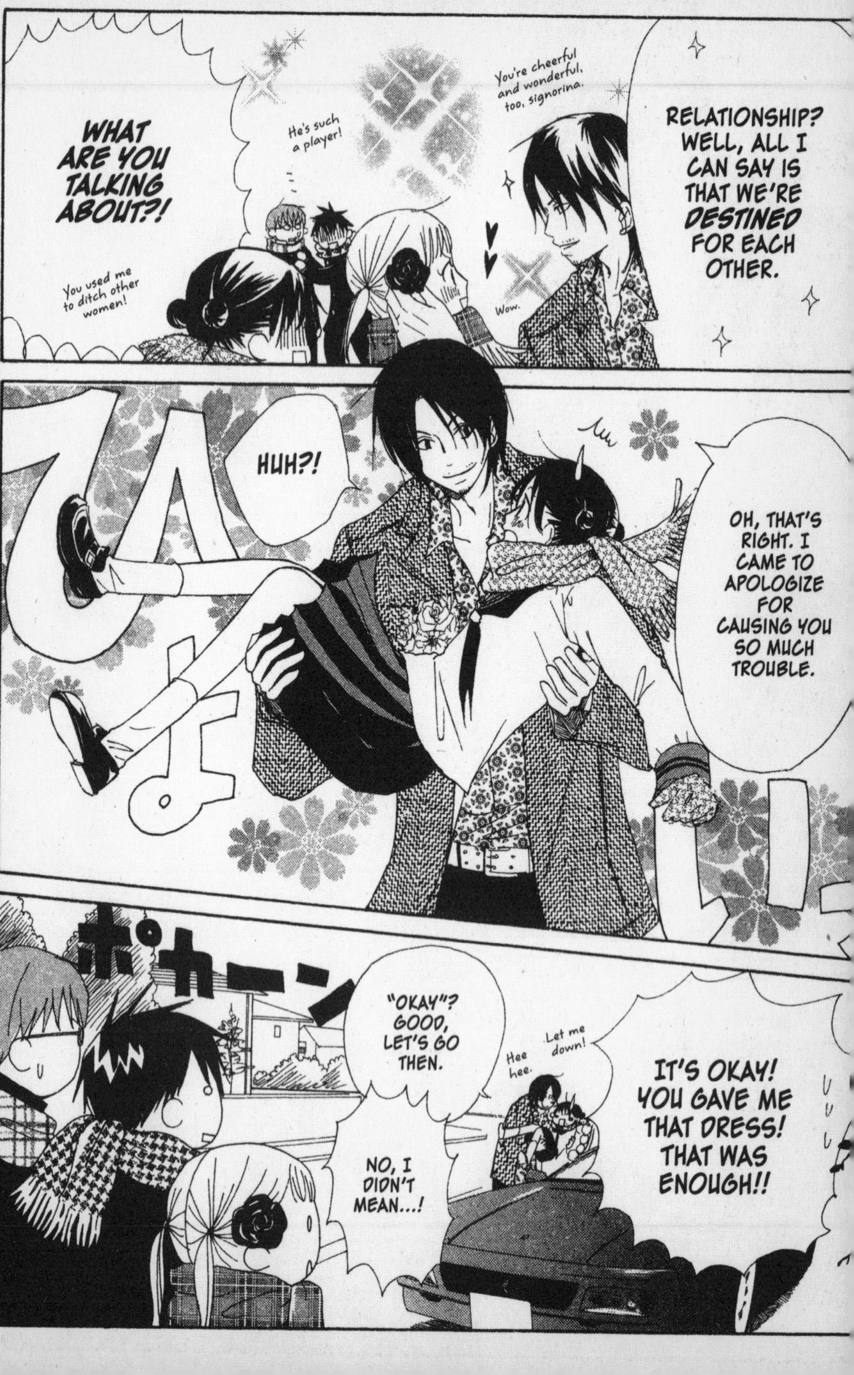
RELATIONSHIP? WELL, ALL I CAN SAY IS THAT WE'RE DESTINED FOR EACH OTHER.
You're cheerful and wonderful, too, signorina.
Wow.
He's such a player!
WHAT ARE YOU TALKING ABOUT?!
You used me to ditch other women!
OH, THAT'S RIGHT. I CAME TO APOLOGIZE FOR CAUSING YOU SO MUCH TROUBLE.
HUH?!
IT'S OKAY! YOU GAVE ME THAT DRESS! THAT WAS ENOUGH!!
Let me down!
Hee hee.
"OKAY"? GOOD, LET'S GO THEN.
NO, I DIDN'T MEAN...!

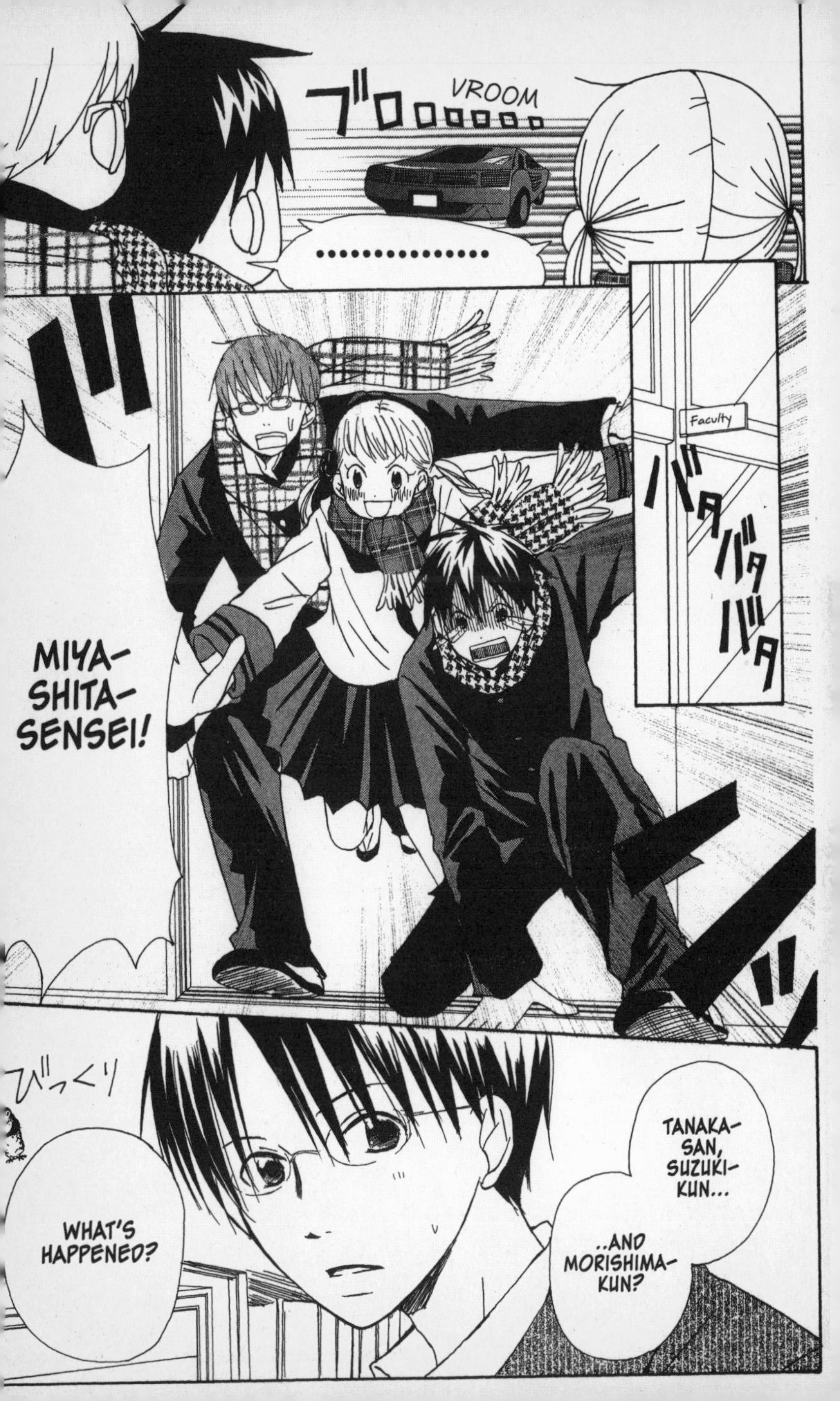

ブロロロロロロ
VROOM
....
バタバタバタ
MIYA-SHITA-SENSEI!
Faculty
びっくり
TANAKA-SAN, SUZUKI-KUN...
..AND MORISHIMA-KUN?
WHAT'S HAPPENED?

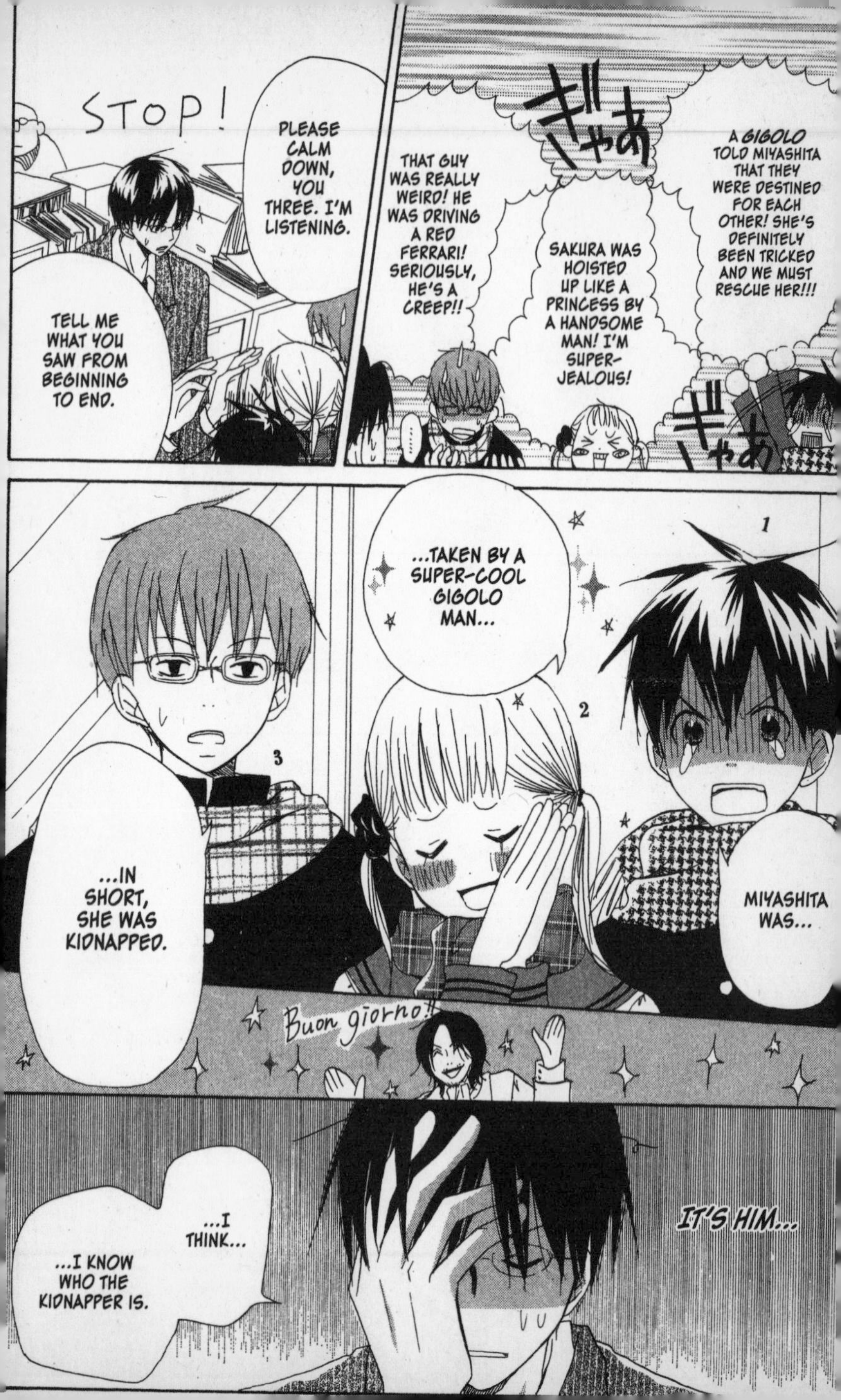
ぎゃあ
A GIGOLO TOLD MIYASHITA THAT THEY WERE DESTINED FOR EACH OTHER! SHE'S DEFINITELY BEEN TRICKED AND WE MUST RESCUE HER!!!
SAKURA WAS HOISTED UP LIKE A PRINCESS BY A HANDSOME MAN! I'M SUPER-JEALOUS!
THAT GUY WAS REALLY WEIRD! HE WAS DRIVING A RED FERRARI! SERIOUSLY, HE'S A CREEP!!
ぎゃあ
...
PLEASE CALM DOWN, YOU THREE. I'M LISTENING.
STOP!
TELL ME WHAT YOU SAW FROM BEGINNING TO END.
1
MIYASHITA WAS...
2
...TAKEN BY A SUPER-COOL GIGOLO MAN...
3
...IN SHORT, SHE WAS KIDNAPPED.
Buon giorno!!
IT'S HIM...
...I THINK...
...I KNOW WHO THE KIDNAPPER IS.

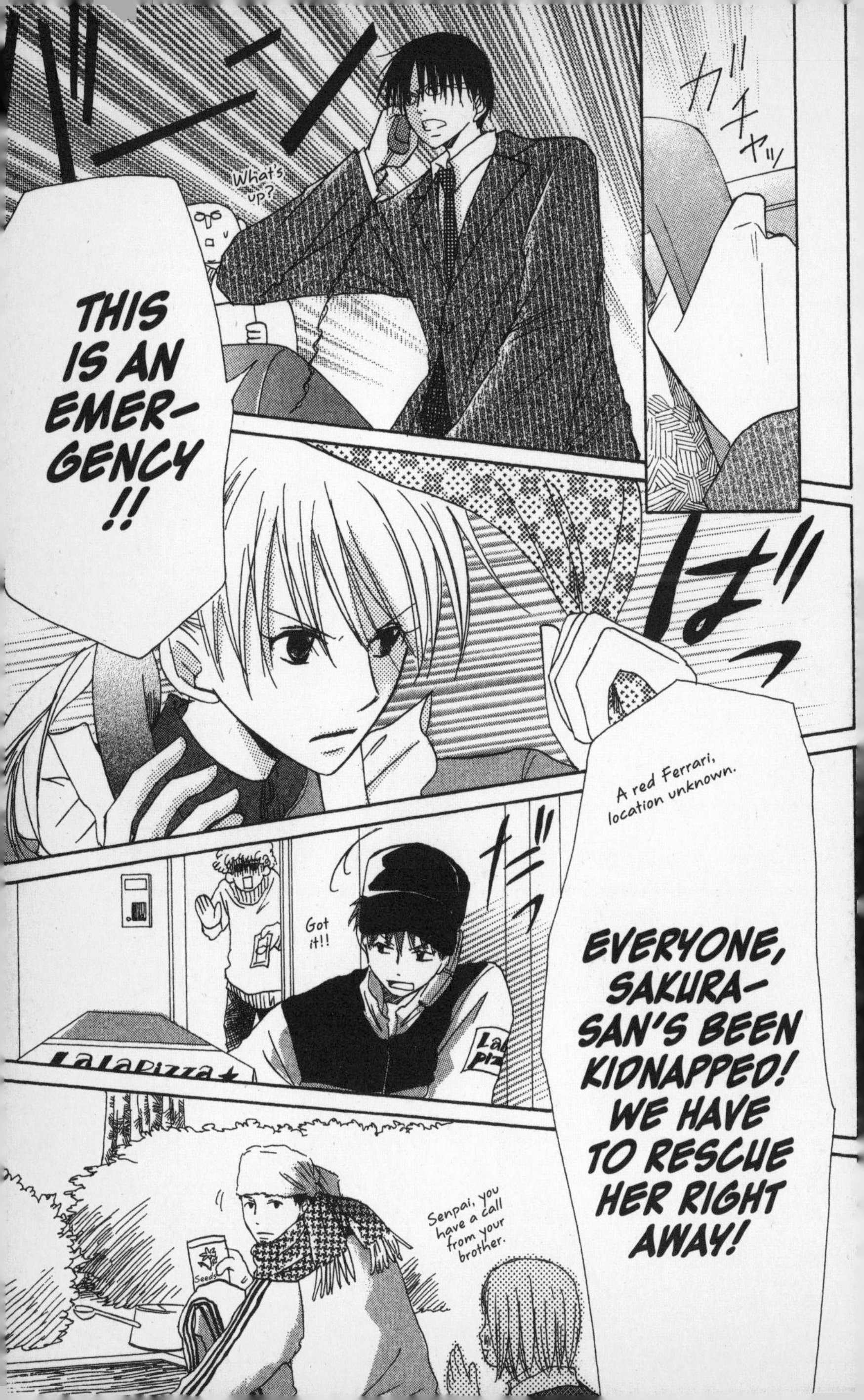

ガチャッ
What's up?
THIS IS AN EMERGENCY!!
ばっ
EVERYONE, SAKURA-SAN'S BEEN KIDNAPPED! WE HAVE TO RESCUE HER RIGHT AWAY!
A red Ferrari, location unknown.
Got it!!
Senpai, you have a call from your brother.

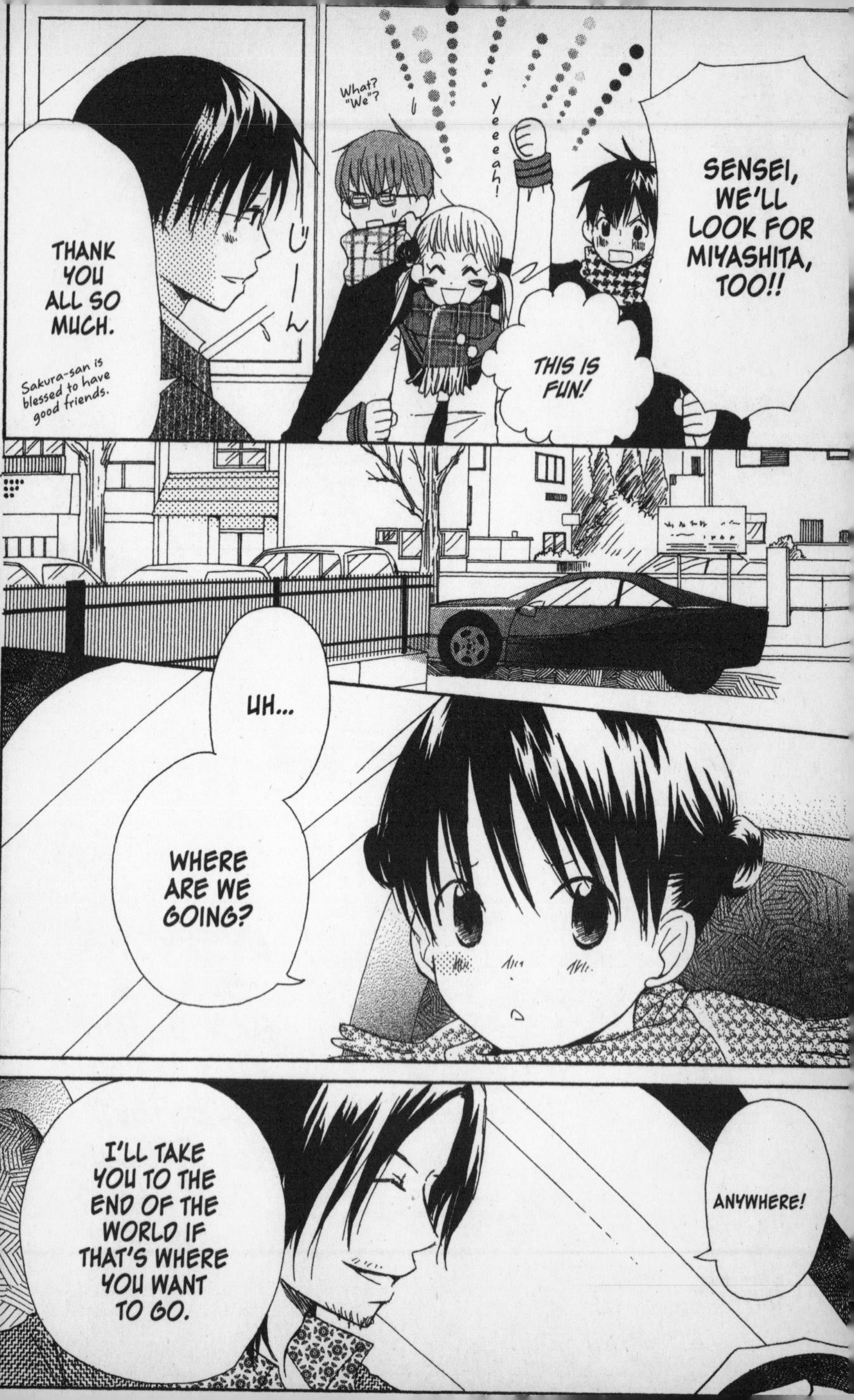
SENSEI, WE'LL LOOK FOR MIYASHITA, TOO!!
Yeeeah!
What? "We"?
THIS IS FUN!
THANK YOU ALL SO MUCH.
Sakura-san is blessed to have good friends.
UH...
WHERE ARE WE GOING?
ANYWHERE!
I'LL TAKE YOU TO THE END OF THE WORLD IF THAT'S WHERE YOU WANT TO GO.

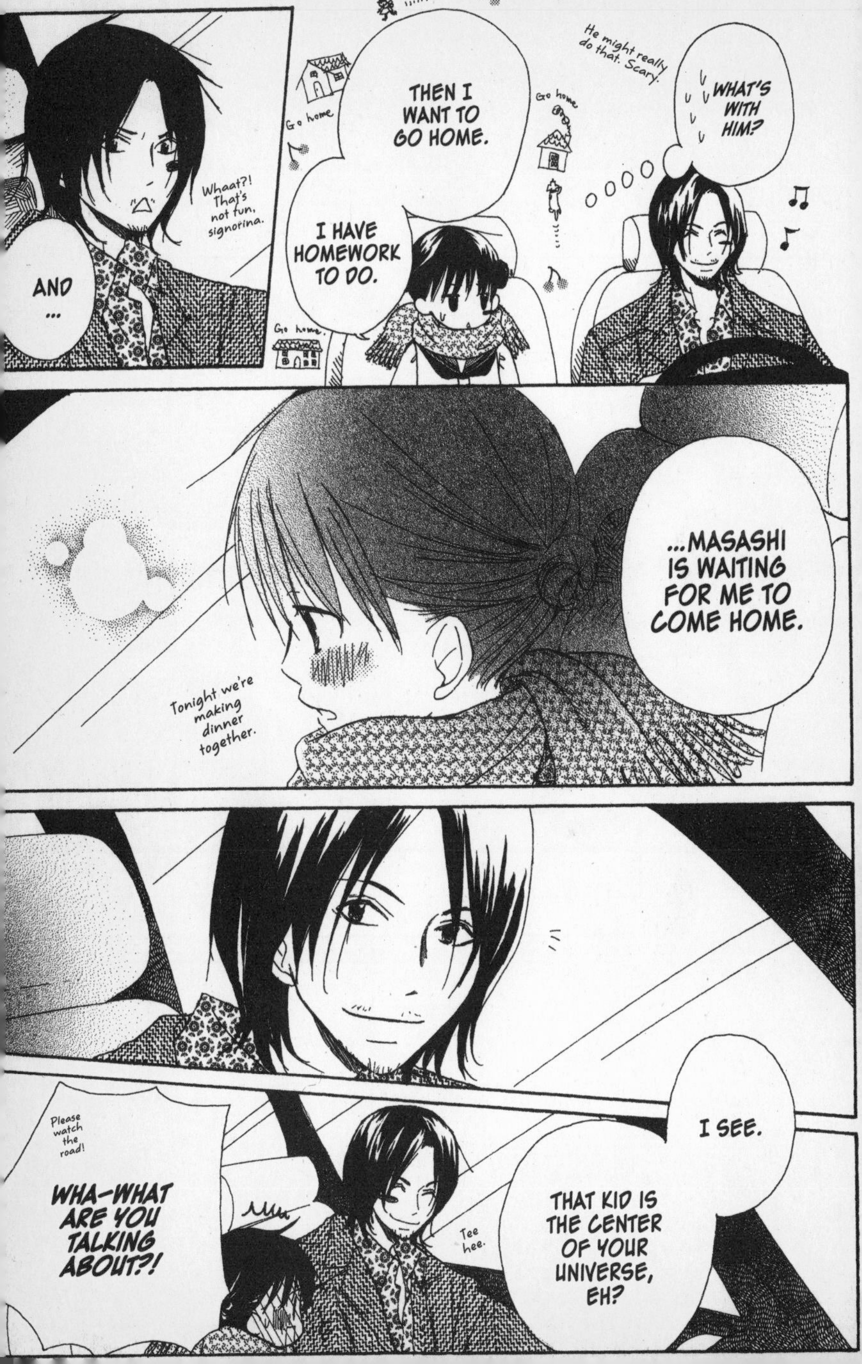
He might really do that. Scary.
WHAT'S WITH HIM?
Go home
THEN I WANT TO GO HOME.
Go home
I HAVE HOMEWORK TO DO.
Go home
Whaat?! That's not fun, signorina.
AND ...
...MASASHI IS WAITING FOR ME TO COME HOME.
Tonight we're making dinner together.
I SEE.
THAT KID IS THE CENTER OF YOUR UNIVERSE, EH?
Tee hee.
WHA-WHAT ARE YOU TALKING ABOUT?!
Please watch the road!

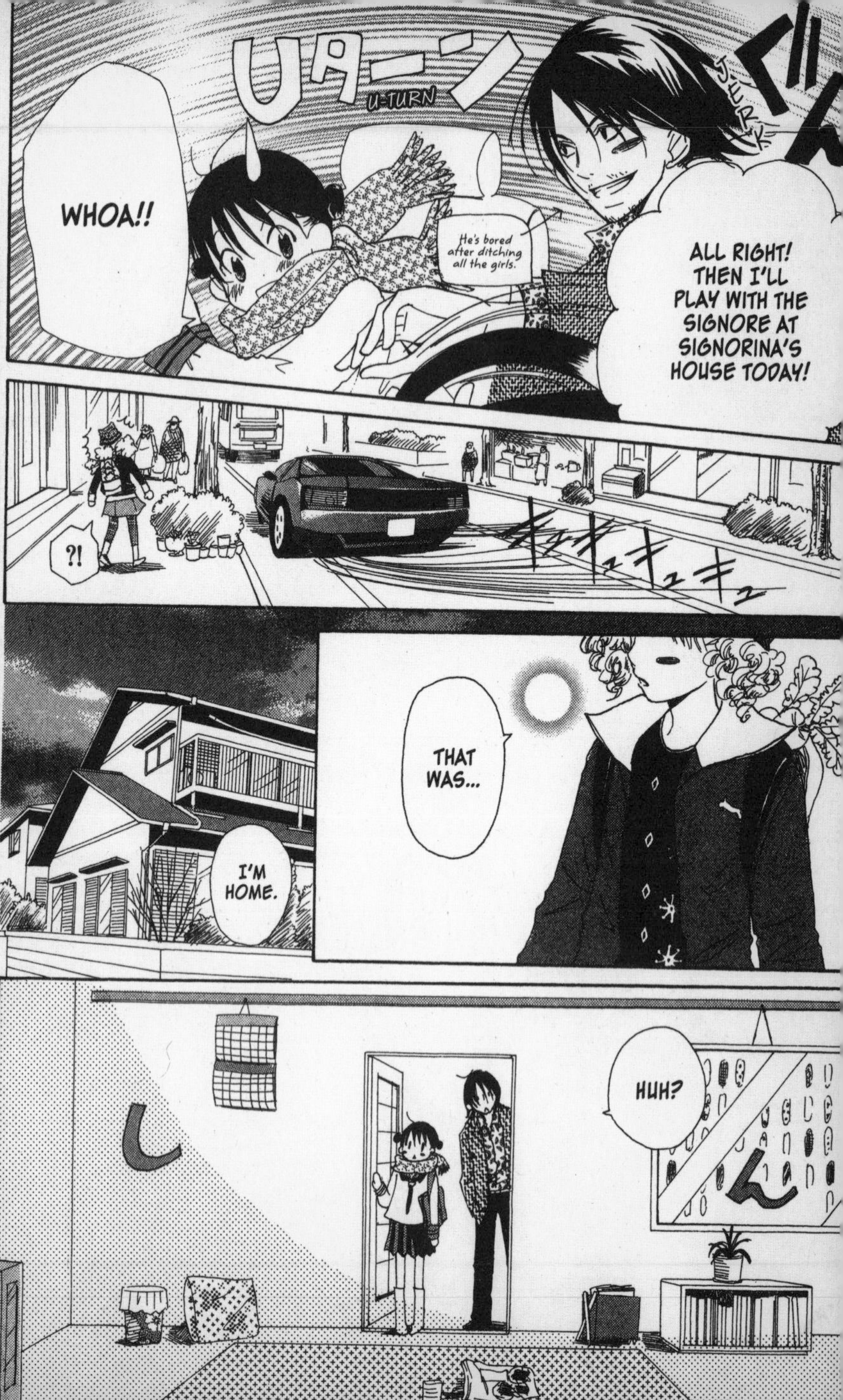
JERK
ALL RIGHT! THEN I'LL PLAY WITH THE SIGNORE AT SIGNORINA'S HOUSE TODAY!
He's bored after ditching all the girls.
Uターン
U-TURN
WHOA!!
?!
THAT WAS...
I'M HOME.
HUH?

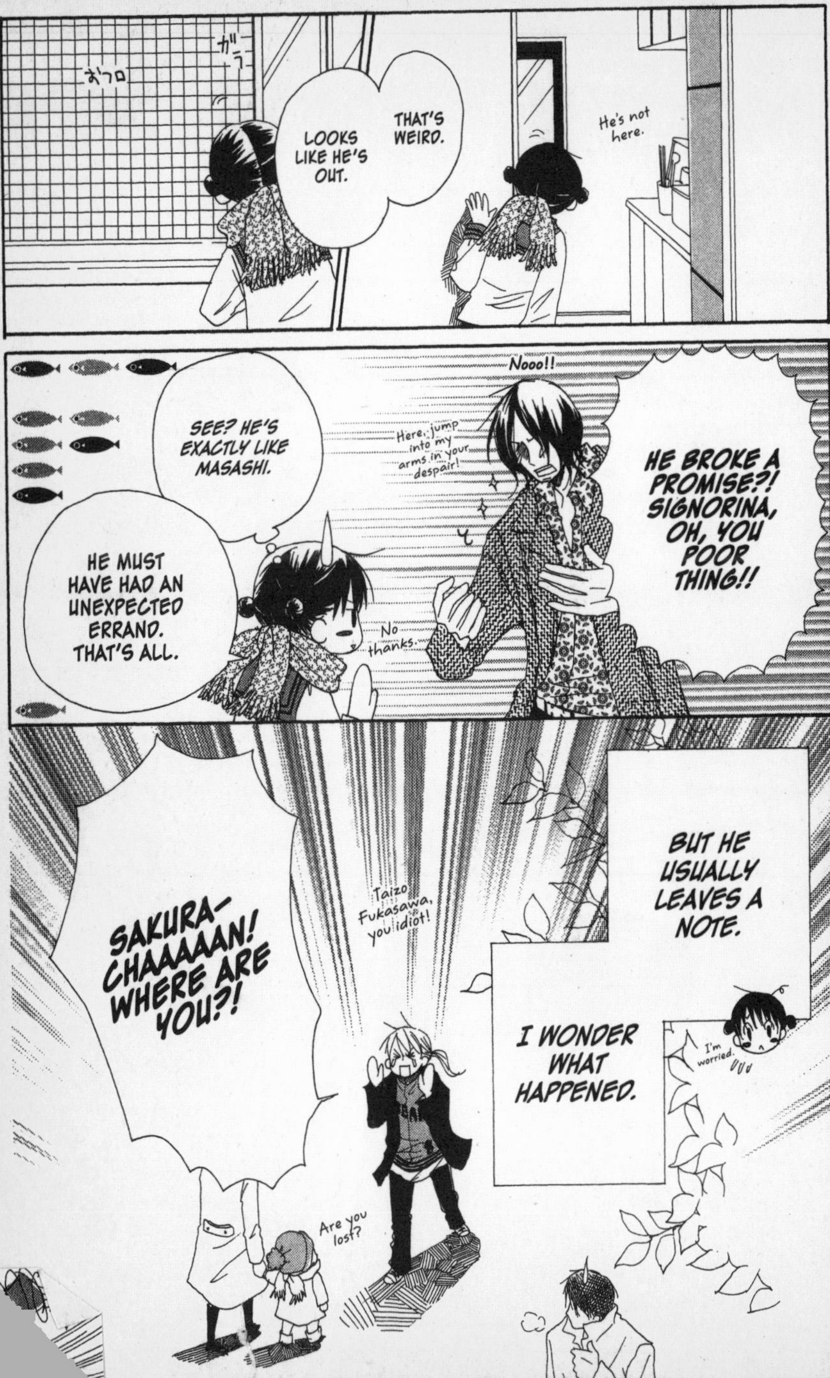
He's not here.
THAT'S WEIRD.
LOOKS LIKE HE'S OUT.
ガラ
おフロ
HE BROKE A PROMISE?! SIGNORINA, OH, YOU POOR THING!!
Nooo!!
Here, jump into my arms in your despair!
SEE? HE'S EXACTLY LIKE MASASHI.
No thanks.
HE MUST HAVE HAD AN UNEXPECTED ERRAND. THAT'S ALL.
BUT HE USUALLY LEAVES A NOTE.
I'm worried.
I WONDER WHAT HAPPENED.
Taizo Fukasawa, you idiot!
SAKURA-CHAAAAAN! WHERE ARE YOU?!
Are you lost?

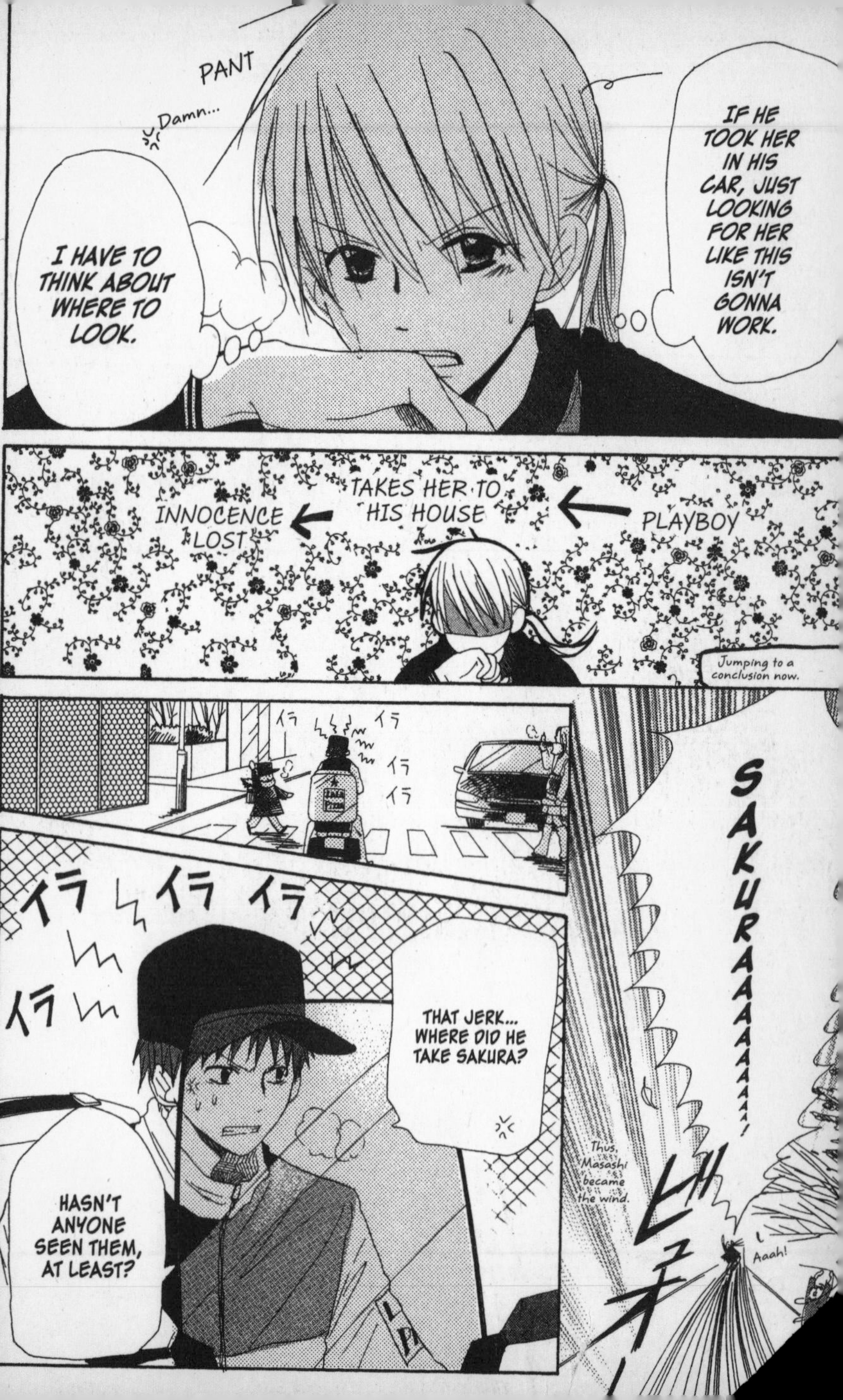
IF HE TOOK HER IN HIS CAR, JUST LOOKING FOR HER LIKE THIS ISN'T GONNA WORK.
PANT
Damn...
I HAVE TO THINK ABOUT WHERE TO LOOK.
PLAYBOY
TAKES HER TO HIS HOUSE
INNOCENCE LOST
Jumping to a conclusion now.
SAKURAAAAAAAAAAA!
ビュオー
Thus, Masashi became the wind.
Aaah!
イラ
イラ
イラ
イラ
イラ
イラ
イラ
イラ
THAT JERK... WHERE DID HE TAKE SAKURA?
HASN'T ANYONE SEEN THEM, AT LEAST?

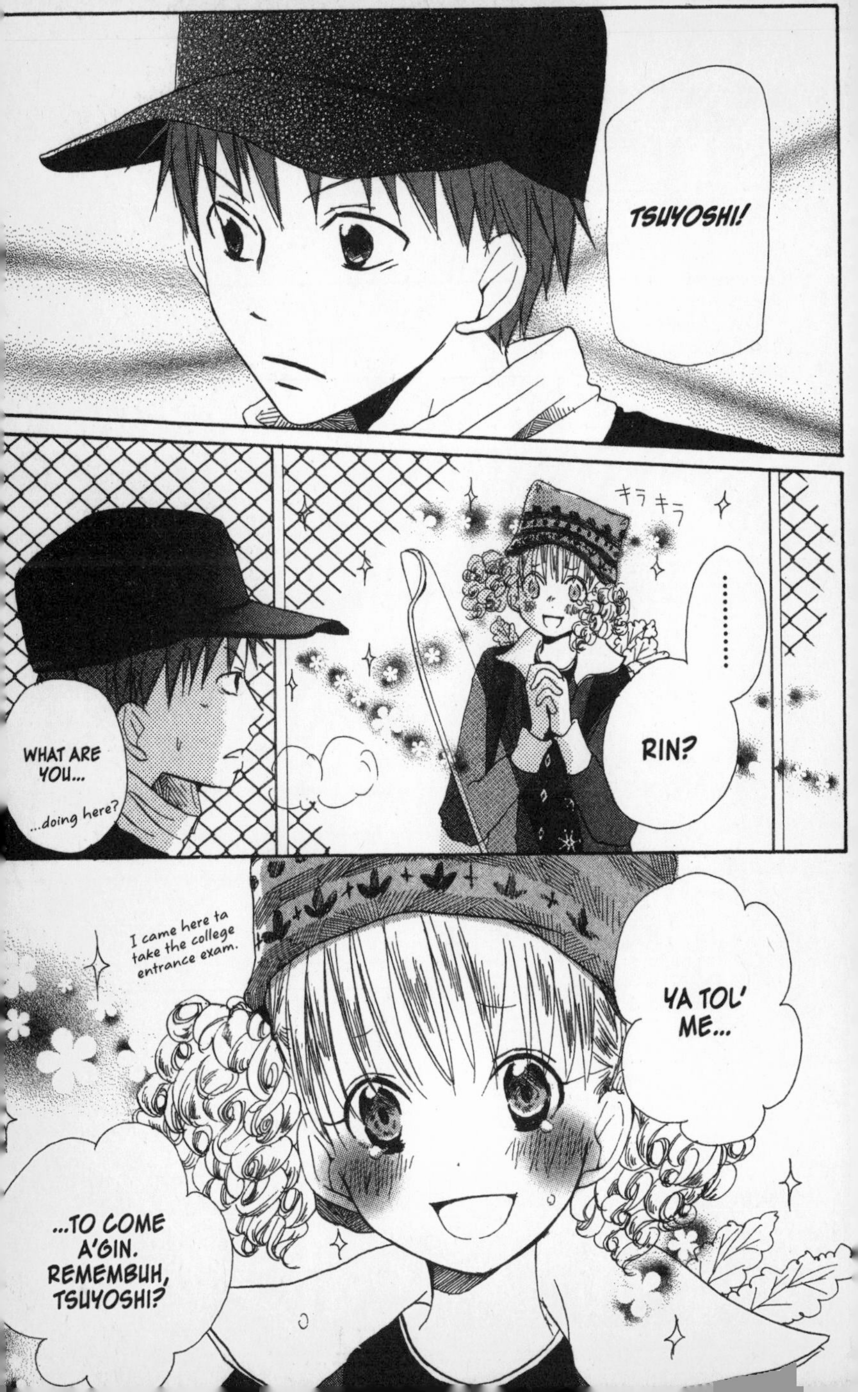

TSUYOSHI!
キラキラ
......
RIN?
WHAT ARE YOU...
...doing here?
YA TOL' ME...
I came here ta take the college entrance exam.
...TO COME A'GIN. REMEMBUH, TSUYOSHI?

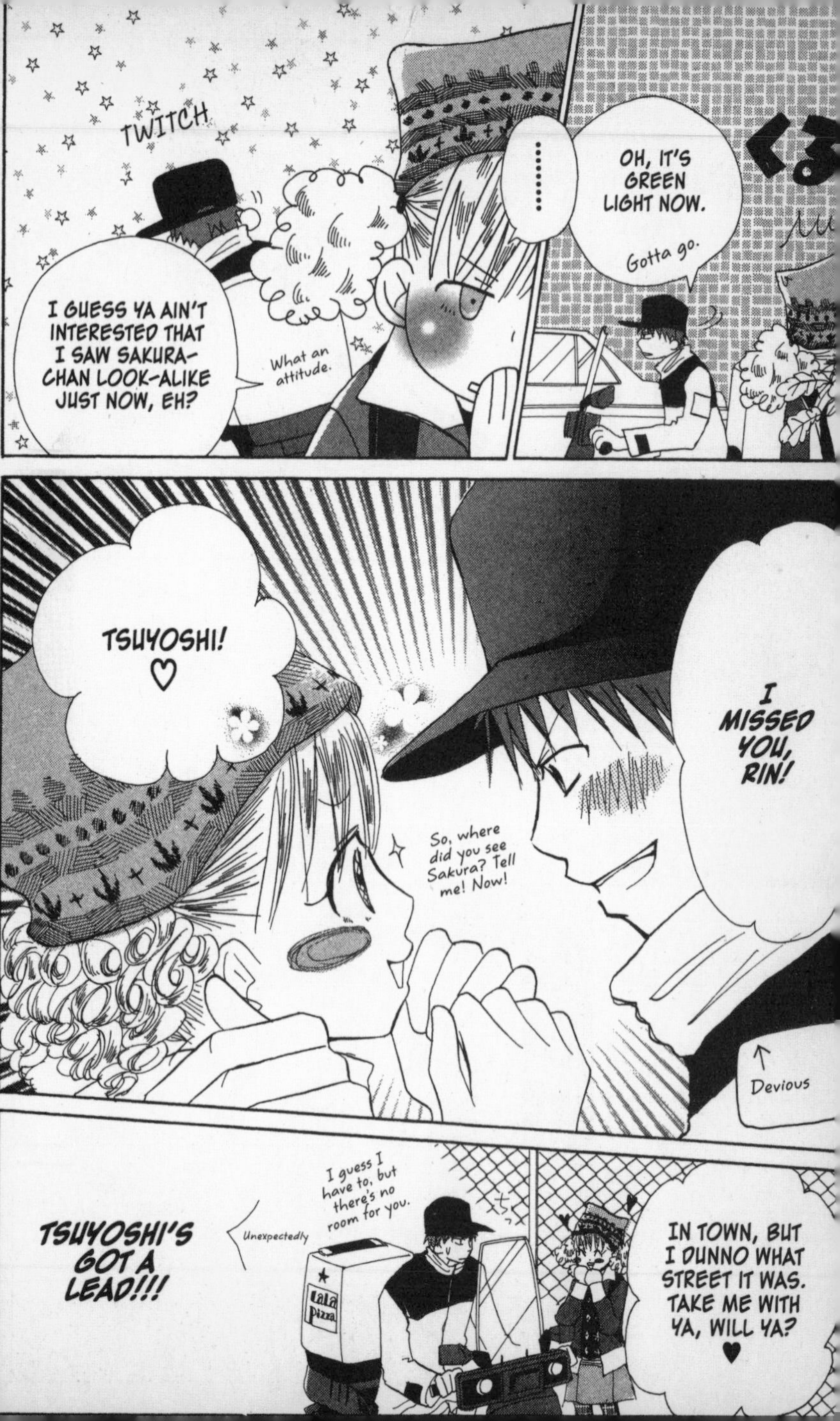

OH, IT'S GREEN LIGHT NOW.
Gotta go.
......
TWITCH
I GUESS YA AIN'T INTERESTED THAT I SAW SAKURA-CHAN LOOK-ALIKE JUST NOW, EH?
What an attitude.
I MISSED YOU, RIN!
Devious
So, where did you see Sakura? Tell me! Now!
TSUYOSHI! ♥
IN TOWN, BUT I DUNNO WHAT STREET IT WAS. TAKE ME WITH YA, WILL YA? ♥
I guess I have to, but there's no room for you.
Unexpectedly
TSUYOSHI'S GOT A LEAD!!!
LaLa Pizza

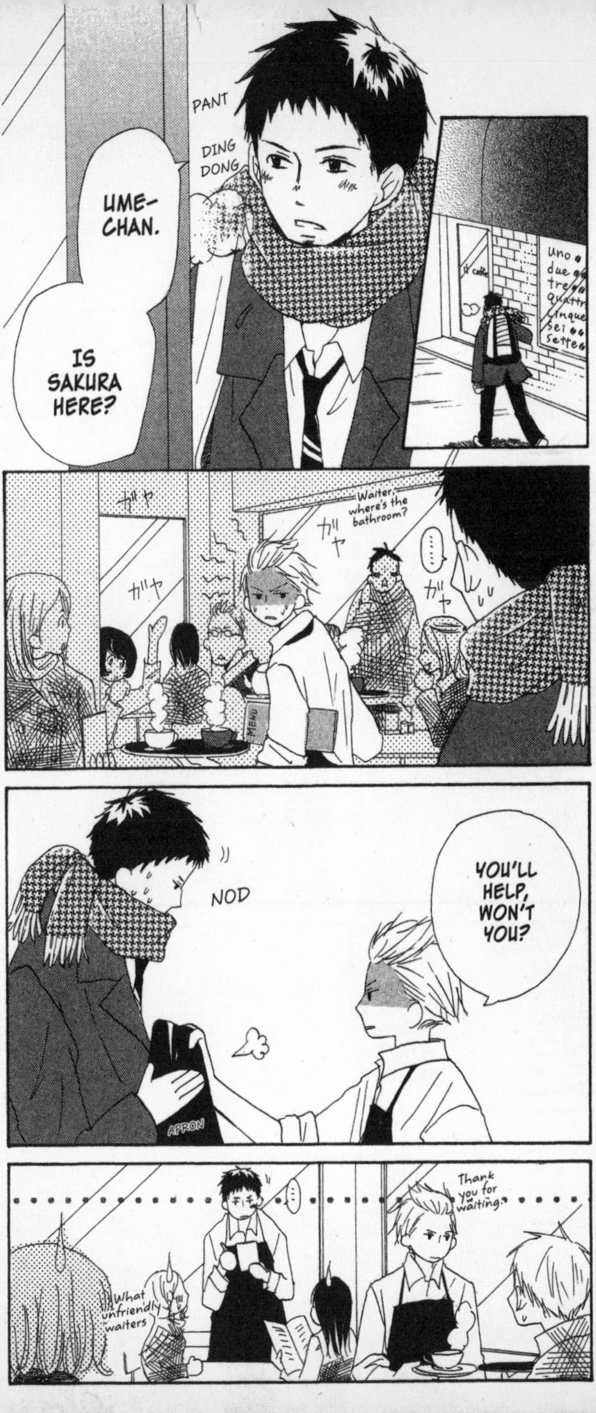
il caffè
uno
due
tre
PANT
DING DONG
UME-CHAN.
IS SAKURA HERE?
ガヤ
Waiter, where's the bathroom?
ガヤ
ガヤ
ガヤ
.....
MENU
YOU'LL HELP, WON'T YOU?
NOD
APRON
Thank you for waiting.
...
What unfriendly waiters

☆ 2 ☆

Well, ahem, I'm in trouble. I can't think of anything to write. So I'll introduce my sister again, I think. I have two sisters. When I made one of my sisters a clock in volume 3, the eldest sister said that if she had to be a clock, she wanted it to be antique.

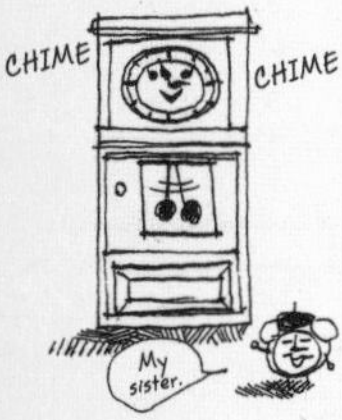
CHIME
CHIME
My sister.

I don't think she'll like it. She might get mad. But I couldn't think of another antique shape... But anyway, the space is filled and that makes everything okay.

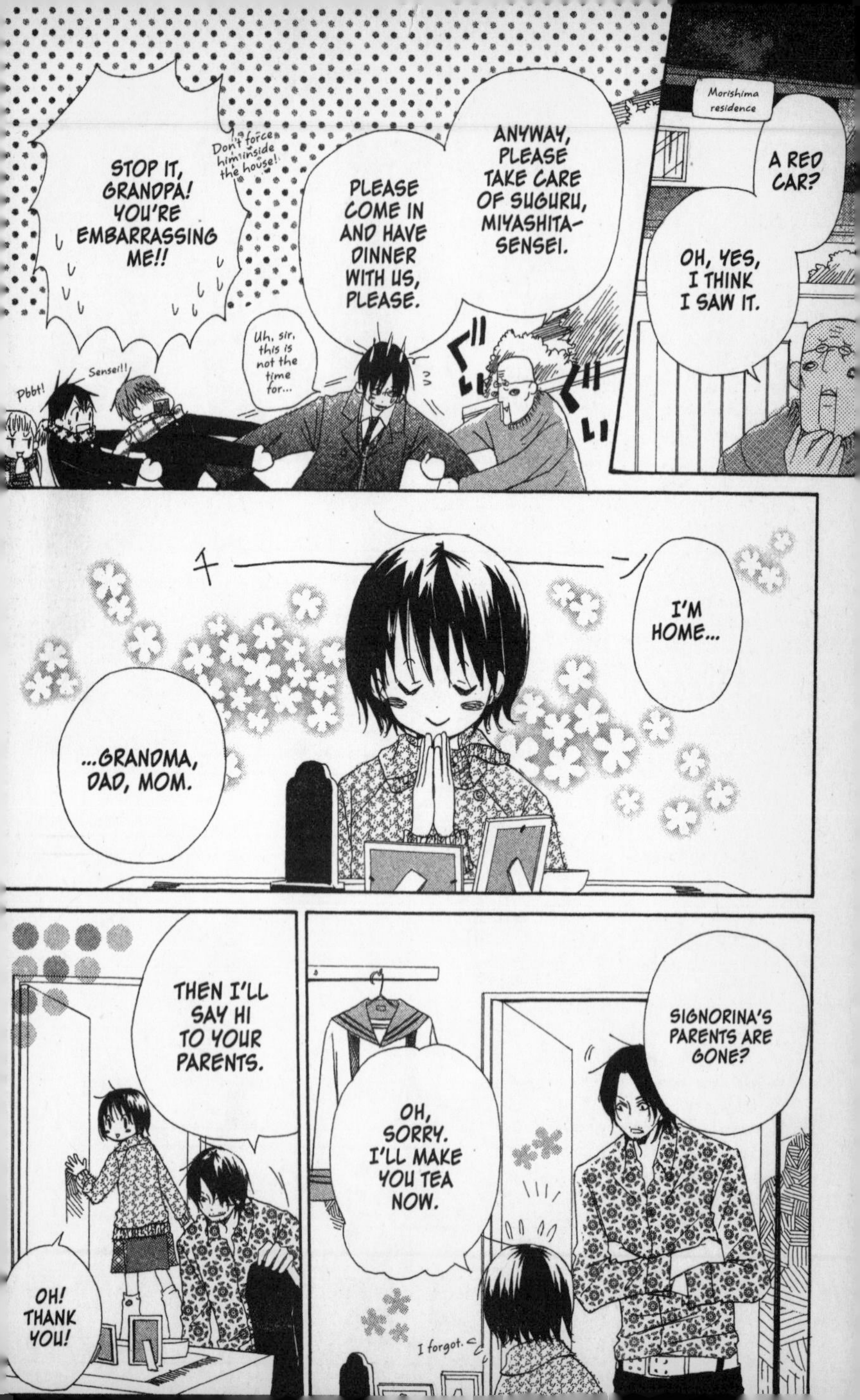
Morishima residence
A RED CAR?
OH, YES, I THINK I SAW IT.
ANYWAY, PLEASE TAKE CARE OF SUGURU, MIYASHITA-SENSEI.
PLEASE COME IN AND HAVE DINNER WITH US, PLEASE.
Don't force him inside the house!
STOP IT, GRANDPA! YOU'RE EMBARRASSING ME!!
Uh, sir, this is not the time for...
Sensei!!
Pbbt!
I'M HOME...
...GRANDMA, DAD, MOM.
SIGNORINA'S PARENTS ARE GONE?
OH, SORRY. I'LL MAKE YOU TEA NOW.
I forgot.
THEN I'LL SAY HI TO YOUR PARENTS.
OH! THANK YOU!

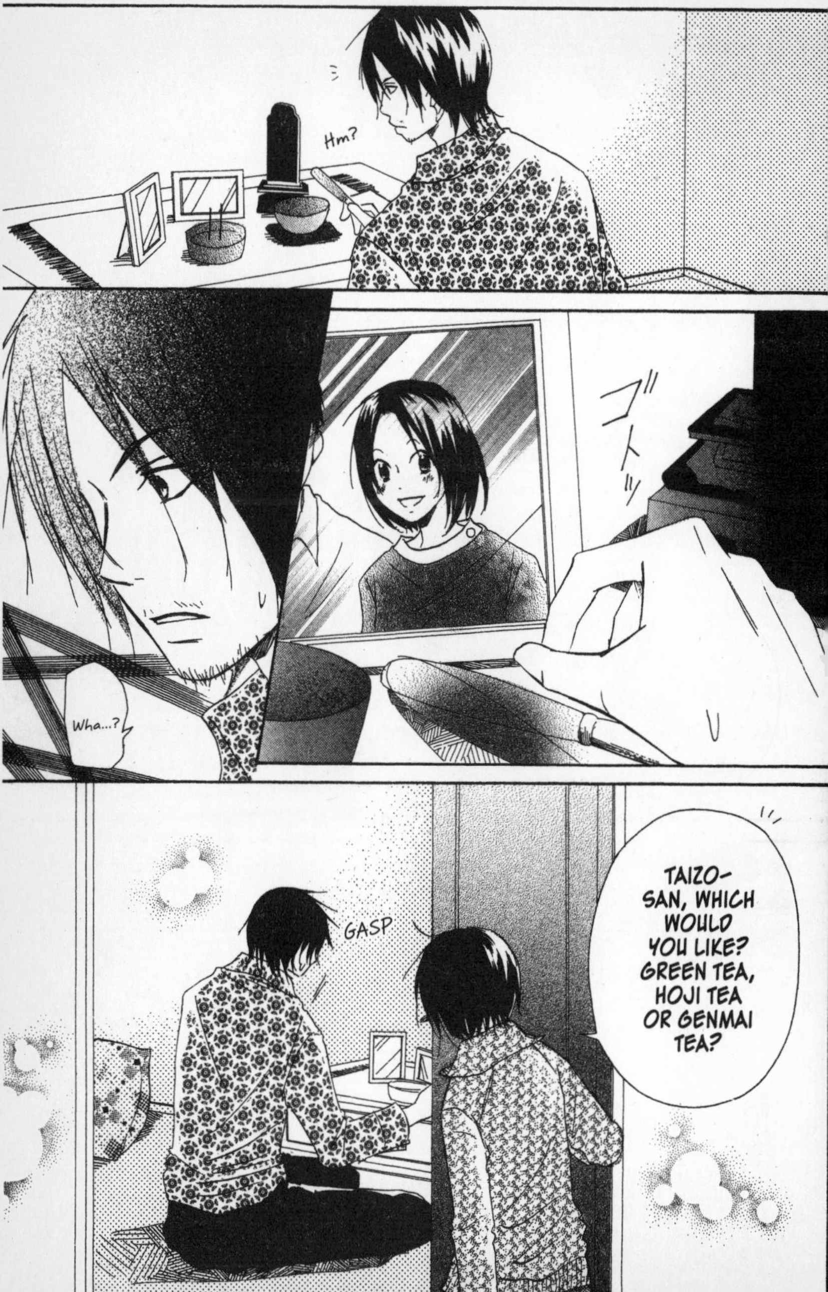
Hm?
ゴトッ
Wha...?
TAIZO-SAN, WHICH WOULD YOU LIKE? GREEN TEA, HOJI TEA OR GENMAI TEA?
GASP

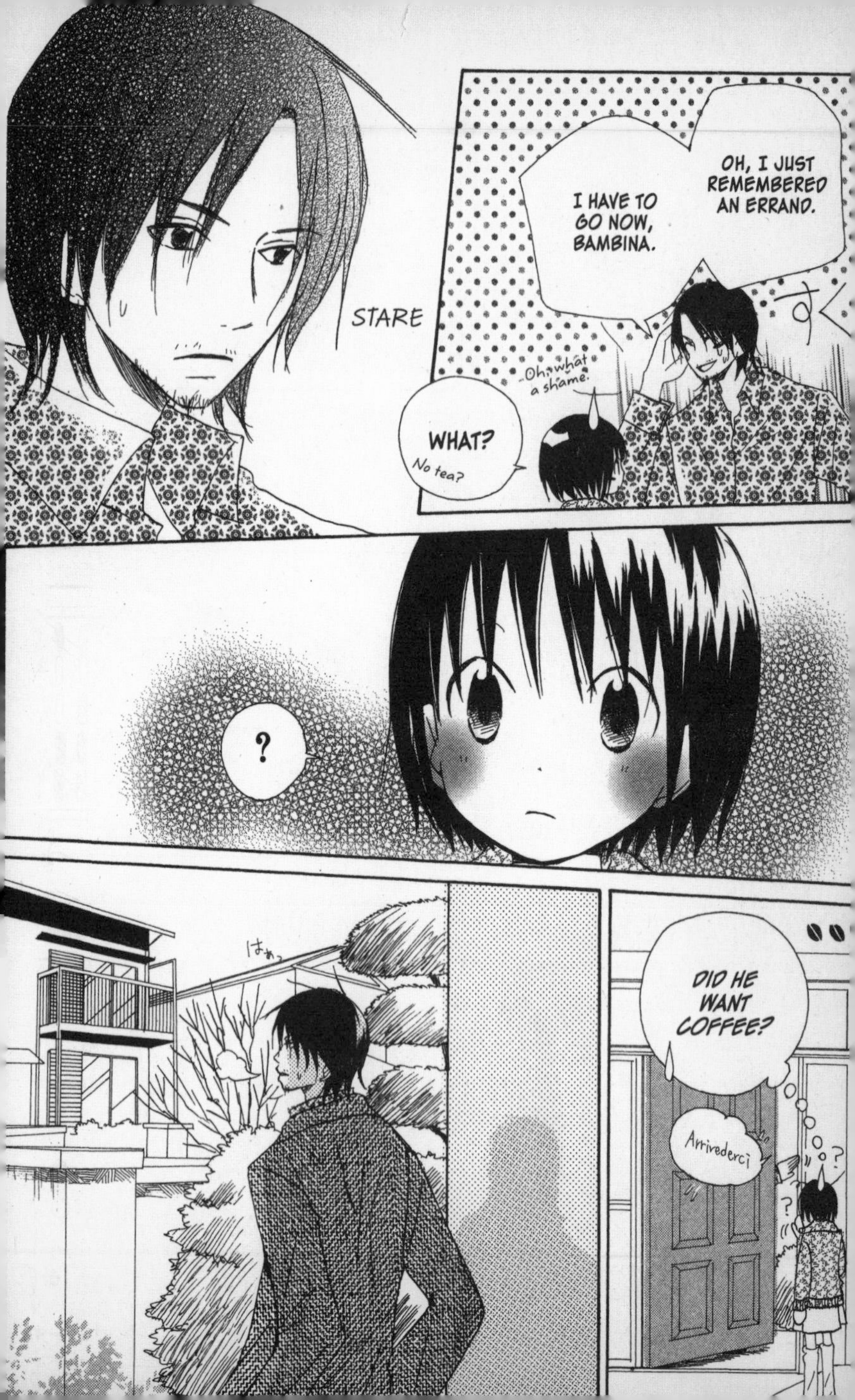
OH, I JUST REMEMBERED AN ERRAND.
I HAVE TO GO NOW, BAMBINA.
すく
Oh, what a shame.
WHAT?
No tea?
STARE
?
DID HE WANT COFFEE?
Arrivederci
?
?
はぁっ

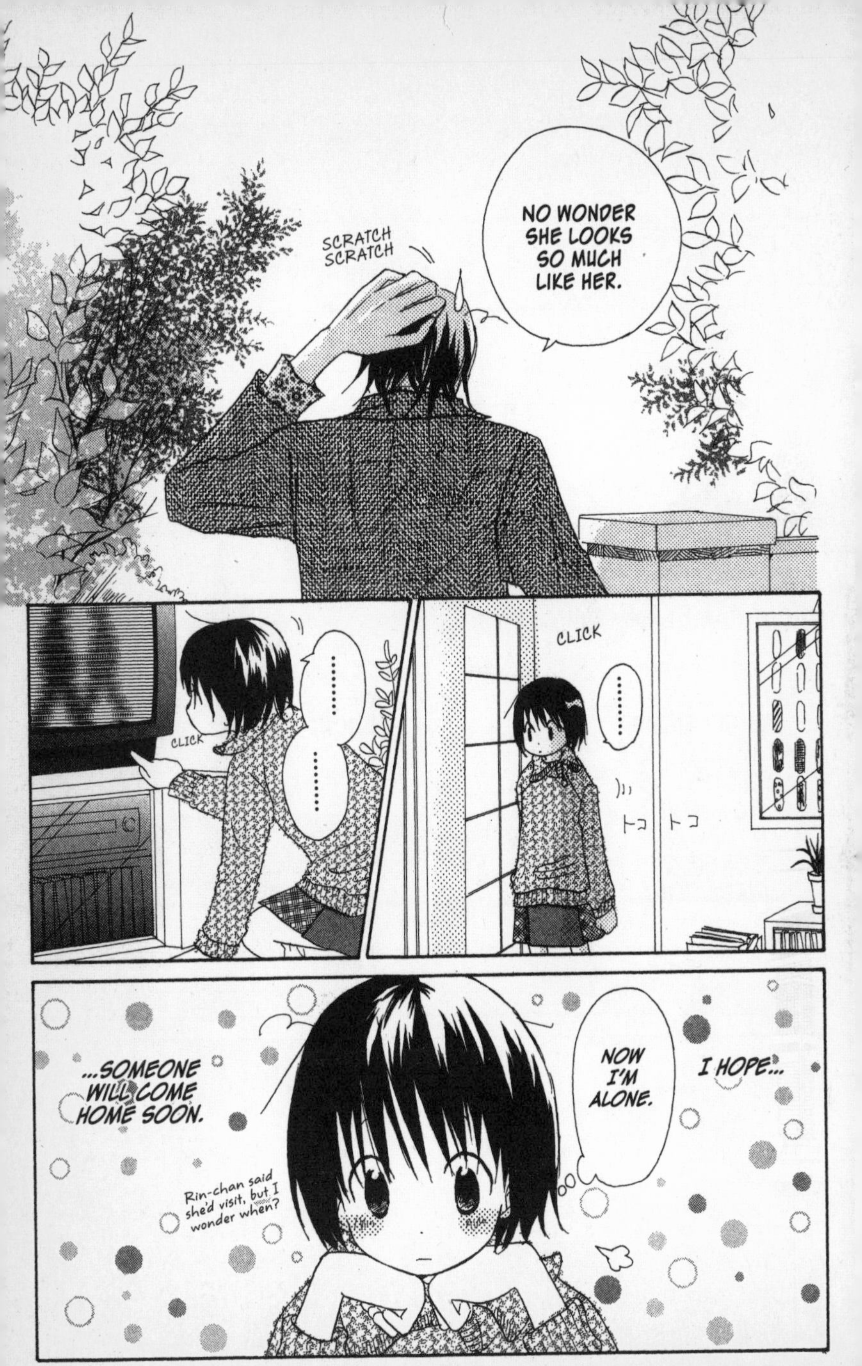
SCRATCH SCRATCH
NO WONDER SHE LOOKS SO MUCH LIKE HER.
CLICK
....
トコ トコ
....
....
CLICK
I HOPE...
NOW I'M ALONE.
...SOMEONE WILL COME HOME SOON.
Rin-chan said she'd visit, but I wonder when?

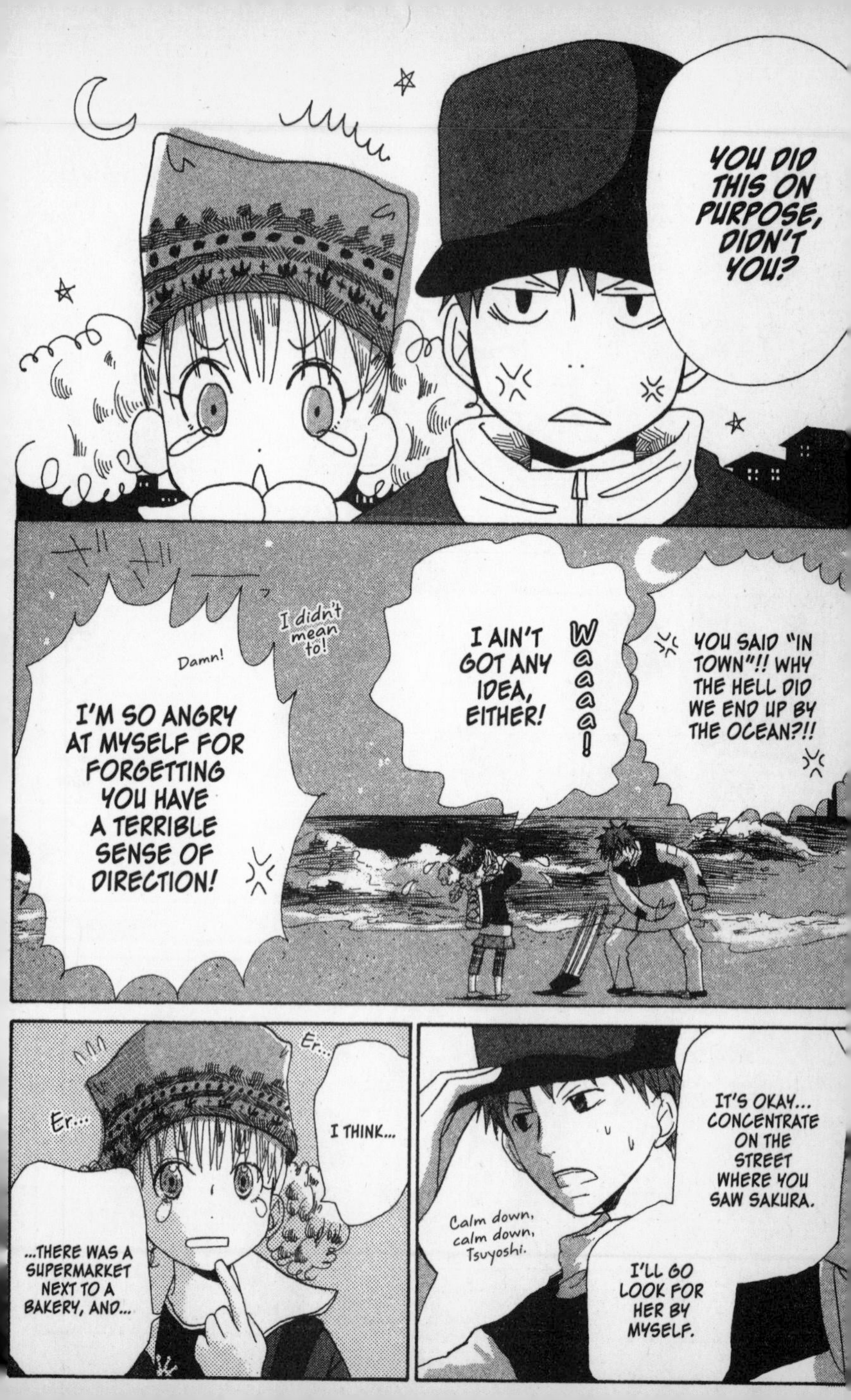
YOU DID THIS ON PURPOSE, DIDN'T YOU?
YOU SAID "IN TOWN"!! WHY THE HELL DID WE END UP BY THE OCEAN?!!
Waaaaa!
I AIN'T GOT ANY IDEA, EITHER!
I didn't mean to!
Damn!
I'M SO ANGRY AT MYSELF FOR FORGETTING YOU HAVE A TERRIBLE SENSE OF DIRECTION!
IT'S OKAY... CONCENTRATE ON THE STREET WHERE YOU SAW SAKURA.
Calm down, calm down, Tsuyoshi.
I'LL GO LOOK FOR HER BY MYSELF.
Er...
Er...
I THINK...
...THERE WAS A SUPERMARKET NEXT TO A BAKERY, AND...

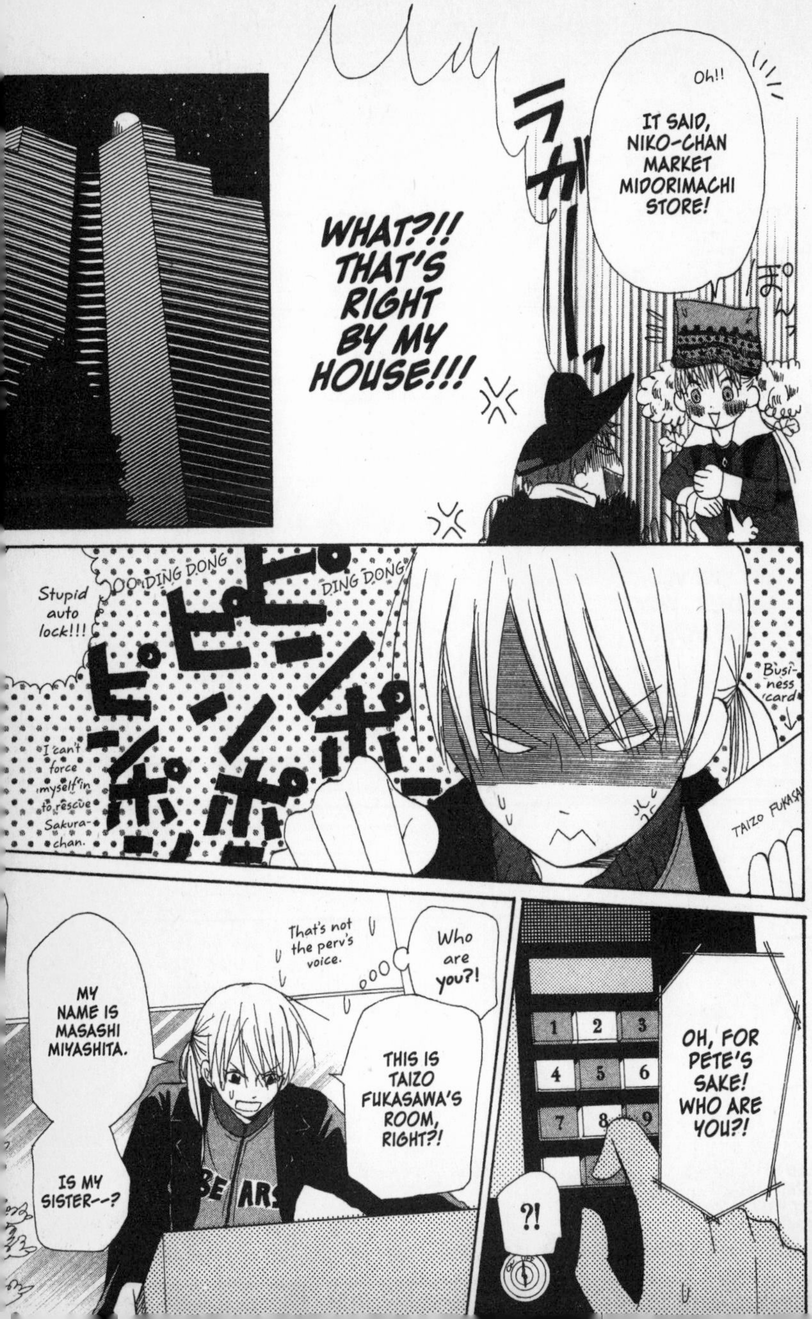
Oh!!
IT SAID, NIKO-CHAN MARKET MIDORIMACHI STORE!
WHAT?!! THAT'S RIGHT BY MY HOUSE!!!
DING DONG
DING DONG
Stupid auto lock!!!
Busi-ness card
TAIZO FUKASA
I can't force myself in to rescue Sakura-chan.
OH, FOR PETE'S SAKE! WHO ARE YOU?!
?!
Who are you?!
That's not the perv's voice.
THIS IS TAIZO FUKASAWA'S ROOM, RIGHT?!
MY NAME IS MASASHI MIYASHITA.
IS MY SISTER--?
BE ARS

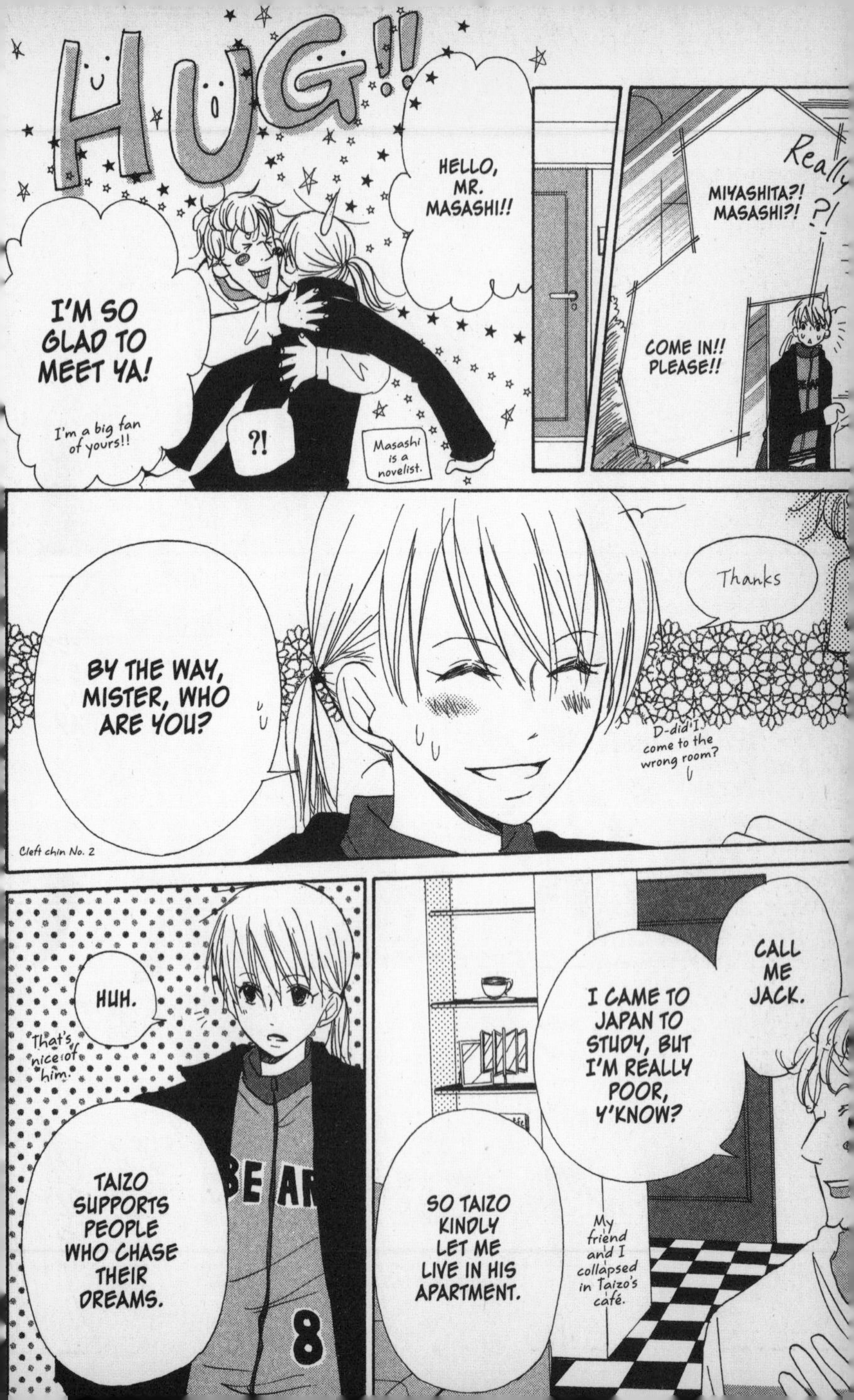
Really ?!
MIYASHITA?! MASASHI?!
COME IN!! PLEASE!!
HUG!!
HELLO, MR. MASASHI!!
?!
I'M SO GLAD TO MEET YA!
I'm a big fan of yours!!
Masashi is a novelist.
Thanks
D-did I come to the wrong room?
BY THE WAY, MISTER, WHO ARE YOU?
Cleft chin No. 2
CALL ME JACK.
I CAME TO JAPAN TO STUDY, BUT I'M REALLY POOR, Y'KNOW?
My friend and I collapsed in Taizo's café.
SO TAIZO KINDLY LET ME LIVE IN HIS APARTMENT.
HUH.
That's nice of him.
TAIZO SUPPORTS PEOPLE WHO CHASE THEIR DREAMS.

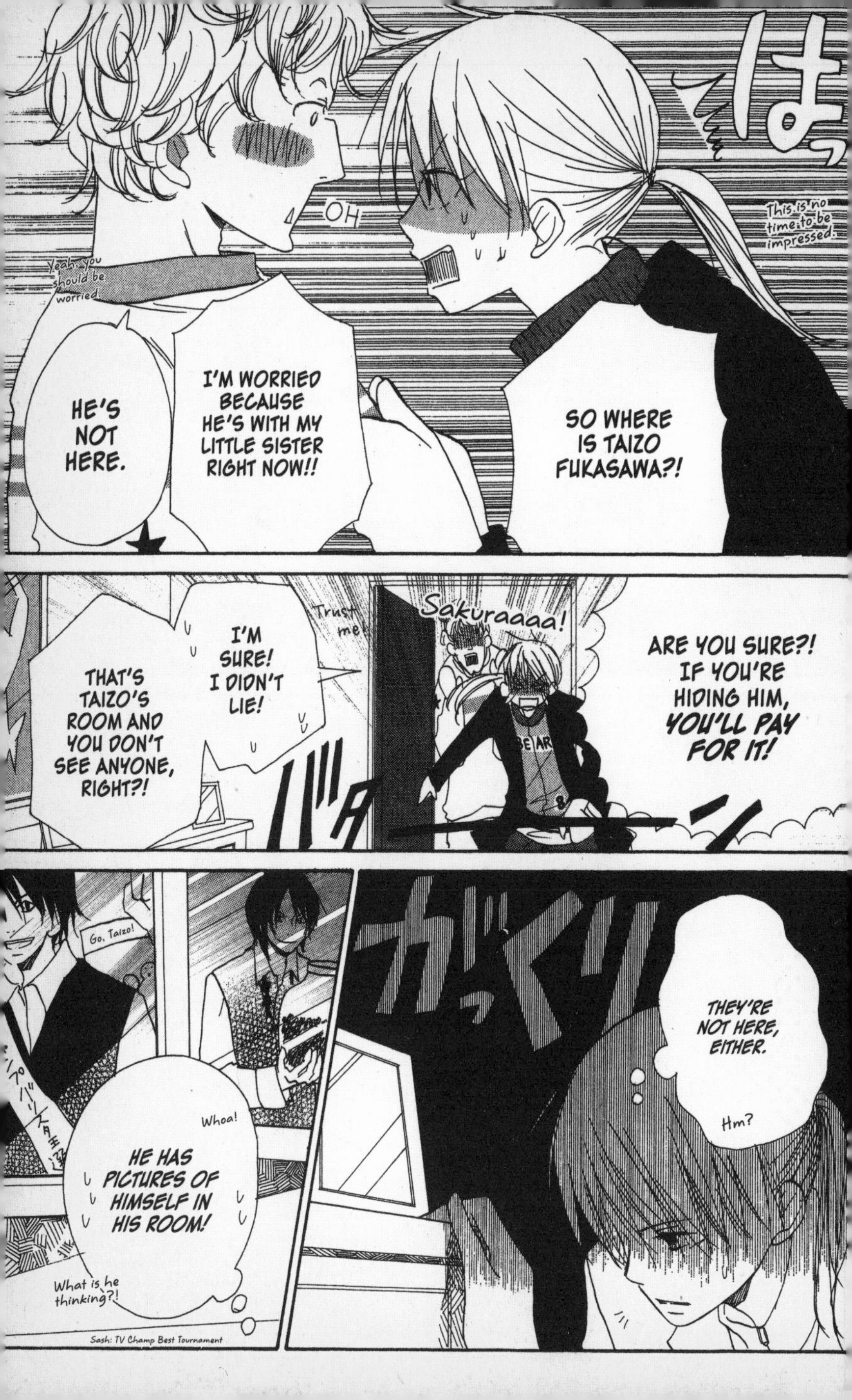

はっ
This is no time to be impressed.
SO WHERE IS TAIZO FUKASAWA?!
OH
I'M WORRIED BECAUSE HE'S WITH MY LITTLE SISTER RIGHT NOW!!
HE'S NOT HERE.
Yeah, you should be worried.
ARE YOU SURE?! IF YOU'RE HIDING HIM, YOU'LL PAY FOR IT!
Sakuraaaaa!
Trust me!
I'M SURE! I DIDN'T LIE!
THAT'S TAIZO'S ROOM AND YOU DON'T SEE ANYONE, RIGHT?!
THEY'RE NOT HERE, EITHER.
Hm?
Go, Taizo!
Whoa!
HE HAS PICTURES OF HIMSELF IN HIS ROOM!
What is he thinking?!
Sash: TV Champ Best Tournament

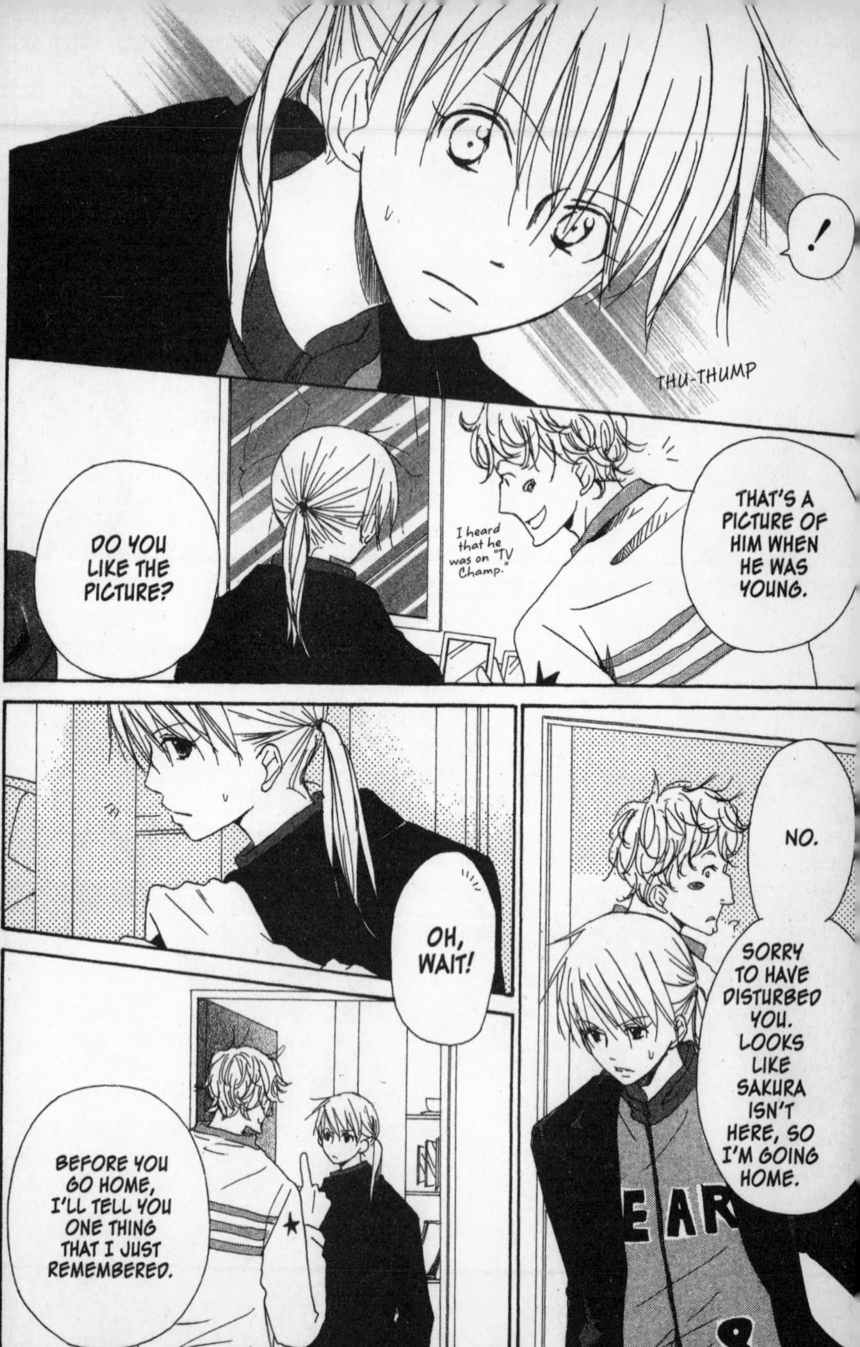
!
THU-THUMP
THAT'S A PICTURE OF HIM WHEN HE WAS YOUNG.
I heard that he was on "TV Champ."
DO YOU LIKE THE PICTURE?
NO.
SORRY TO HAVE DISTURBED YOU. LOOKS LIKE SAKURA ISN'T HERE, SO I'M GOING HOME.
OH, WAIT!
BEFORE YOU GO HOME, I'LL TELL YOU ONE THING THAT I JUST REMEMBERED.

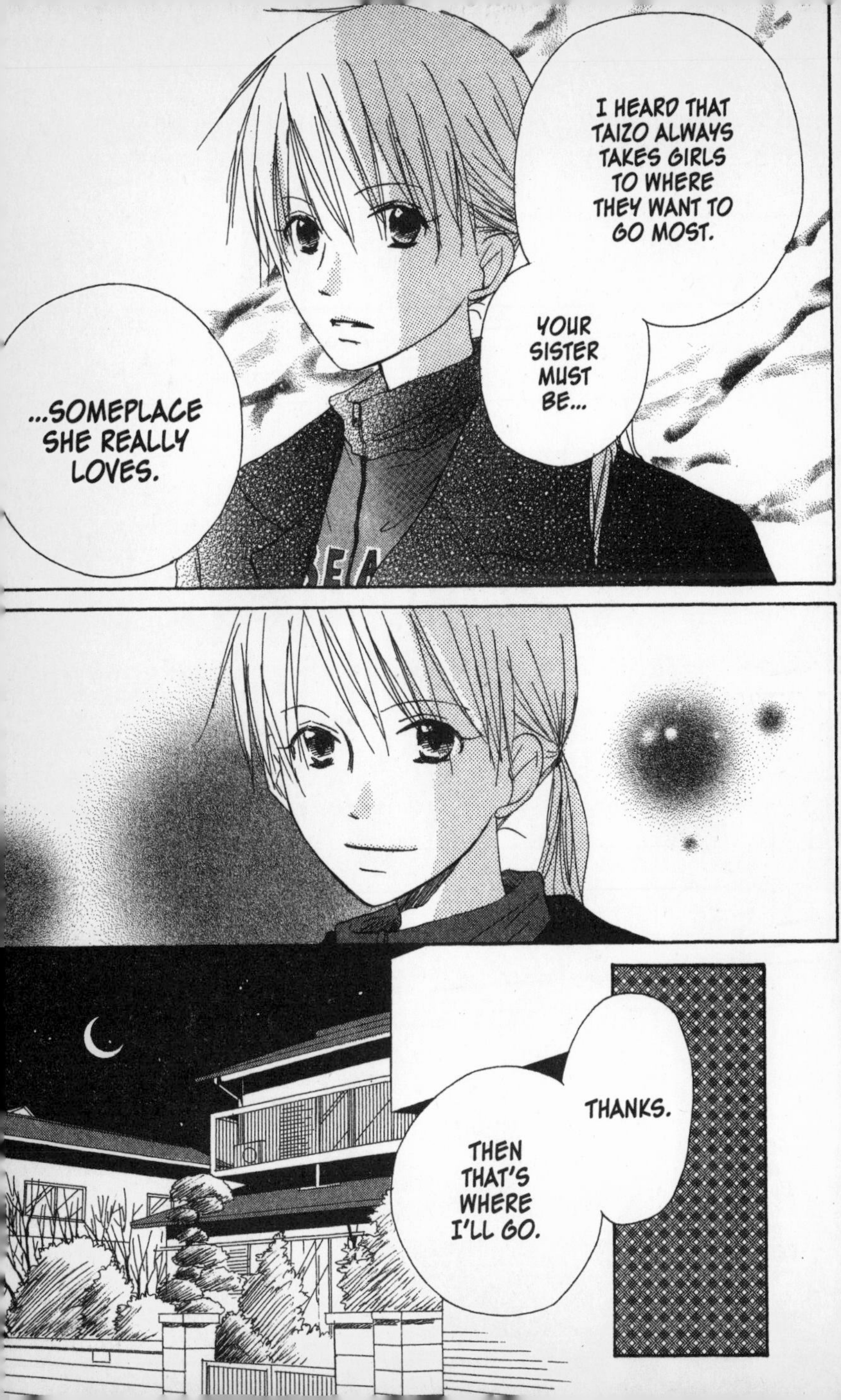
I HEARD THAT TAIZO ALWAYS TAKES GIRLS TO WHERE THEY WANT TO GO MOST.
YOUR SISTER MUST BE...
...SOMEPLACE SHE REALLY LOVES.
THANKS.
THEN THAT'S WHERE I'LL GO.

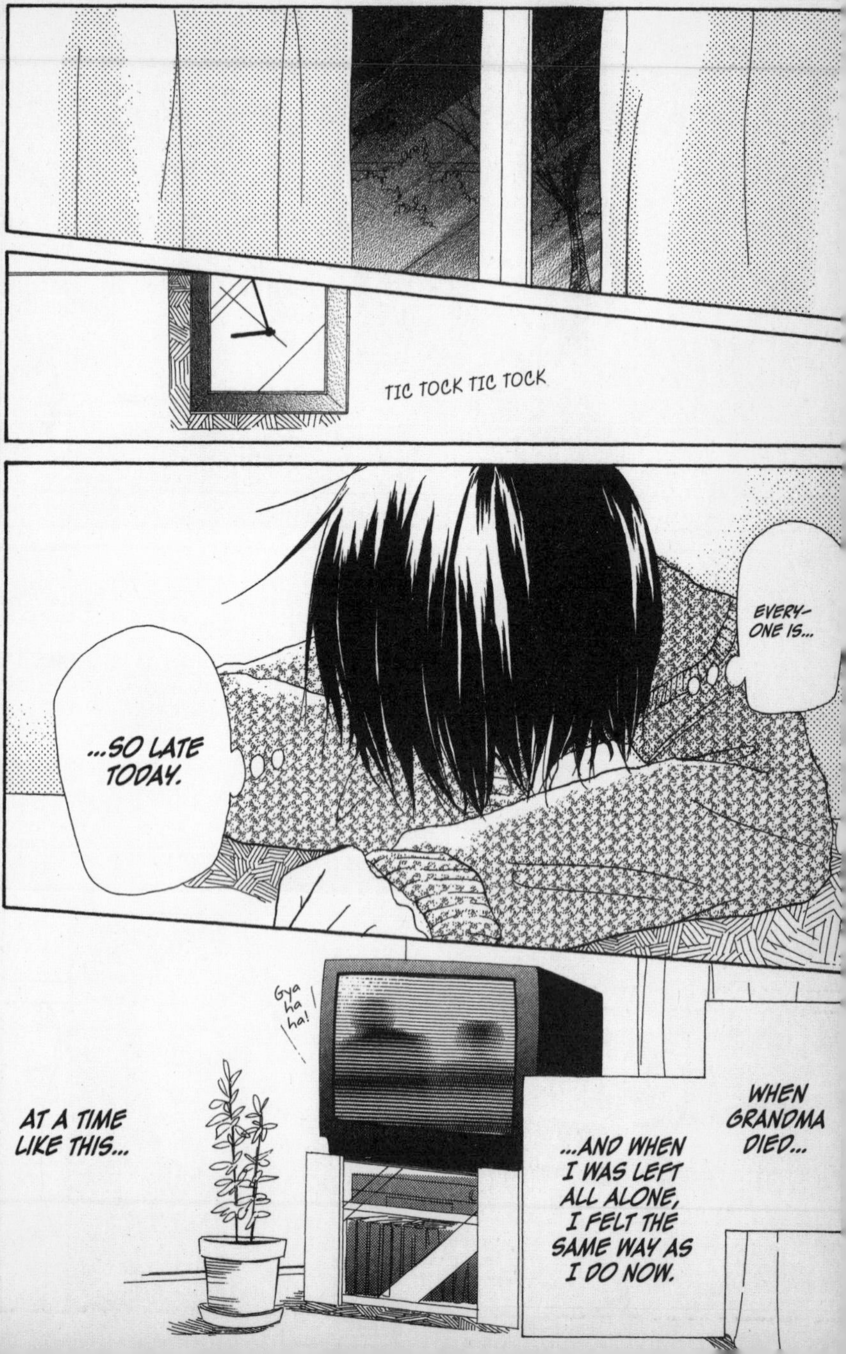
TIC TOCK TIC TOCK
EVERY-ONE IS...
...SO LATE TODAY.
WHEN GRANDMA DIED...
...AND WHEN I WAS LEFT ALL ALONE, I FELT THE SAME WAY AS I DO NOW.
Gya ha ha!
AT A TIME LIKE THIS...

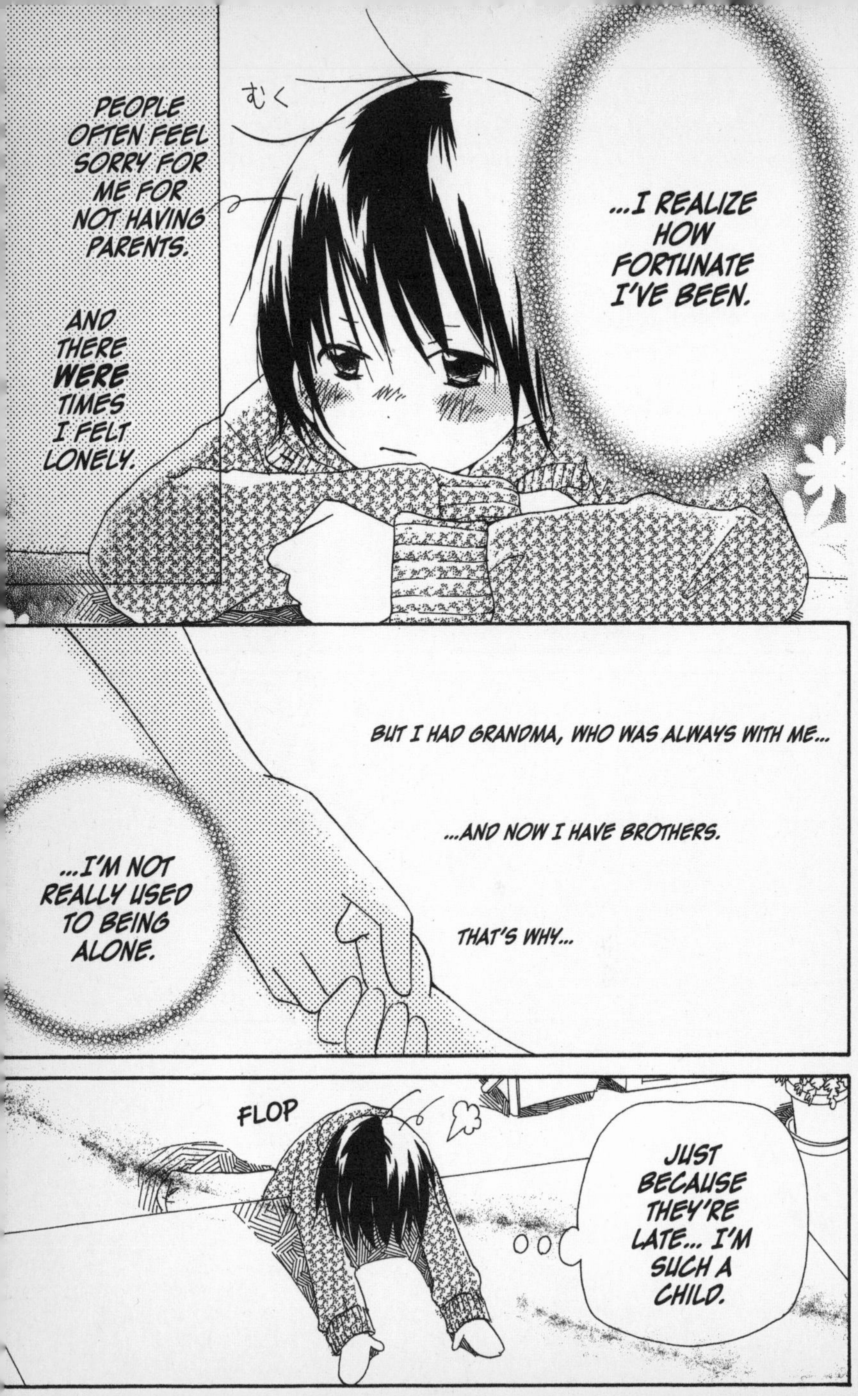
...I REALIZE HOW FORTUNATE I'VE BEEN.
むく
PEOPLE OFTEN FEEL SORRY FOR ME FOR NOT HAVING PARENTS.
AND THERE WERE TIMES I FELT LONELY.
BUT I HAD GRANDMA, WHO WAS ALWAYS WITH ME...
...AND NOW I HAVE BROTHERS.
THAT'S WHY...
...I'M NOT REALLY USED TO BEING ALONE.
JUST BECAUSE THEY'RE LATE... I'M SUCH A CHILD.
FLOP

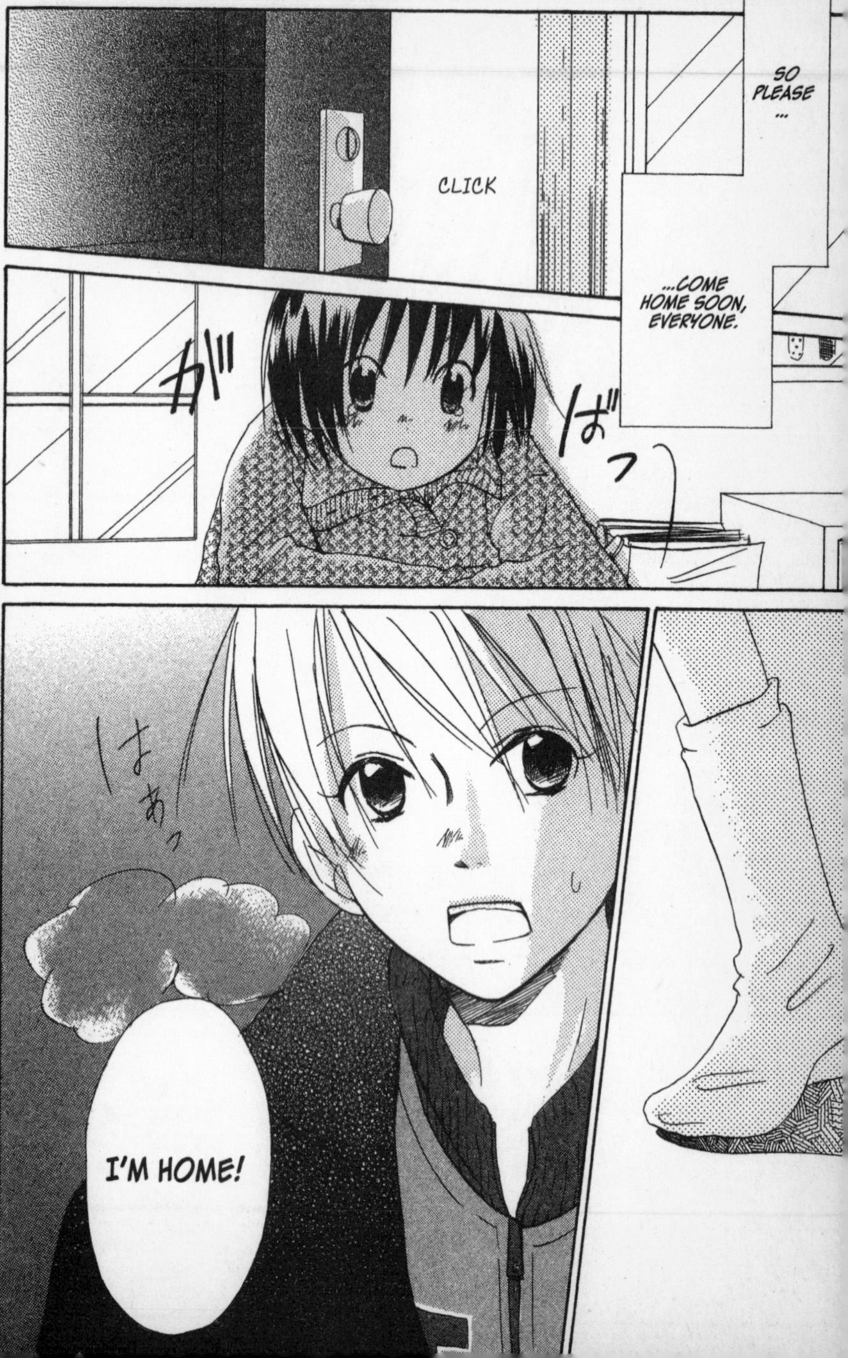
SO PLEASE ...
CLICK
...COME HOME SOON, EVERYONE.
ばっ
ガ
はあっ
I'M HOME!

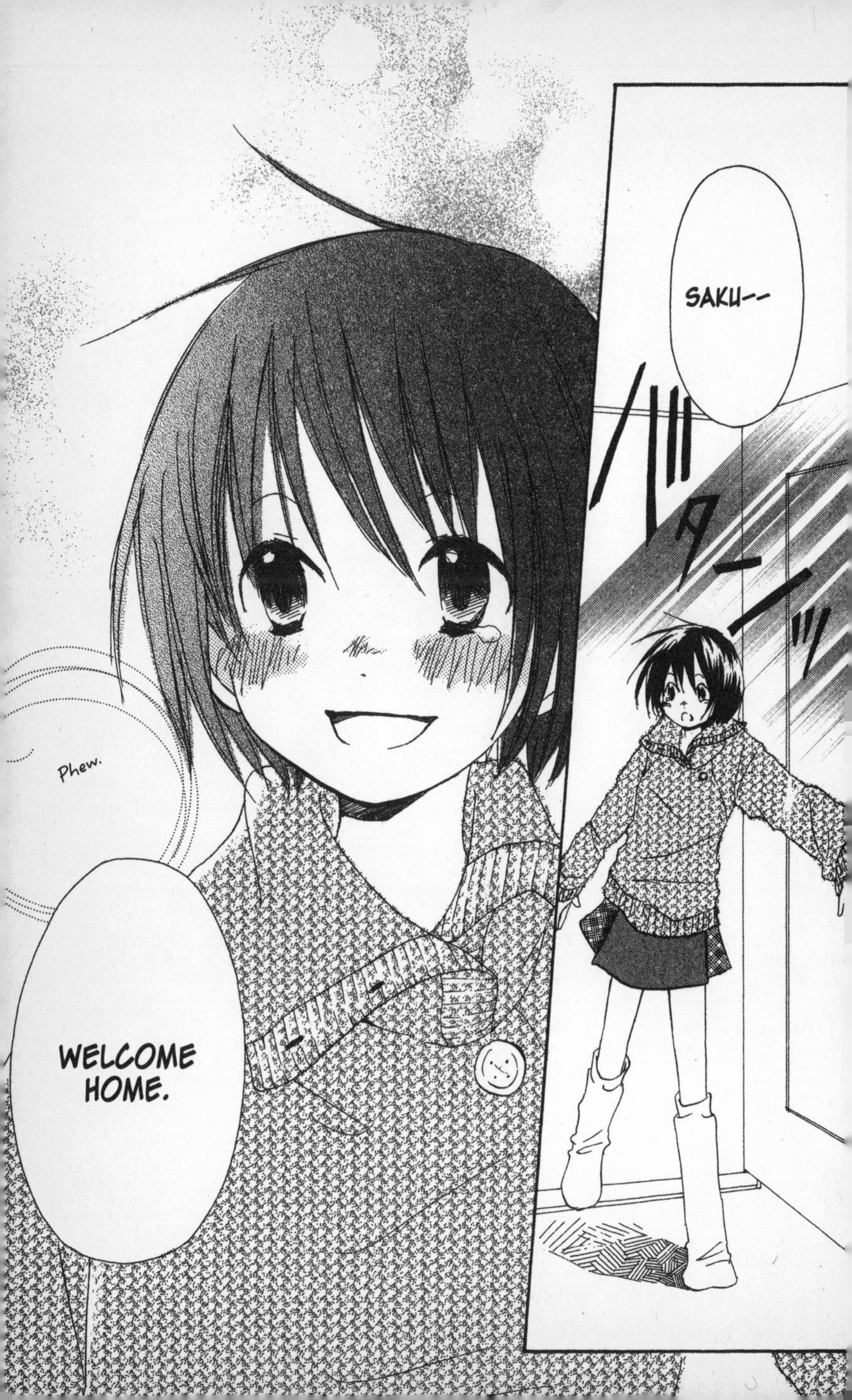
SAKU--
バターーッ
Phew.
WELCOME HOME.

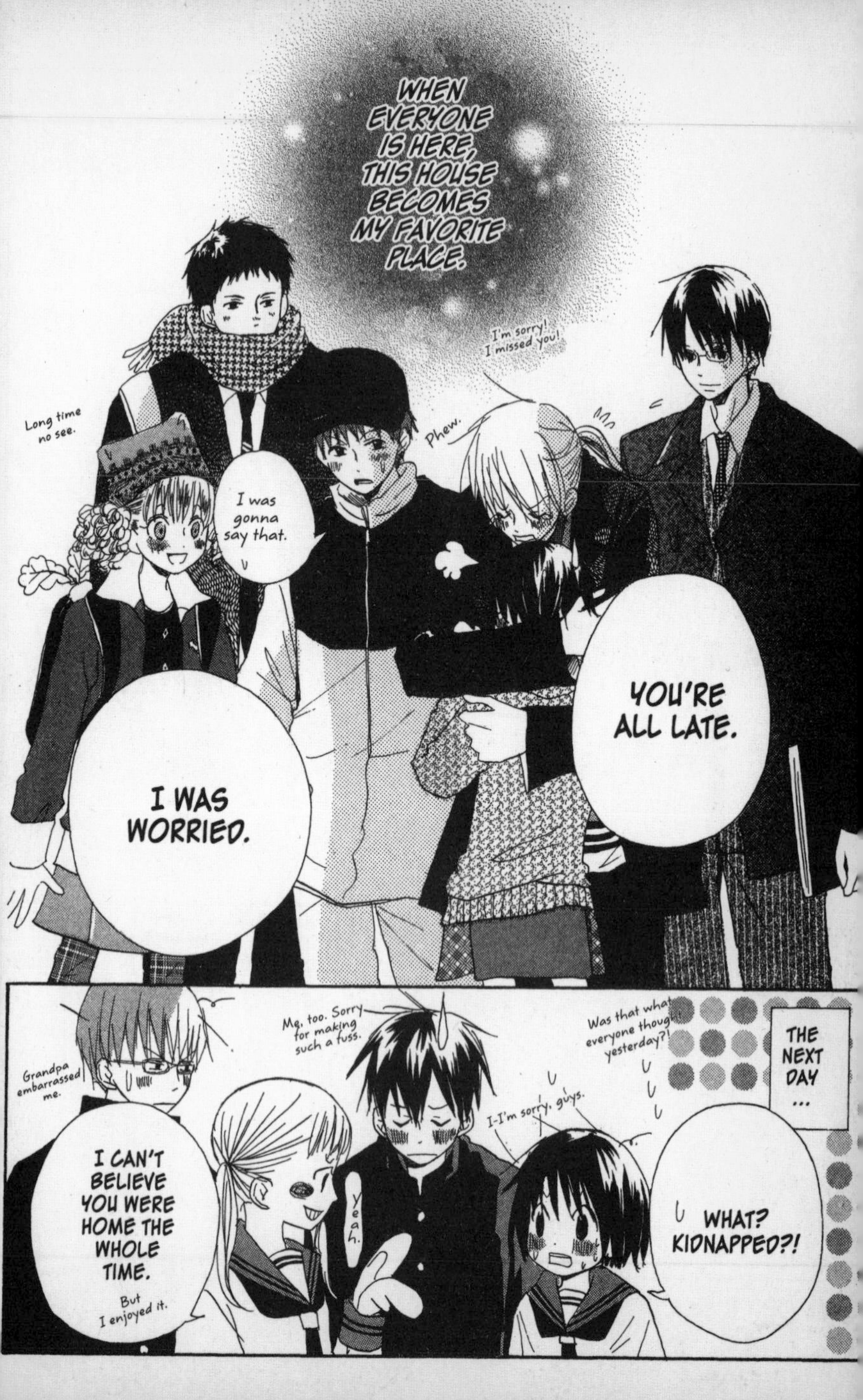
WHEN EVERYONE IS HERE, THIS HOUSE BECOMES MY FAVORITE PLACE.
I'm sorry! I missed you!
YOU'RE ALL LATE.
Phew.
Long time no see.
I was gonna say that.
I WAS WORRIED.
THE NEXT DAY ...
Was that what everyone though yesterday?!
WHAT? KIDNAPPED?!
I-I'm sorry, guys.
Me, too. Sorry for making such a fuss.
Yeah.
Grandpa embarrassed me.
I CAN'T BELIEVE YOU WERE HOME THE WHOLE TIME.
But I enjoyed it.

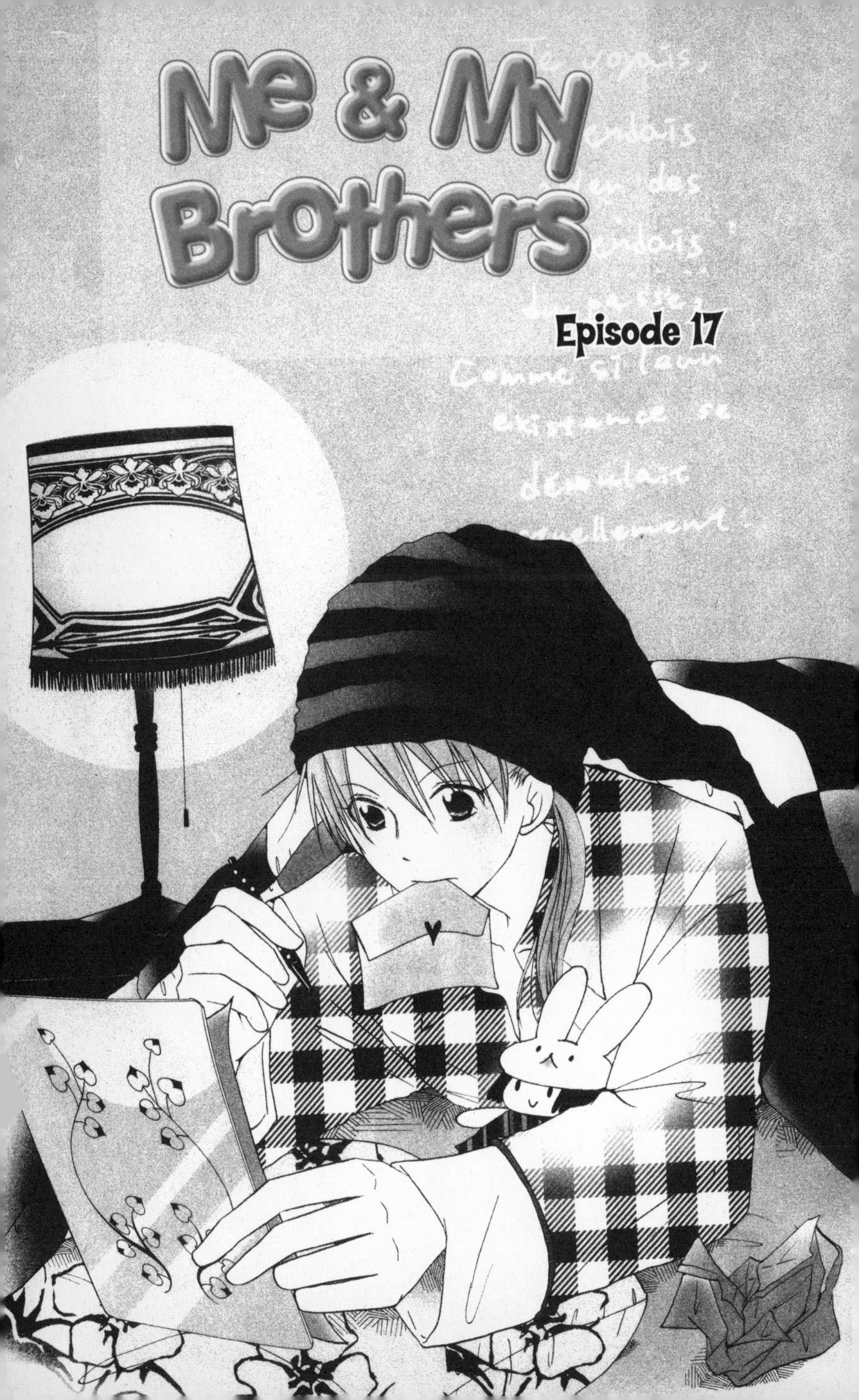
Me & My Brothers
Episode 17

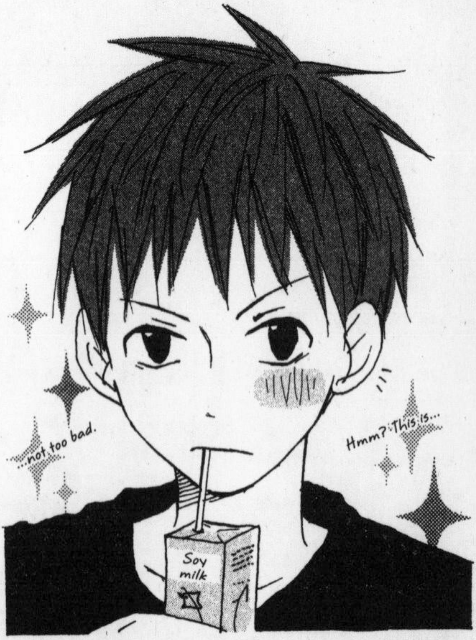
Hmm? This is...
...not too bad.
Soy milk

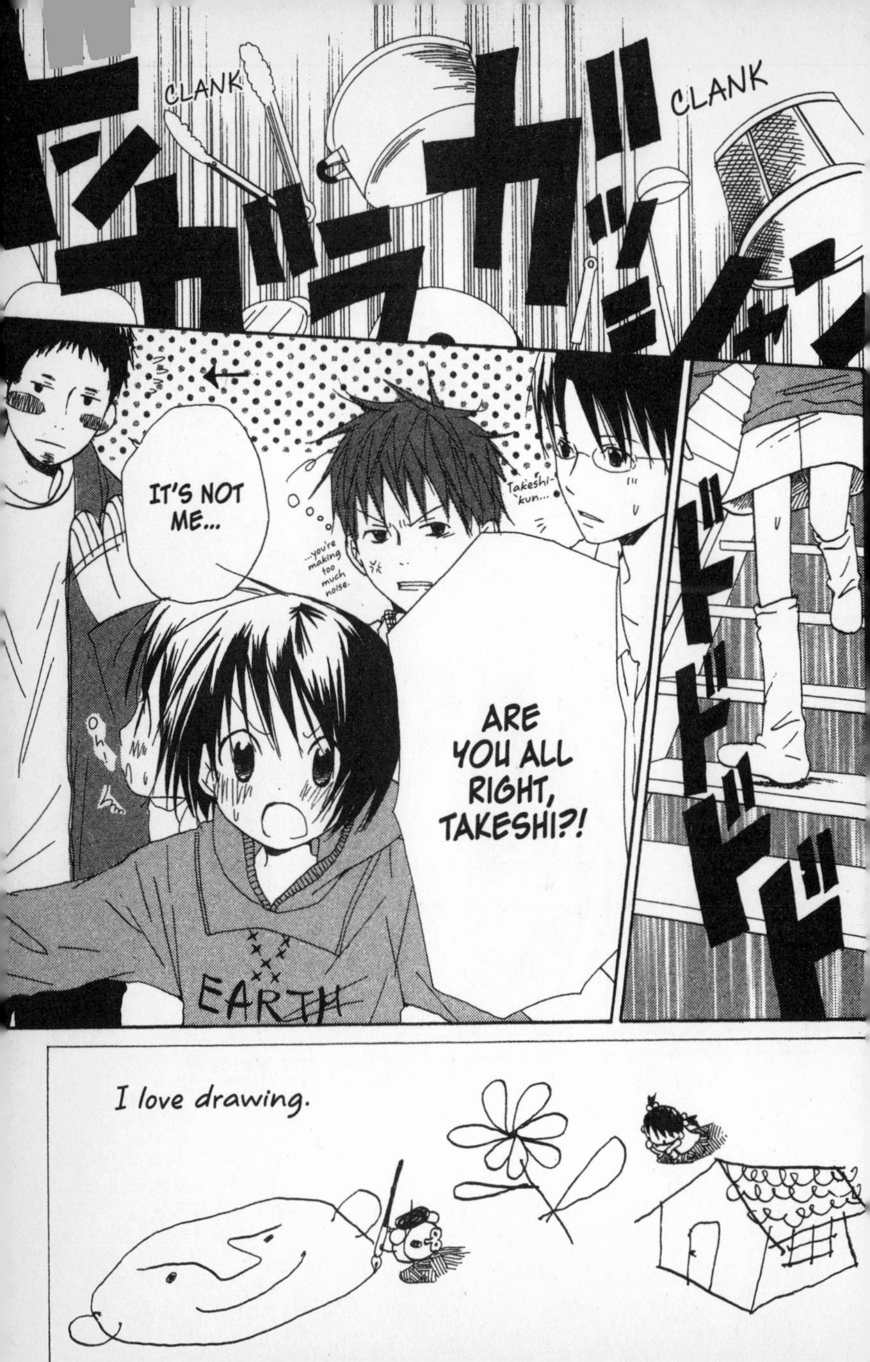
CLANK
CLANK
Takeshi-kun...
ARE YOU ALL RIGHT, TAKESHI?!
...you're making too much noise.
IT'S NOT ME...
I love drawing.

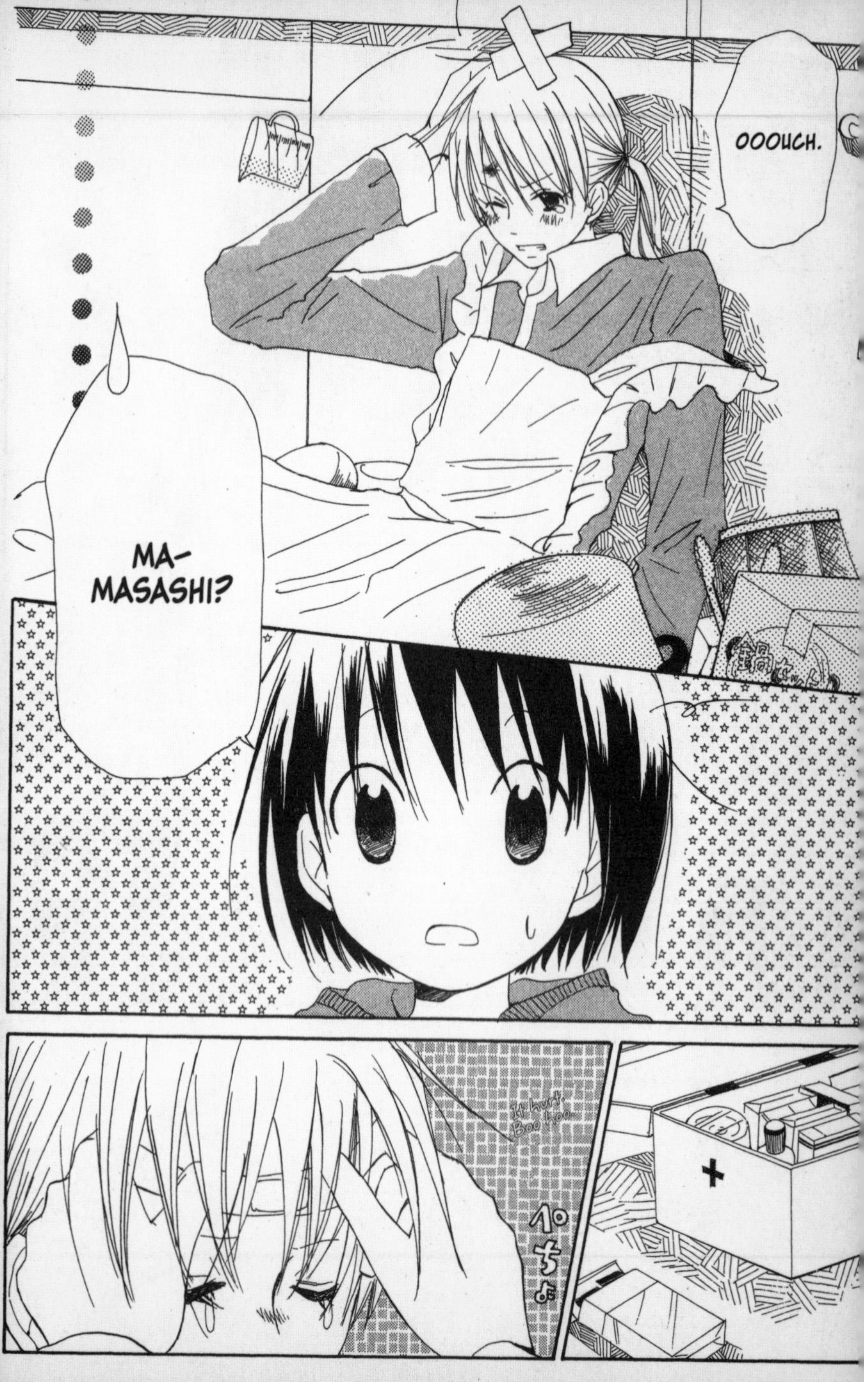
OOOUCH.
MA- MASASHI?
It hurt. Boo hoo.

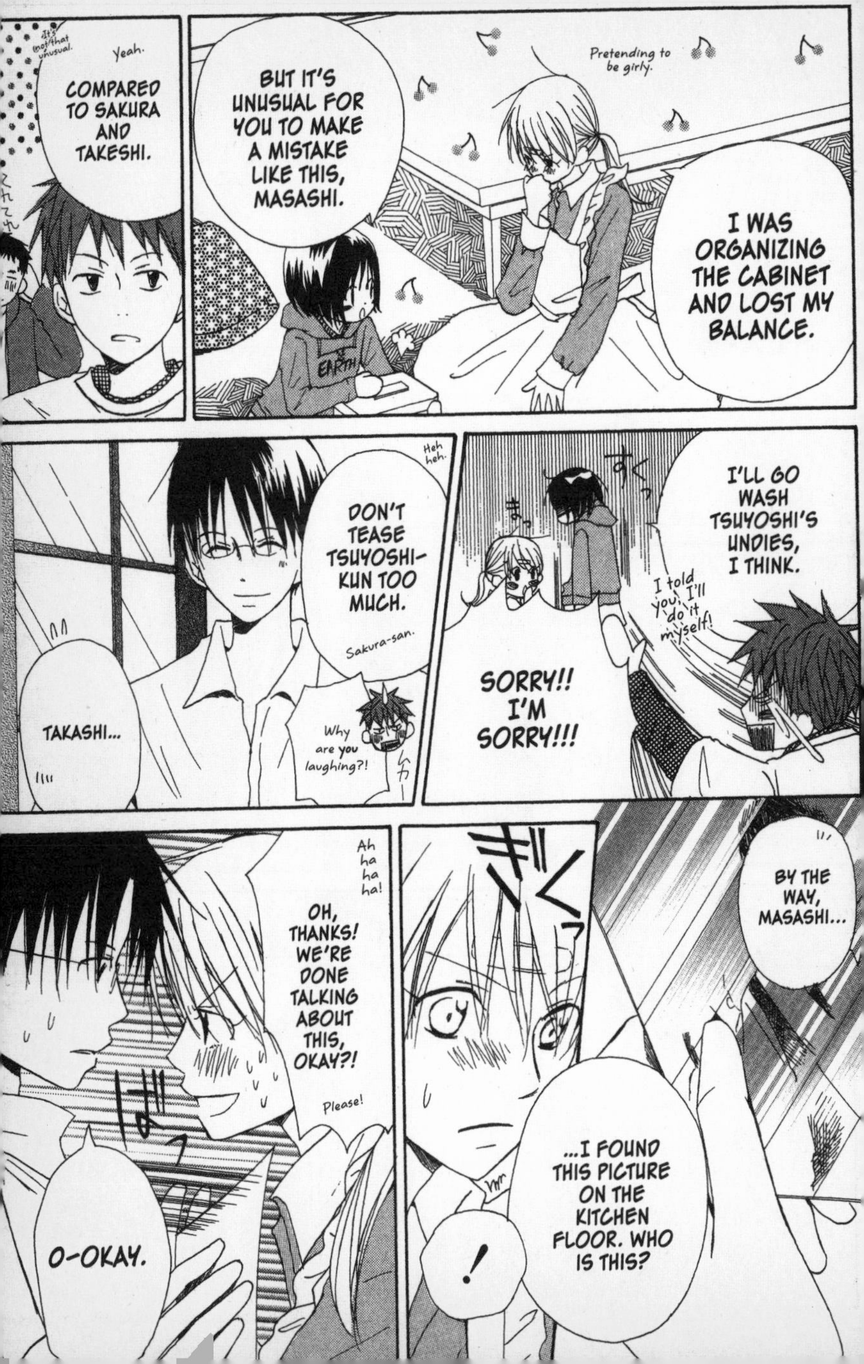
Pretending to be girly.
I WAS ORGANIZING THE CABINET AND LOST MY BALANCE.
BUT IT'S UNUSUAL FOR YOU TO MAKE A MISTAKE LIKE THIS, MASASHI.
It's not that unusual.
Yeah.
COMPARED TO SAKURA AND TAKESHI.
I'LL GO WASH TSUYOSHI'S UNDIES, I THINK.
I told you, I'll do it myself!
SORRY!! I'M SORRY!!!
Heh heh.
DON'T TEASE TSUYOSHI-KUN TOO MUCH.
Sakura-san.
Why are you laughing?!
TAKASHI...
BY THE WAY, MASASHI...
...I FOUND THIS PICTURE ON THE KITCHEN FLOOR. WHO IS THIS?
!
Ah ha ha ha!
OH, THANKS! WE'RE DONE TALKING ABOUT THIS, OKAY?!
Please!
O-OKAY.

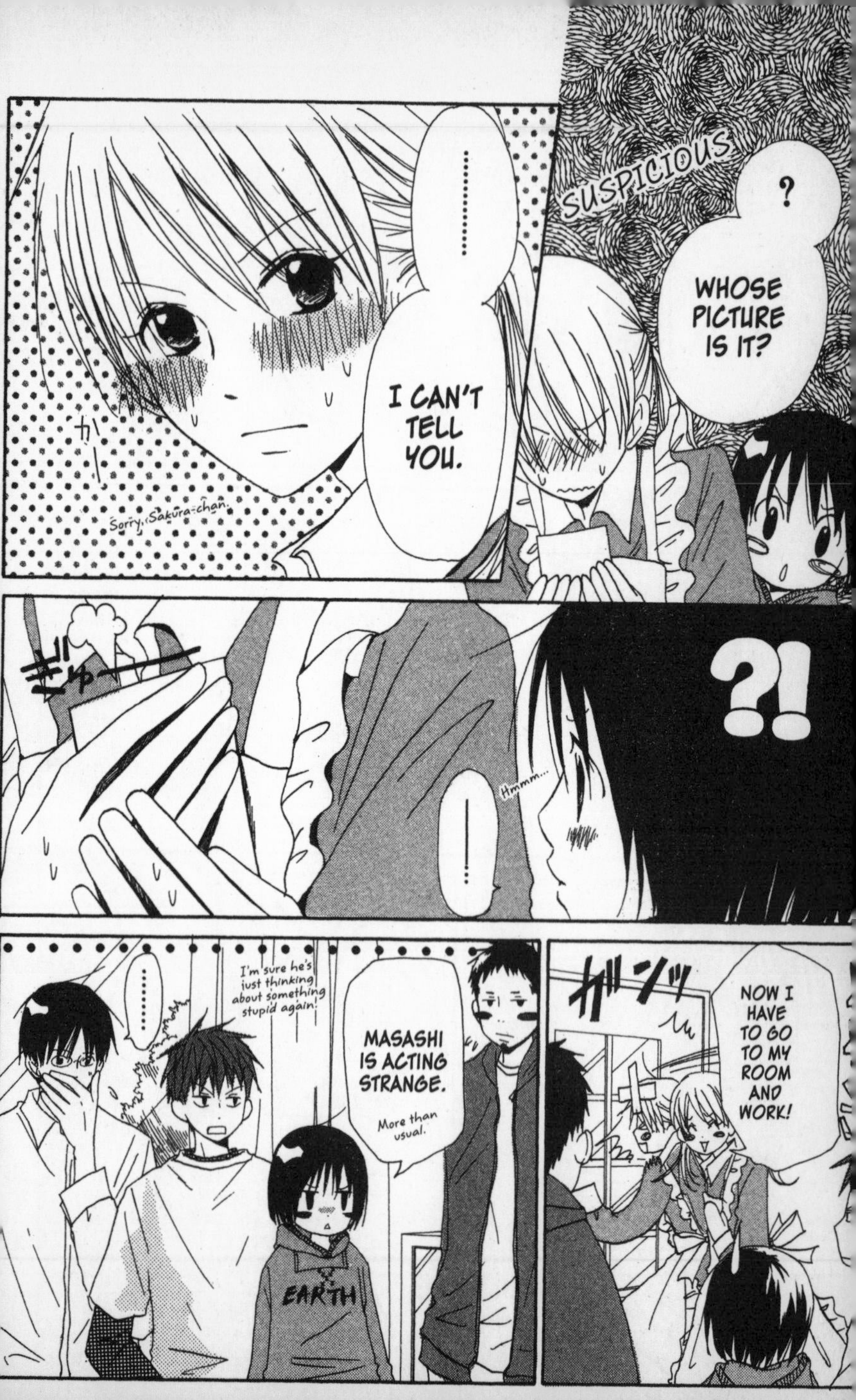
SUSPICIOUS
?
WHOSE PICTURE IS IT?
......
I CAN'T TELL YOU.
Sorry, Sakura-chan.
?!
Hmmm...
...!
NOW I HAVE TO GO TO MY ROOM AND WORK!
MASASHI IS ACTING STRANGE.
More than usual.
I'm sure he's just thinking about something stupid again!
......
EARTH

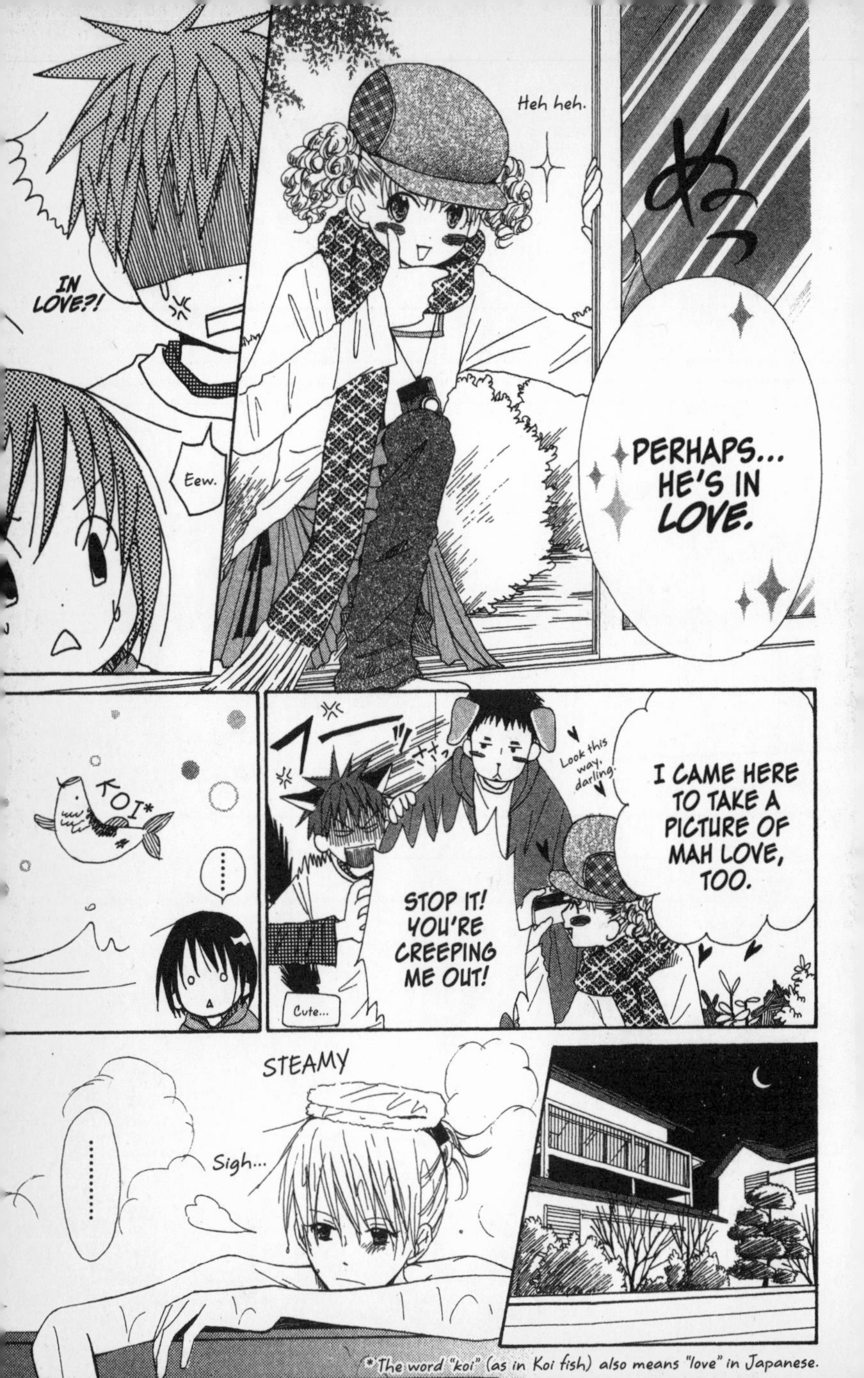
Heh heh.
ぬっ
PERHAPS... HE'S IN LOVE.
IN LOVE?!
Eew.
I CAME HERE TO TAKE A PICTURE OF MAH LOVE, TOO.
Look this way, darling.
STOP IT! YOU'RE CREEPING ME OUT!
Cute...
KOI*
......
STEAMY
Sigh...
......

*The word "koi" (as in Koi fish) also means "love" in Japanese.

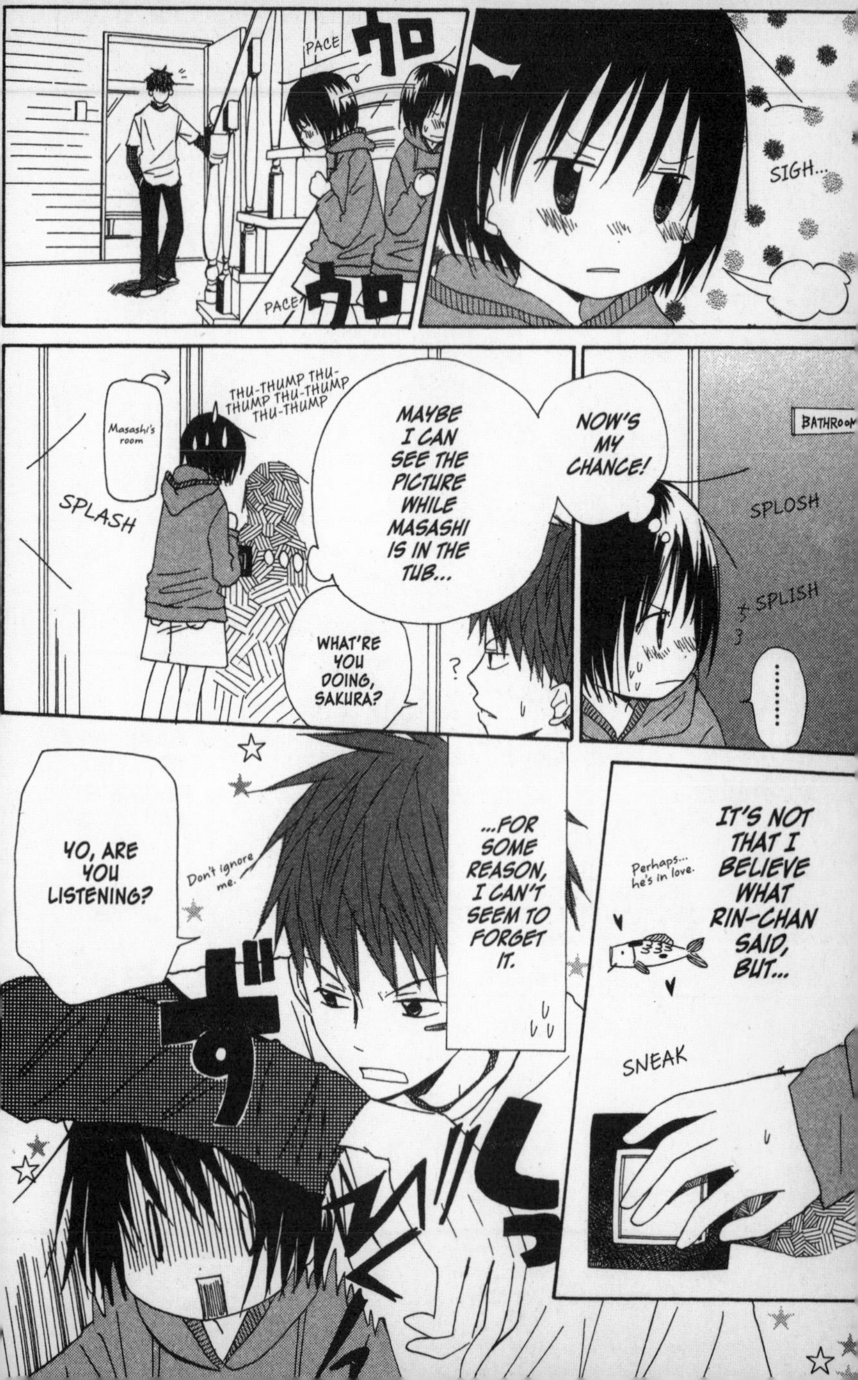
SIGH...
PACE
PACE
NOW'S MY CHANCE!
BATHROOM
SPLOSH
SPLISH
......
MAYBE I CAN SEE THE PICTURE WHILE MASASHI IS IN THE TUB...
THU-THUMP THU-THUMP THU-THUMP THU-THUMP
Masashi's room
SPLASH
WHAT'RE YOU DOING, SAKURA?
?
IT'S NOT THAT I BELIEVE WHAT RIN-CHAN SAID, BUT...
Perhaps... he's in love.
SNEAK
...FOR SOME REASON, I CAN'T SEEM TO FORGET IT.
YO, ARE YOU LISTENING?
Don't ignore me.

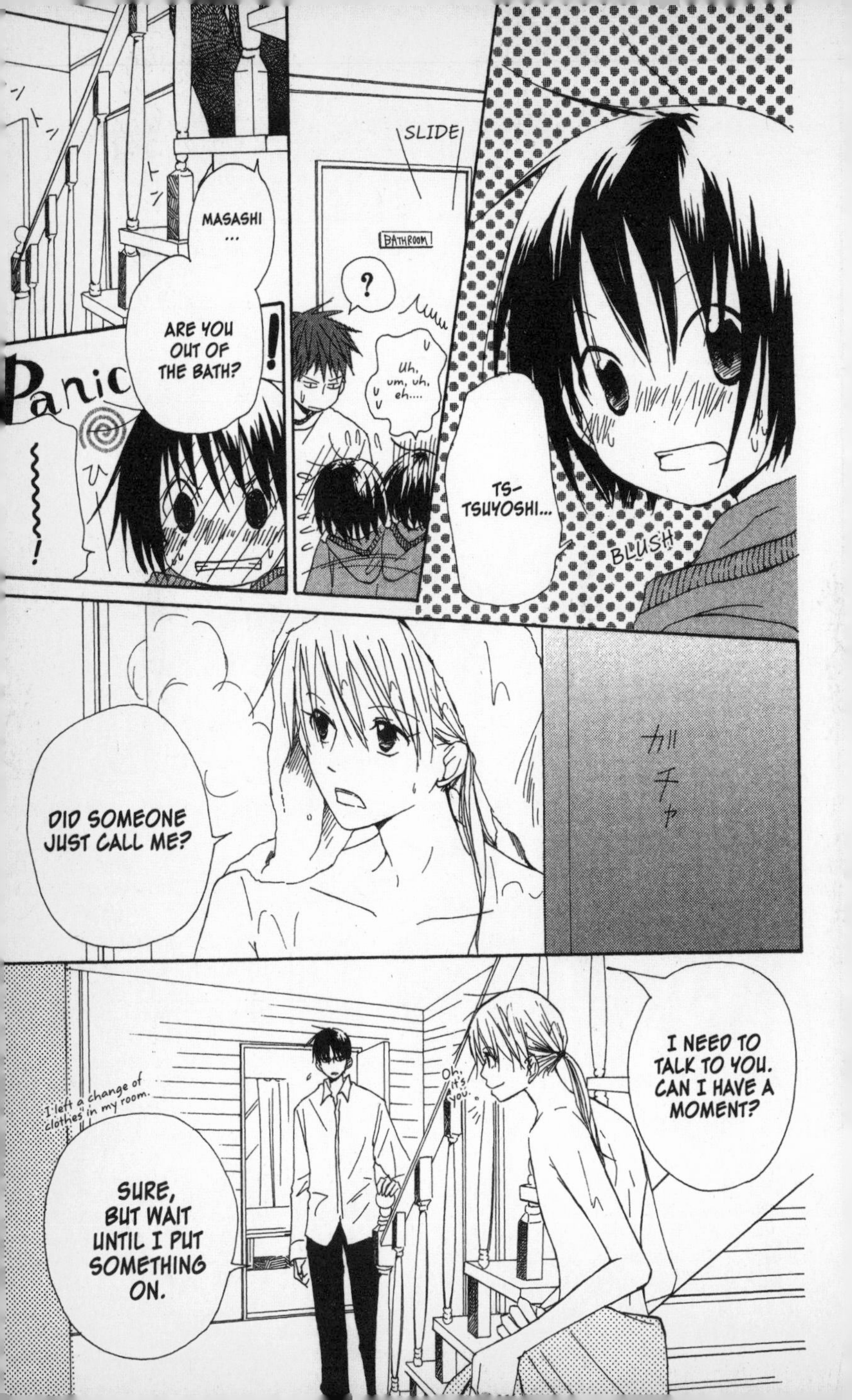

TS-TSUYOSHI...
BLUSH
SLIDE
BATHROOM
?
Uh, um, uh, eh....
MASASHI ...
ARE YOU OUT OF THE BATH?
!
Panic
ガチャ
DID SOMEONE JUST CALL ME?
I NEED TO TALK TO YOU. CAN I HAVE A MOMENT?
Oh, it's you.
I left a change of clothes in my room.
SURE, BUT WAIT UNTIL I PUT SOMETHING ON.

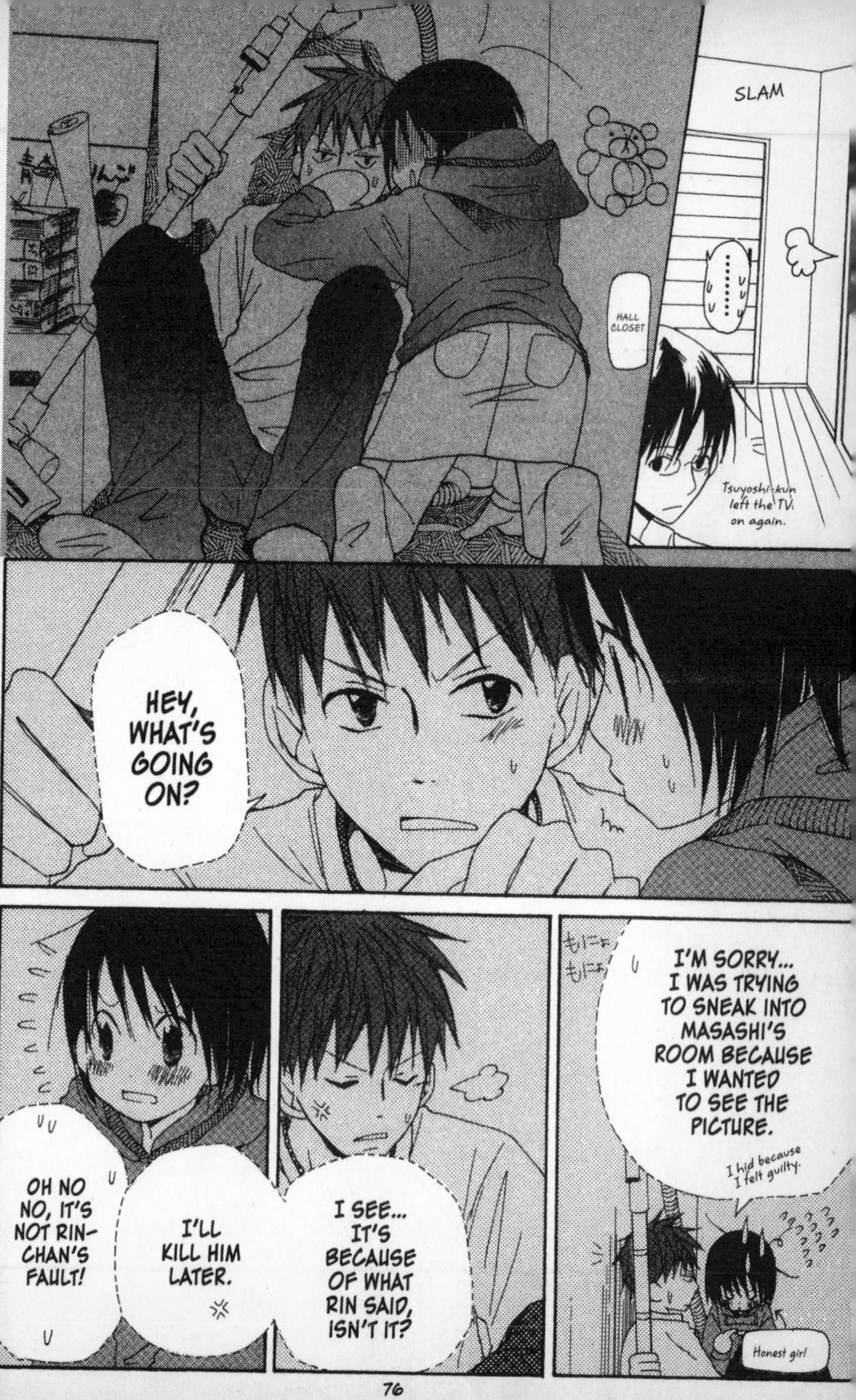
SLAM
HALL CLOSET
……
Tsuyoshi-kun left the TV on again.
HEY, WHAT'S GOING ON?
I'M SORRY... I WAS TRYING TO SNEAK INTO MASASHI'S ROOM BECAUSE I WANTED TO SEE THE PICTURE.
I hid because I felt guilty.
Honest girl
I SEE... IT'S BECAUSE OF WHAT RIN SAID, ISN'T IT?
I'LL KILL HIM LATER.
OH NO NO, IT'S NOT RIN-CHAN'S FAULT!

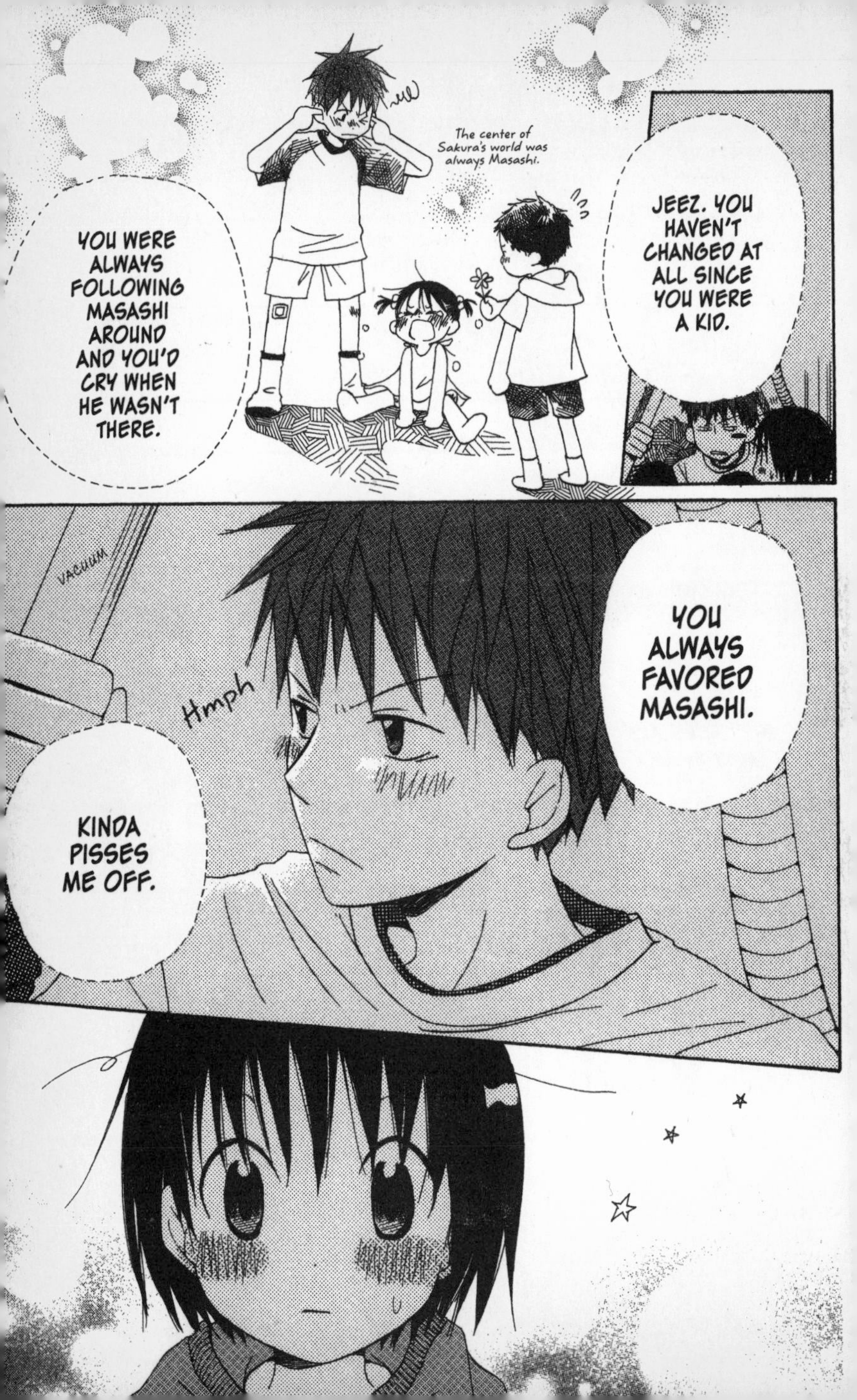

JEEZ. YOU HAVEN'T CHANGED AT ALL SINCE YOU WERE A KID.
The center of Sakura's world was always Masashi.
YOU WERE ALWAYS FOLLOWING MASASHI AROUND AND YOU'D CRY WHEN HE WASN'T THERE.
YOU ALWAYS FAVORED MASASHI.
VACUUM
Hmph
KINDA PISSES ME OFF.

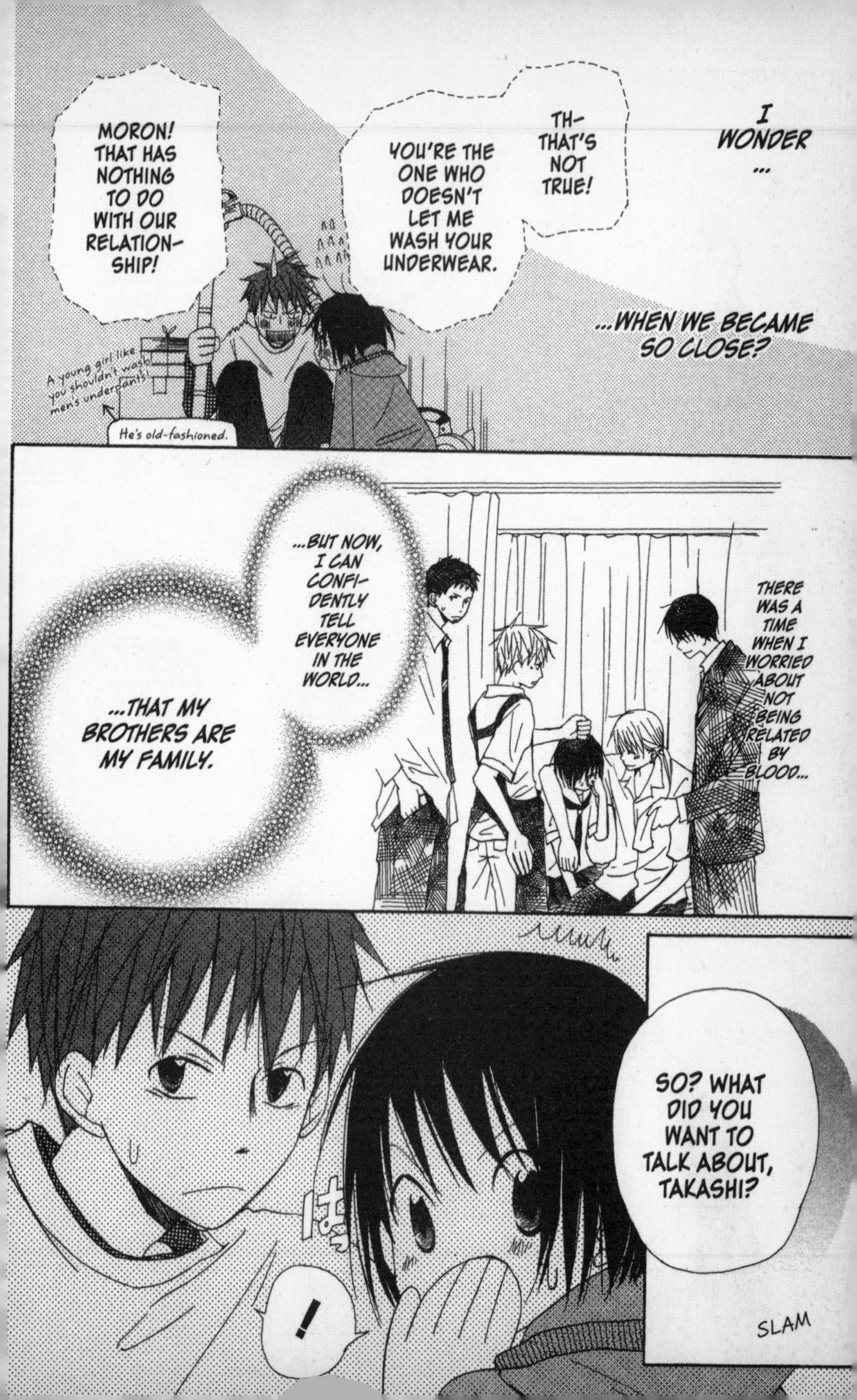
I WONDER ...
TH- THAT'S NOT TRUE!
YOU'RE THE ONE WHO DOESN'T LET ME WASH YOUR UNDERWEAR.
MORON! THAT HAS NOTHING TO DO WITH OUR RELATION-SHIP!
...WHEN WE BECAME SO CLOSE?
A young girl like you shouldn't wash men's underpants!
He's old-fashioned.
THERE WAS A TIME WHEN I WORRIED ABOUT NOT BEING RELATED BY BLOOD...
...BUT NOW, I CAN CONFI-DENTLY TELL EVERYONE IN THE WORLD...
...THAT MY BROTHERS ARE MY FAMILY.
SO? WHAT DID YOU WANT TO TALK ABOUT, TAKASHI?
SLAM
はっ
!

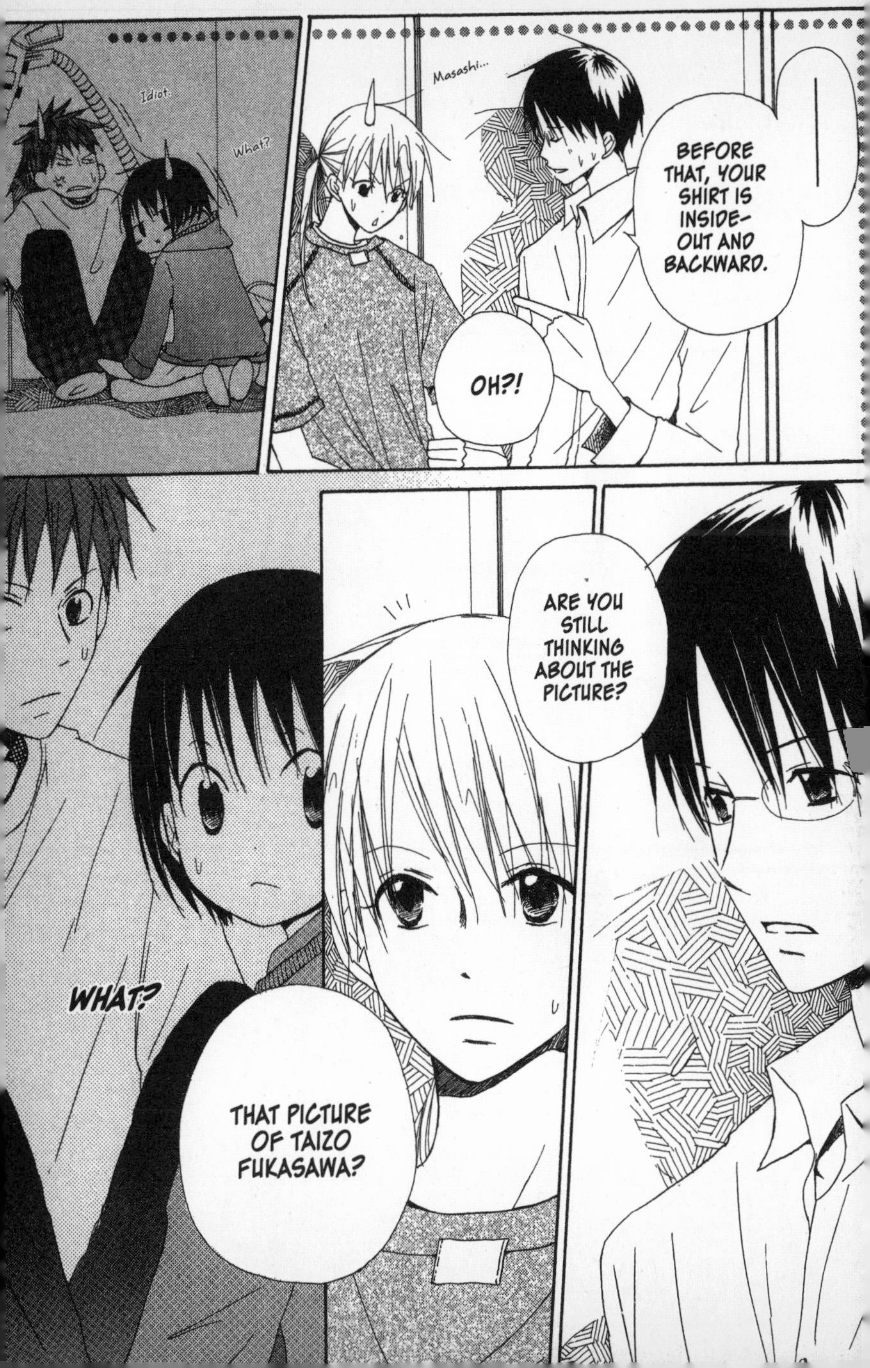
Masashi...
BEFORE THAT, YOUR SHIRT IS INSIDE-OUT AND BACKWARD.
OH?!
Idiot.
What?
ARE YOU STILL THINKING ABOUT THE PICTURE?
THAT PICTURE OF TAIZO FUKASAWA?
WHAT?

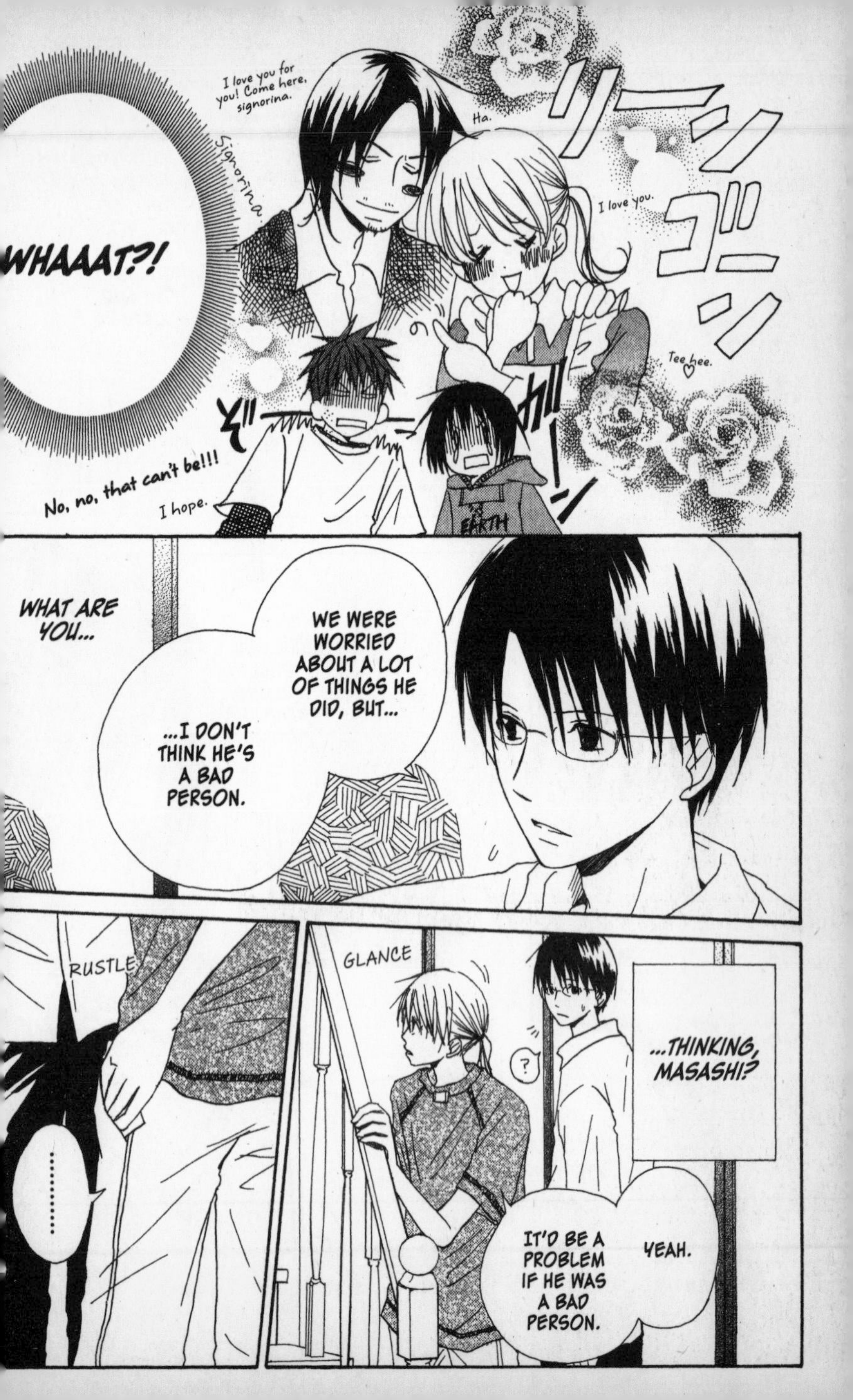

リーンゴーン
Ha.
I love you.
I love you for you! Come here, signorina.
Signorina
Tee hee.
WHAAAT?!
No, no, that can't be!!!
I hope.
EARTH
WE WERE WORRIED ABOUT A LOT OF THINGS HE DID, BUT...
...I DON'T THINK HE'S A BAD PERSON.
WHAT ARE YOU...
...THINKING, MASASHI?
?
GLANCE
YEAH.
IT'D BE A PROBLEM IF HE WAS A BAD PERSON.
RUSTLE
......

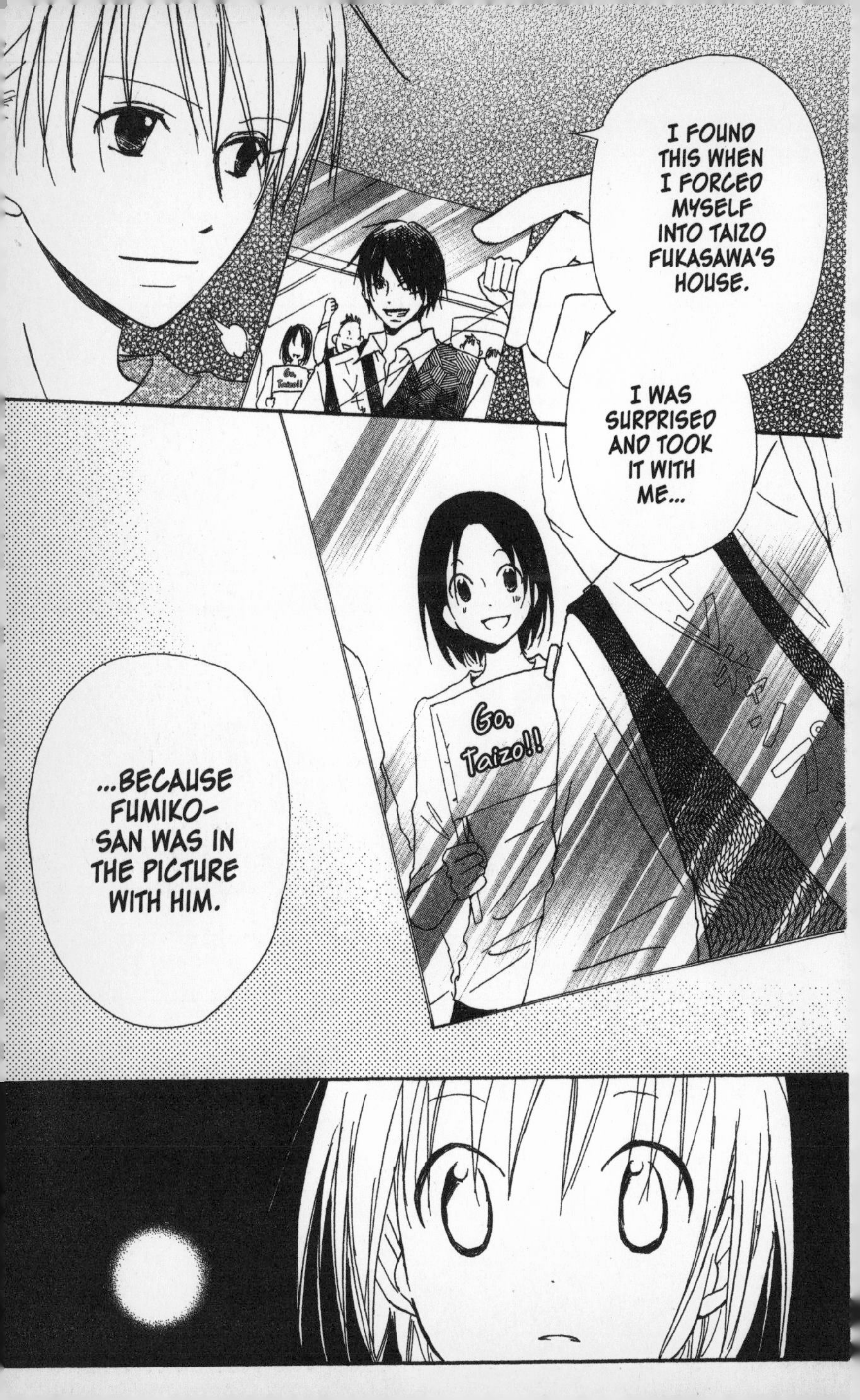
I FOUND THIS WHEN I FORCED MYSELF INTO TAIZO FUKASAWA'S HOUSE.
Go, Taizo!!
I WAS SURPRISED AND TOOK IT WITH ME...
Go, Taizo!!
...BECAUSE FUMIKO-SAN WAS IN THE PICTURE WITH HIM.

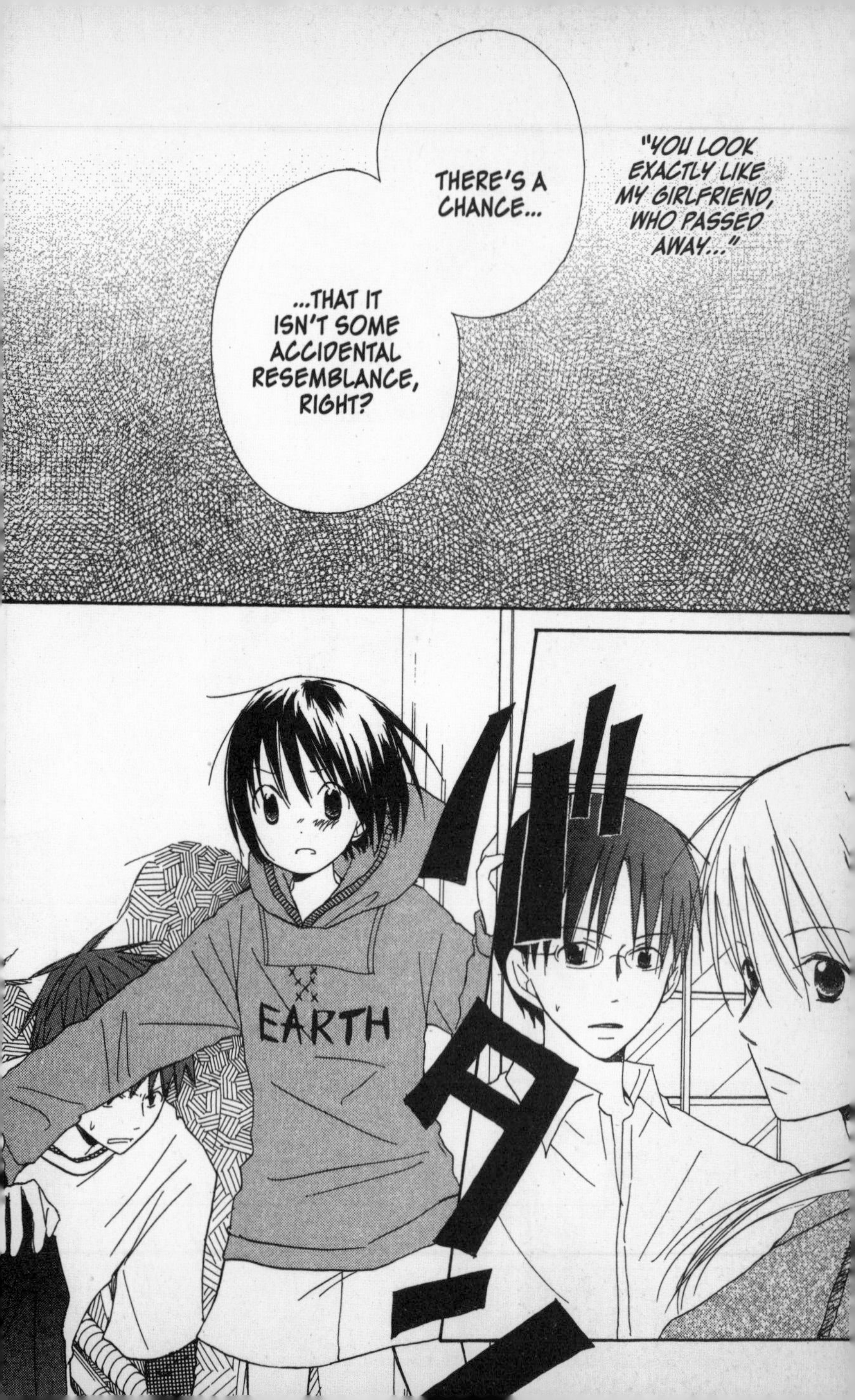
"YOU LOOK EXACTLY LIKE MY GIRLFRIEND, WHO PASSED AWAY..."
THERE'S A CHANCE...
...THAT IT ISN'T SOME ACCIDENTAL RESEMBLANCE, RIGHT?
EARTH

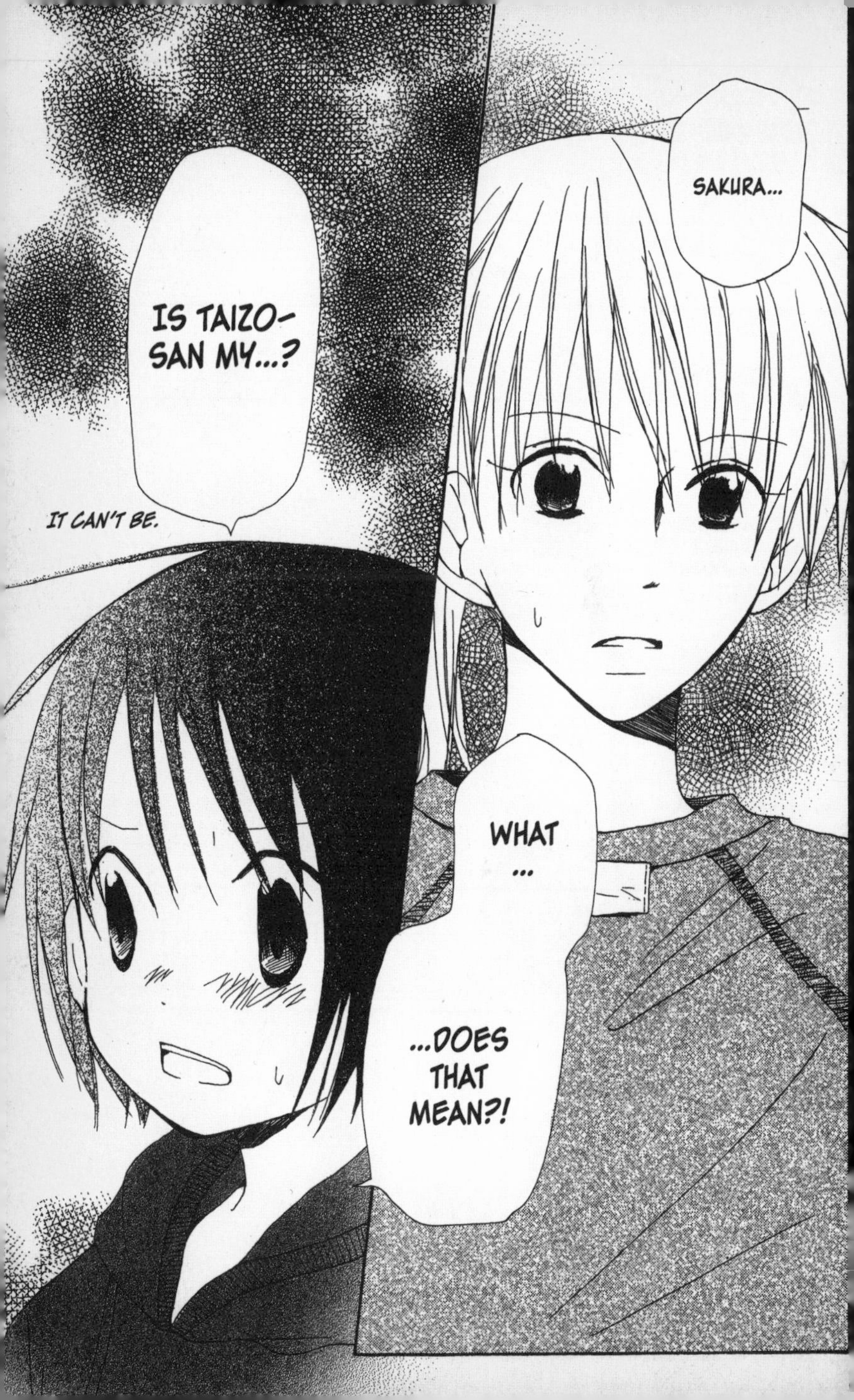
SAKURA...
IS TAIZO-SAN MY...?
IT CAN'T BE.
WHAT ...
...DOES THAT MEAN?!

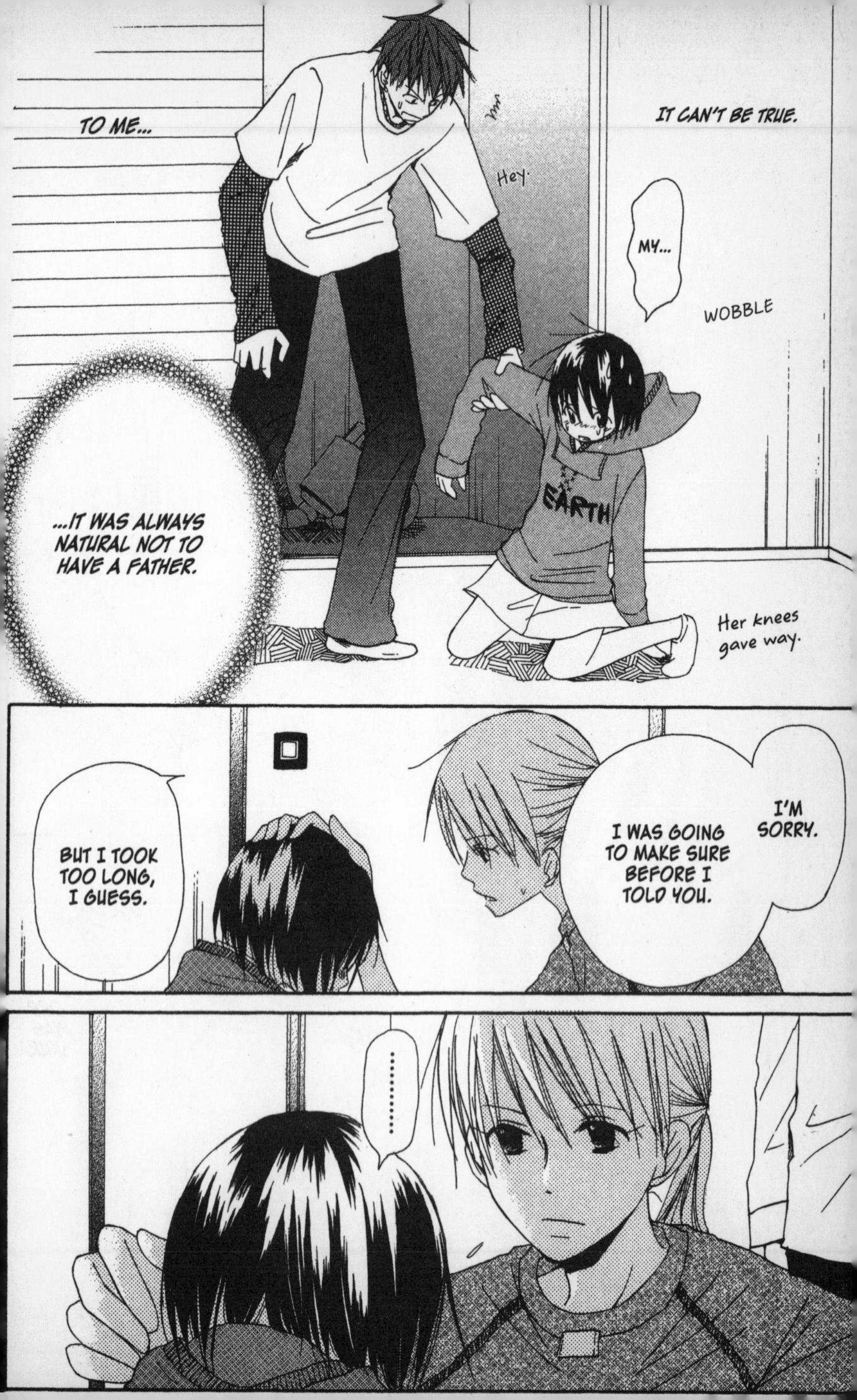
IT CAN'T BE TRUE.
MY...
WOBBLE
Hey.
TO ME...
Her knees gave way.
...IT WAS ALWAYS NATURAL NOT TO HAVE A FATHER.
I'M SORRY.
I WAS GOING TO MAKE SURE BEFORE I TOLD YOU.
BUT I TOOK TOO LONG, I GUESS.
....

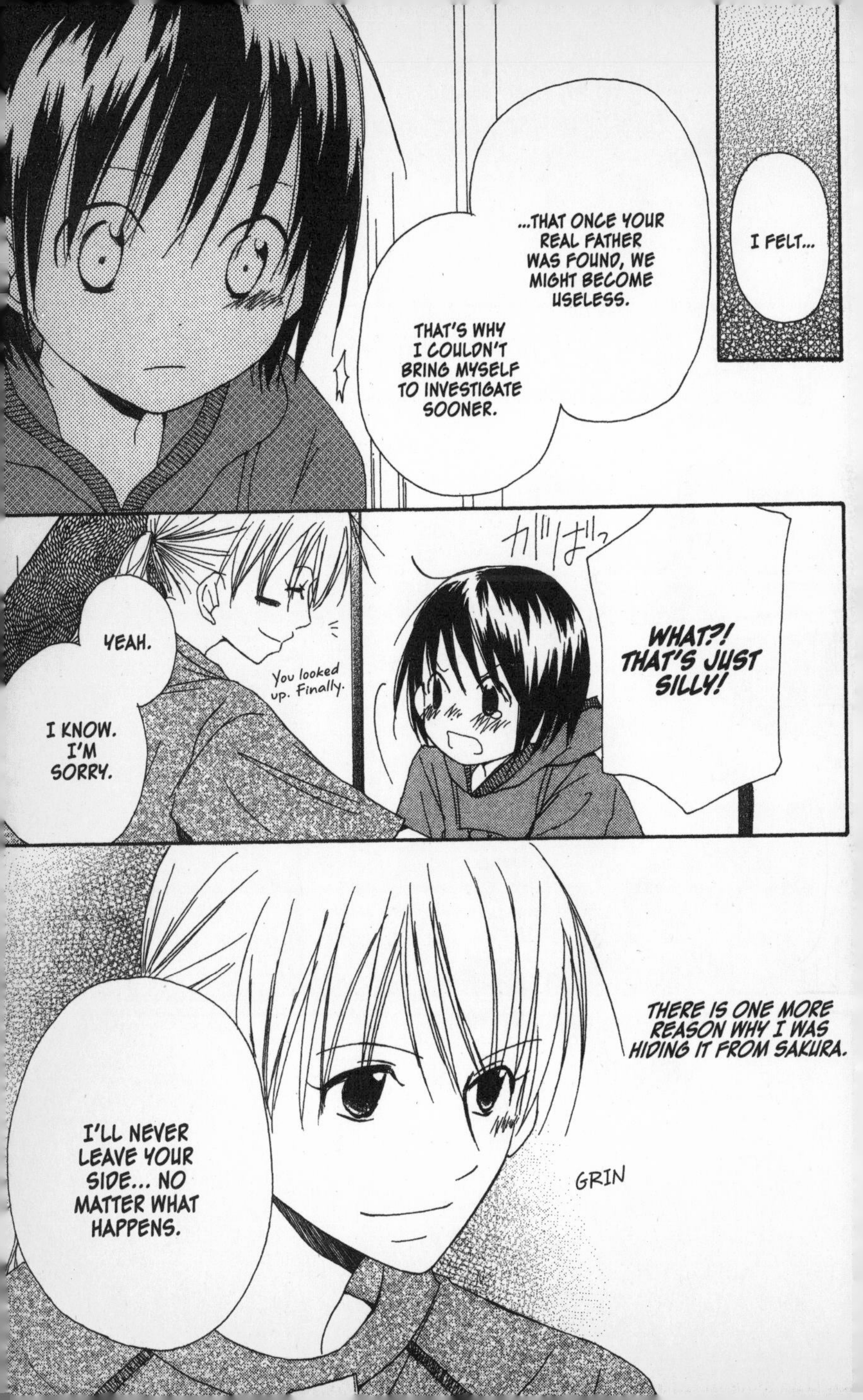
I FELT...
...THAT ONCE YOUR REAL FATHER WAS FOUND, WE MIGHT BECOME USELESS.
THAT'S WHY I COULDN'T BRING MYSELF TO INVESTIGATE SOONER.
がばっ
WHAT?! THAT'S JUST SILLY!
YEAH.
You looked up. Finally.
I KNOW. I'M SORRY.
THERE IS ONE MORE REASON WHY I WAS HIDING IT FROM SAKURA.
GRIN
I'LL NEVER LEAVE YOUR SIDE... NO MATTER WHAT HAPPENS.

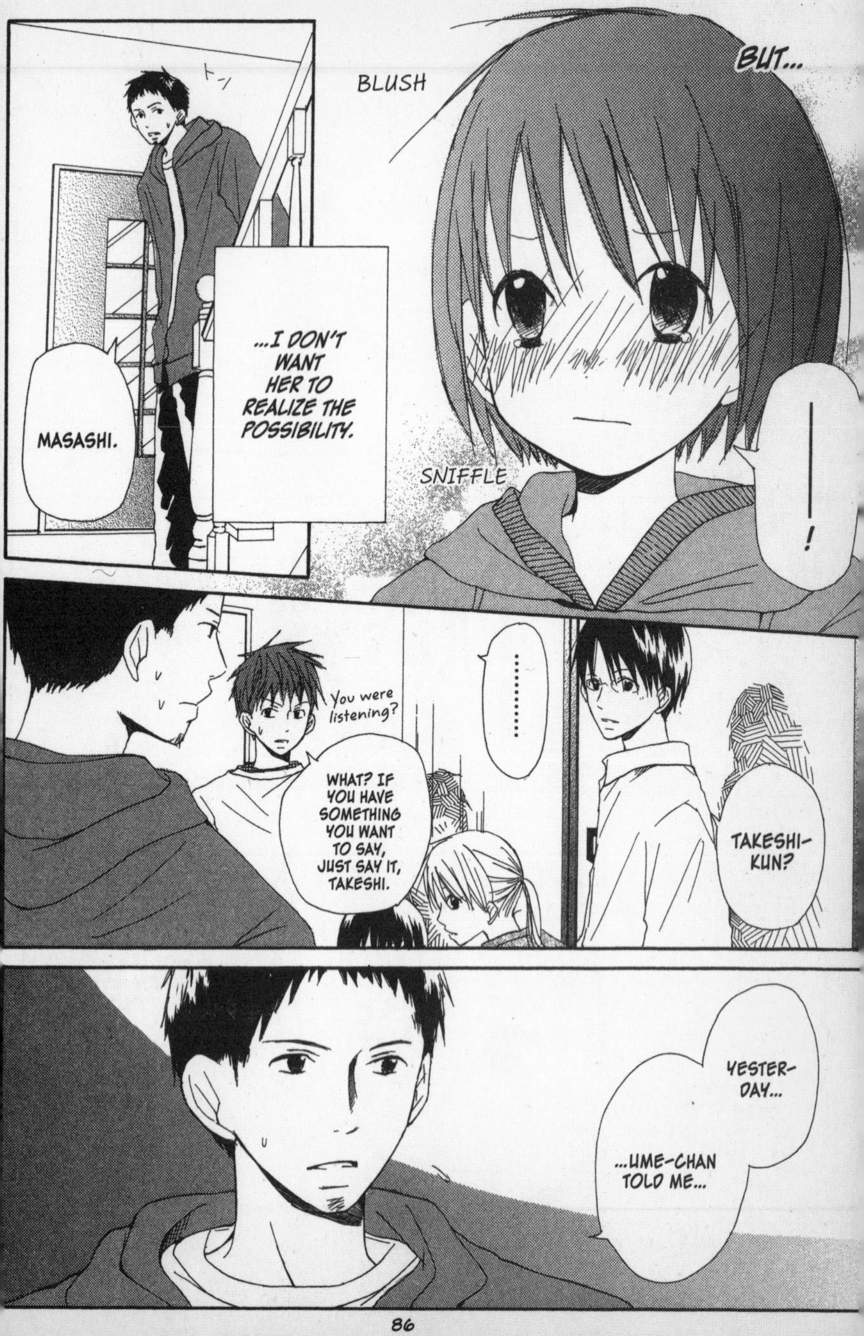

BUT...
BLUSH
—!
SNIFFLE
...I DON'T WANT HER TO REALIZE THE POSSIBILITY.
MASASHI.
TAKESHI-KUN?
......
You were listening?
WHAT? IF YOU HAVE SOMETHING YOU WANT TO SAY, JUST SAY IT, TAKESHI.
YESTER-DAY...
...UME-CHAN TOLD ME...

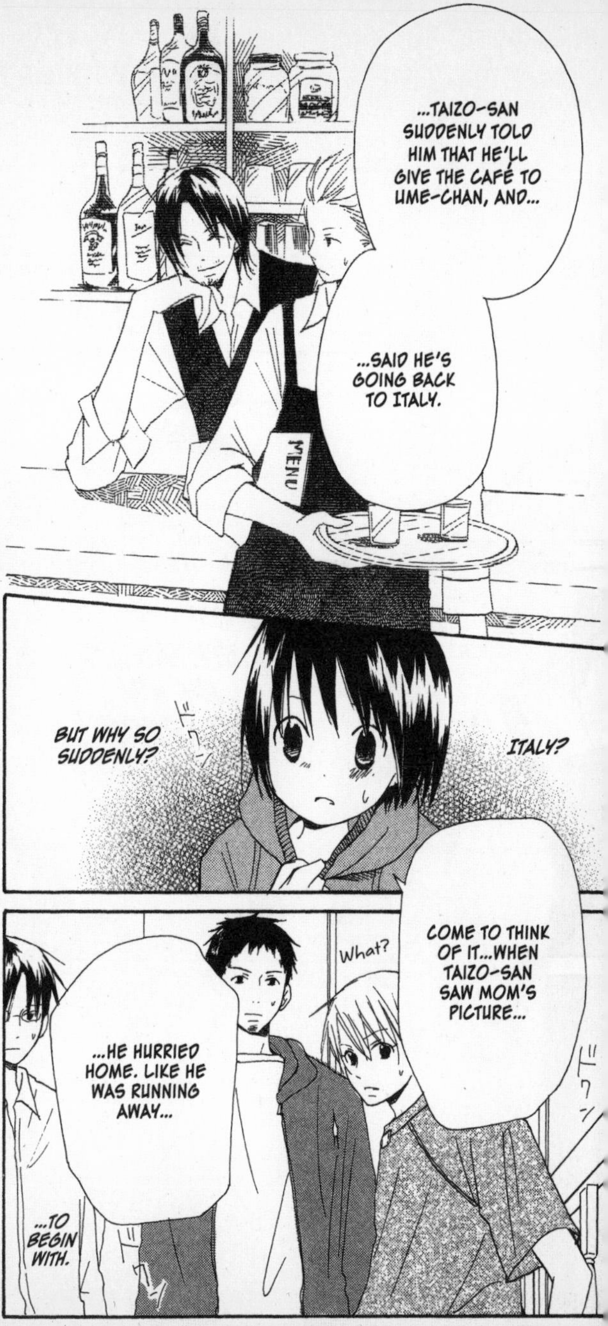
...TAIZO-SAN SUDDENLY TOLD HIM THAT HE'LL GIVE THE CAFÉ TO UME-CHAN, AND...
...SAID HE'S GOING BACK TO ITALY.
MENU
ITALY?
BUT WHY SO SUDDENLY?
COME TO THINK OF IT...WHEN TAIZO-SAN SAW MOM'S PICTURE...
What?
...HE HURRIED HOME. LIKE HE WAS RUNNING AWAY...
...TO BEGIN WITH.

☆ 3 ☆

Er...uh...um... oh no, I don't know what to write! I guess I'll write about this manga. Let's see, let's see... Sakura-chan became a high school student in Episode 19. Surprising. It can't be helped because everyone looks young in my drawings, but...

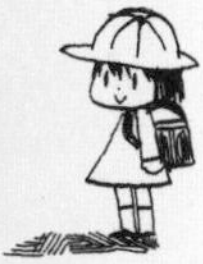

...she's a little like an elementary student, isn't she? I'll try and make her grow up inside and outside. Also, I have to do something about all those new characters I created despite my lack of drawing skills. There are characters that only appeared in one episode.

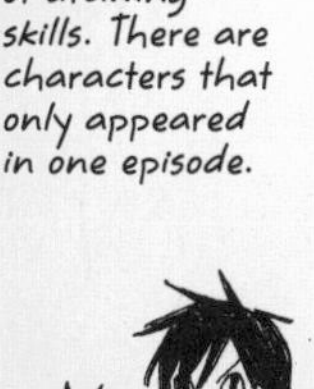

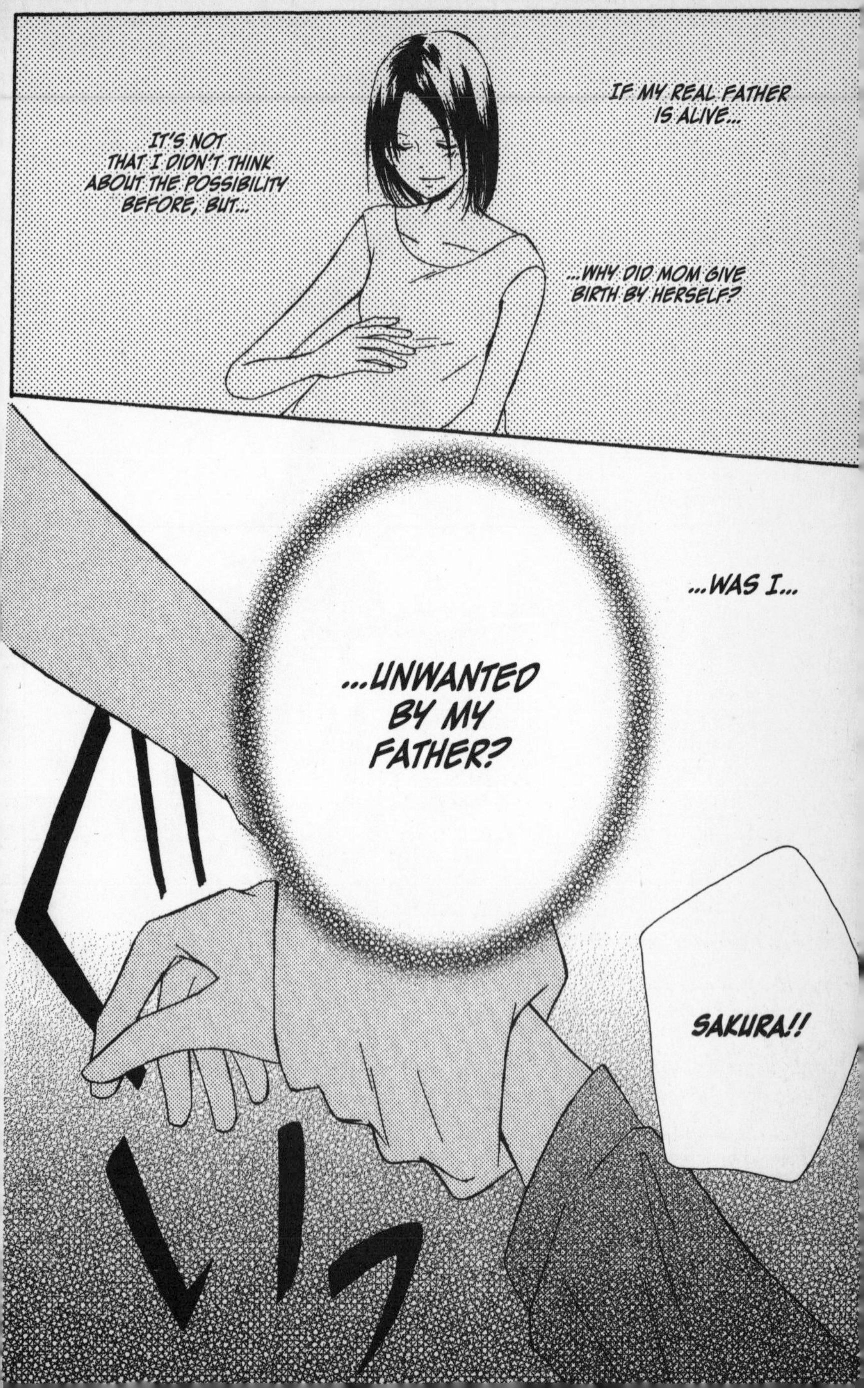
IF MY REAL FATHER IS ALIVE...
IT'S NOT THAT I DIDN'T THINK ABOUT THE POSSIBILITY BEFORE, BUT...
...WHY DID MOM GIVE BIRTH BY HERSELF?
...WAS I...
...UNWANTED BY MY FATHER?
SAKURA!!

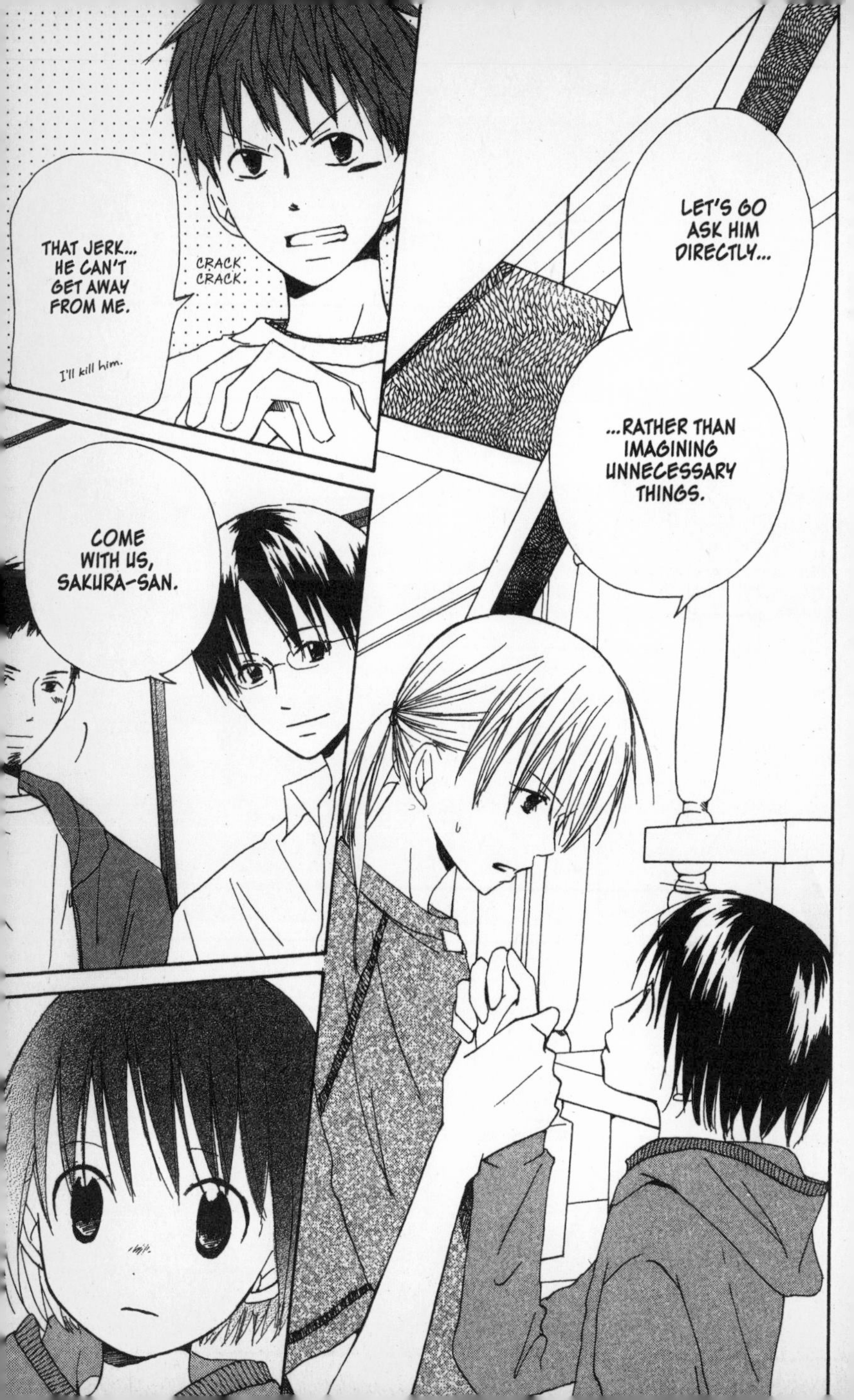
LET'S GO ASK HIM DIRECTLY...
...RATHER THAN IMAGINING UNNECESSARY THINGS.
THAT JERK... HE CAN'T GET AWAY FROM ME.
CRACK CRACK
I'll kill him.
COME WITH US, SAKURA-SAN.

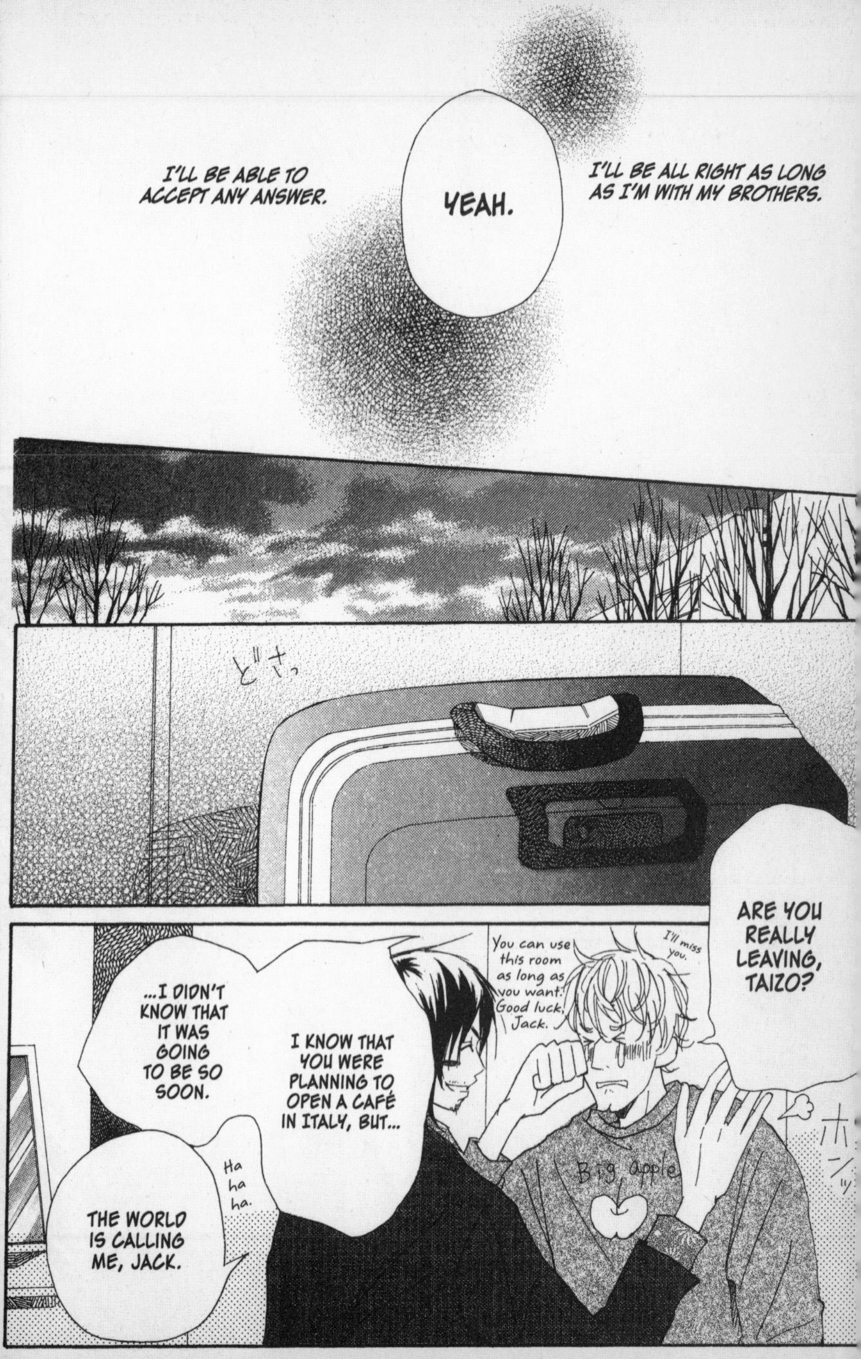
I'LL BE ALL RIGHT AS LONG AS I'M WITH MY BROTHERS.
YEAH.
I'LL BE ABLE TO ACCEPT ANY ANSWER.
どさっ
ARE YOU REALLY LEAVING, TAIZO?
I'll miss you.
You can use this room as long as you want. Good luck, Jack.
Big apple
I KNOW THAT YOU WERE PLANNING TO OPEN A CAFÉ IN ITALY, BUT...
...I DIDN'T KNOW THAT IT WAS GOING TO BE SO SOON.
Ha ha ha.
THE WORLD IS CALLING ME, JACK.

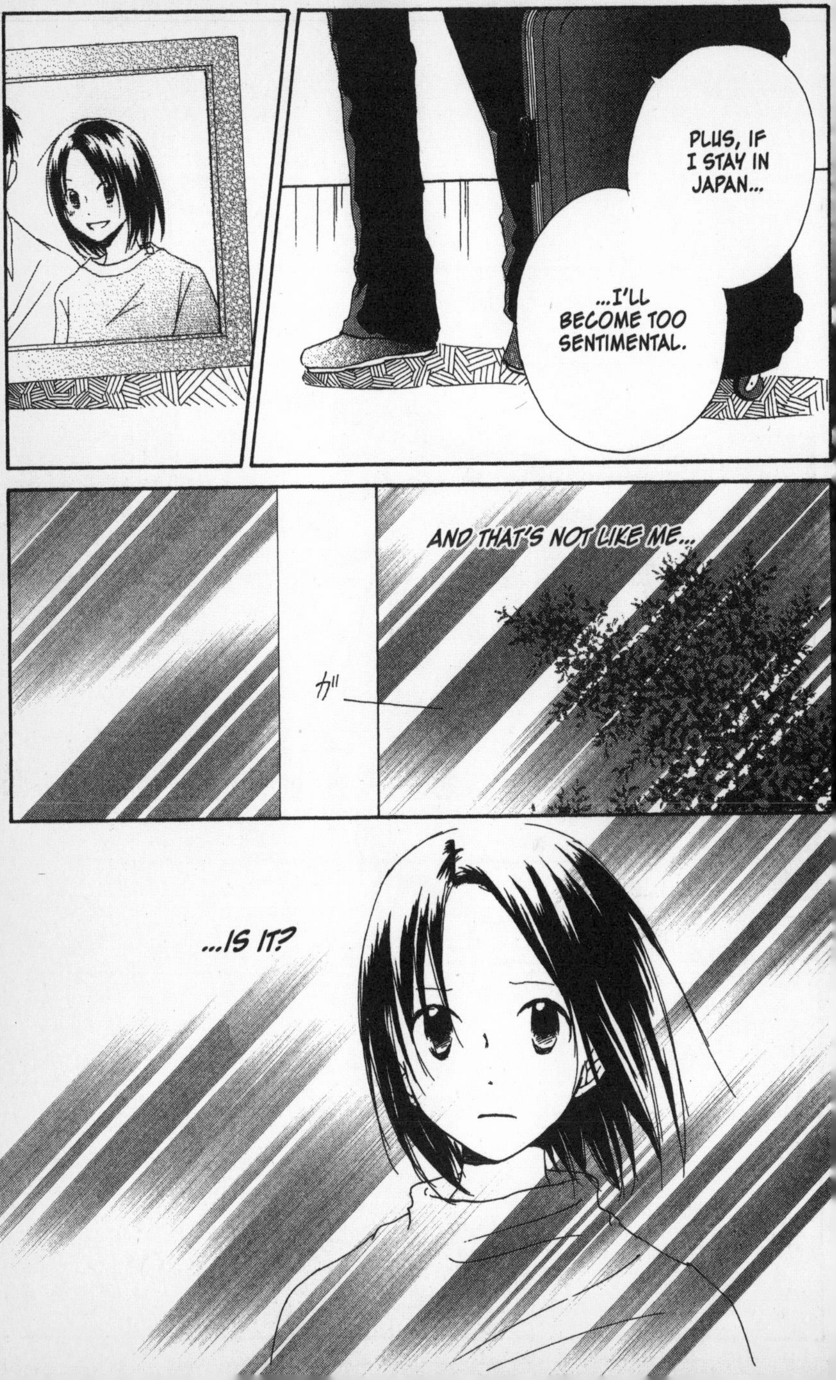
PLUS, IF I STAY IN JAPAN...
...I'LL BECOME TOO SENTIMENTAL.
AND THAT'S NOT LIKE ME...
ガ
...IS IT?

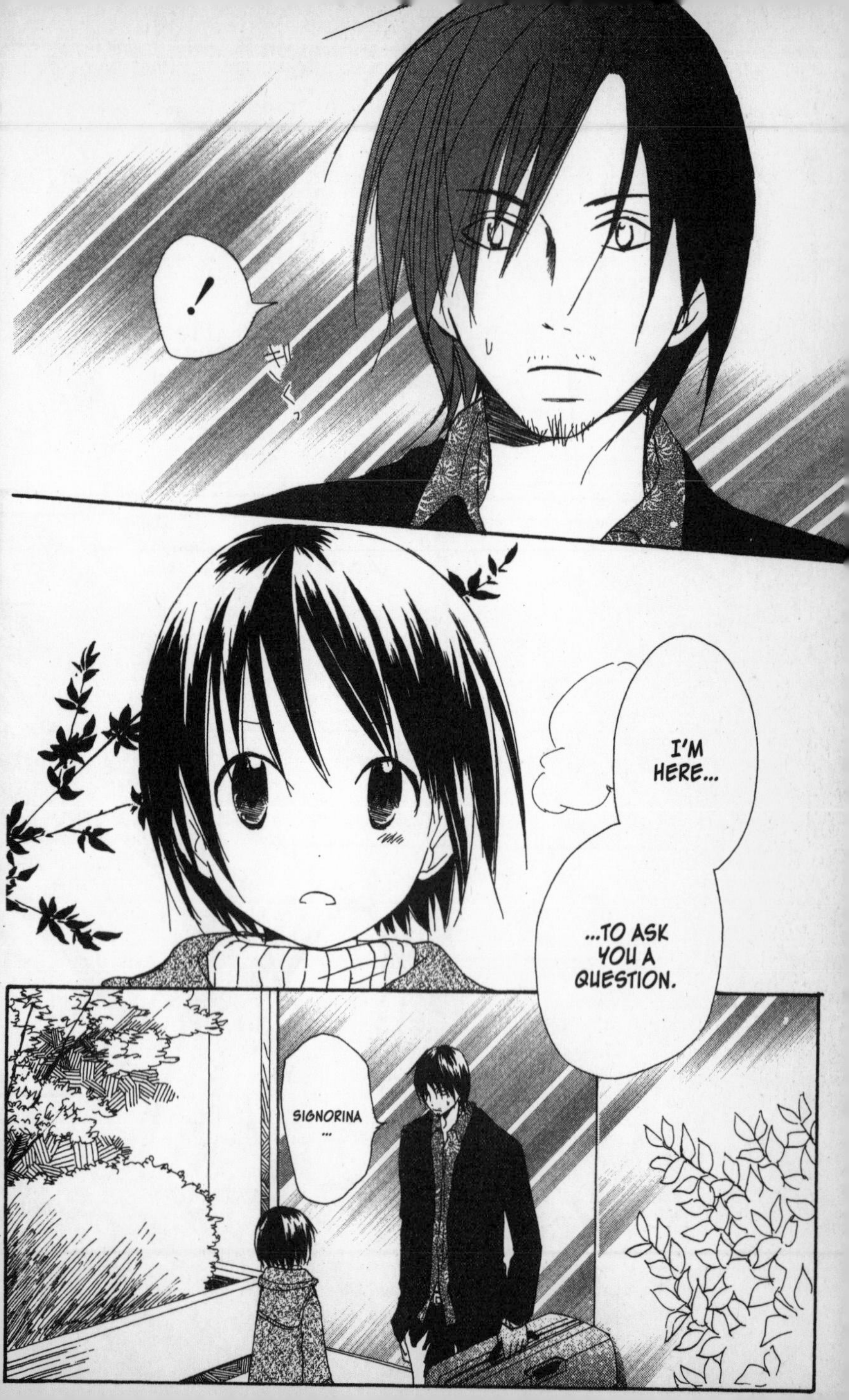
!
I'M HERE...
...TO ASK YOU A QUESTION.
SIGNORINA ...

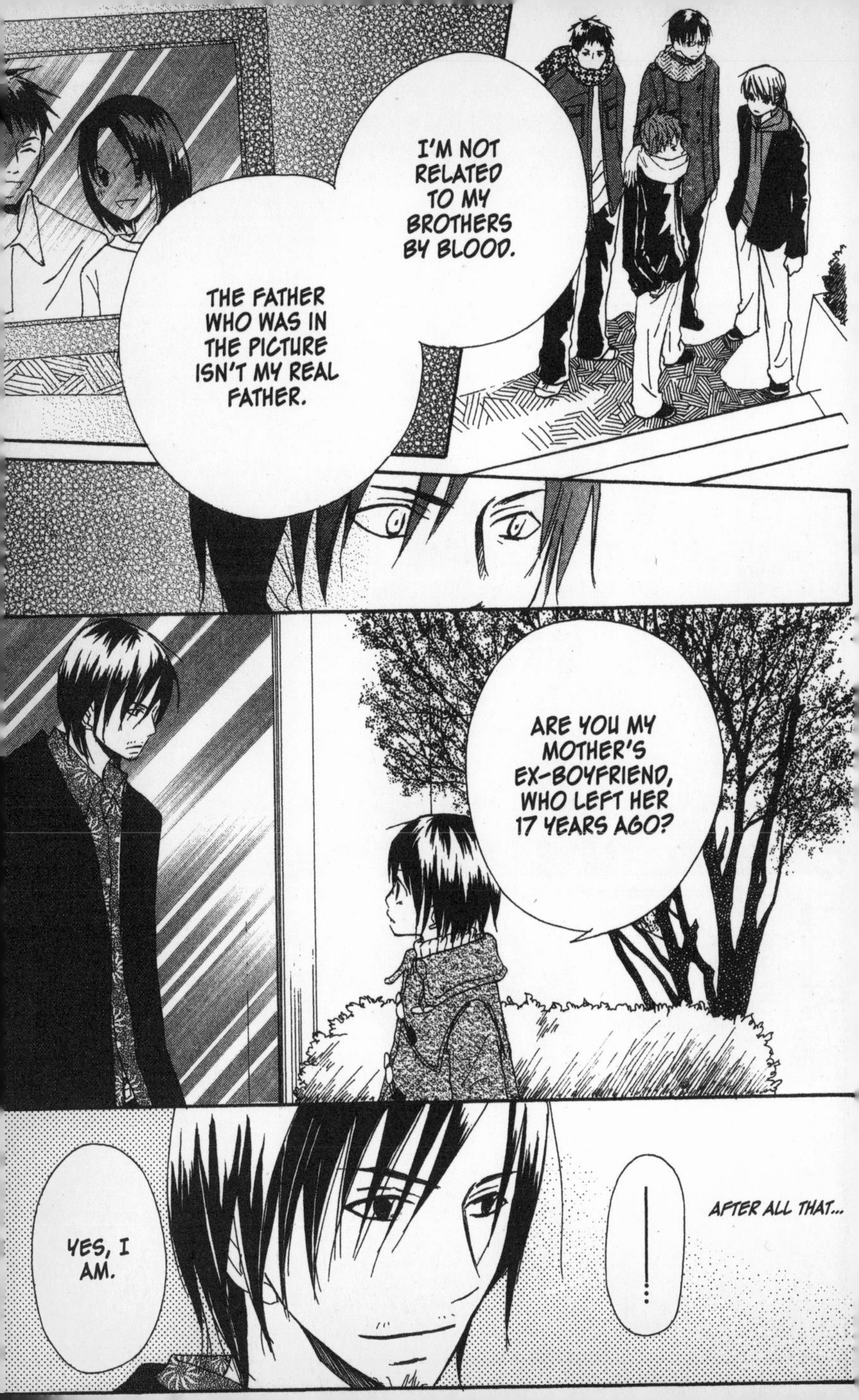
I'M NOT RELATED TO MY BROTHERS BY BLOOD.
THE FATHER WHO WAS IN THE PICTURE ISN'T MY REAL FATHER.
ARE YOU MY MOTHER'S EX-BOYFRIEND, WHO LEFT HER 17 YEARS AGO?
AFTER ALL THAT...
!......
YES, I AM.

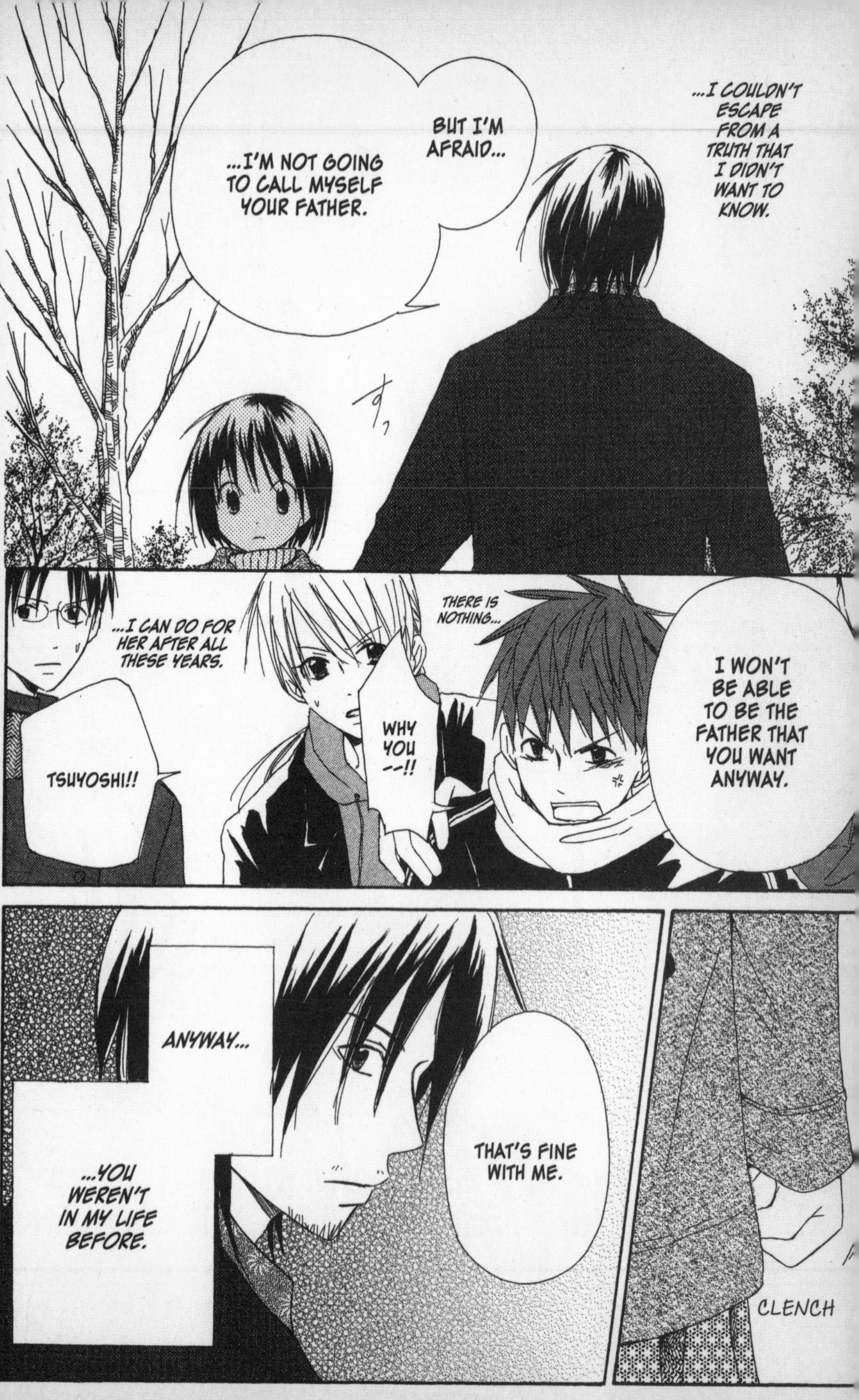
...I COULDN'T ESCAPE FROM A TRUTH THAT I DIDN'T WANT TO KNOW.
BUT I'M AFRAID...
...I'M NOT GOING TO CALL MYSELF YOUR FATHER.
すっ
I WON'T BE ABLE TO BE THE FATHER THAT YOU WANT ANYWAY.
THERE IS NOTHING...
WHY YOU--!!
...I CAN DO FOR HER AFTER ALL THESE YEARS.
TSUYOSHI!!
CLENCH
THAT'S FINE WITH ME.
ANYWAY...
...YOU WEREN'T IN MY LIFE BEFORE.

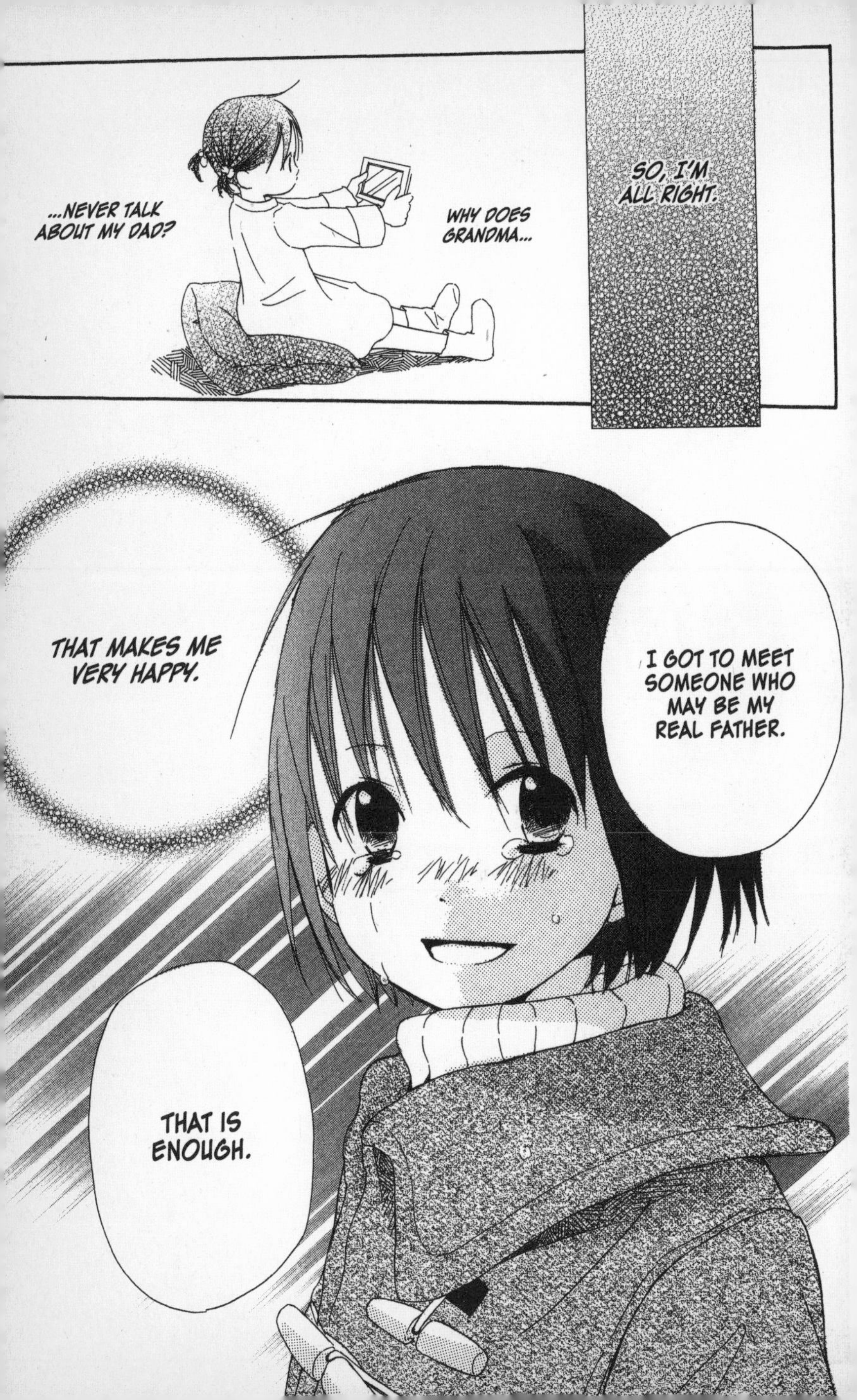
SO, I'M ALL RIGHT.
WHY DOES GRANDMA...
...NEVER TALK ABOUT MY DAD?
I GOT TO MEET SOMEONE WHO MAY BE MY REAL FATHER.
THAT MAKES ME VERY HAPPY.
THAT IS ENOUGH.

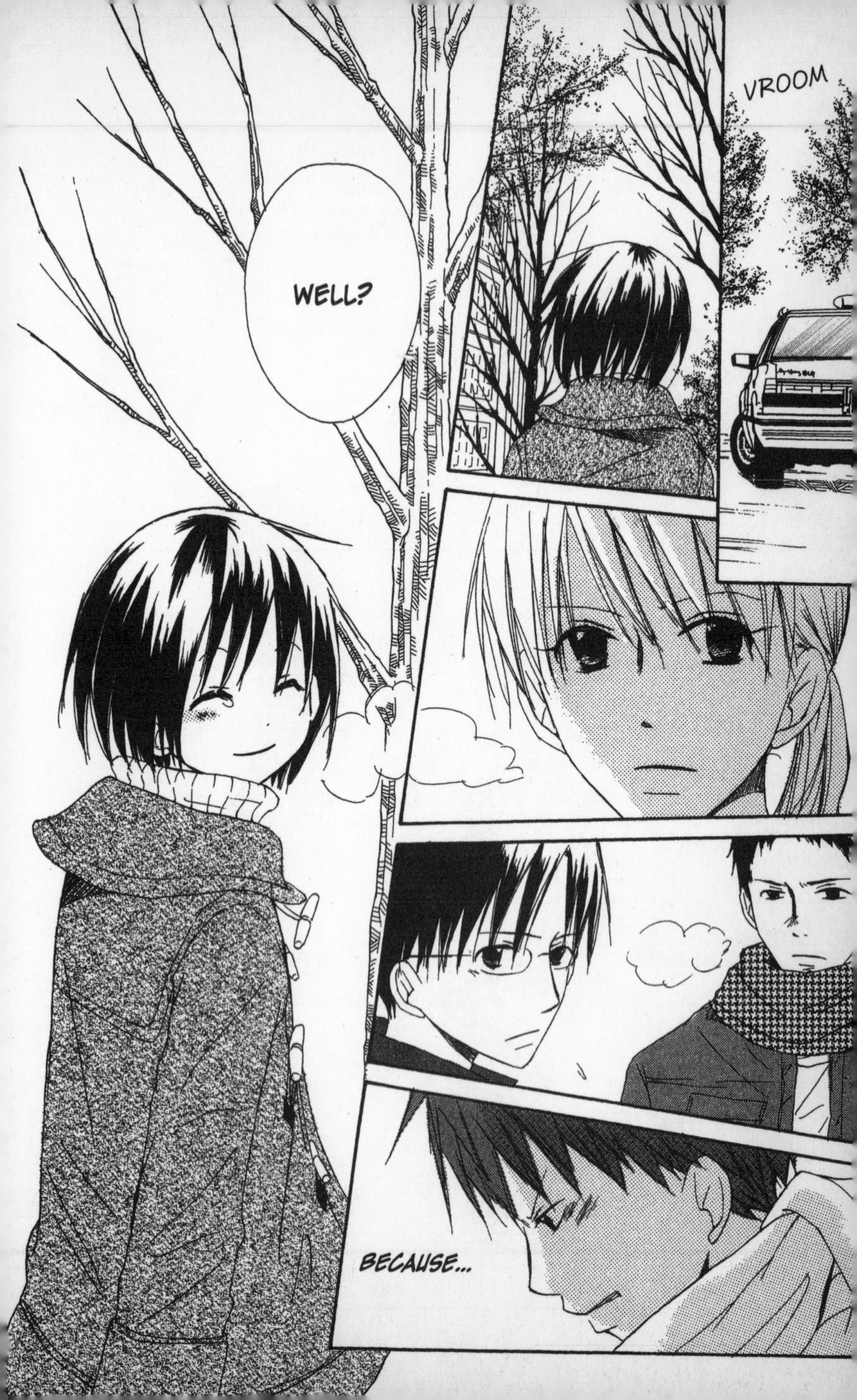
VROOM
BECAUSE...
WELL?

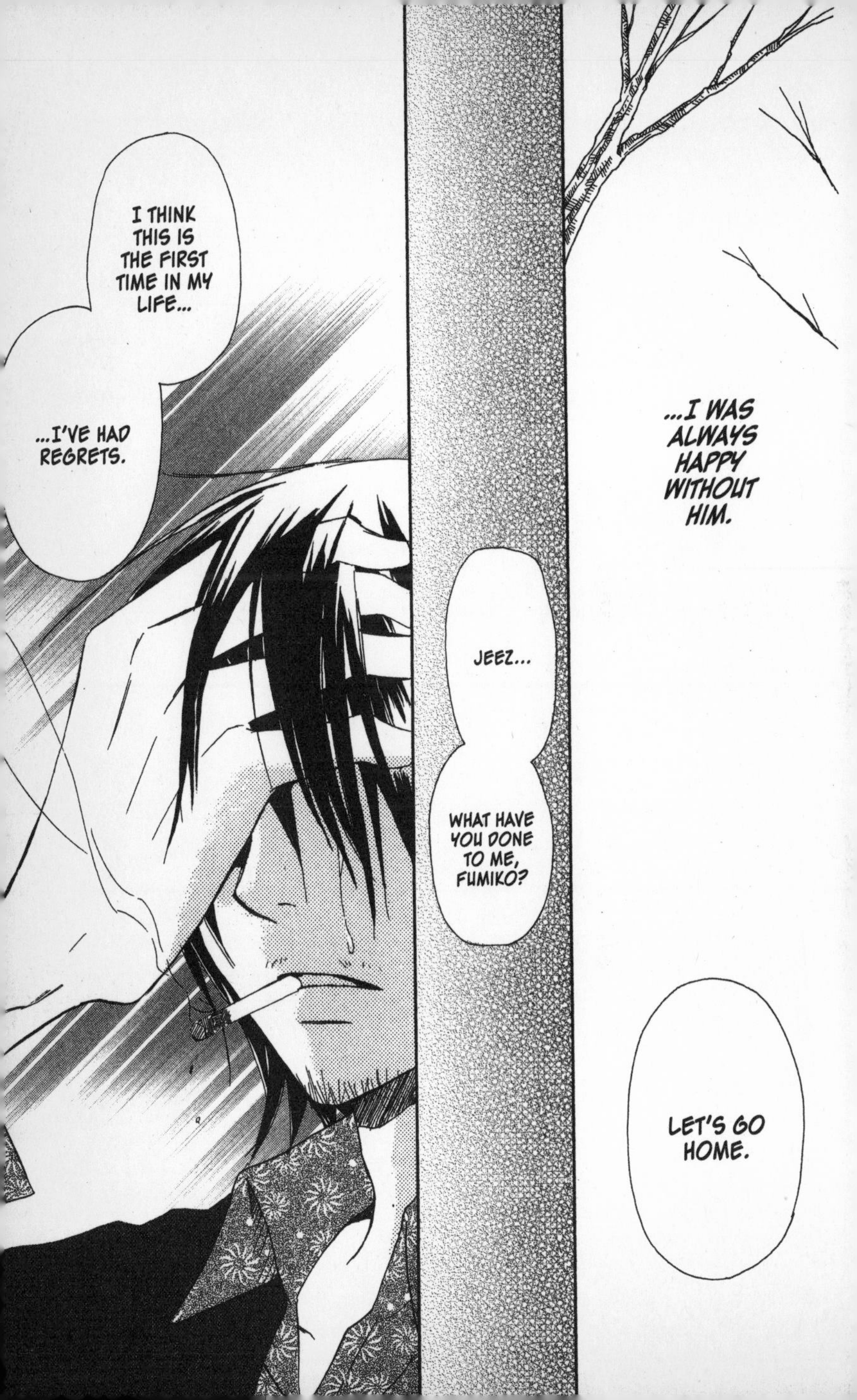
...I WAS ALWAYS HAPPY WITHOUT HIM.
LET'S GO HOME.
JEEZ...
WHAT HAVE YOU DONE TO ME, FUMIKO?
I THINK THIS IS THE FIRST TIME IN MY LIFE...
...I'VE HAD REGRETS.

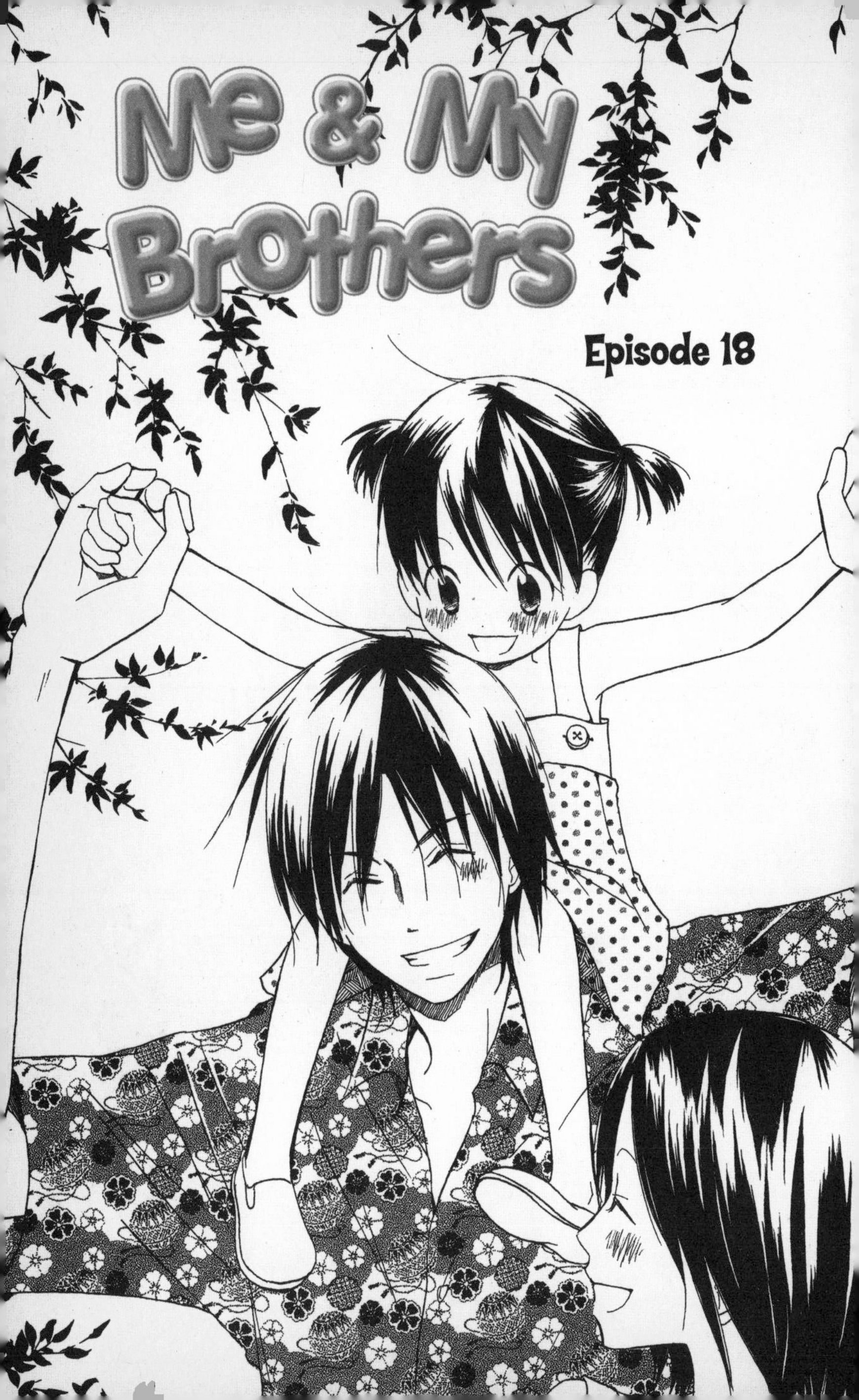
Me & My Brothers
Episode 18

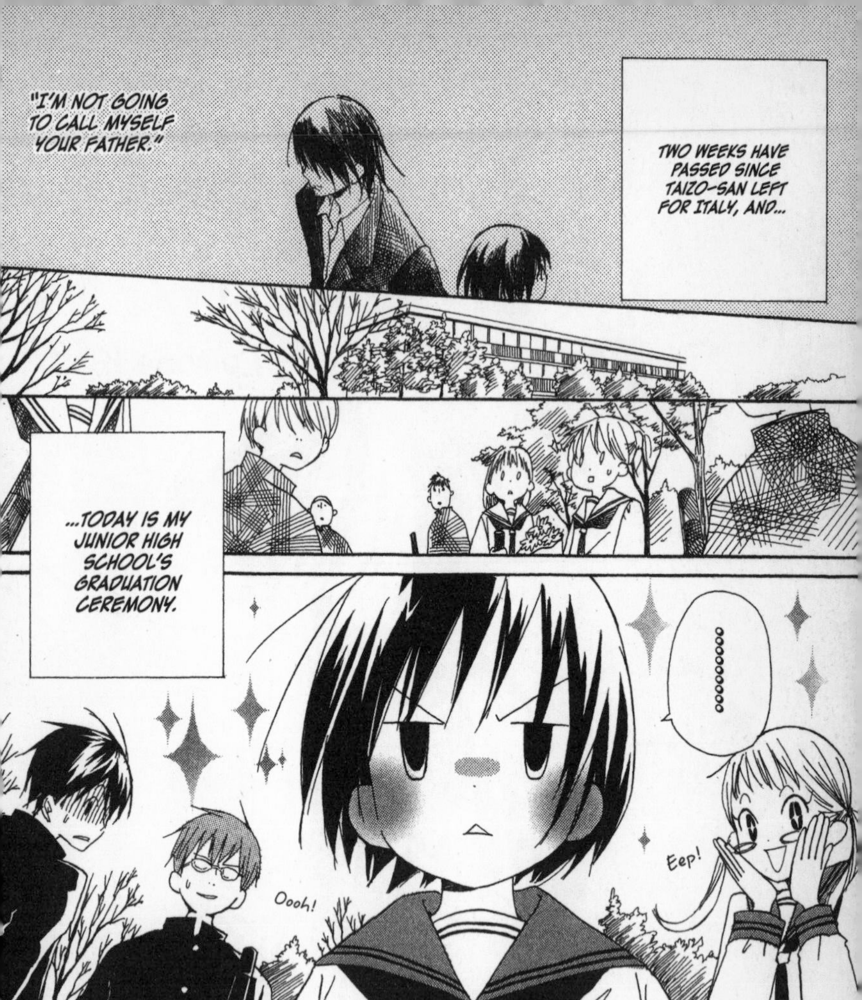
TWO WEEKS HAVE PASSED SINCE TAIZO-SAN LEFT FOR ITALY, AND...
"I'M NOT GOING TO CALL MYSELF YOUR FATHER."
...TODAY IS MY JUNIOR HIGH SCHOOL'S GRADUATION CEREMONY.
....
Eep!
Oooh!

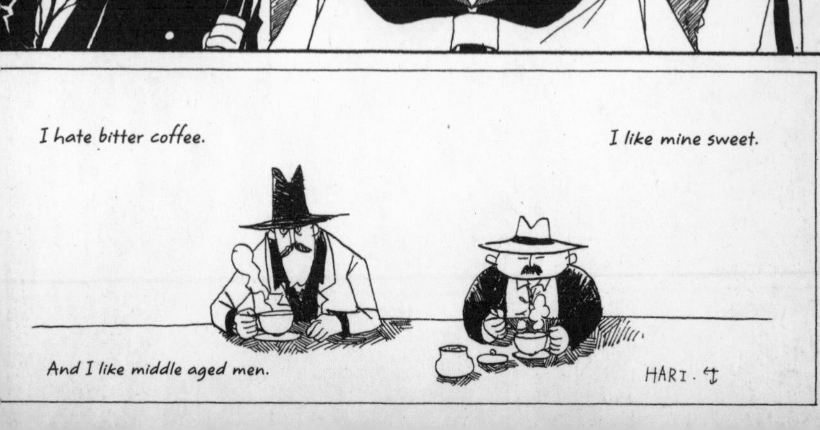
I hate bitter coffee.
I like mine sweet.
And I like middle aged men.
HARI.

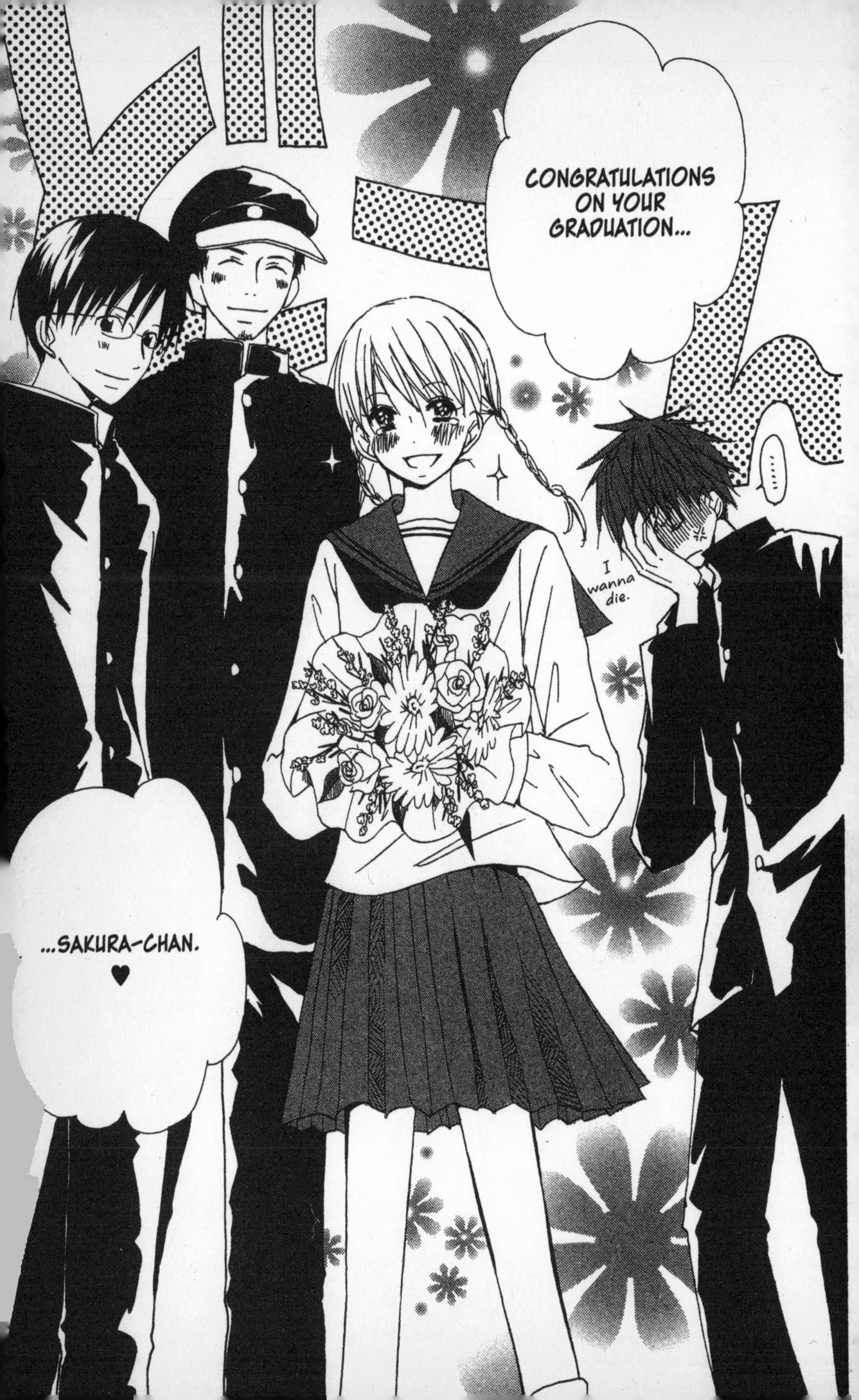
CONGRATULATIONS ON YOUR GRADUATION...
......
I wanna die.
...SAKURA-CHAN. ♥

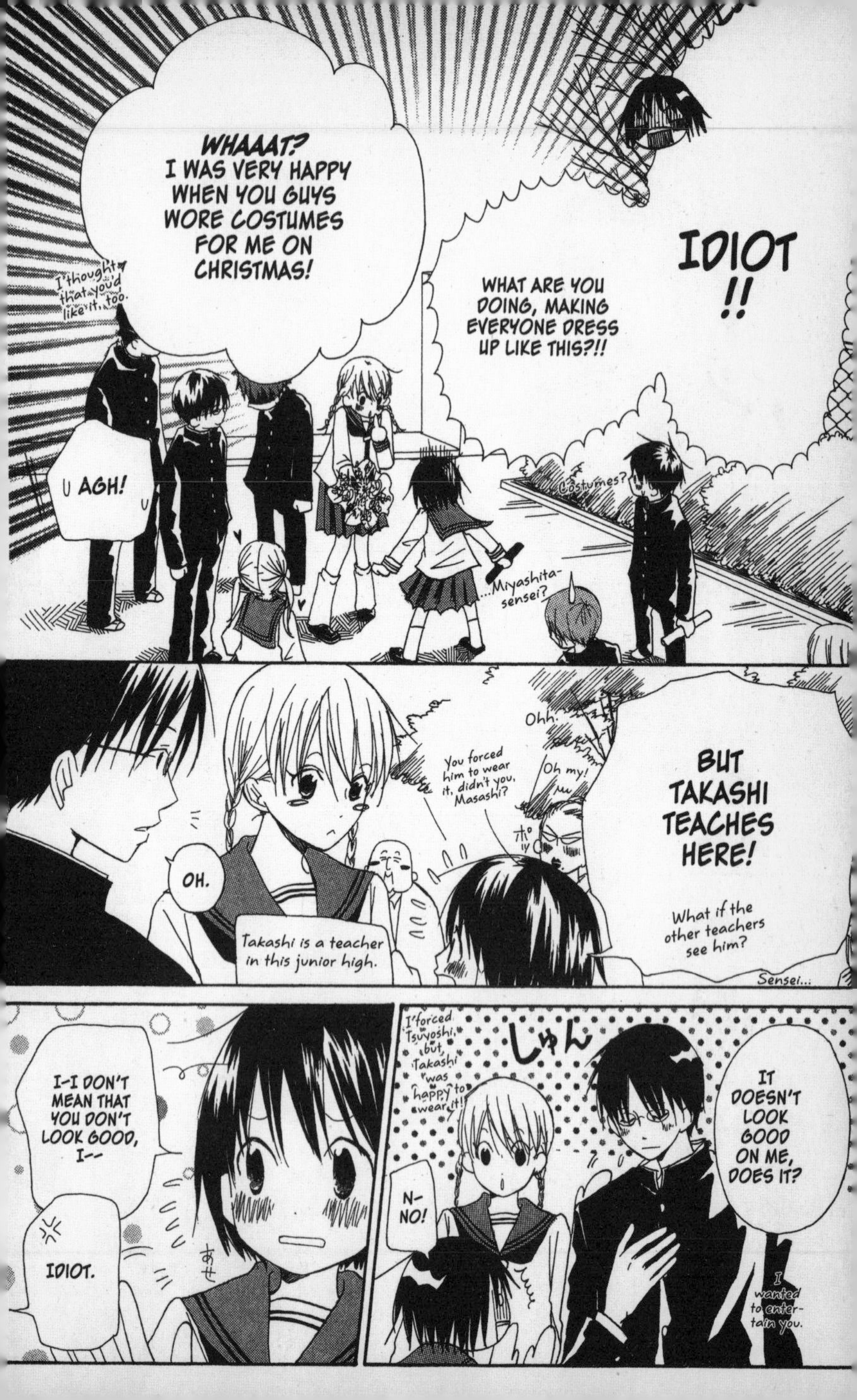
IDIOT!!
WHAT ARE YOU DOING, MAKING EVERYONE DRESS UP LIKE THIS?!!
WHAAAT? I WAS VERY HAPPY WHEN YOU GUYS WORE COSTUMES FOR ME ON CHRISTMAS!
I thought that you'd like it, too.
Costumes?
...Miyashita-sensei?
AGH!
BUT TAKASHI TEACHES HERE!
What if the other teachers see him?
Sensei...
Oh my!
Ohh.
ポ
You forced him to wear it, didn't you, Masashi?
Takashi is a teacher in this junior high.
OH.
IT DOESN'T LOOK GOOD ON ME, DOES IT?
I wanted to enter-tain you.
じゅん
I forced Tsuyoshi, but, Takashi was happy to wear it!
N-NO!
I-I DON'T MEAN THAT YOU DON'T LOOK GOOD, I--
あせ
IDIOT.

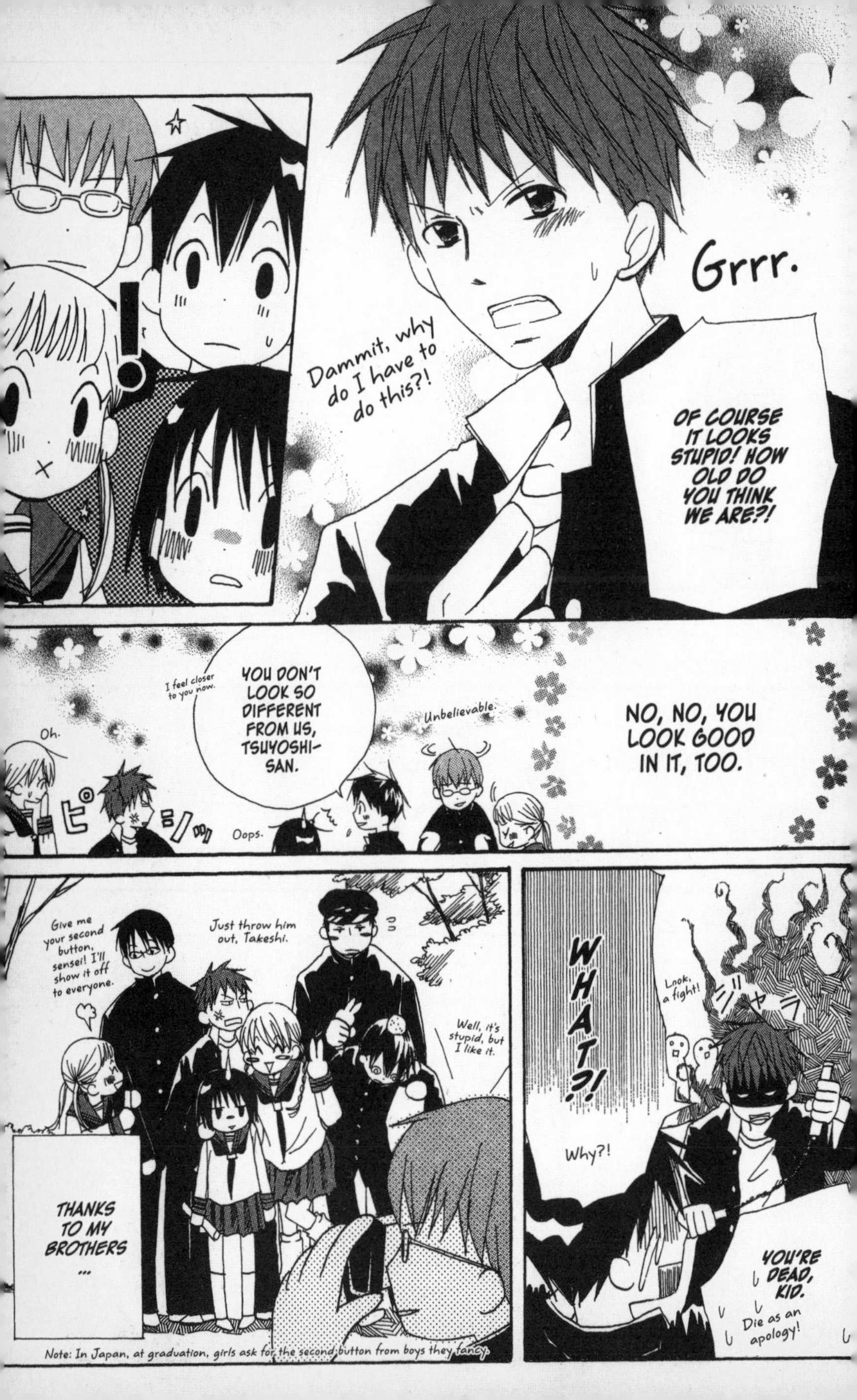
Grrr.
Of course it looks stupid! How old do you think we are?!
Dammit, why do I have to do this?!
No, no, you look good in it, too.
Unbelievable.
You don't look so different from us, Tsuyoshi-san.
I feel closer to you now.
Oops.
Oh.
WHAT?!
Look, a fight!
Why?!
You're dead, kid.
Die as an apology!
Just throw him out, Takeshi.
Give me your second button, sensei! I'll show it off to everyone.
Well, it's stupid, but I like it.
Thanks to my brothers...

Note: In Japan, at graduation, girls ask for the second button from boys they fancy.

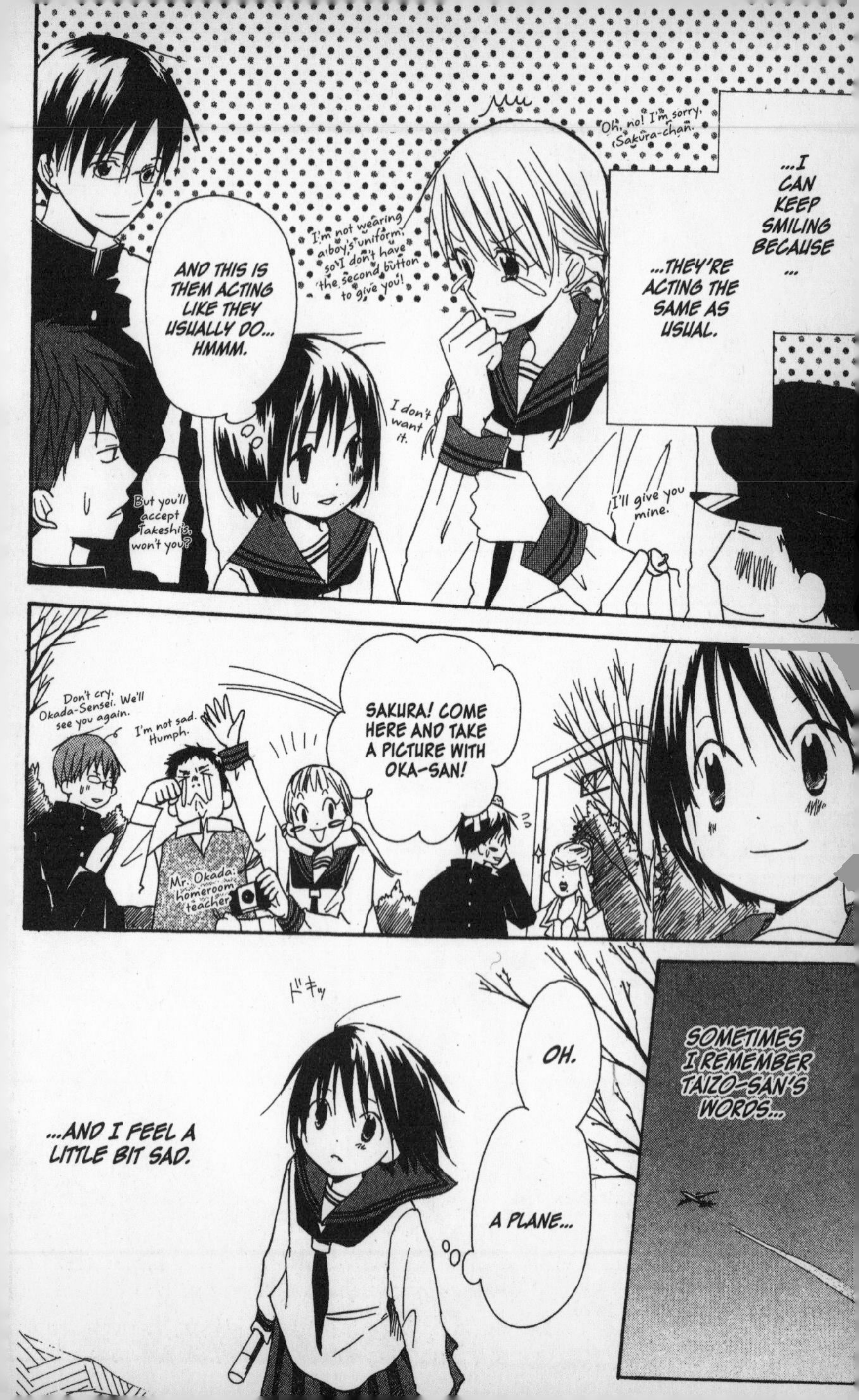
...I CAN KEEP SMILING BECAUSE ...
...THEY'RE ACTING THE SAME AS USUAL.
Oh, no! I'm sorry, Sakura-chan.
I'm not wearing a boy's uniform, so I don't have the second button to give you!
I'll give you mine.
I don't want it.
AND THIS IS THEM ACTING LIKE THEY USUALLY DO... HMMM.
But you'll accept Takeshi's, won't you?
SAKURA! COME HERE AND TAKE A PICTURE WITH OKA-SAN!
I'm not sad. Humph.
Don't cry, Okada-Sensei. We'll see you again.
Mr. Okada: homeroom teacher
SOMETIMES I REMEMBER TAIZO-SAN'S WORDS...
OH.
A PLANE...
ドキッ
...AND I FEEL A LITTLE BIT SAD.

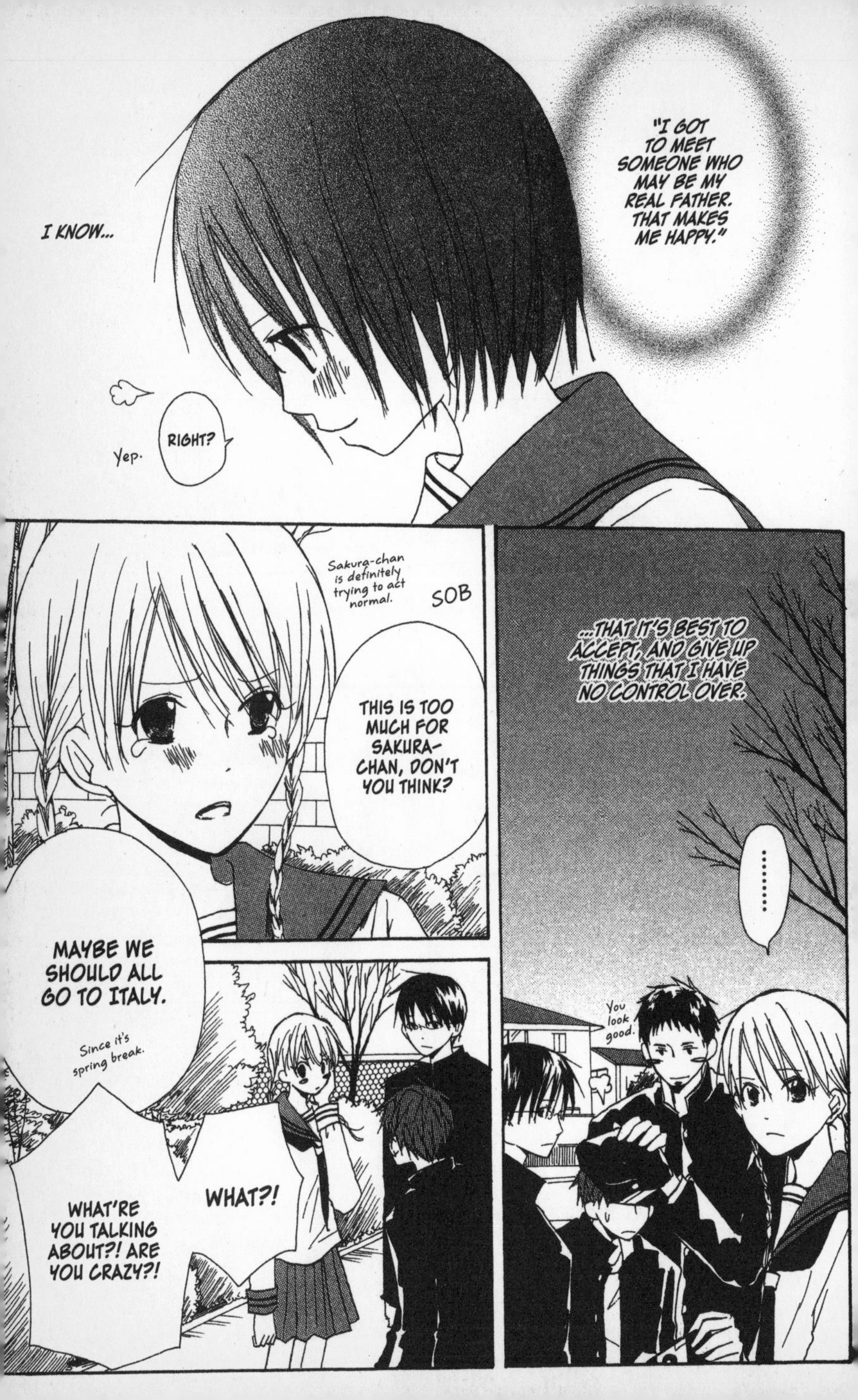
"I GOT TO MEET SOMEONE WHO MAY BE MY REAL FATHER. THAT MAKES ME HAPPY."
I KNOW...
RIGHT?
Yep.
...THAT IT'S BEST TO ACCEPT, AND GIVE UP THINGS THAT I HAVE NO CONTROL OVER.
......
You look good.
Sakura-chan is definitely trying to act normal.
SOB
THIS IS TOO MUCH FOR SAKURA-CHAN, DON'T YOU THINK?
MAYBE WE SHOULD ALL GO TO ITALY.
Since it's spring break.
WHAT?!
WHAT'RE YOU TALKING ABOUT?! ARE YOU CRAZY?!

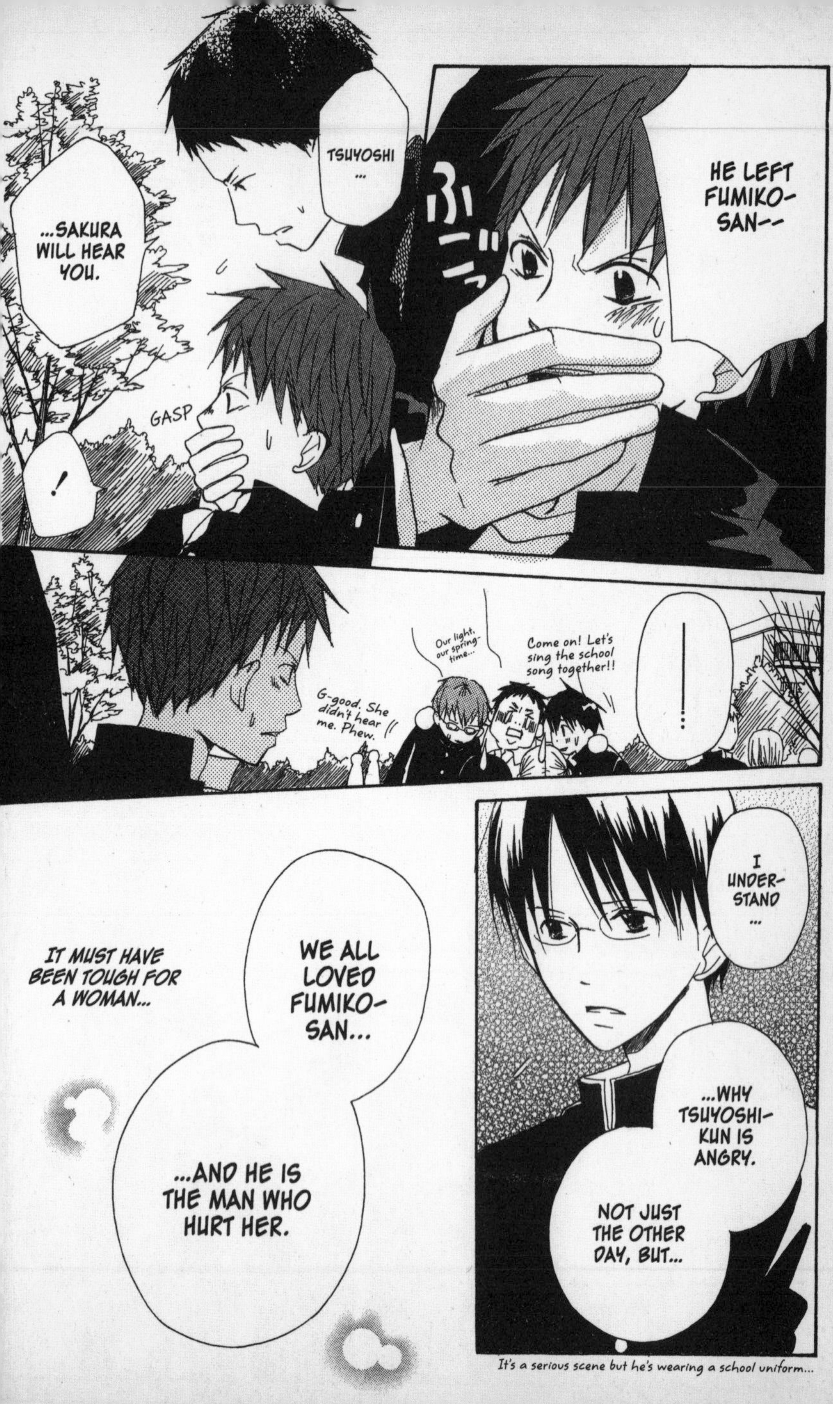
HE LEFT FUMIKO-SAN--
TSUYOSHI...
...SAKURA WILL HEAR YOU.
GASP
!
!
Come on! Let's sing the school song together!!
Our light, our spring-time...
G-good. She didn't hear me. Phew.
I UNDERSTAND...
...WHY TSUYOSHI-KUN IS ANGRY.
NOT JUST THE OTHER DAY, BUT...
WE ALL LOVED FUMIKO-SAN...
...AND HE IS THE MAN WHO HURT HER.
IT MUST HAVE BEEN TOUGH FOR A WOMAN...

It's a serious scene but he's wearing a school uniform...

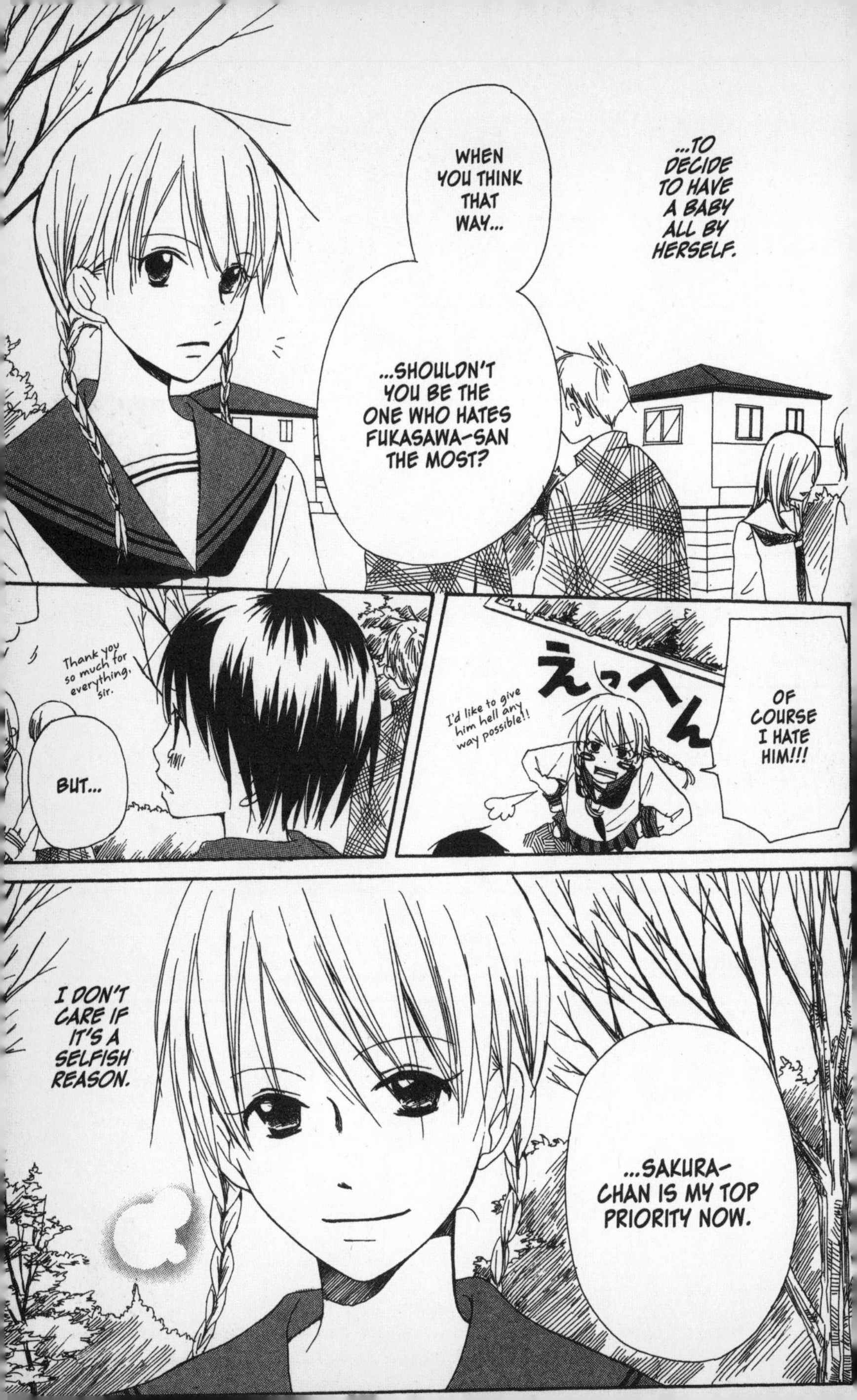
...TO DECIDE TO HAVE A BABY ALL BY HERSELF.
WHEN YOU THINK THAT WAY...
...SHOULDN'T YOU BE THE ONE WHO HATES FUKASAWA-SAN THE MOST?
OF COURSE I HATE HIM!!!
えっへん
I'd like to give him hell any way possible!!
Thank you so much for everything, sir.
BUT...
...SAKURA-CHAN IS MY TOP PRIORITY NOW.
I DON'T CARE IF IT'S A SELFISH REASON.

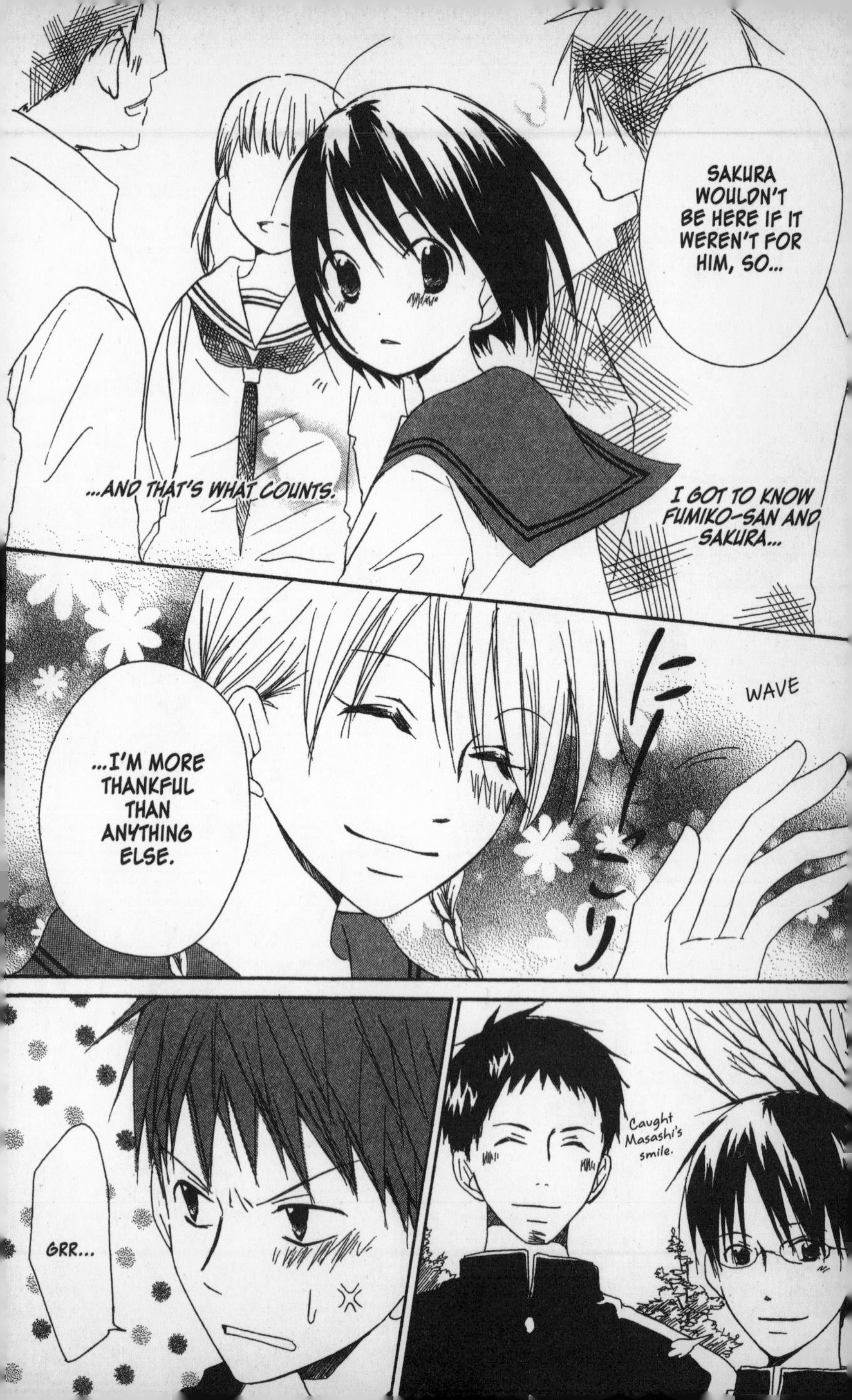
SAKURA WOULDN'T BE HERE IF IT WEREN'T FOR HIM, SO...
I GOT TO KNOW FUMIKO-SAN AND SAKURA...
...AND THAT'S WHAT COUNTS.
WAVE
...I'M MORE THANKFUL THAN ANYTHING ELSE.
Caught Masashi's smile.
GRR...

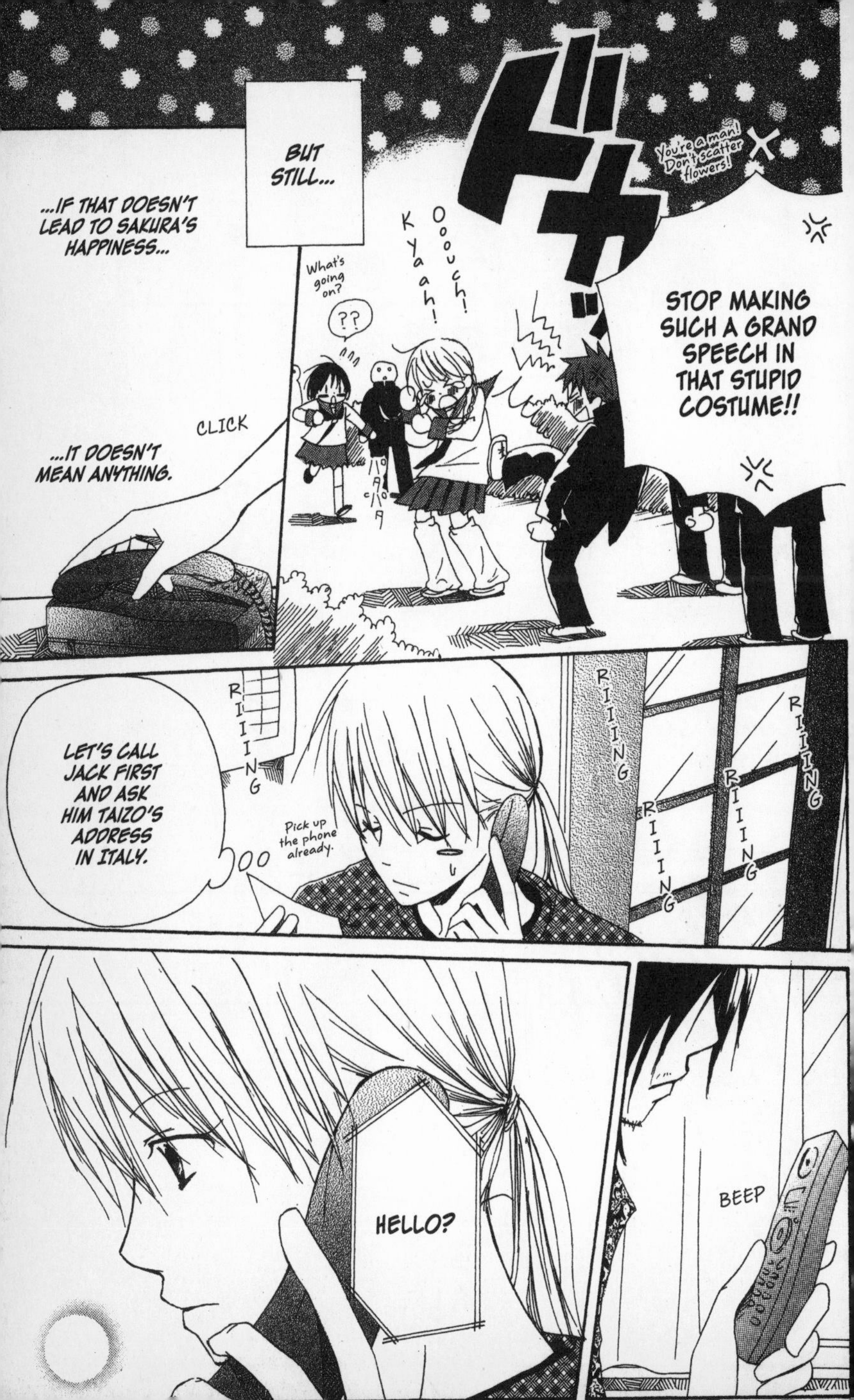
You're a man! Don't scatter flowers!
STOP MAKING SUCH A GRAND SPEECH IN THAT STUPID COSTUME!!
BUT STILL...
Oooouch!
Kyaah!
What's going on?
??
...IF THAT DOESN'T LEAD TO SAKURA'S HAPPINESS...
CLICK
...IT DOESN'T MEAN ANYTHING.
RIIIING
RIIIING
RIIING
RIIIING
RIIIING
RIIIING
Pick up the phone already.
LET'S CALL JACK FIRST AND ASK HIM TAIZO'S ADDRESS IN ITALY.
BEEP
HELLO?

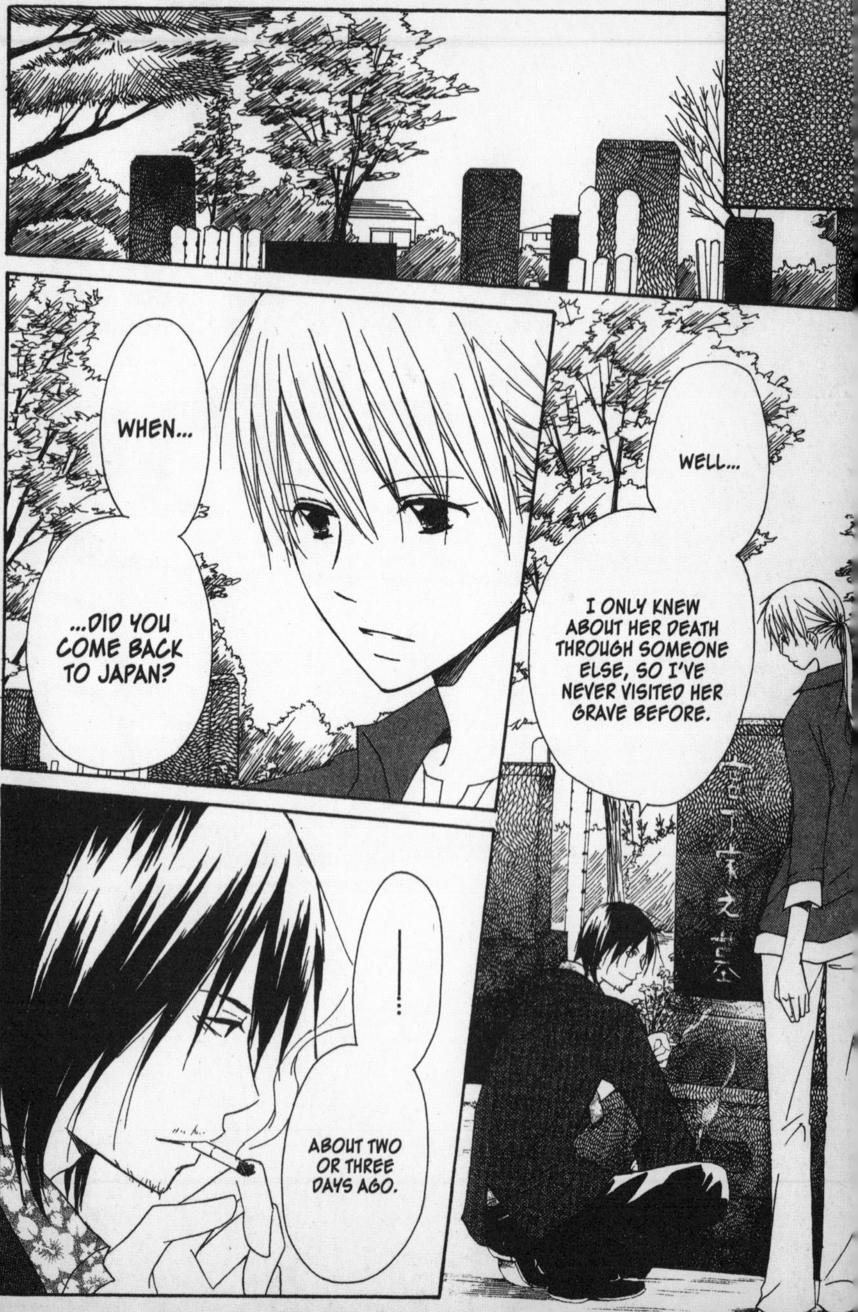
WELL...
I ONLY KNEW ABOUT HER DEATH THROUGH SOMEONE ELSE, SO I'VE NEVER VISITED HER GRAVE BEFORE.
WHEN...
...DID YOU COME BACK TO JAPAN?
—...
ABOUT TWO OR THREE DAYS AGO.

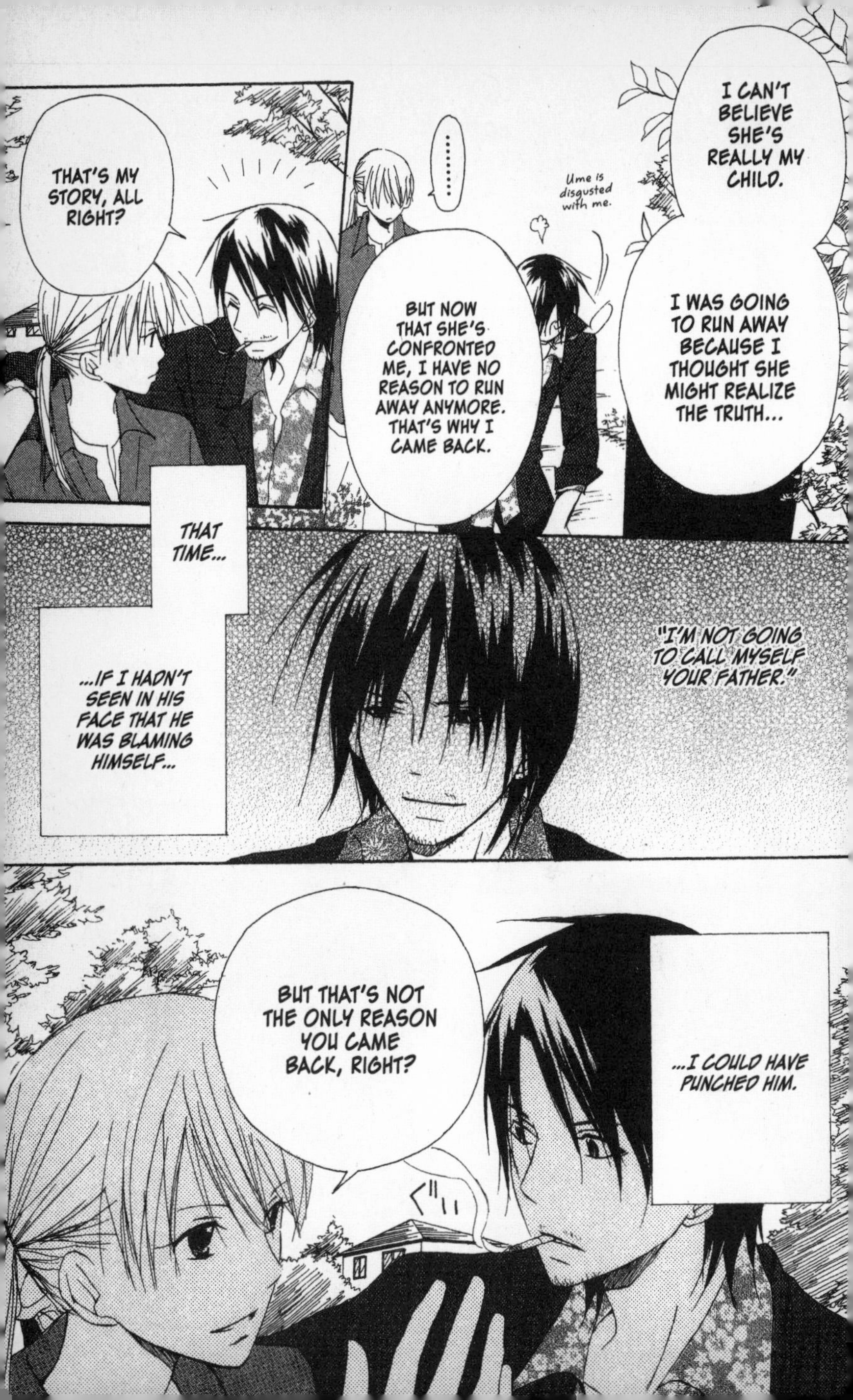
I CAN'T BELIEVE SHE'S REALLY MY CHILD.
I WAS GOING TO RUN AWAY BECAUSE I THOUGHT SHE MIGHT REALIZE THE TRUTH...
Ume is disgusted with me.
BUT NOW THAT SHE'S CONFRONTED ME, I HAVE NO REASON TO RUN AWAY ANYMORE. THAT'S WHY I CAME BACK.
....
THAT'S MY STORY, ALL RIGHT?
THAT TIME...
"I'M NOT GOING TO CALL MYSELF YOUR FATHER."
...IF I HADN'T SEEN IN HIS FACE THAT HE WAS BLAMING HIMSELF...
...I COULD HAVE PUNCHED HIM.
BUT THAT'S NOT THE ONLY REASON YOU CAME BACK, RIGHT?

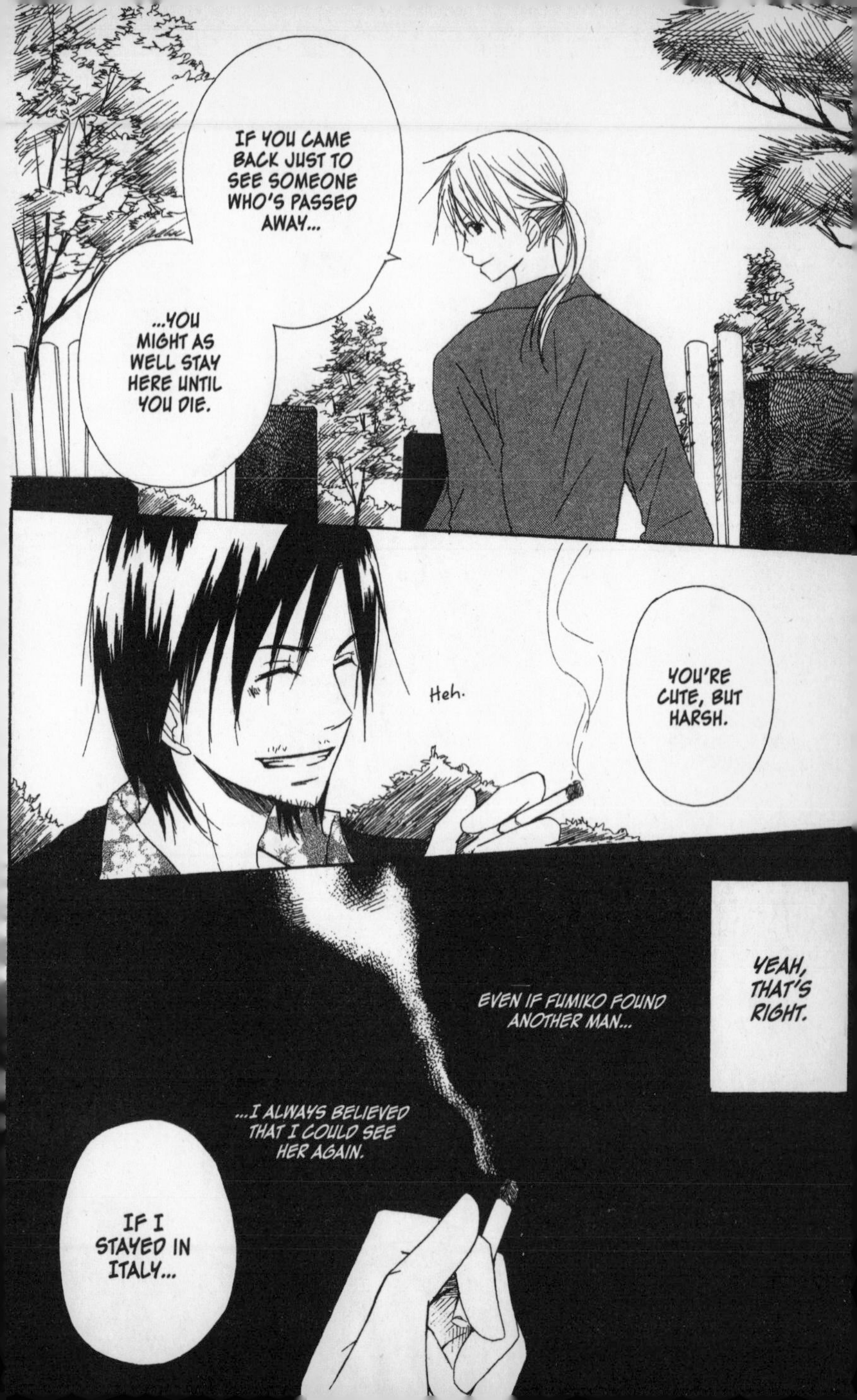
IF YOU CAME BACK JUST TO SEE SOMEONE WHO'S PASSED AWAY...
...YOU MIGHT AS WELL STAY HERE UNTIL YOU DIE.
YOU'RE CUTE, BUT HARSH.
Heh.
YEAH, THAT'S RIGHT.
EVEN IF FUMIKO FOUND ANOTHER MAN...
...I ALWAYS BELIEVED THAT I COULD SEE HER AGAIN.
IF I STAYED IN ITALY...

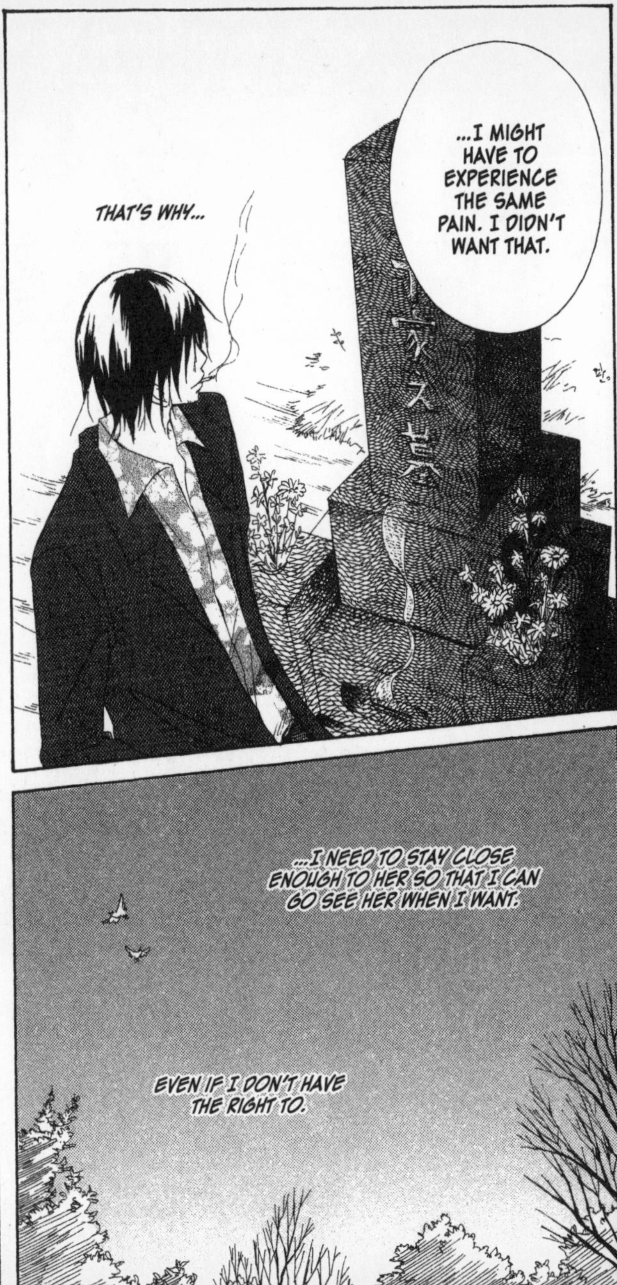
...I MIGHT HAVE TO EXPERIENCE THE SAME PAIN. I DIDN'T WANT THAT.
THAT'S WHY...
...I NEED TO STAY CLOSE ENOUGH TO HER SO THAT I CAN GO SEE HER WHEN I WANT.
EVEN IF I DON'T HAVE THE RIGHT TO.

☆ 4 ☆

I've been doing things like the soccer club and studying soccer abroad and stuff, but I'm only a pseudo soccer fan who doesn't know much about it.

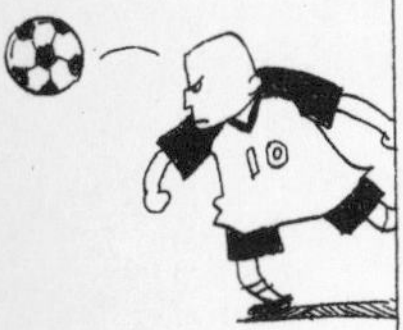
10

I love Shinji Ono. This is out of date, but I also love Miyamoto the Masked Man. (He was wearing a mask at the World Cup, wasn't he...?) I lived in Chiba for a long time, so I'm a JEF fan. I don't know what kind of team it is, but it makes me happy when they win.

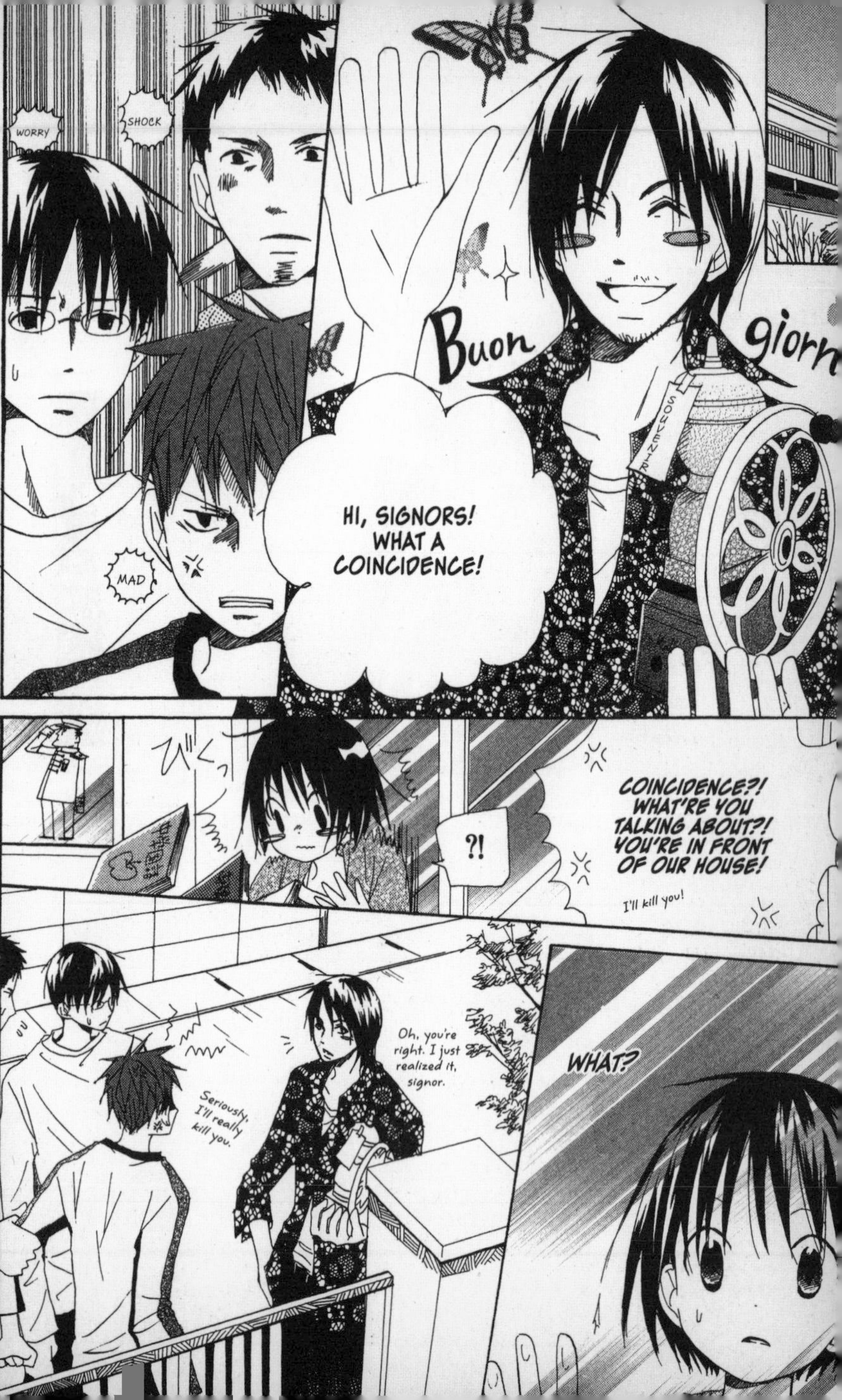

Buon
giorn
SOUVENIR
HI, SIGNORS! WHAT A COINCIDENCE!
SHOCK
WORRY
MAD
COINCIDENCE?! WHAT'RE YOU TALKING ABOUT?! YOU'RE IN FRONT OF OUR HOUSE!
I'll kill you!
?!
びくっ
WHAT?
Oh, you're right. I just realized it, signor.
Seriously, I'll really kill you.

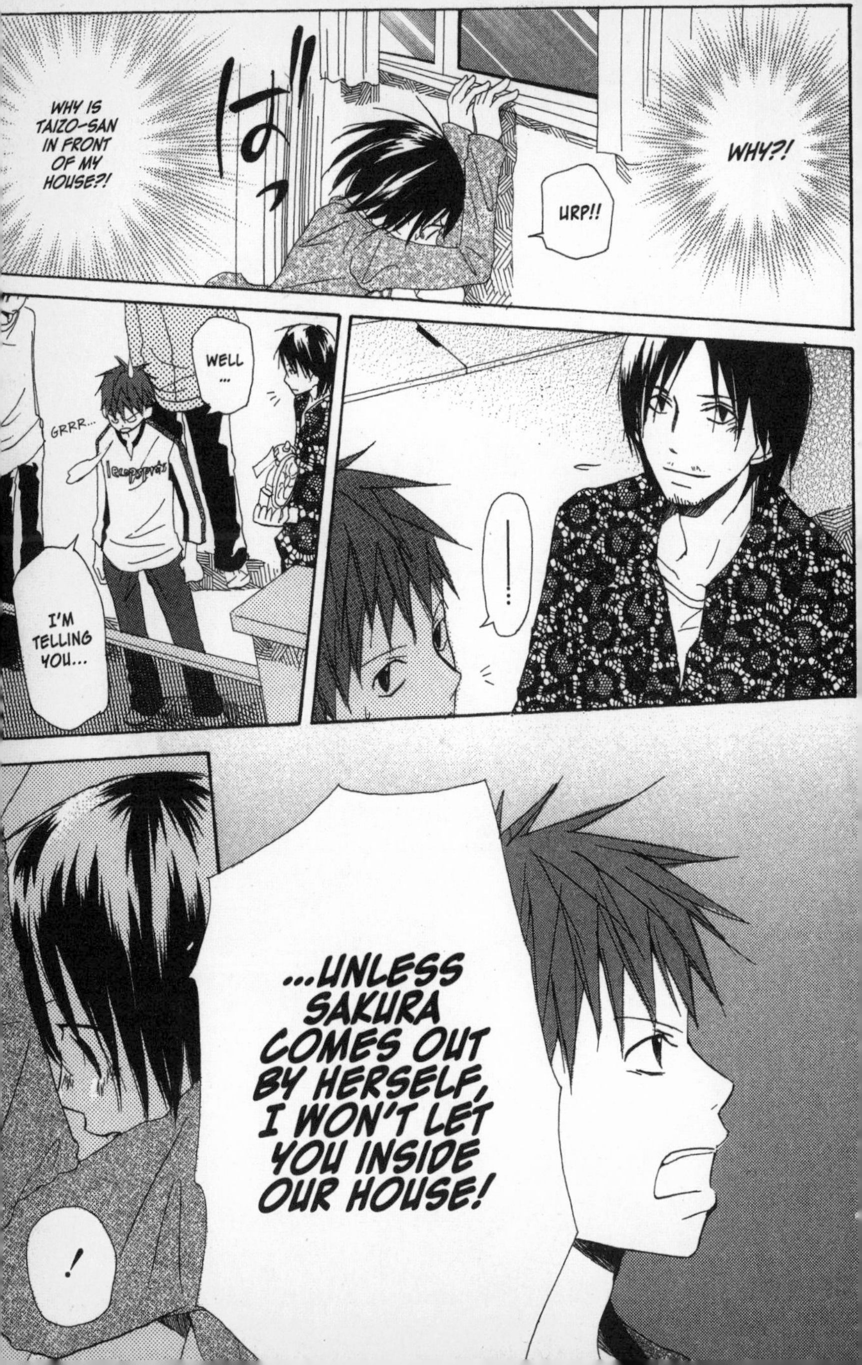
WHY?!
URP!!
はっ
WHY IS TAIZO-SAN IN FRONT OF MY HOUSE?!
!...!
WELL ...
GRRR...
I'M TELLING YOU...
...UNLESS SAKURA COMES OUT BY HERSELF, I WON'T LET YOU INSIDE OUR HOUSE!
!

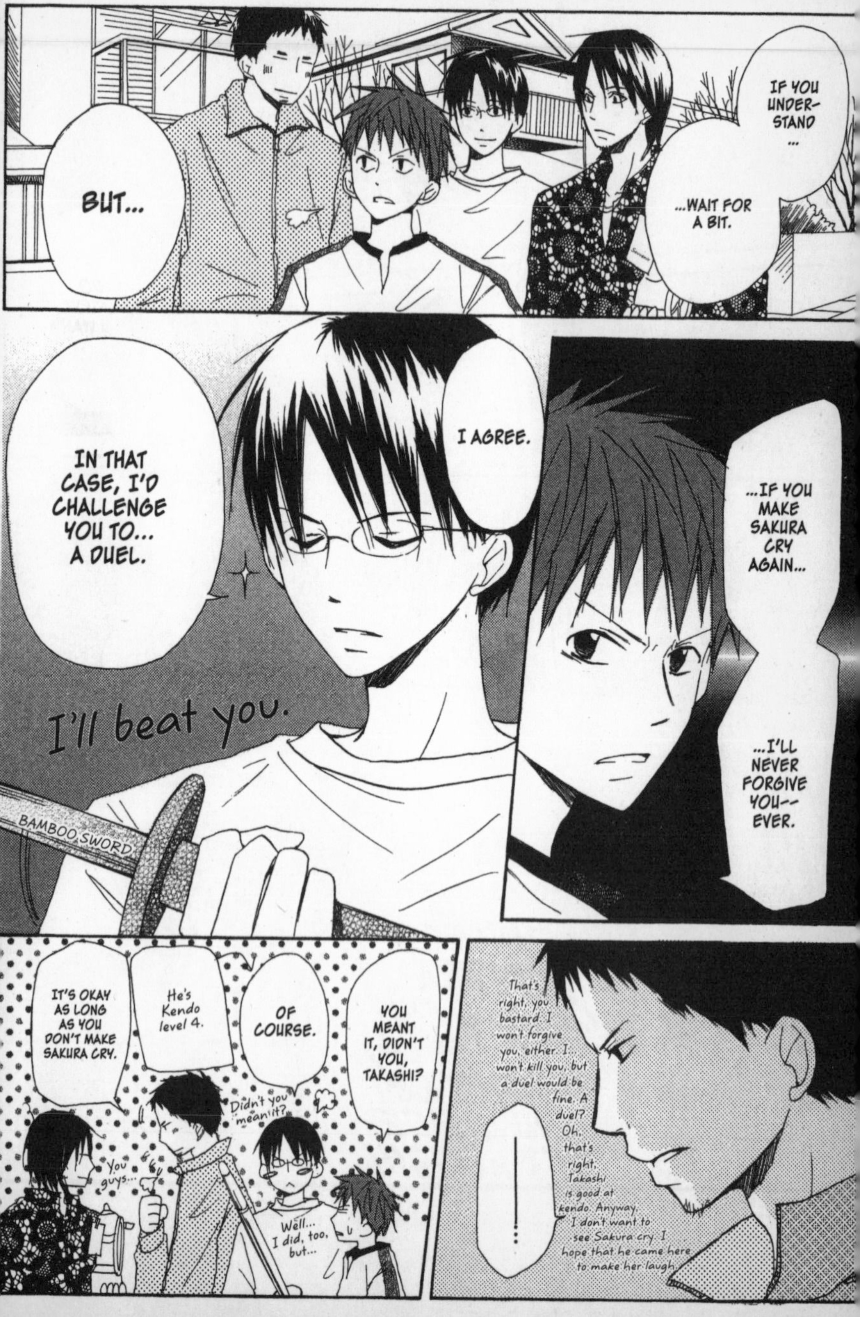
IF YOU UNDER-STAND ...
...WAIT FOR A BIT.
BUT...
...IF YOU MAKE SAKURA CRY AGAIN...
...I'LL NEVER FORGIVE YOU-- EVER.
I AGREE.
IN THAT CASE, I'D CHALLENGE YOU TO... A DUEL.
I'll beat you.
BAMBOO SWORD
That's right, you bastard. I won't forgive you, either. I... won't kill you, but a duel would be fine. A duel? Oh, that's right, Takashi is good at kendo. Anyway, I don't want to see Sakura cry. I hope that he came here to make her laugh.
!......
YOU MEANT IT, DIDN'T YOU, TAKASHI?
OF COURSE.
He's Kendo level 4.
IT'S OKAY AS LONG AS YOU DON'T MAKE SAKURA CRY.
Didn't you mean it?
Well... I did, too, but...
You guys...

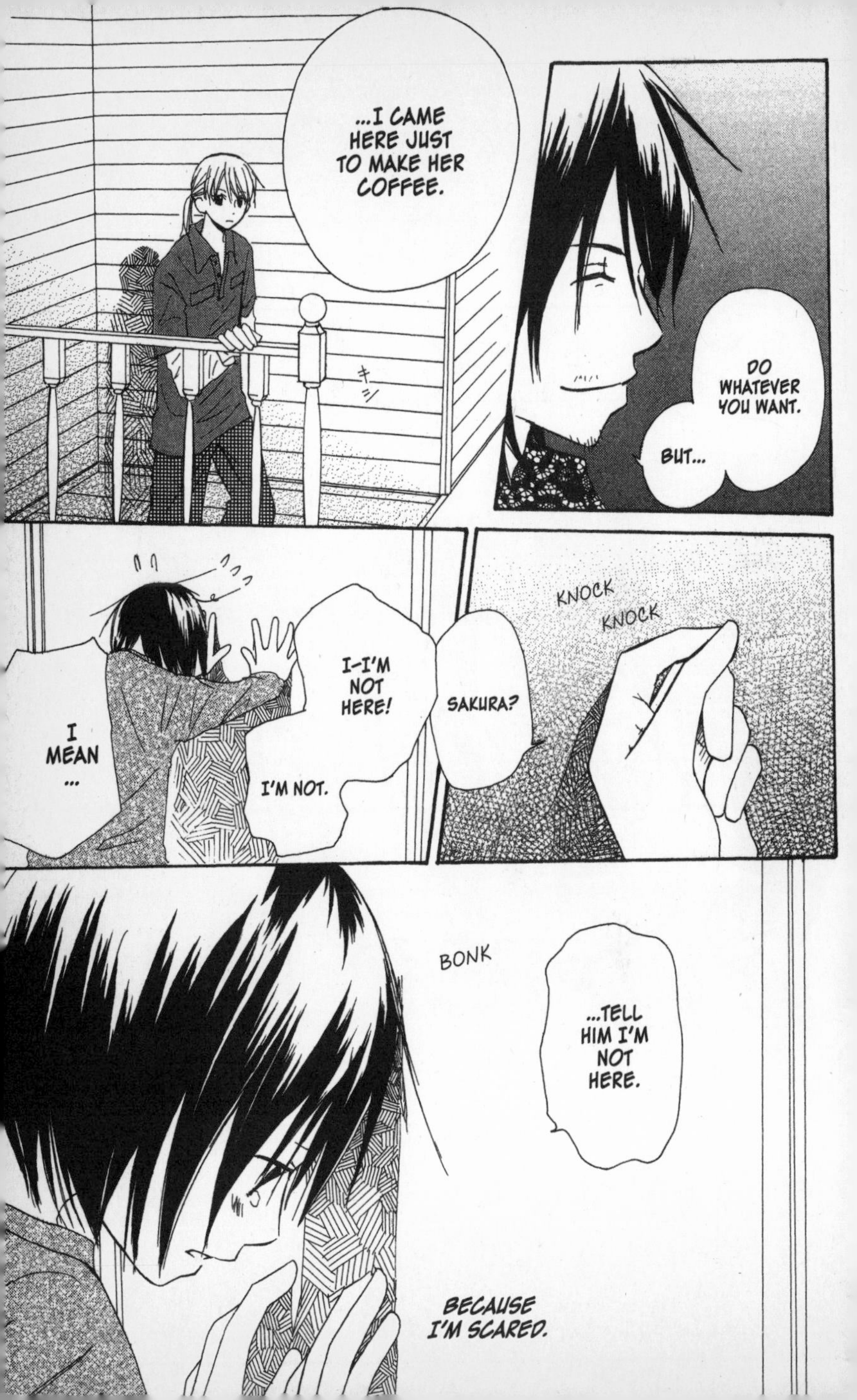
DO WHATEVER YOU WANT.
BUT...
...I CAME HERE JUST TO MAKE HER COFFEE.
キシ
KNOCK
KNOCK
SAKURA?
I-I'M NOT HERE!
I'M NOT.
I MEAN ...
BONK
...TELL HIM I'M NOT HERE.
BECAUSE I'M SCARED.

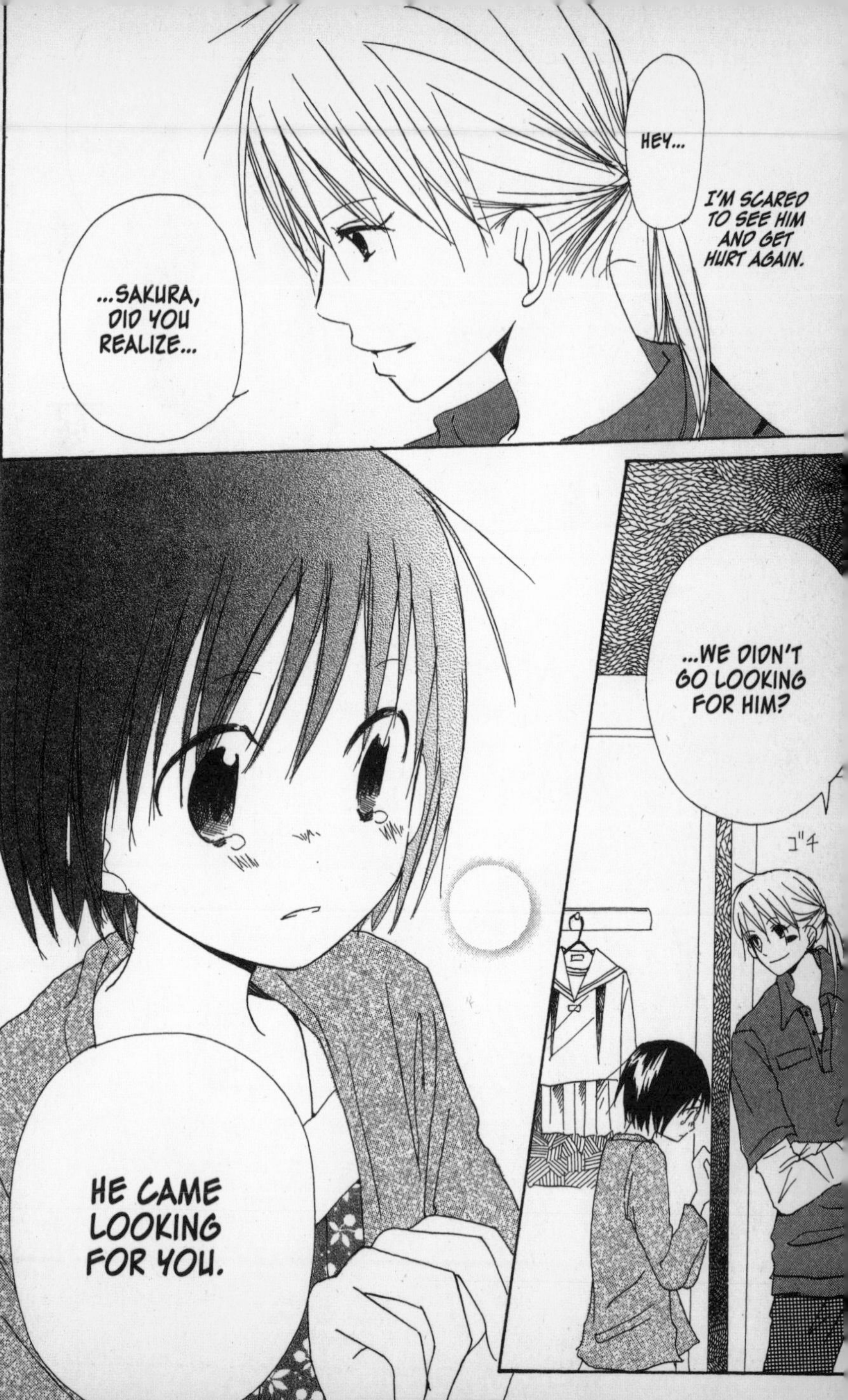
HEY...
I'M SCARED TO SEE HIM AND GET HURT AGAIN.
...SAKURA, DID YOU REALIZE...
...WE DIDN'T GO LOOKING FOR HIM?
ゴチ
HE CAME LOOKING FOR YOU.

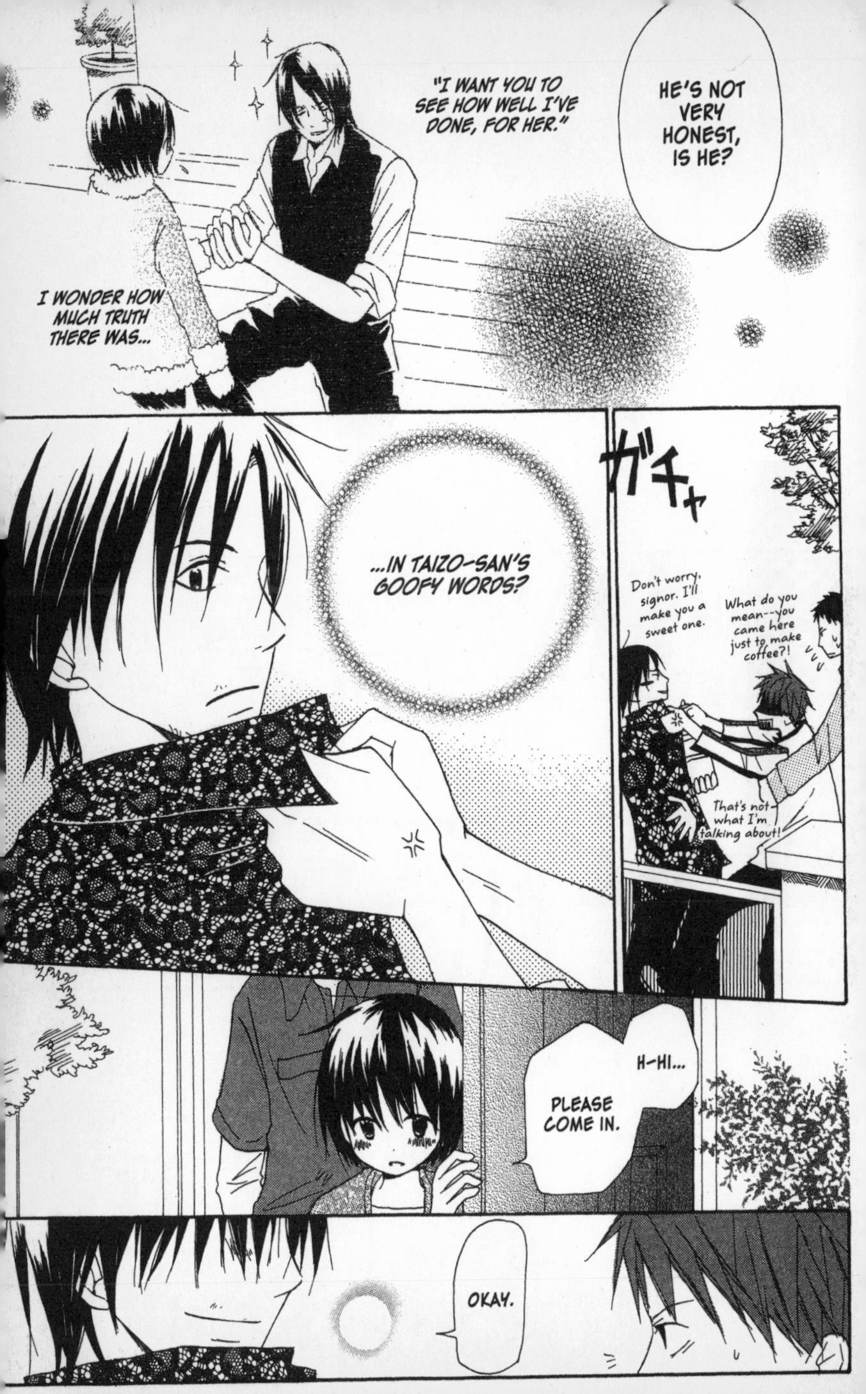
HE'S NOT VERY HONEST, IS HE?
"I WANT YOU TO SEE HOW WELL I'VE DONE, FOR HER."
I WONDER HOW MUCH TRUTH THERE WAS...
ガチャ
What do you mean--you came here just to make coffee?!
Don't worry, signor. I'll make you a sweet one.
That's not what I'm talking about!
...IN TAIZO-SAN'S GOOFY WORDS?
H-HI...
PLEASE COME IN.
OKAY.

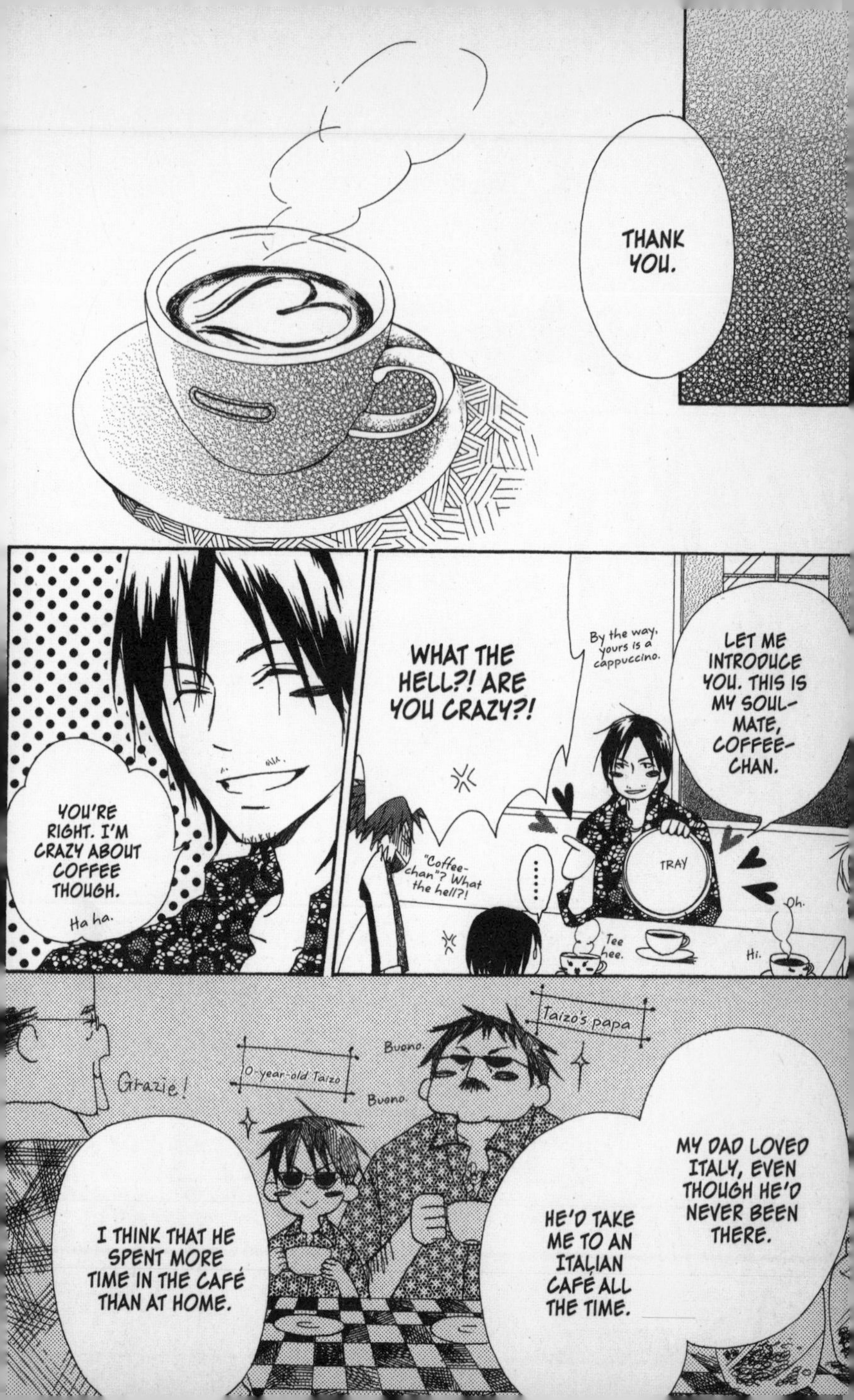
THANK YOU.
LET ME INTRODUCE YOU. THIS IS MY SOUL-MATE, COFFEE-CHAN.
By the way, yours is a cappuccino.
Oh.
Hi.
TRAY
WHAT THE HELL?! ARE YOU CRAZY?!
Tee hee.
......
"Coffee-chan"? What the hell?!
YOU'RE RIGHT. I'M CRAZY ABOUT COFFEE THOUGH.
Ha ha.
Taizo's papa
MY DAD LOVED ITALY, EVEN THOUGH HE'D NEVER BEEN THERE.
HE'D TAKE ME TO AN ITALIAN CAFÉ ALL THE TIME.
Buono.
Buono.
10-year-old Taizo
Grazie!
I THINK THAT HE SPENT MORE TIME IN THE CAFÉ THAN AT HOME.

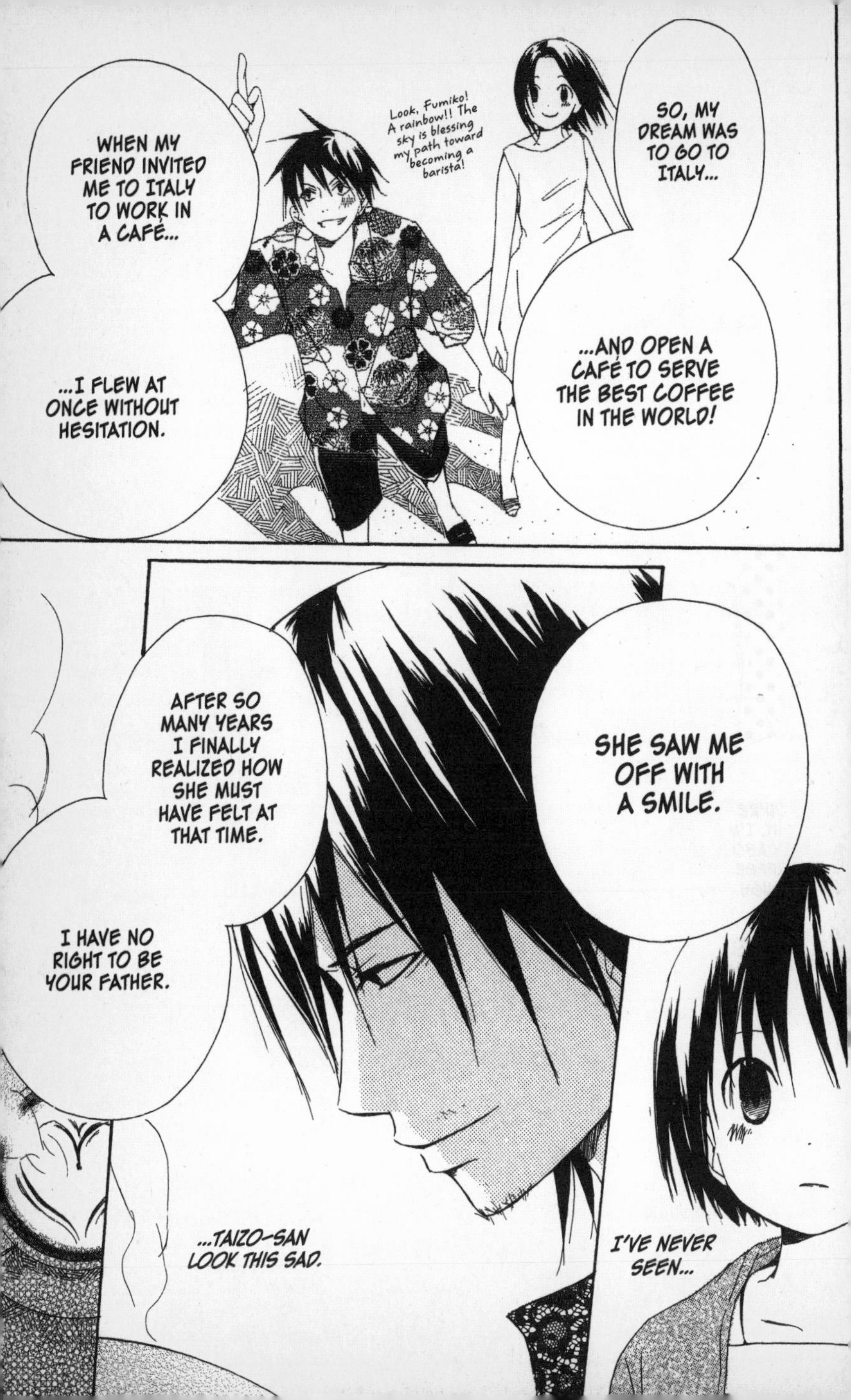
SO, MY DREAM WAS TO GO TO ITALY...
...AND OPEN A CAFÉ TO SERVE THE BEST COFFEE IN THE WORLD!
Look, Fumiko! A rainbow!! The sky is blessing my path toward becoming a barista!
WHEN MY FRIEND INVITED ME TO ITALY TO WORK IN A CAFÉ...
...I FLEW AT ONCE WITHOUT HESITATION.
SHE SAW ME OFF WITH A SMILE.
AFTER SO MANY YEARS I FINALLY REALIZED HOW SHE MUST HAVE FELT AT THAT TIME.
I HAVE NO RIGHT TO BE YOUR FATHER.
I'VE NEVER SEEN...
...TAIZO-SAN LOOK THIS SAD.

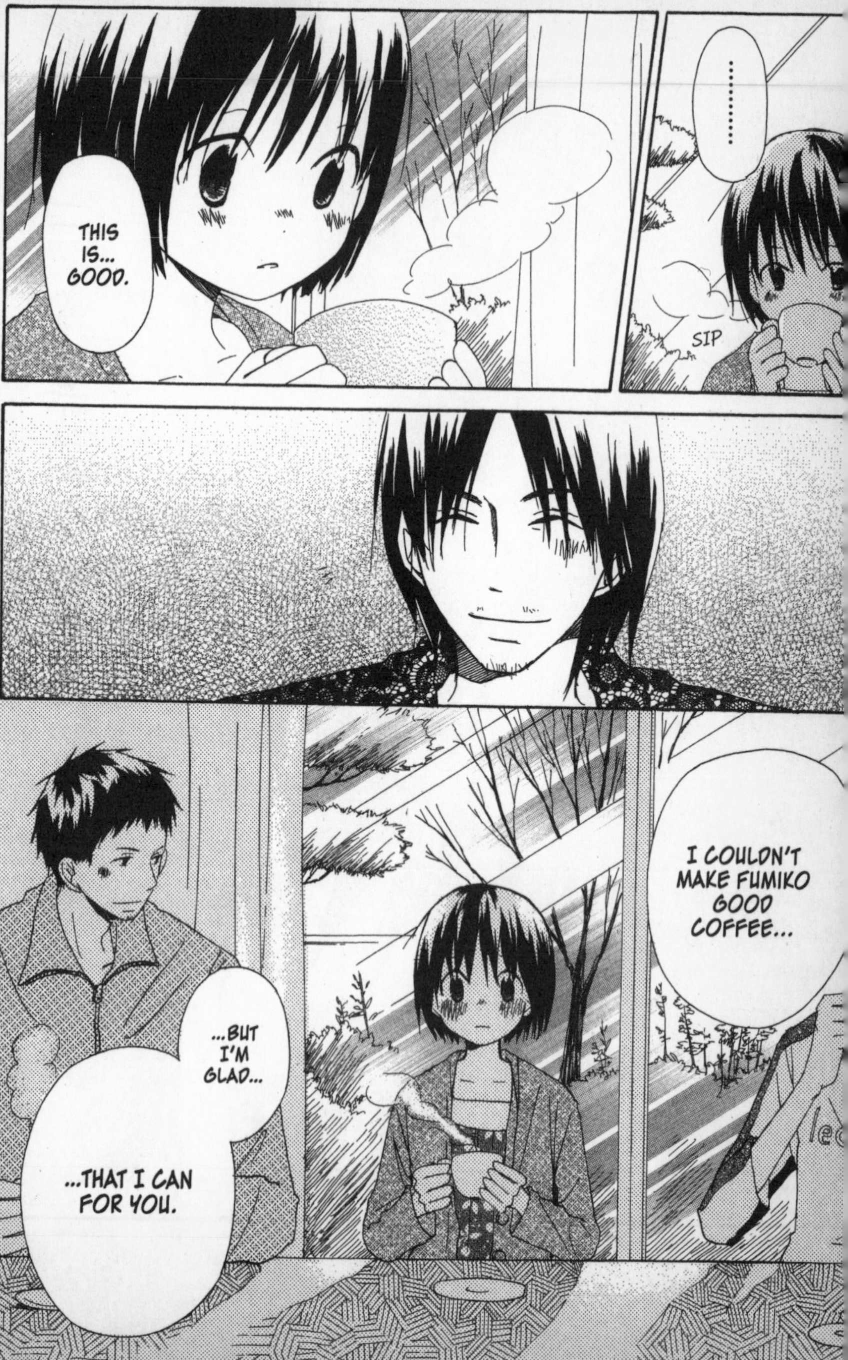

......
SIP
THIS IS... GOOD.
I COULDN'T MAKE FUMIKO GOOD COFFEE...
...BUT I'M GLAD...
...THAT I CAN FOR YOU.

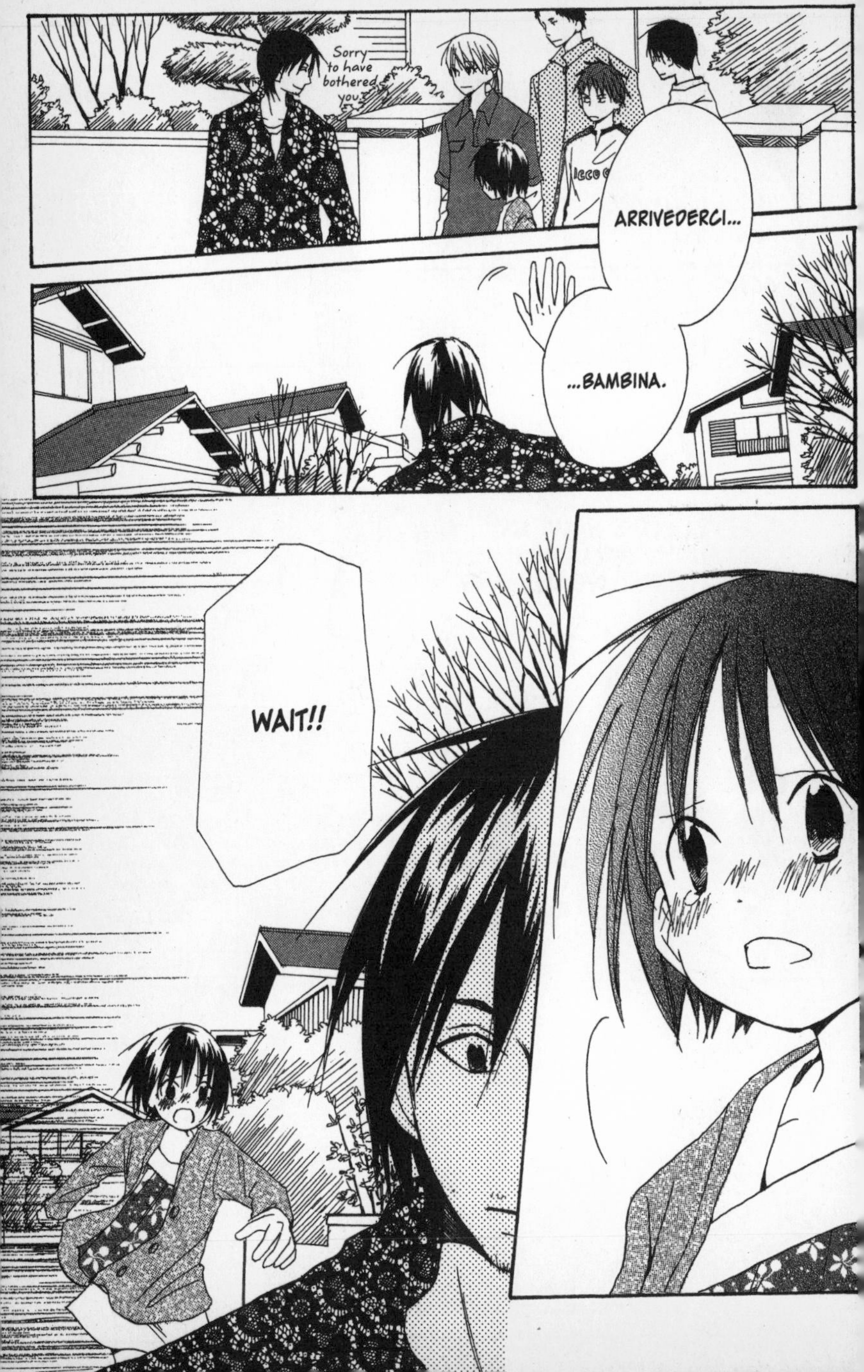
Sorry to have bothered you.
ARRIVEDERCI...
...BAMBINA.
WAIT!!

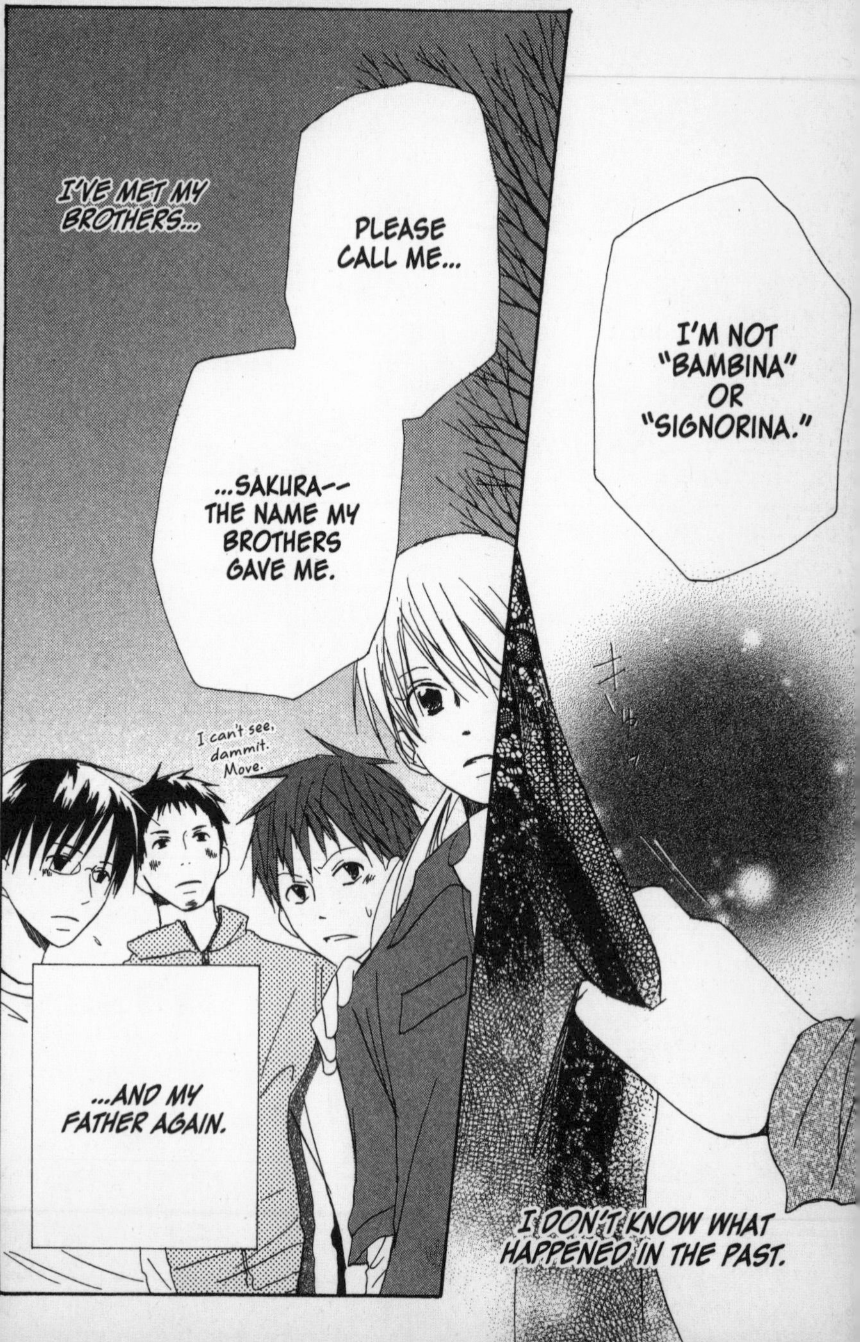
I'M NOT "BAMBINA" OR "SIGNORINA."
I DON'T KNOW WHAT HAPPENED IN THE PAST.
I'VE MET MY BROTHERS...
PLEASE CALL ME...
...SAKURA-- THE NAME MY BROTHERS GAVE ME.
I can't see, dammit. Move.
...AND MY FATHER AGAIN.

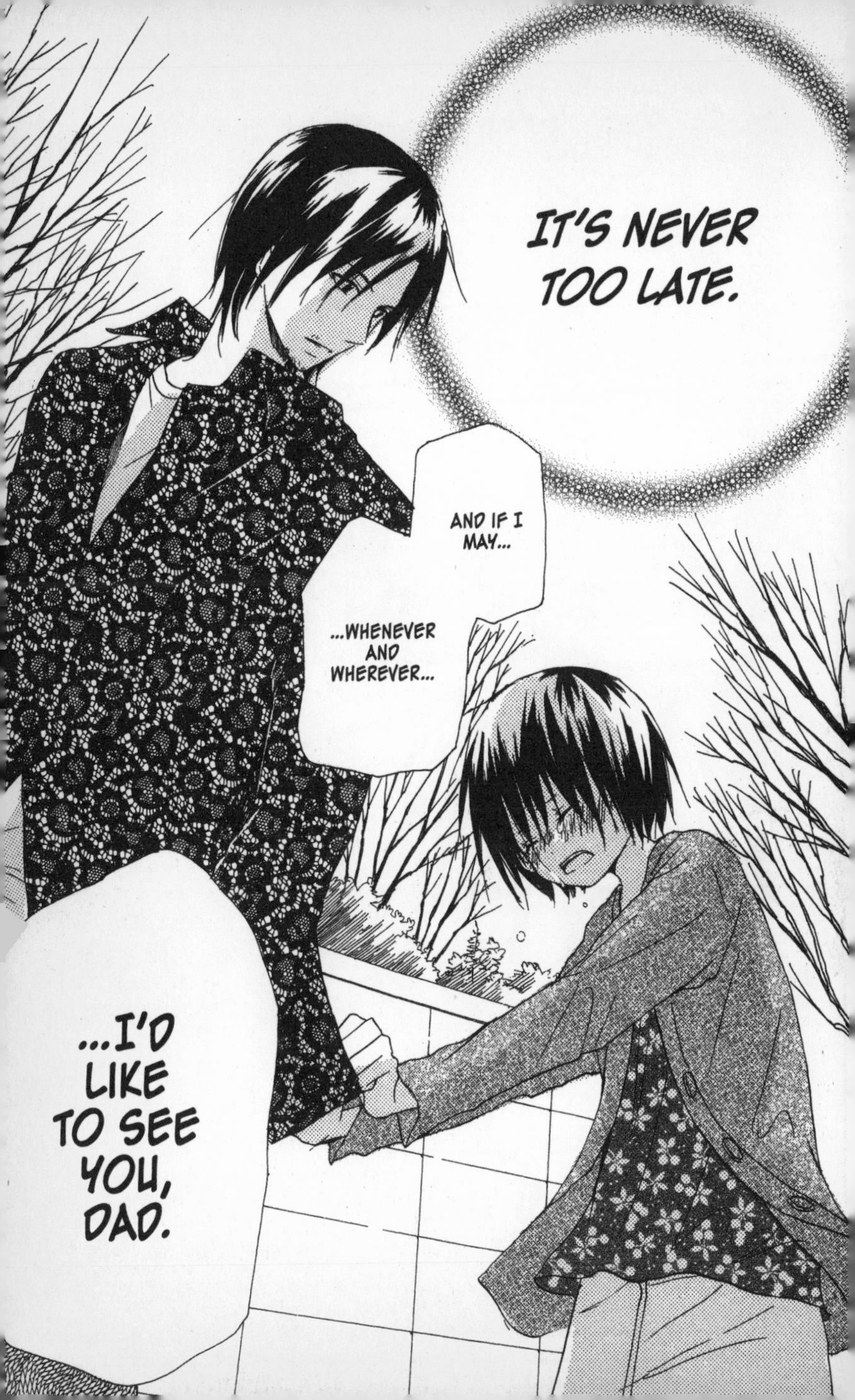
IT'S NEVER TOO LATE.
AND IF I MAY...
...WHENEVER AND WHEREVER...
...I'D LIKE TO SEE YOU, DAD.

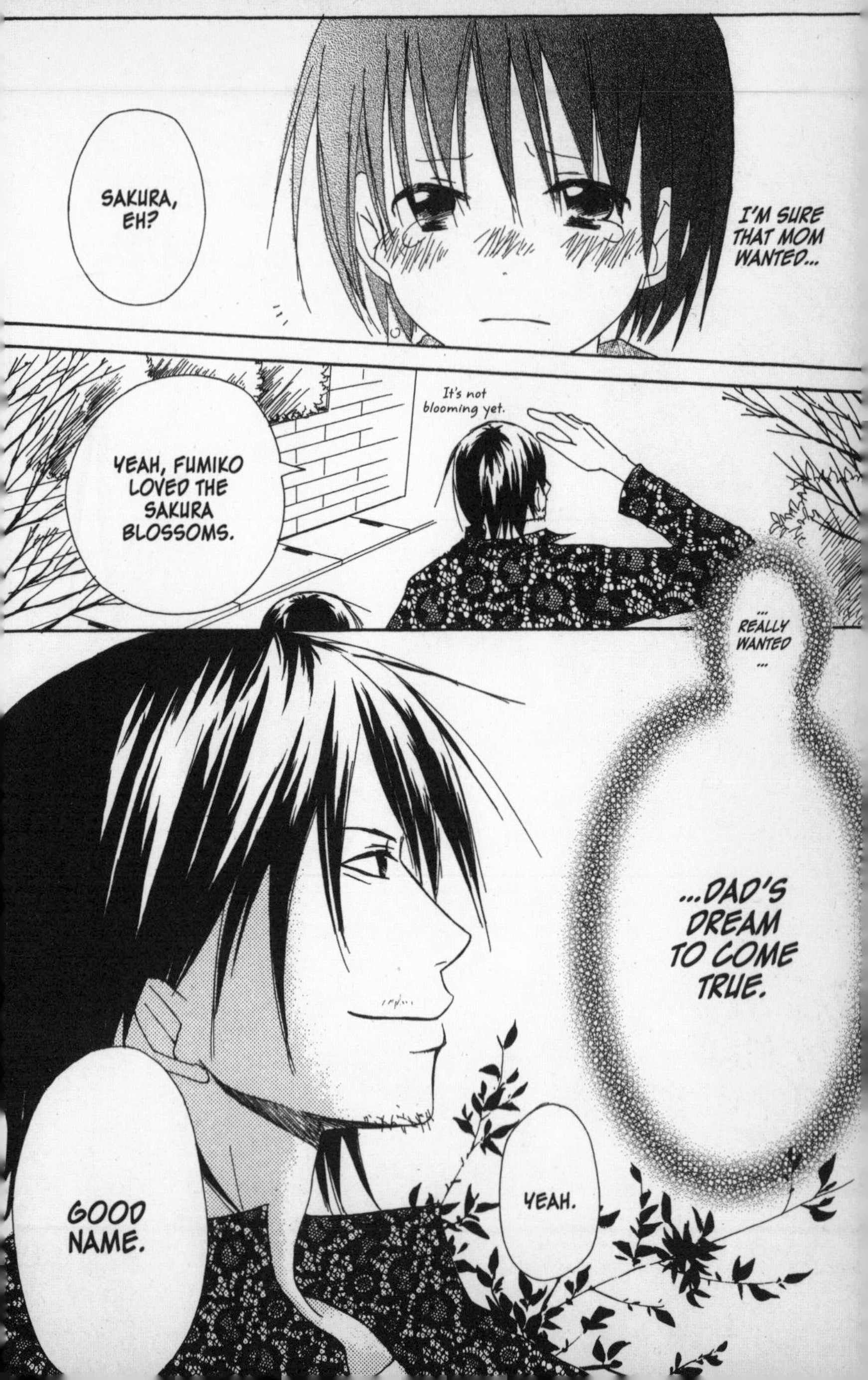
I'M SURE THAT MOM WANTED...
SAKURA, EH?
It's not blooming yet.
YEAH, FUMIKO LOVED THE SAKURA BLOSSOMS.
...REALLY WANTED...
...DAD'S DREAM TO COME TRUE.
YEAH.
GOOD NAME.

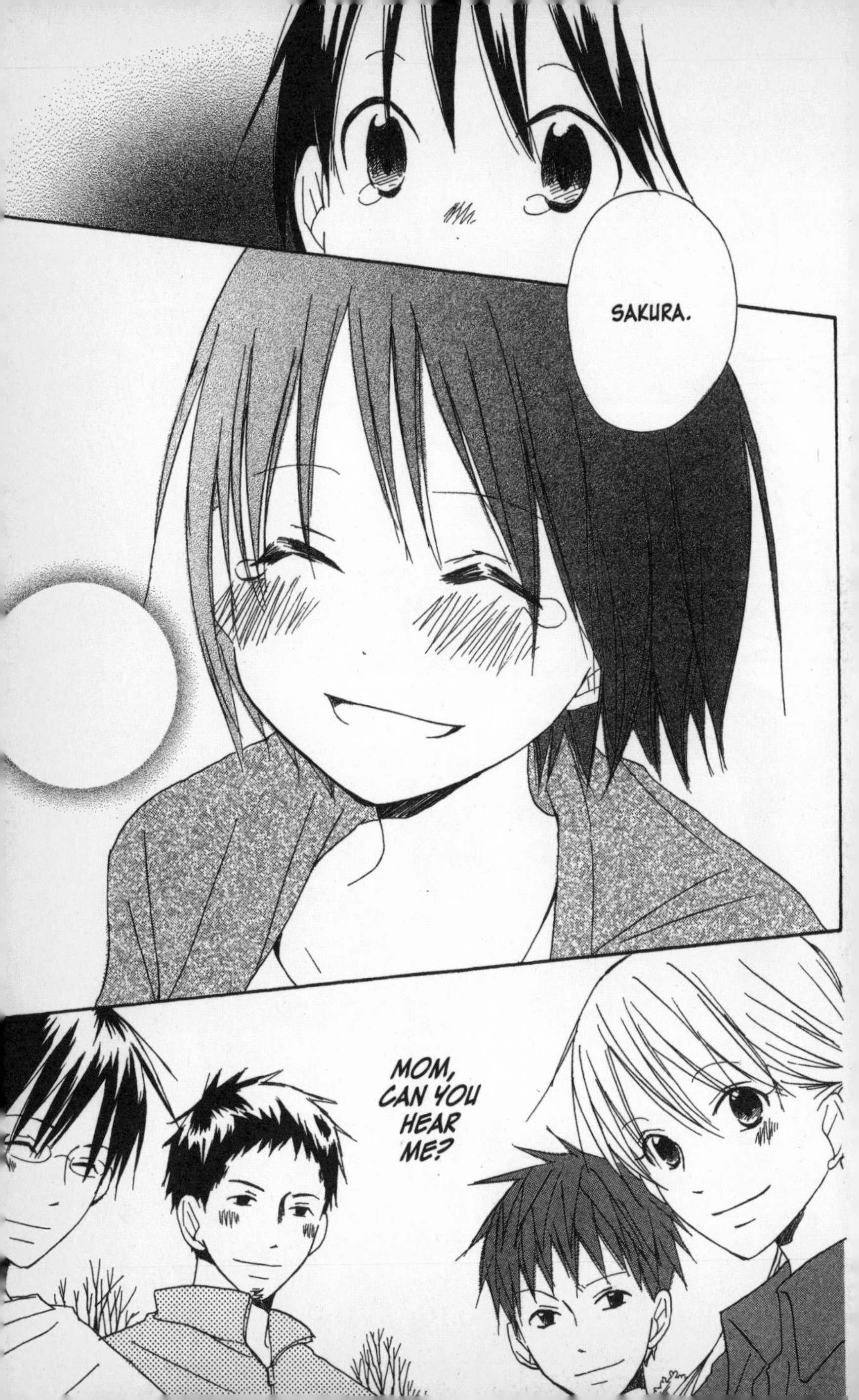
SAKURA.
MOM, CAN YOU HEAR ME?

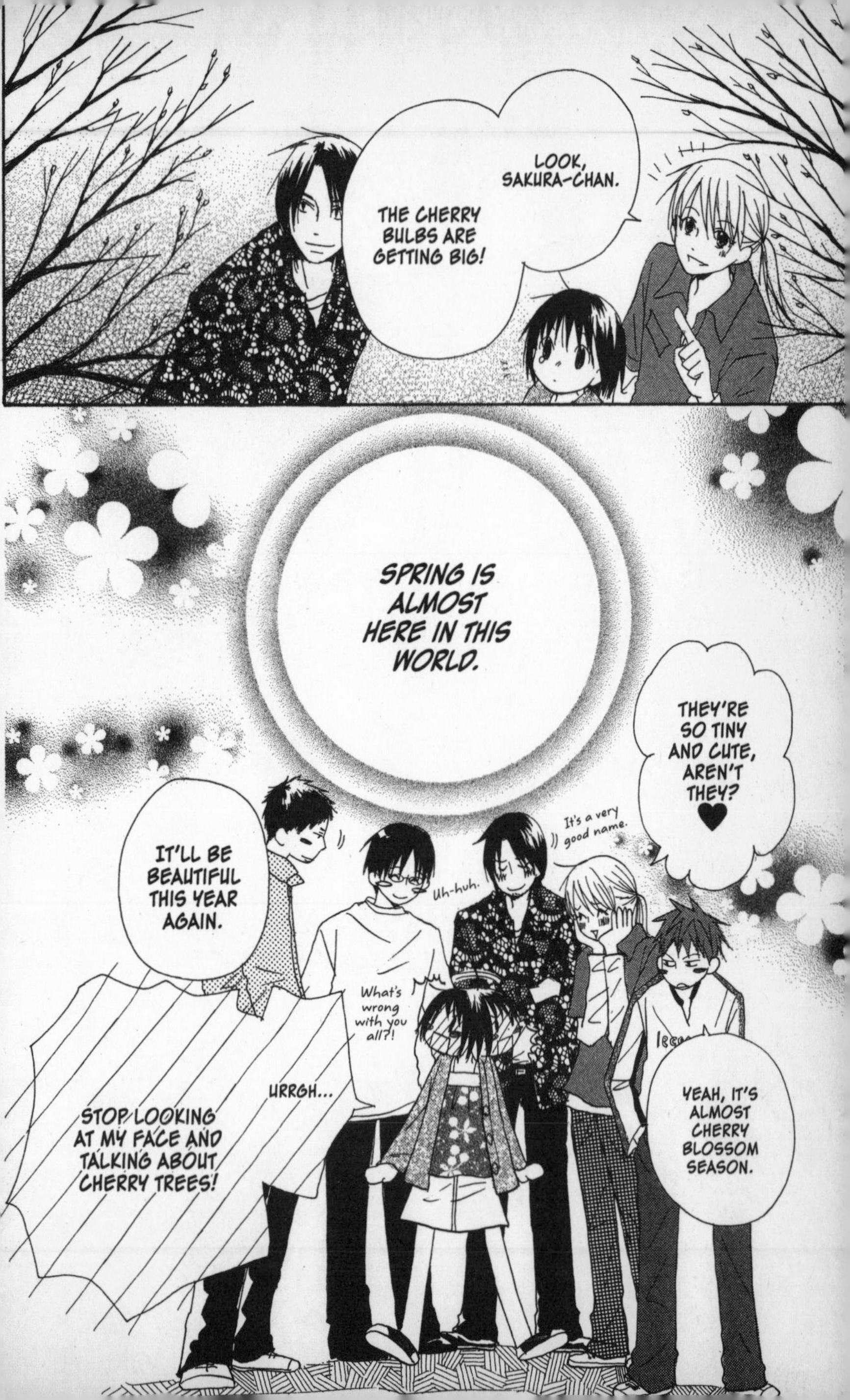
LOOK, SAKURA-CHAN.
THE CHERRY BULBS ARE GETTING BIG!
SPRING IS ALMOST HERE IN THIS WORLD.
THEY'RE SO TINY AND CUTE, AREN'T THEY? ♥
It's a very good name.
IT'LL BE BEAUTIFUL THIS YEAR AGAIN.
Uh-huh.
YEAH, IT'S ALMOST CHERRY BLOSSOM SEASON.
What's wrong with you all?!
URRGH...
STOP LOOKING AT MY FACE AND TALKING ABOUT CHERRY TREES!

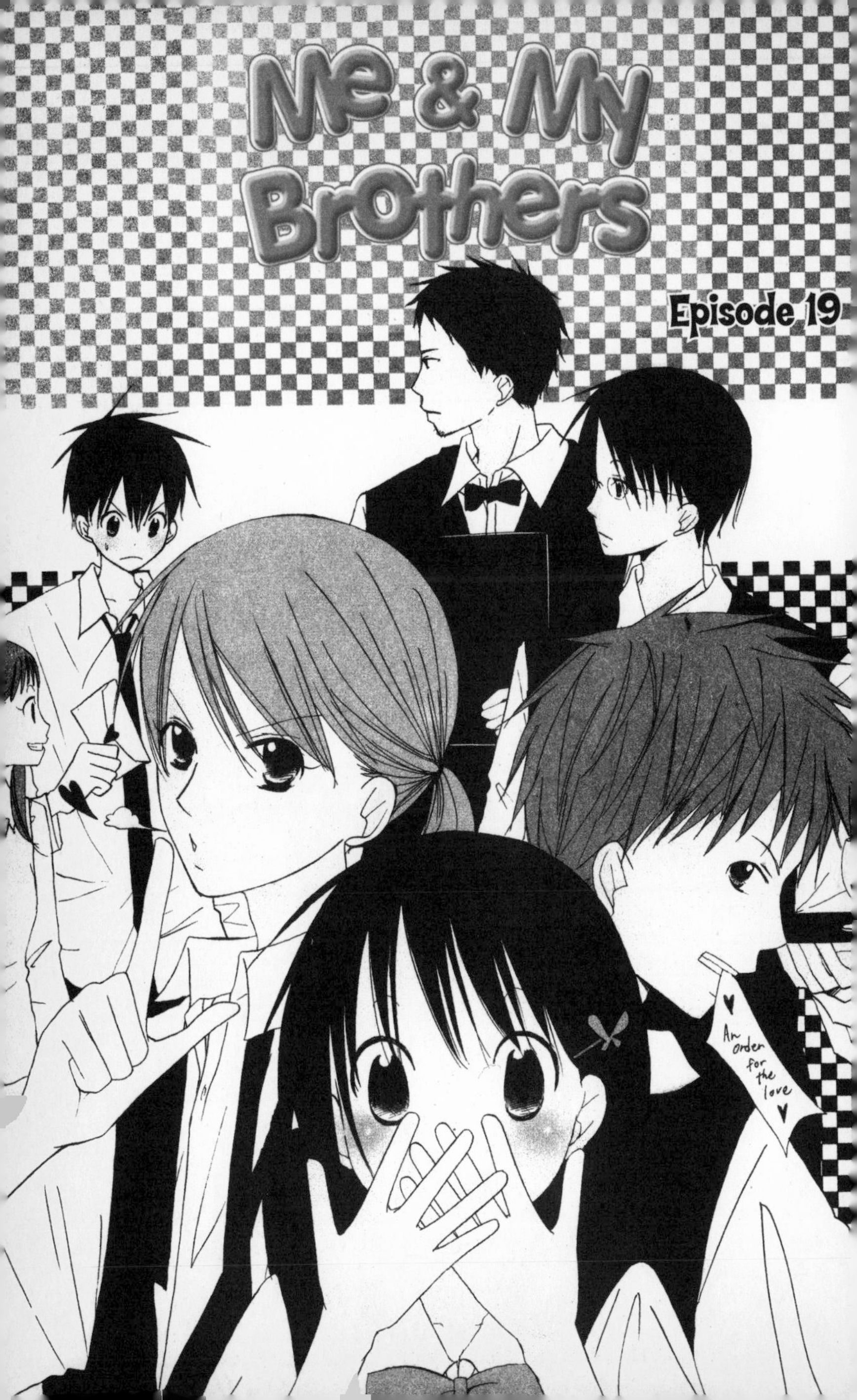
Me & My Brothers
Episode 19
An order for the love

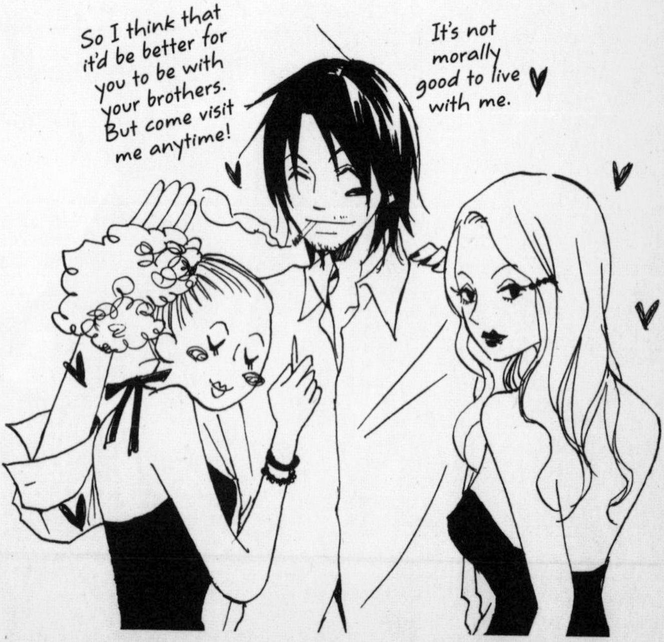
It's not morally good to live with me.
So I think that it'd be better for you to be with your brothers. But come visit me anytime!

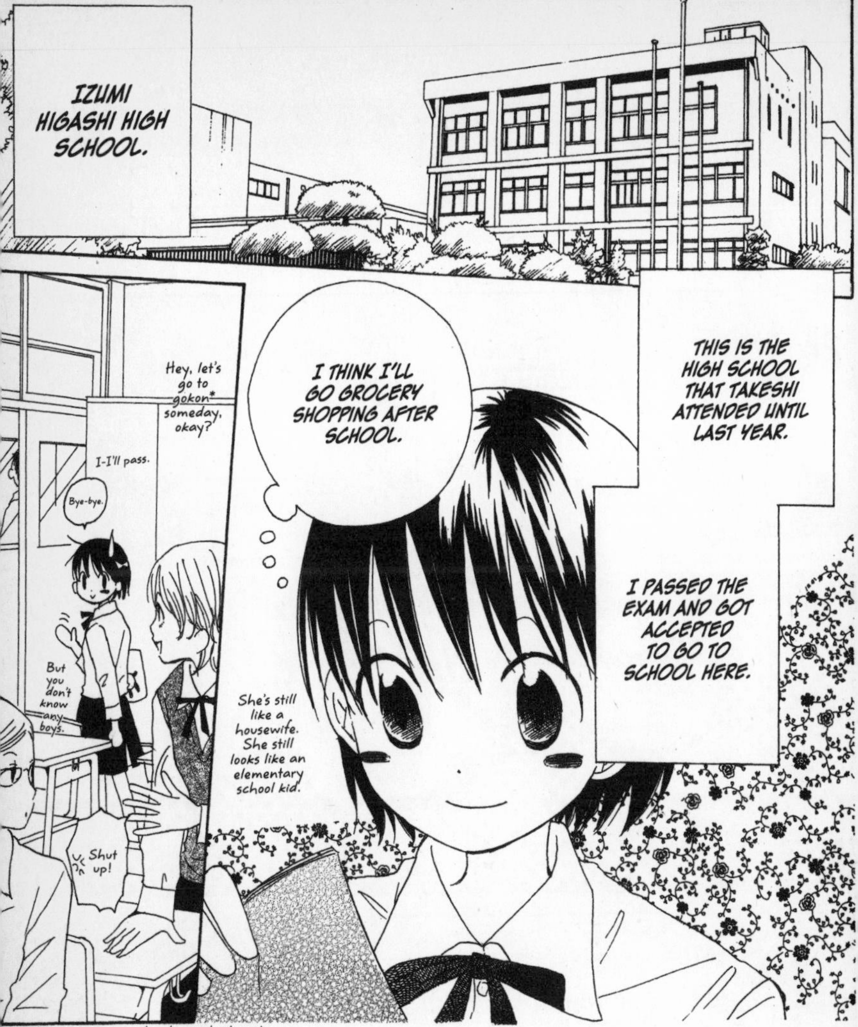
IZUMI HIGASHI HIGH SCHOOL.
THIS IS THE HIGH SCHOOL THAT TAKESHI ATTENDED UNTIL LAST YEAR.
I PASSED THE EXAM AND GOT ACCEPTED TO GO TO SCHOOL HERE.
I THINK I'LL GO GROCERY SHOPPING AFTER SCHOOL.
Hey, let's go to gokon* someday, okay?
I-I'll pass.
Bye-bye.
But you don't know any boys.
She's still like a housewife. She still looks like an elementary school kid.
Shut up!

* A gokon is a party where boys and girls meet.

If you'd like to send me comments about my book, here's the address:

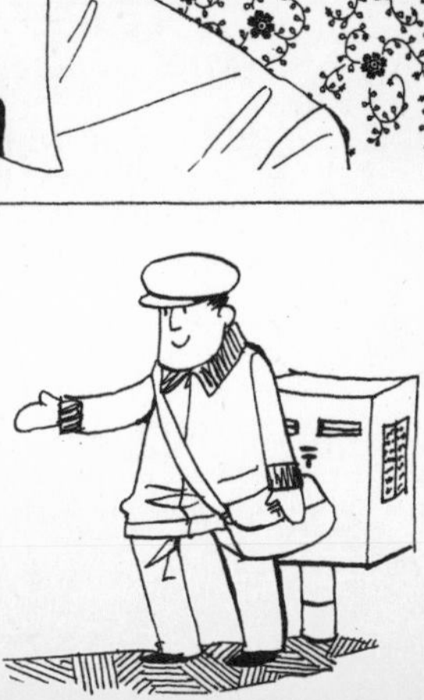

TOKYOPOP
c/o Hyun Joo Kim
5900 Wilshire Blvd. Ste 2000
Los Angeles, CA 90036

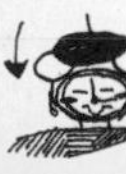

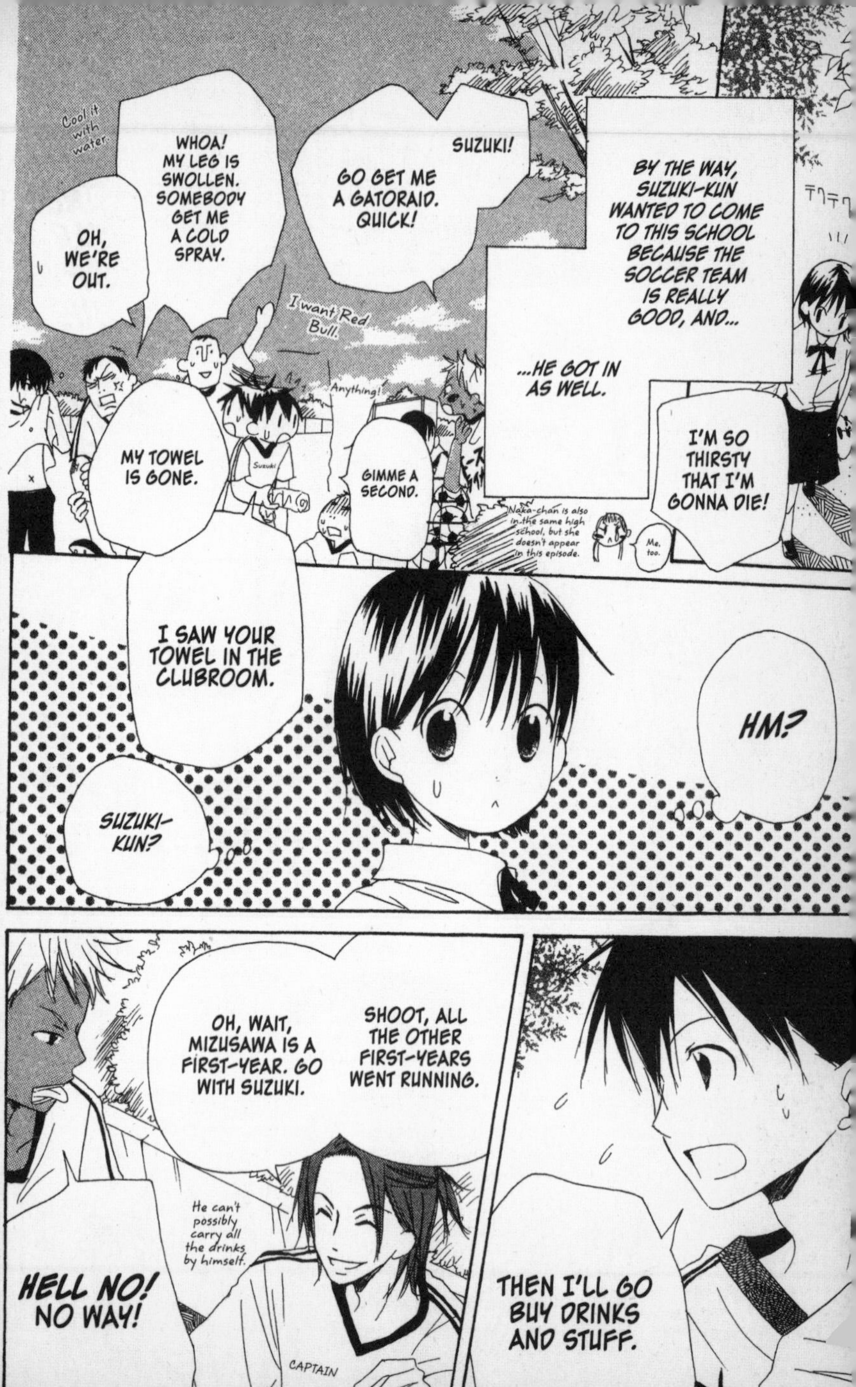
BY THE WAY, SUZUKI-KUN WANTED TO COME TO THIS SCHOOL BECAUSE THE SOCCER TEAM IS REALLY GOOD, AND...
...HE GOT IN AS WELL.
I'M SO THIRSTY THAT I'M GONNA DIE!
Me, too.
Naka-chan is also in the same high school, but she doesn't appear in this episode.
SUZUKI!
GO GET ME A GATORAID. QUICK!
I want Red Bull.
Anything!
GIMME A SECOND.
WHOA! MY LEG IS SWOLLEN. SOMEBODY GET ME A COLD SPRAY.
OH, WE'RE OUT.
Cool it with water.
MY TOWEL IS GONE.
HM?
SUZUKI-KUN?
I SAW YOUR TOWEL IN THE CLUBROOM.
THEN I'LL GO BUY DRINKS AND STUFF.
SHOOT, ALL THE OTHER FIRST-YEARS WENT RUNNING.
OH, WAIT, MIZUSAWA IS A FIRST-YEAR. GO WITH SUZUKI.
He can't possibly carry all the drinks by himself.
CAPTAIN
HELL NO! NO WAY!

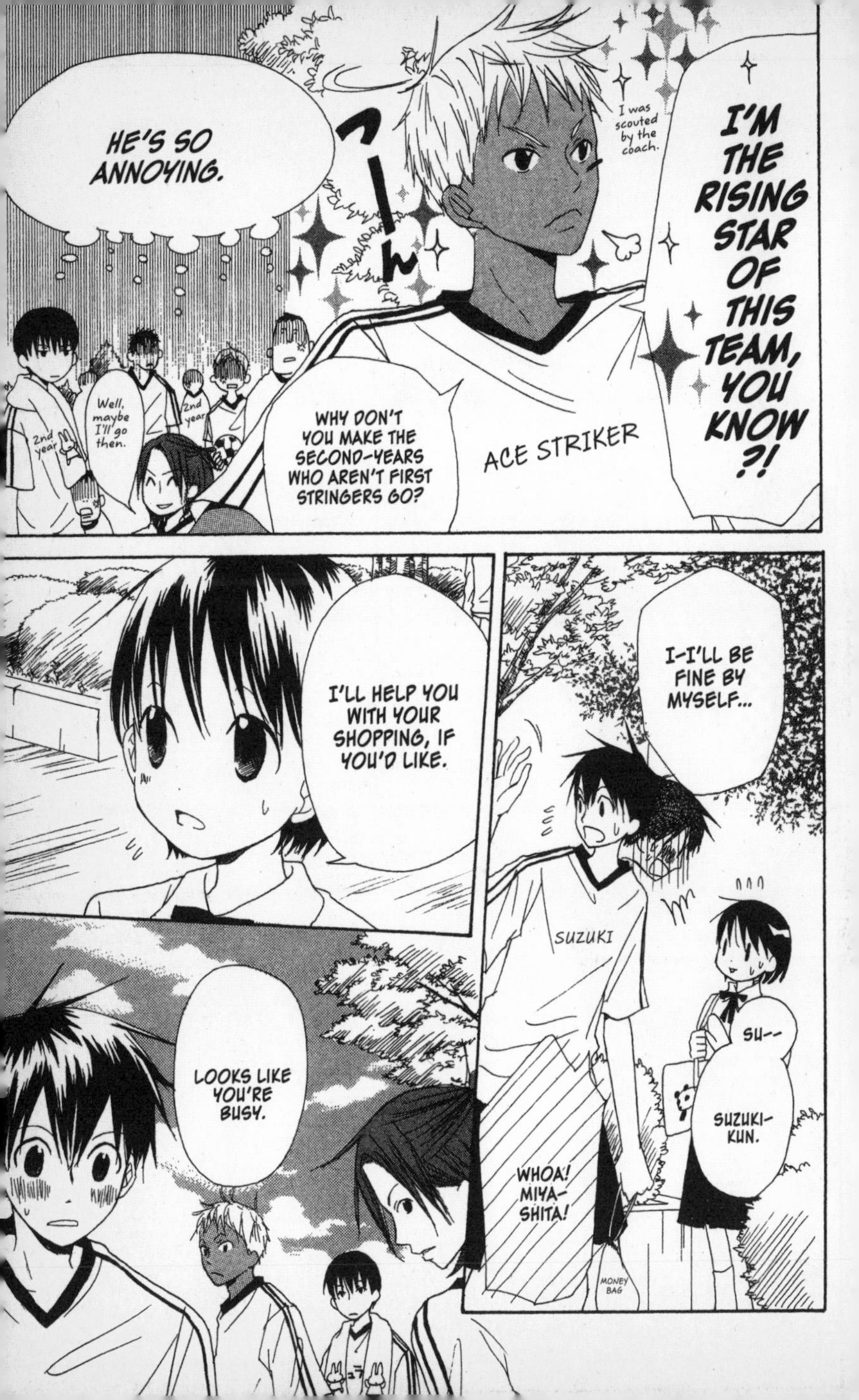
I'M THE RISING STAR OF THIS TEAM, YOU KNOW?!
I was scouted by the coach.
ACE STRIKER
WHY DON'T YOU MAKE THE SECOND-YEARS WHO AREN'T FIRST STRINGERS GO?
HE'S SO ANNOYING.
2nd year
Well, maybe I'll go then.
2nd year
I-I'LL BE FINE BY MYSELF...
SU--
SUZUKI-KUN.
SUZUKI
WHOA! MIYA-SHITA!
MONEY BAG
I'LL HELP YOU WITH YOUR SHOPPING, IF YOU'D LIKE.
LOOKS LIKE YOU'RE BUSY.

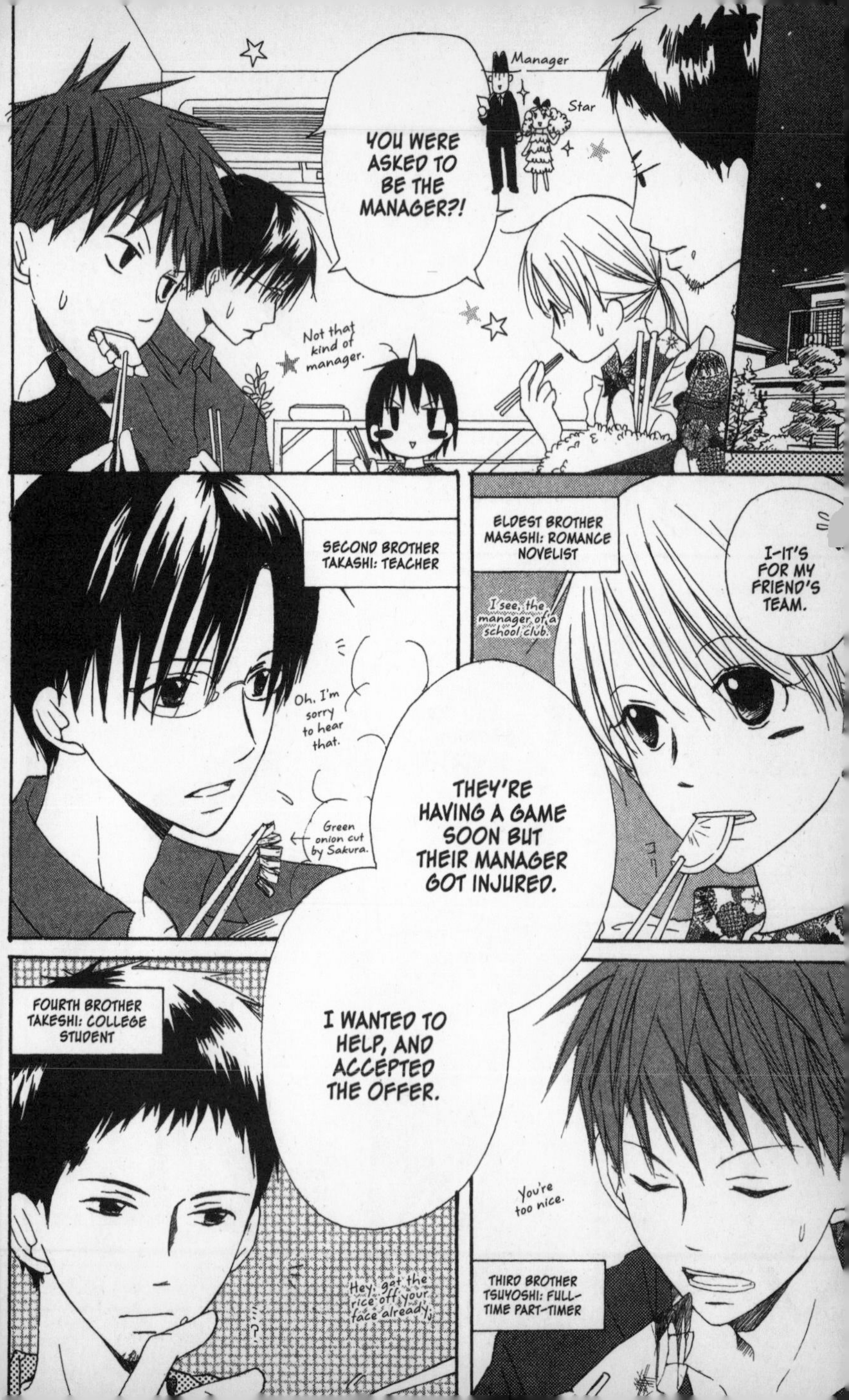
YOU WERE ASKED TO BE THE MANAGER?!
Manager
Star
Not that kind of manager.
ELDEST BROTHER MASASHI: ROMANCE NOVELIST
I-IT'S FOR MY FRIEND'S TEAM.
I see, the manager of a school club.
THEY'RE HAVING A GAME SOON BUT THEIR MANAGER GOT INJURED.
SECOND BROTHER TAKASHI: TEACHER
Oh, I'm sorry to hear that.
Green onion cut by Sakura.
I WANTED TO HELP, AND ACCEPTED THE OFFER.
You're too nice.
THIRD BROTHER TSUYOSHI: FULL-TIME PART-TIMER
FOURTH BROTHER TAKESHI: COLLEGE STUDENT
Hey, get the rice off your face already.
?

☆5☆

Two more of these 1/4 columns. Oh well, I've run out of things to write again. Then let's talk about my family. My parents are leading a country life. They even built their own house.

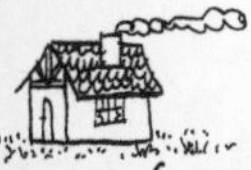

They raise fancy chickens and their eggs are delicious. Thank you for sending them to me! If you buy this type of chicken's eggs at the store, they cost...

...500 yen each! !!

← Each! Not per carton!

Even though I'm not a gourmet, I think these eggs are delicious.

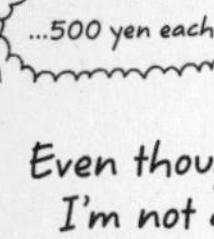

Does this column sound gossipy?

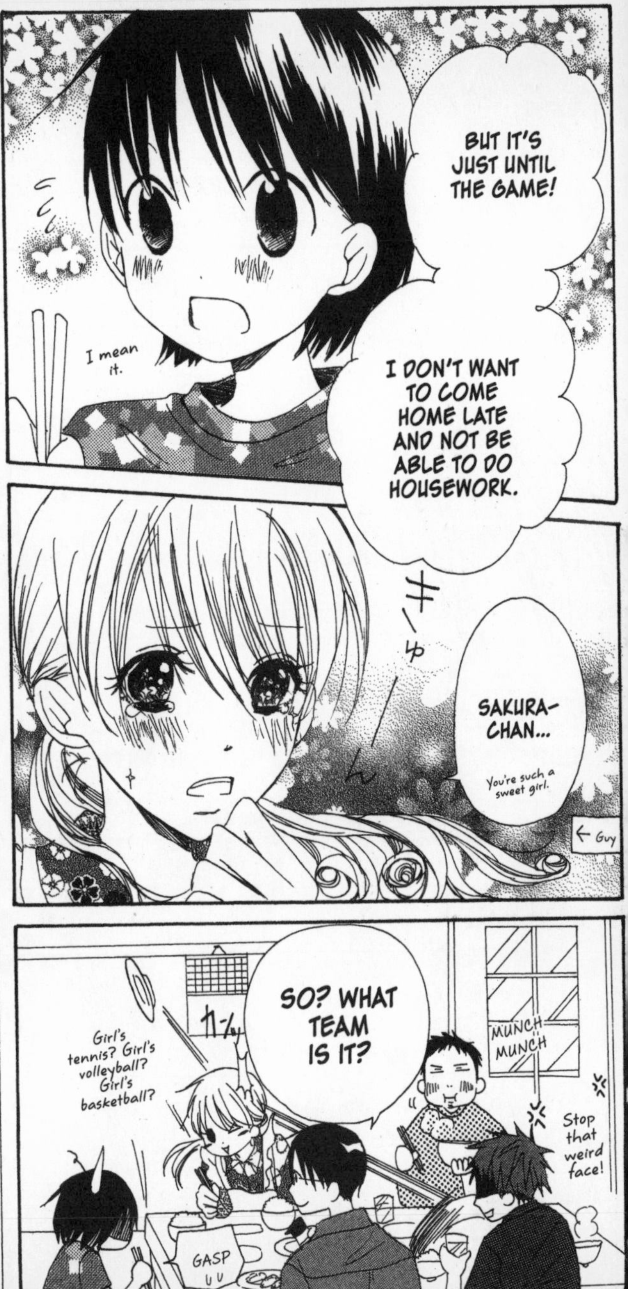

BUT IT'S JUST UNTIL THE GAME!
I DON'T WANT TO COME HOME LATE AND NOT BE ABLE TO DO HOUSEWORK.
I mean it.
キゅん
SAKURA-CHAN...
You're such a sweet girl.
← Guy
SO? WHAT TEAM IS IT?
MUNCH MUNCH
Stop that weird face!
Girl's tennis? Girl's volleyball? Girl's basketball?
GASP

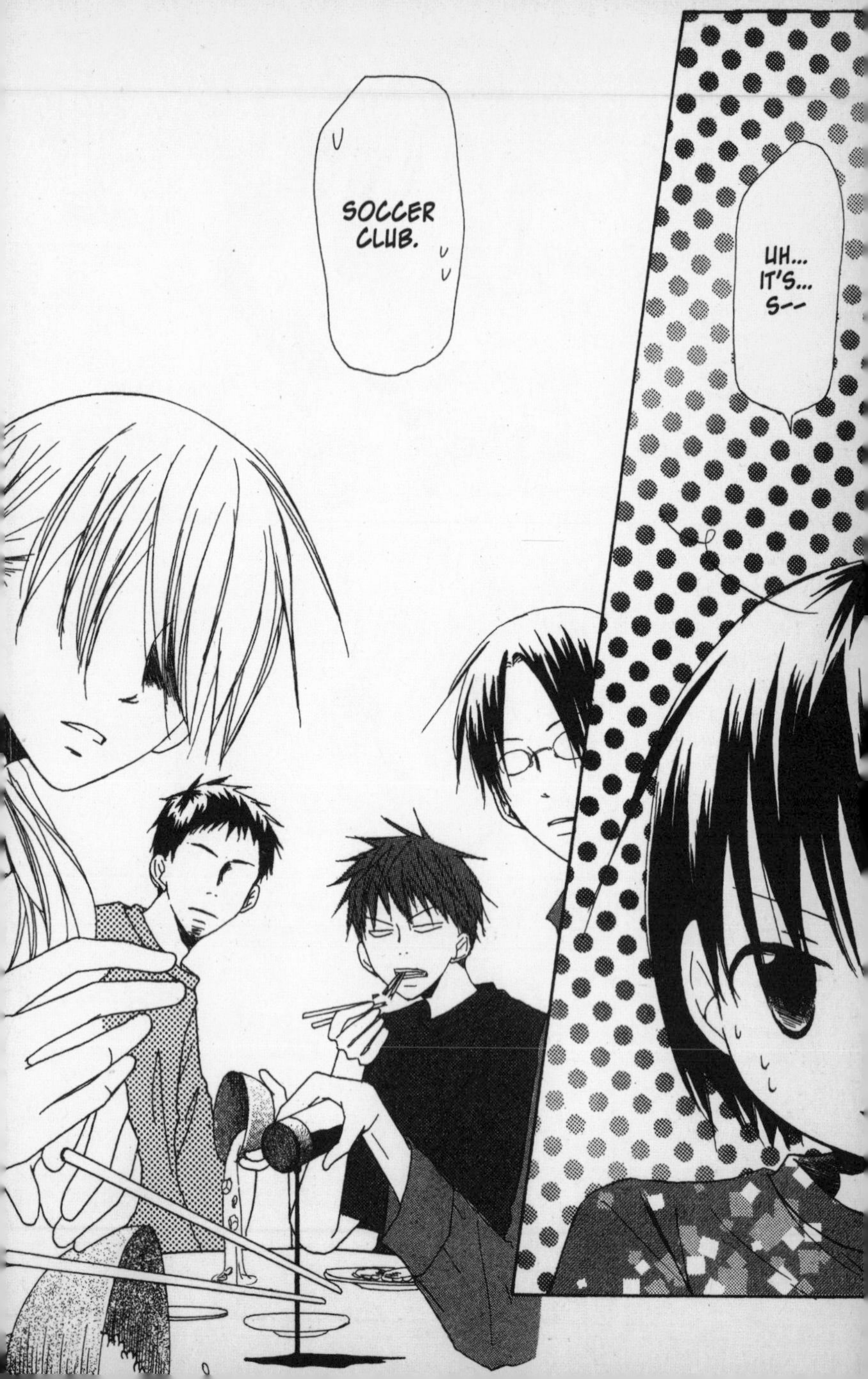
UH... IT'S... S--
SOCCER CLUB.

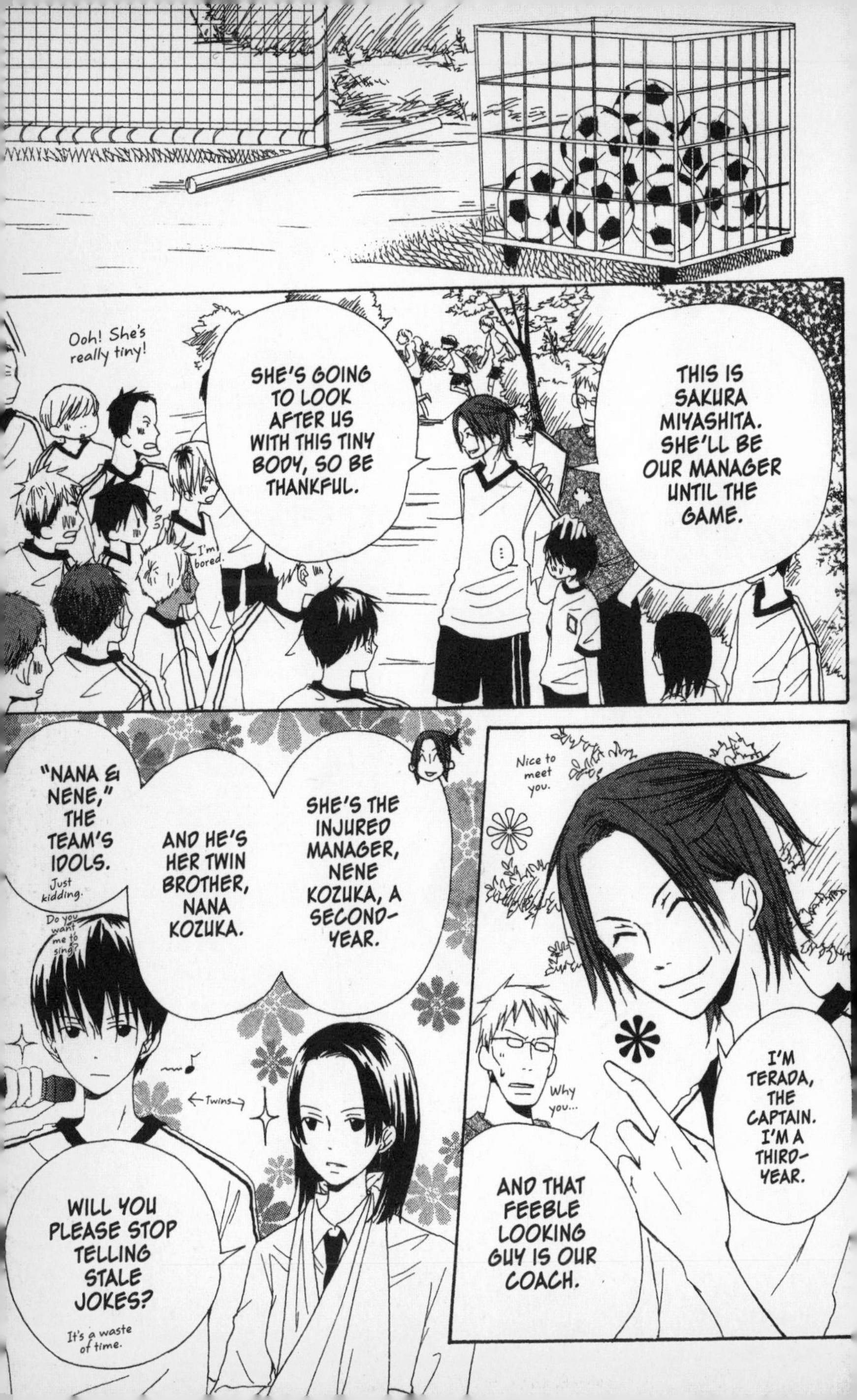
THIS IS SAKURA MIYASHITA. SHE'LL BE OUR MANAGER UNTIL THE GAME.
SHE'S GOING TO LOOK AFTER US WITH THIS TINY BODY, SO BE THANKFUL.
...
Ooh! She's really tiny!
I'm bored.
Nice to meet you.
I'M TERADA, THE CAPTAIN. I'M A THIRD-YEAR.
AND THAT FEEBLE LOOKING GUY IS OUR COACH.
Why you...
SHE'S THE INJURED MANAGER, NENE KOZUKA, A SECOND-YEAR.
AND HE'S HER TWIN BROTHER, NANA KOZUKA.
"NANA & NENE," THE TEAM'S IDOLS.
Just kidding.
Do you want me to sing?
←Twins→
WILL YOU PLEASE STOP TELLING STALE JOKES?
It's a waste of time.

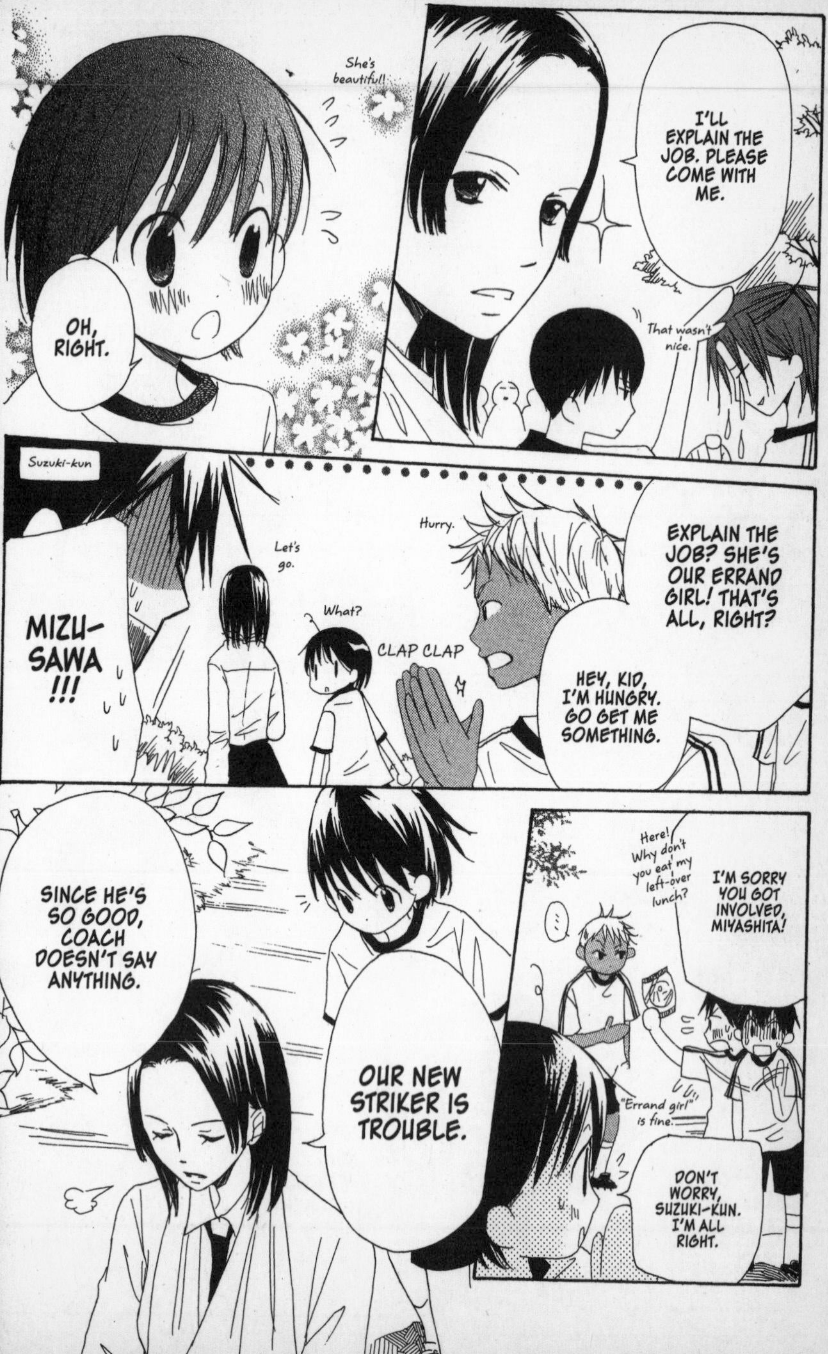
I'LL EXPLAIN THE JOB. PLEASE COME WITH ME.
That wasn't nice.
She's beautiful!
OH, RIGHT.
EXPLAIN THE JOB? SHE'S OUR ERRAND GIRL! THAT'S ALL, RIGHT?
HEY, KID, I'M HUNGRY. GO GET ME SOMETHING.
Hurry.
CLAP CLAP
Let's go.
What?
Suzuki-kun
MIZU-SAWA!!!
I'M SORRY YOU GOT INVOLVED, MIYASHITA!
Here! Why don't you eat my left-over lunch?
...
"Errand girl" is fine.
DON'T WORRY, SUZUKI-KUN. I'M ALL RIGHT.
OUR NEW STRIKER IS TROUBLE.
SINCE HE'S SO GOOD, COACH DOESN'T SAY ANYTHING.

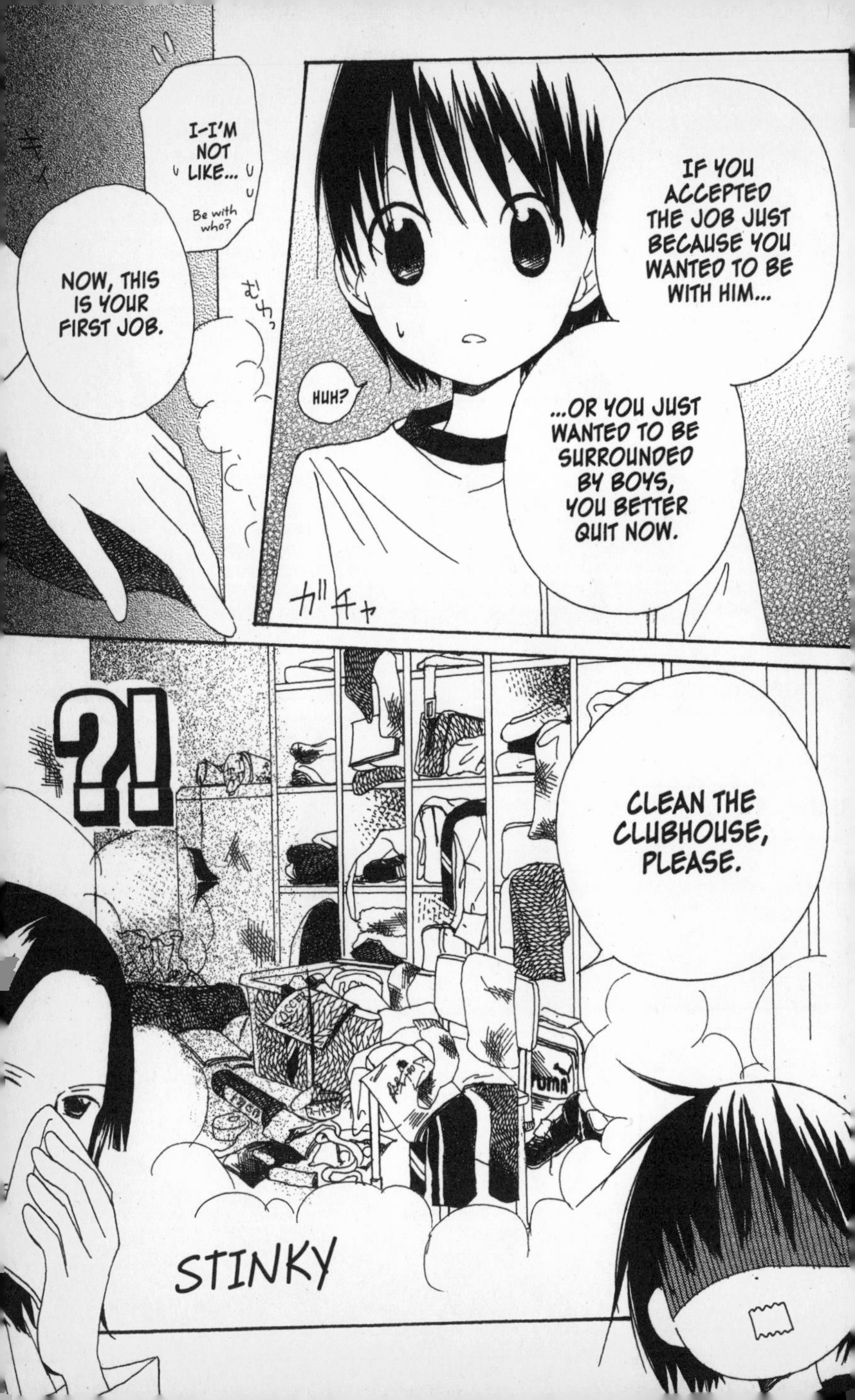
IF YOU ACCEPTED THE JOB JUST BECAUSE YOU WANTED TO BE WITH HIM...
...OR YOU JUST WANTED TO BE SURROUNDED BY BOYS, YOU BETTER QUIT NOW.
HUH?
ガチャ
I-I'M NOT LIKE...
Be with who?
むかっ
NOW, THIS IS YOUR FIRST JOB.
キィ
CLEAN THE CLUBHOUSE, PLEASE.
?!
PUMA
STINKY

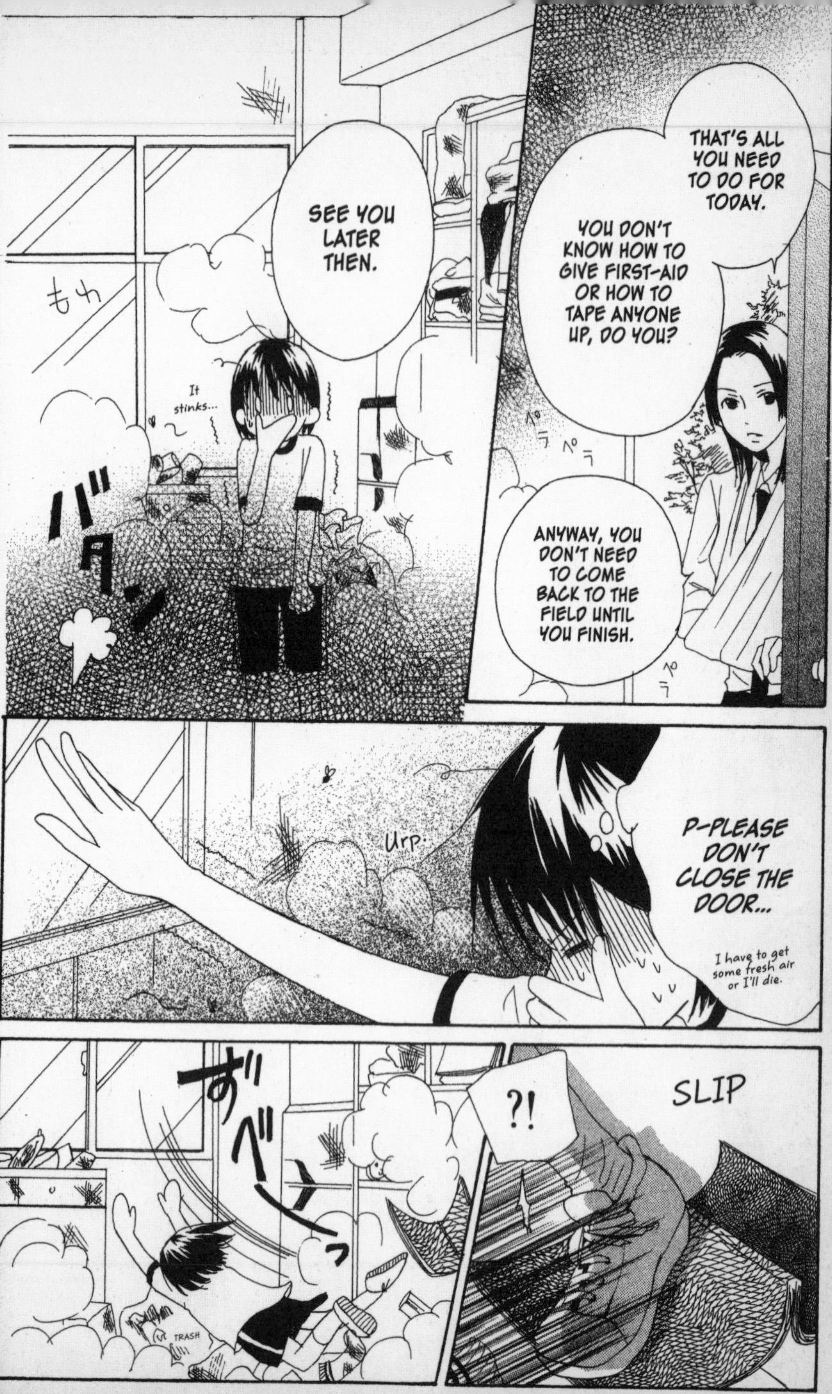
THAT'S ALL YOU NEED TO DO FOR TODAY.
YOU DON'T KNOW HOW TO GIVE FIRST-AID OR HOW TO TAPE ANYONE UP, DO YOU?
ペラ ペラ
ANYWAY, YOU DON'T NEED TO COME BACK TO THE FIELD UNTIL YOU FINISH.
ペラ
SEE YOU LATER THEN.
もわ
It stinks...
バタン
P-PLEASE DON'T CLOSE THE DOOR...
I have to get some fresh air or I'll die.
Urp.
SLIP
?!
ずべーっ
TRASH

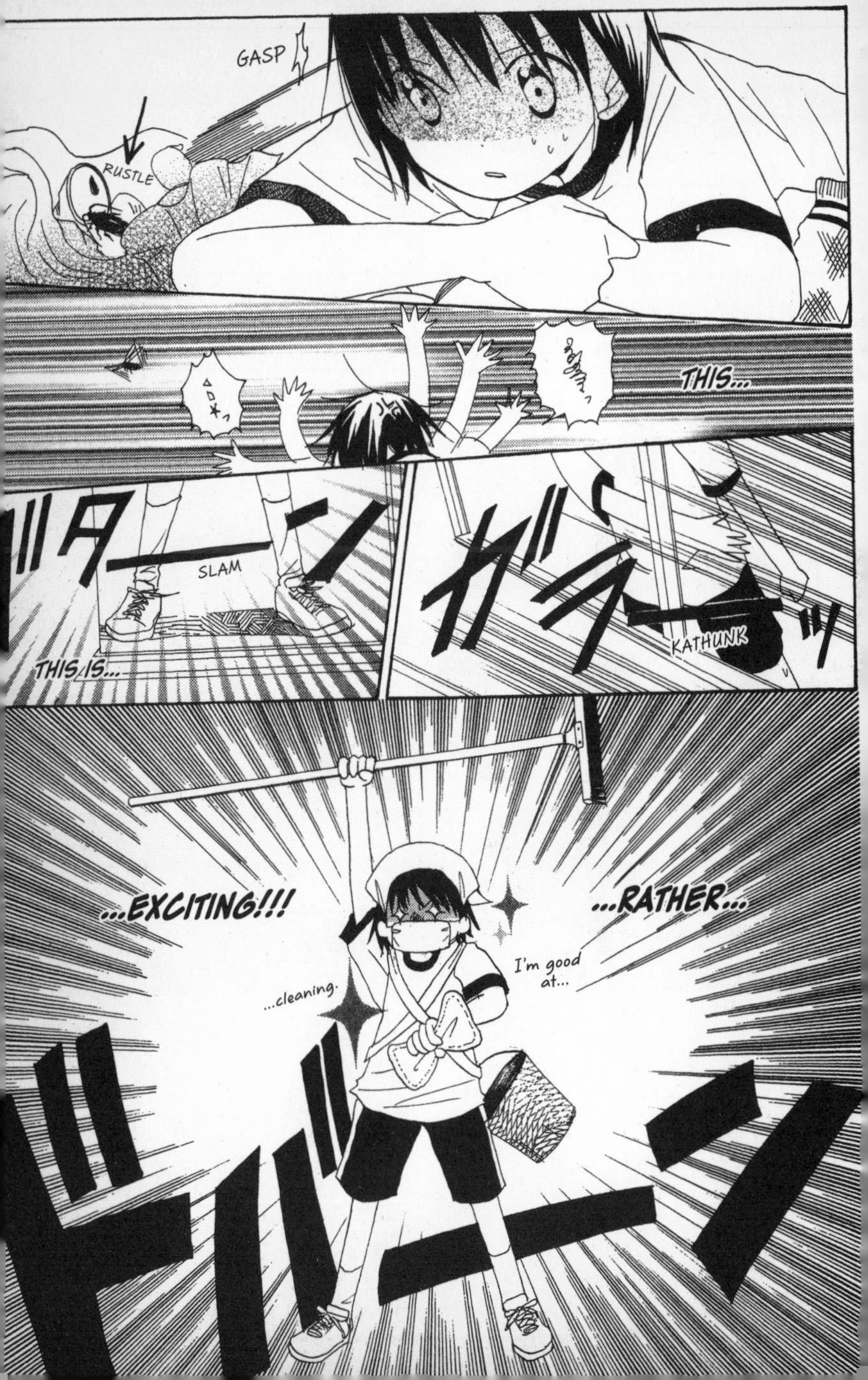
GASP
RUSTLE
THIS...
KATHUNK
SLAM
THIS IS...
...RATHER...
I'm good at...
...cleaning.
...EXCITING!!!

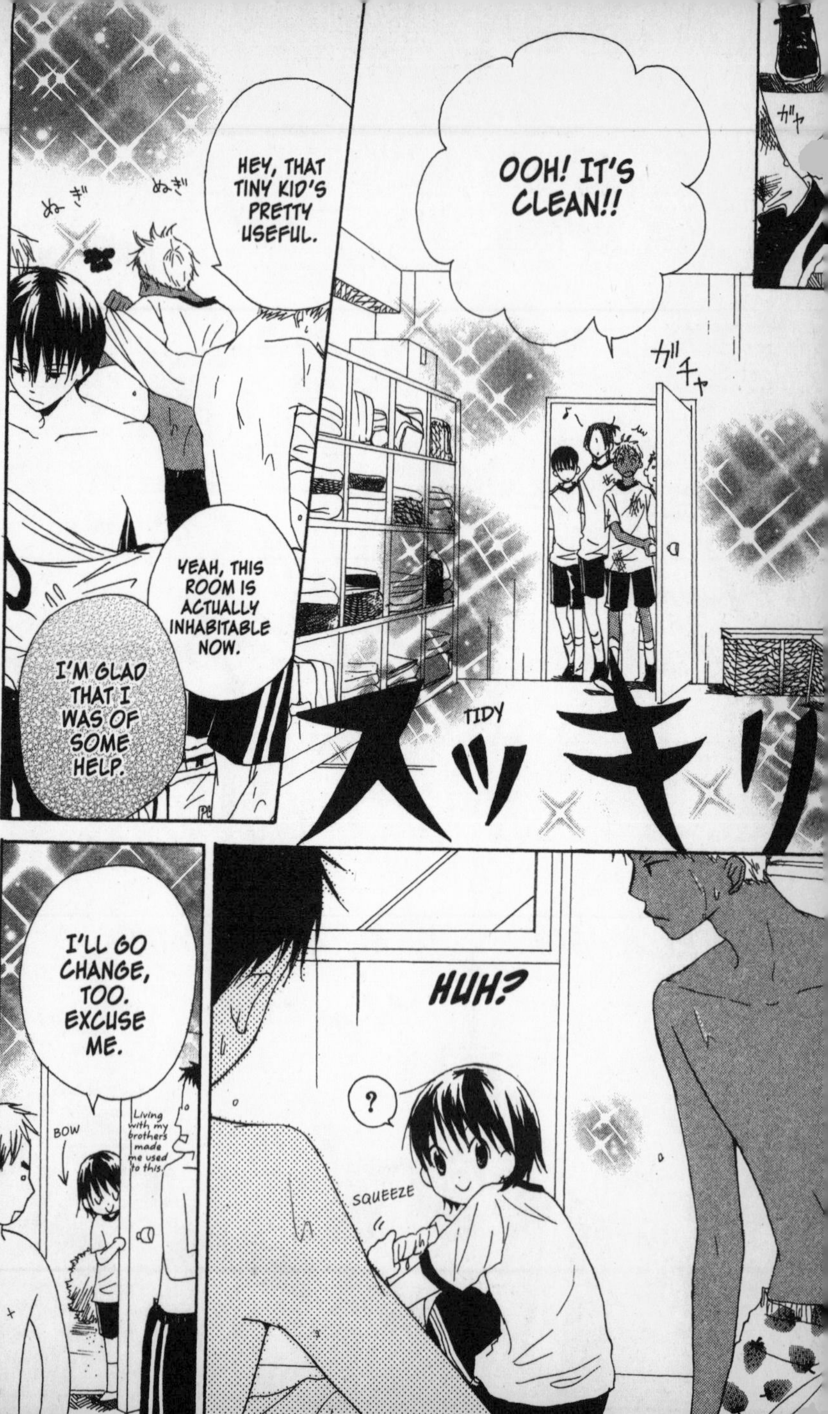
ガヤ
OOH! IT'S CLEAN!!
ガチャ
TIDY
スッキリ
HEY, THAT TINY KID'S PRETTY USEFUL.
ぬぎ
ぬぎ
YEAH, THIS ROOM IS ACTUALLY INHABITABLE NOW.
I'M GLAD THAT I WAS OF SOME HELP.
HUH?
?
SQUEEZE
I'LL GO CHANGE, TOO. EXCUSE ME.
BOW
Living with my brothers made me used to this.

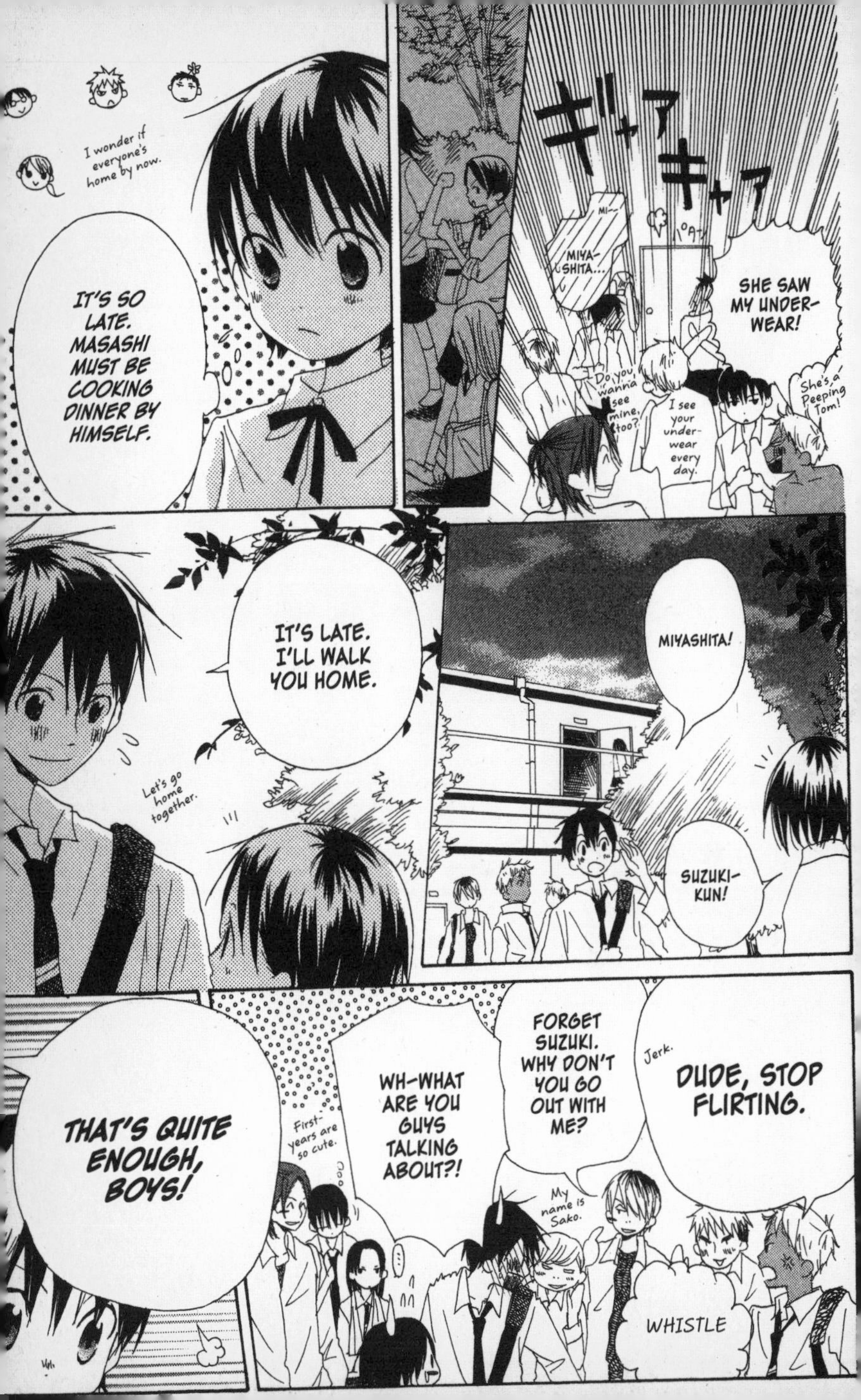
ギャア
キャア
MI-
MIYA-SHITA...
SHE SAW MY UNDER-WEAR!
She's a Peeping Tom!
I see your under-wear every day.
Do you wanna see mine, too?
I wonder if everyone's home by now.
IT'S SO LATE. MASASHI MUST BE COOKING DINNER BY HIMSELF.
MIYASHITA!
SUZUKI-KUN!
IT'S LATE. I'LL WALK YOU HOME.
Let's go home together.
DUDE, STOP FLIRTING.
Jerk.
FORGET SUZUKI. WHY DON'T YOU GO OUT WITH ME?
My name is Sako.
WH-WHAT ARE YOU GUYS TALKING ABOUT?!
First-years are so cute.
WHISTLE
THAT'S QUITE ENOUGH, BOYS!

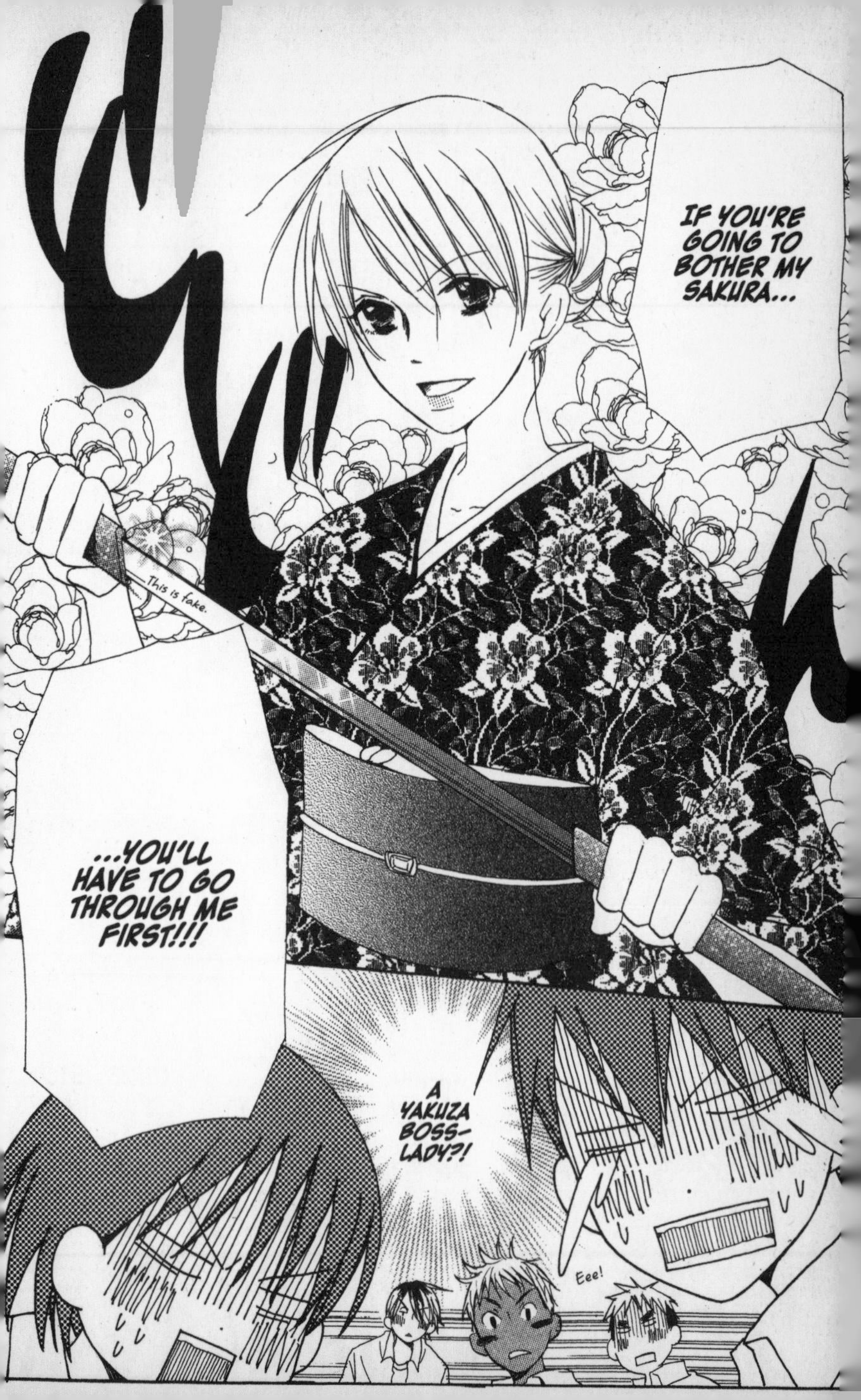
IF YOU'RE GOING TO BOTHER MY SAKURA...
This is fake.
...YOU'LL HAVE TO GO THROUGH ME FIRST!!!
A YAKUZA BOSS-LADY?!
Eee!

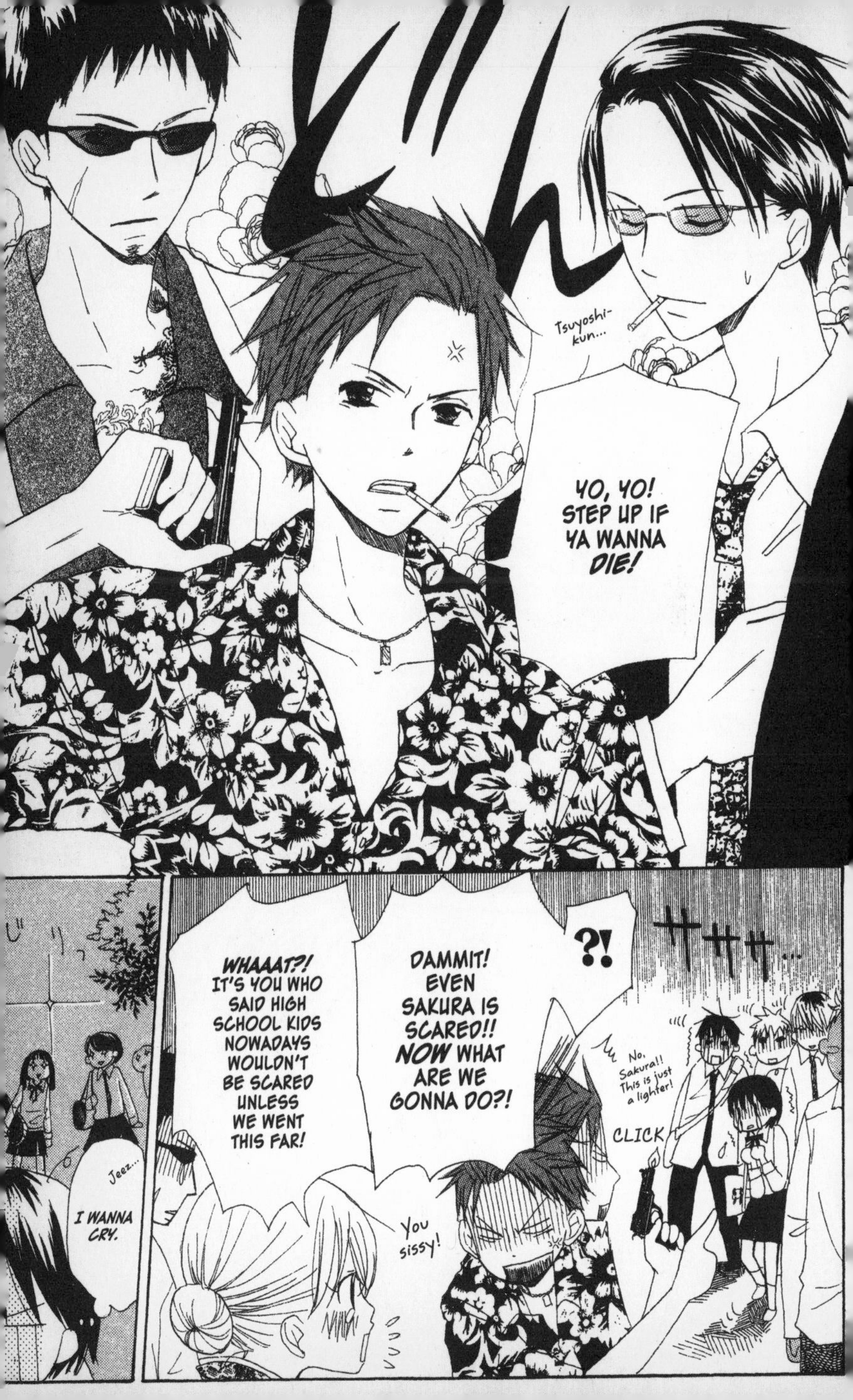
Tsuyoshi-kun...
YO, YO! STEP UP IF YA WANNA DIE!
?!
No, Sakura!! This is just a lighter!
CLICK
DAMMIT! EVEN SAKURA IS SCARED!! NOW WHAT ARE WE GONNA DO?!
You sissy!
WHAAAT?! IT'S YOU WHO SAID HIGH SCHOOL KIDS NOWADAYS WOULDN'T BE SCARED UNLESS WE WENT THIS FAR!
Jeez...
I WANNA CRY.

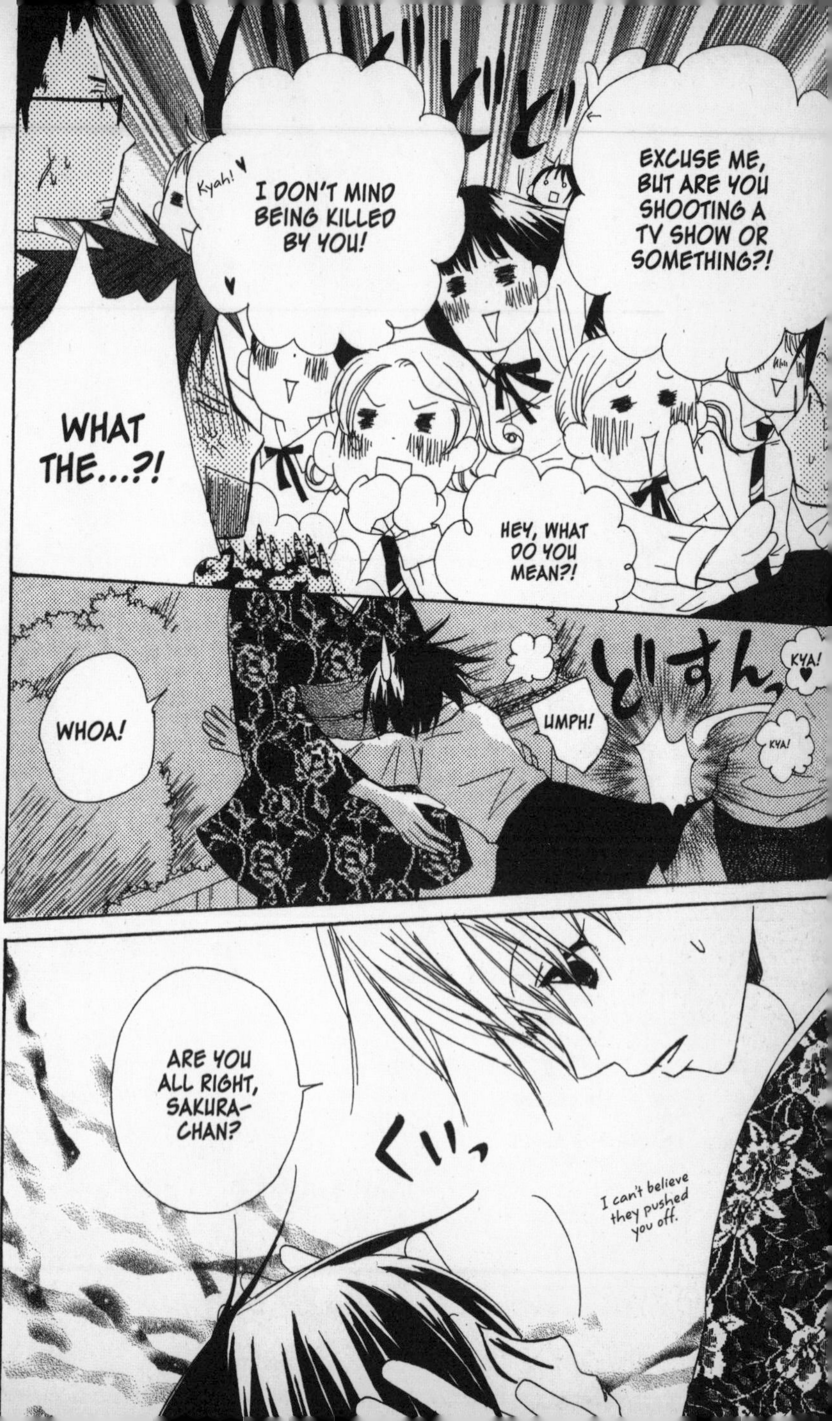
EXCUSE ME, BUT ARE YOU SHOOTING A TV SHOW OR SOMETHING?!
Kyah!
I DON'T MIND BEING KILLED BY YOU!
HEY, WHAT DO YOU MEAN?!
WHAT THE...?!
KYA!
KYA!
どすん
UMPH!
WHOA!
ARE YOU ALL RIGHT, SAKURA-CHAN?
I can't believe they pushed you off.
ぐいっ

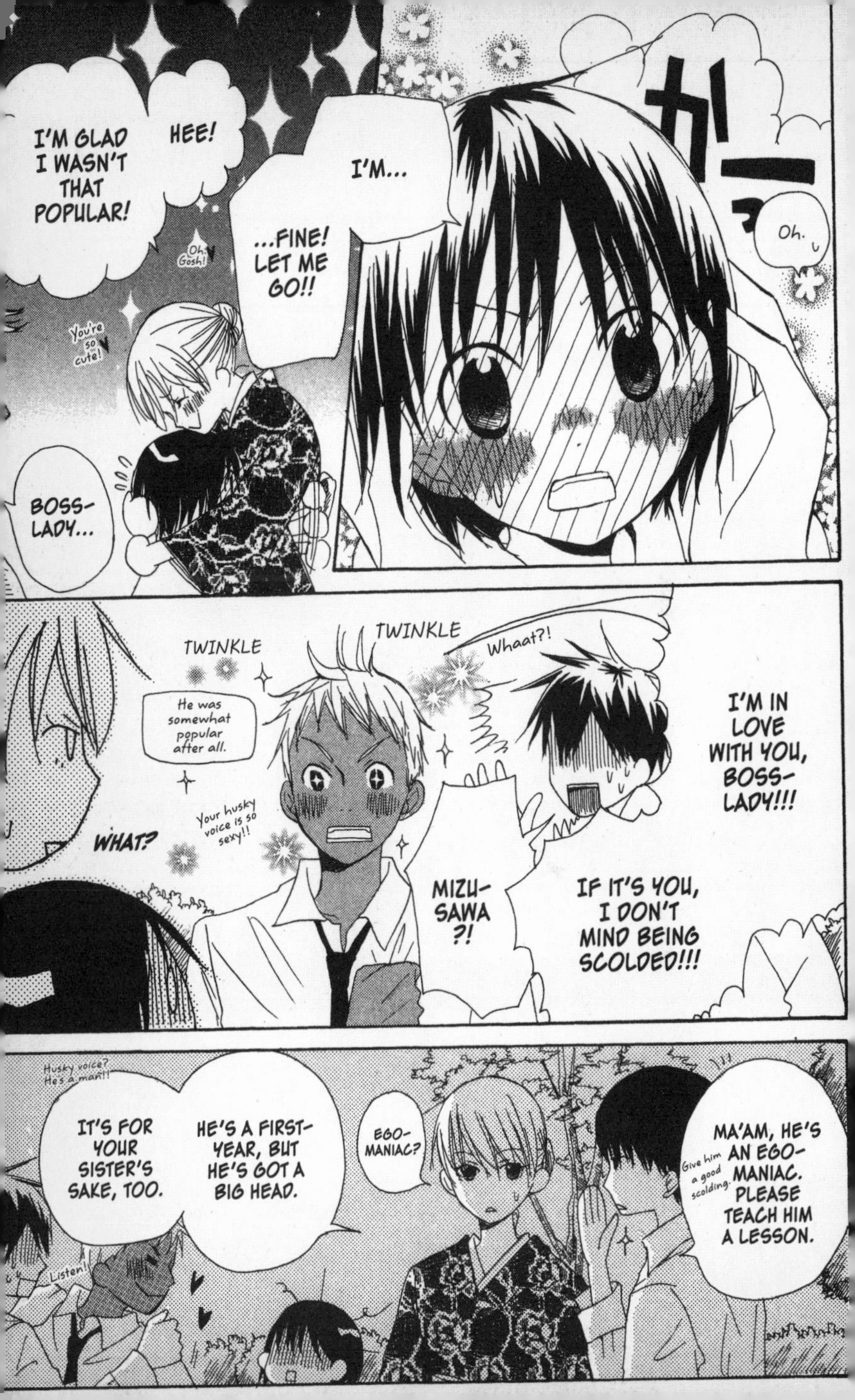
カー
Oh.
I'M...
...FINE! LET ME GO!!
HEE!
I'M GLAD I WASN'T THAT POPULAR!
Oh. Gosh!
You're so cute!
BOSS-LADY...
I'M IN LOVE WITH YOU, BOSS-LADY!!!
Whaat?!
IF IT'S YOU, I DON'T MIND BEING SCOLDED!!!
MIZU-SAWA?!
TWINKLE
TWINKLE
He was somewhat popular after all.
Your husky voice is so sexy!!
WHAT?
MA'AM, HE'S AN EGO-MANIAC. PLEASE TEACH HIM A LESSON.
Give him a good scolding.
EGO-MANIAC?
HE'S A FIRST-YEAR, BUT HE'S GOT A BIG HEAD.
IT'S FOR YOUR SISTER'S SAKE, TOO.
Husky voice? He's a man!!
Listen!

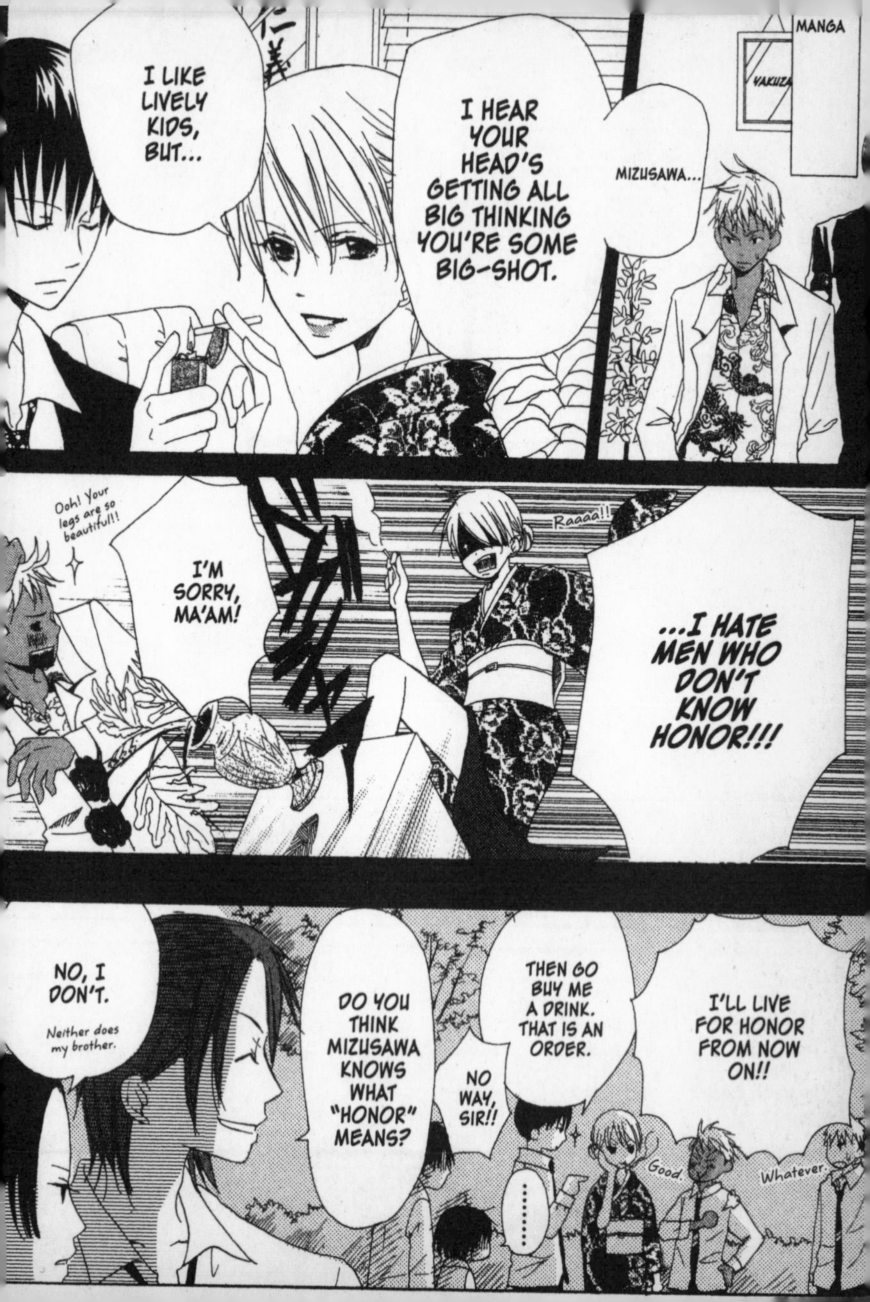
MANGA
YAKUZA
MIZUSAWA...
I HEAR YOUR HEAD'S GETTING ALL BIG THINKING YOU'RE SOME BIG-SHOT.
I LIKE LIVELY KIDS, BUT...
...I HATE MEN WHO DON'T KNOW HONOR!!!
Raaaa!!
I'M SORRY, MA'AM!
Ooh! Your legs are so beautiful!!
I'LL LIVE FOR HONOR FROM NOW ON!!
THEN GO BUY ME A DRINK. THAT IS AN ORDER.
NO WAY, SIR!!
Whatever.
Good.
......
DO YOU THINK MIZUSAWA KNOWS WHAT "HONOR" MEANS?
NO, I DON'T.
Neither does my brother.

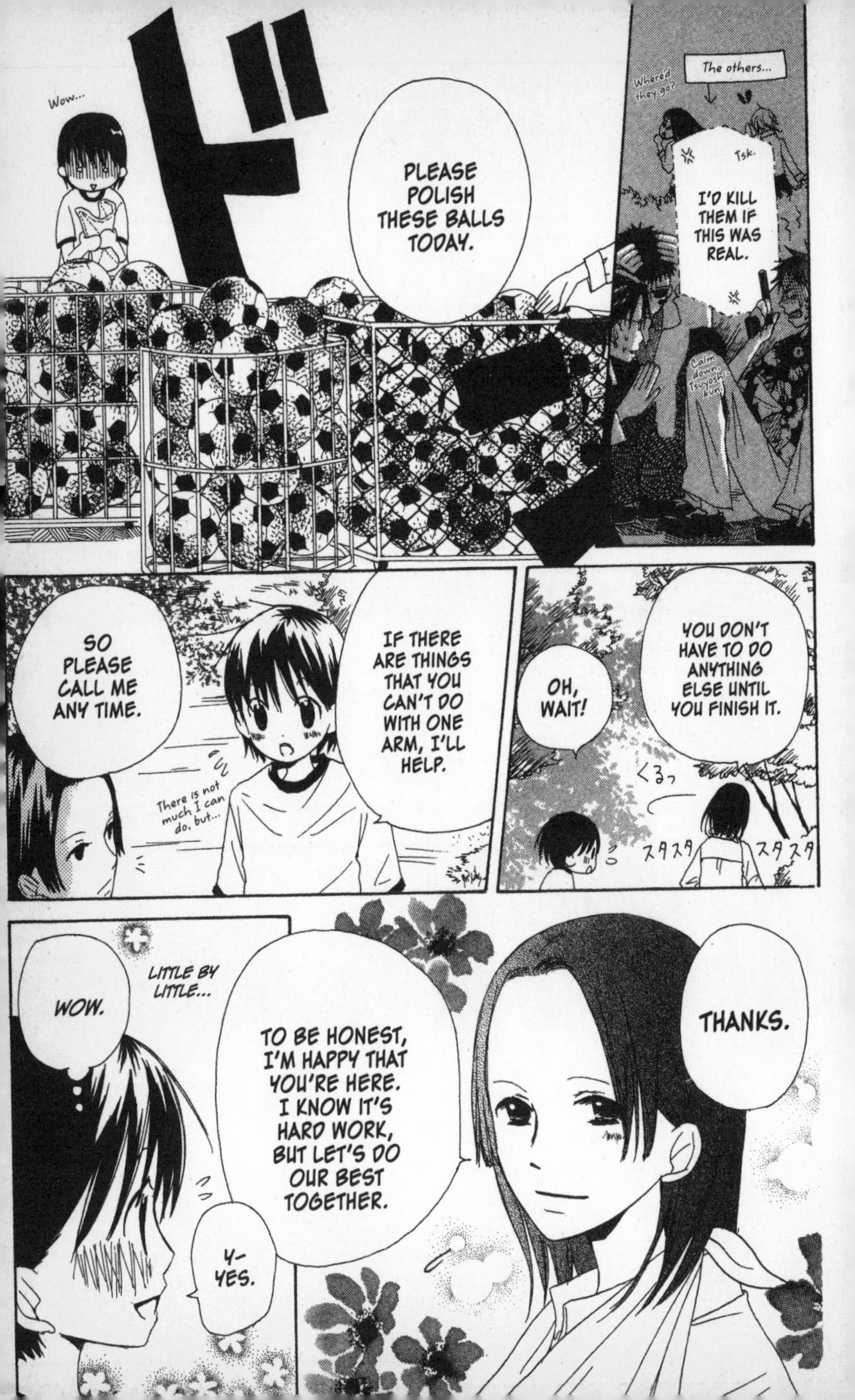
The others...
Where'd they go?
Tsk.
I'D KILL THEM IF THIS WAS REAL.
Calm down, Tsuyoshi-kun.
PLEASE POLISH THESE BALLS TODAY.
ド
Wow...
YOU DON'T HAVE TO DO ANYTHING ELSE UNTIL YOU FINISH IT.
OH, WAIT!
くるっ
スタスタ
スタスタ
IF THERE ARE THINGS THAT YOU CAN'T DO WITH ONE ARM, I'LL HELP.
There is not much I can do, but...
SO PLEASE CALL ME ANY TIME.
THANKS.
TO BE HONEST, I'M HAPPY THAT YOU'RE HERE. I KNOW IT'S HARD WORK, BUT LET'S DO OUR BEST TOGETHER.
Y-YES.
LITTLE BY LITTLE...
WOW.

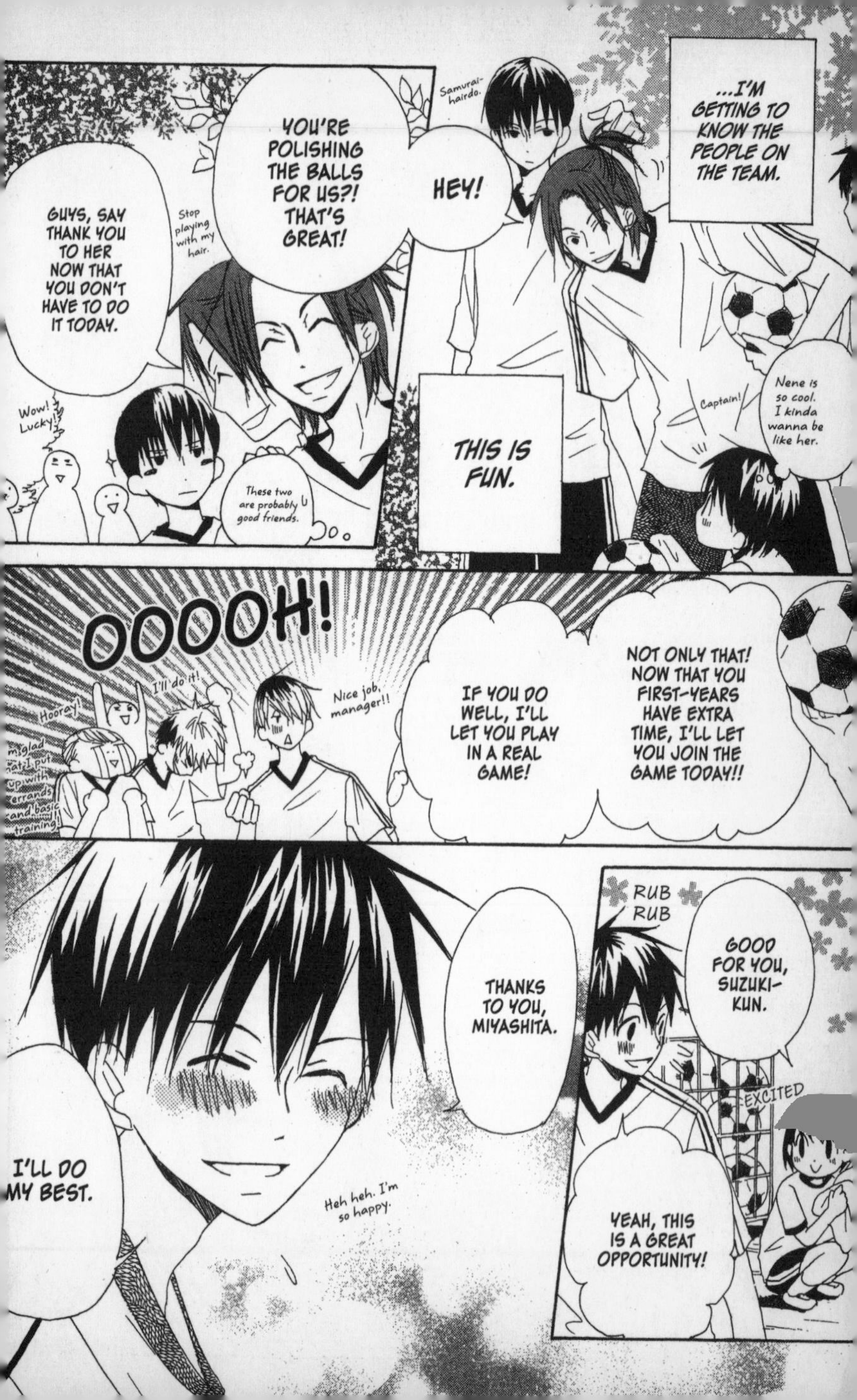
...I'M GETTING TO KNOW THE PEOPLE ON THE TEAM.
Samurai-hairdo.
HEY!
Nene is so cool. I kinda wanna be like her.
Captain!
THIS IS FUN.
YOU'RE POLISHING THE BALLS FOR US?! THAT'S GREAT!
Stop playing with my hair.
GUYS, SAY THANK YOU TO HER NOW THAT YOU DON'T HAVE TO DO IT TODAY.
These two are probably good friends.
Wow! Lucky!
NOT ONLY THAT! NOW THAT YOU FIRST-YEARS HAVE EXTRA TIME, I'LL LET YOU JOIN THE GAME TODAY!!
IF YOU DO WELL, I'LL LET YOU PLAY IN A REAL GAME!
OOOOH!
Nice job, manager!!
I'll do it!
Hooray!
m glad hat I put up with errands and basic training!
RUB RUB
GOOD FOR YOU, SUZUKI-KUN.
EXCITED
YEAH, THIS IS A GREAT OPPORTUNITY!
THANKS TO YOU, MIYASHITA.
I'LL DO MY BEST.
Heh heh. I'm so happy.

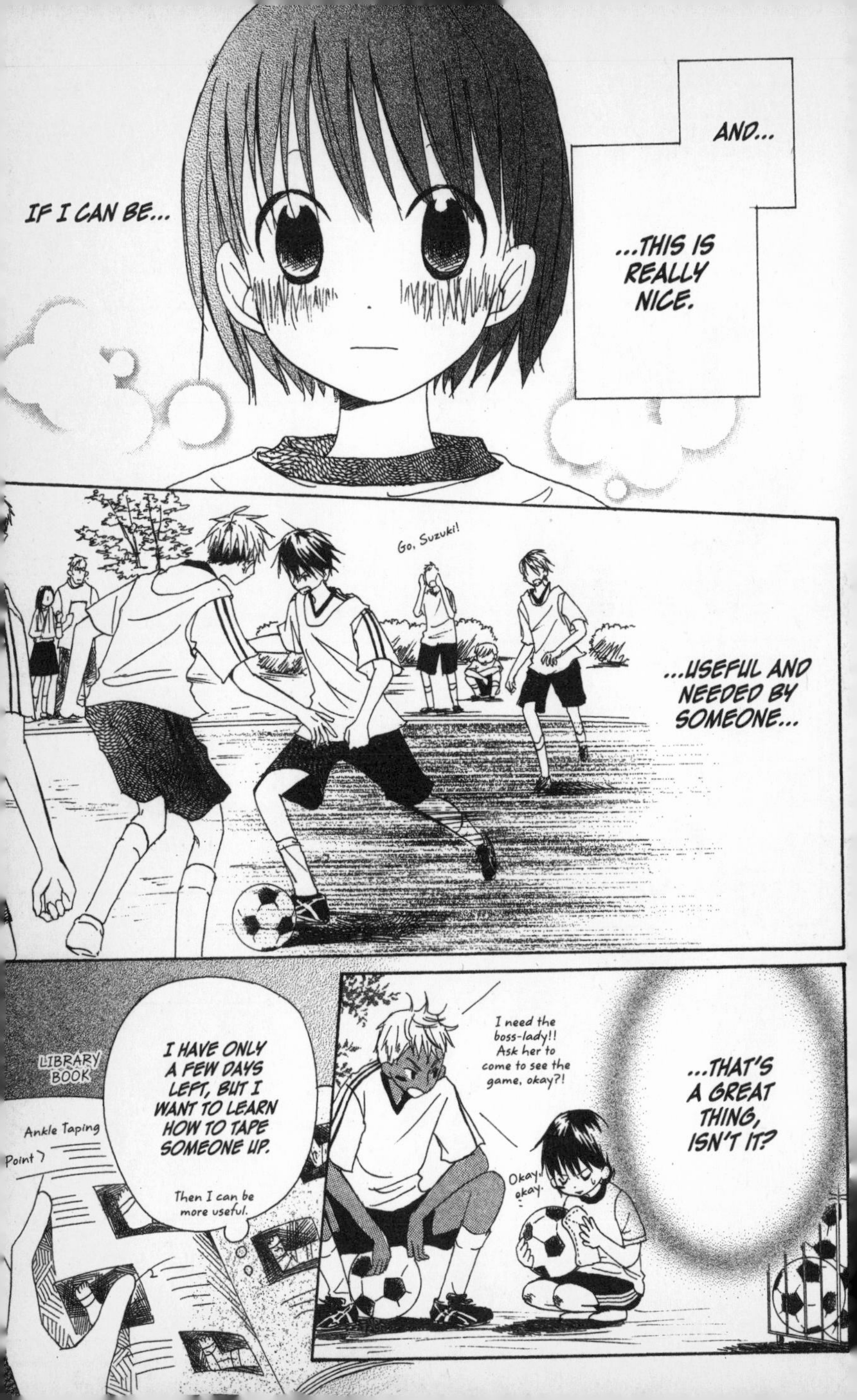
AND...
...THIS IS REALLY NICE.
IF I CAN BE...
...USEFUL AND NEEDED BY SOMEONE...
Go, Suzuki!
...THAT'S A GREAT THING, ISN'T IT?
I need the boss-lady!! Ask her to come to see the game, okay?!
Okay, okay.
I HAVE ONLY A FEW DAYS LEFT, BUT I WANT TO LEARN HOW TO TAPE SOMEONE UP.
Then I can be more useful.
LIBRARY BOOK
Ankle Taping
Point

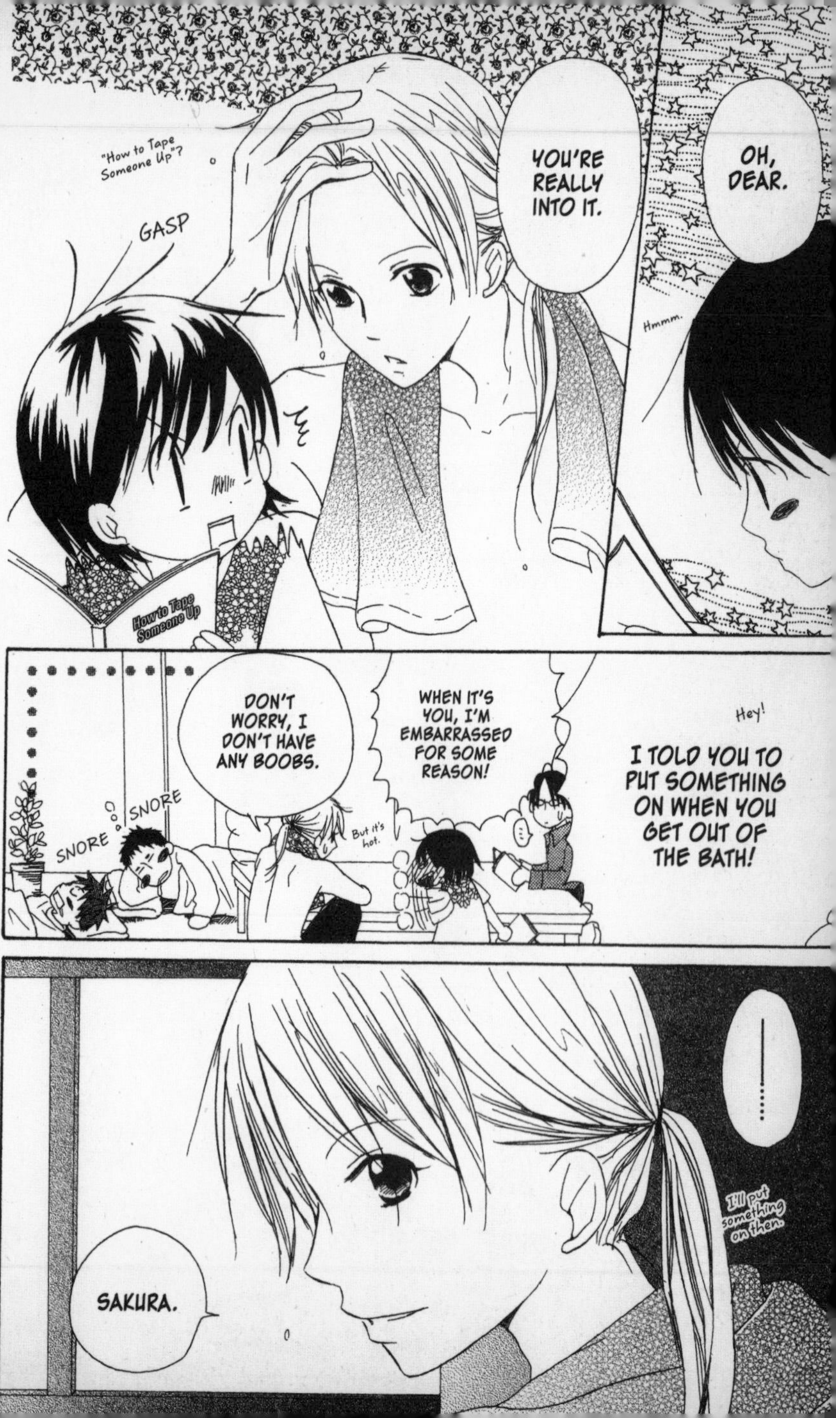
OH, DEAR.
Hmmm.
YOU'RE REALLY INTO IT.
GASP
"How to Tape Someone Up"?
How to Tape Someone Up
Hey!
I TOLD YOU TO PUT SOMETHING ON WHEN YOU GET OUT OF THE BATH!
WHEN IT'S YOU, I'M EMBARRASSED FOR SOME REASON!
DON'T WORRY, I DON'T HAVE ANY BOOBS.
But it's hot.
SNORE
SNORE
......
I'll put something on then.
SAKURA.

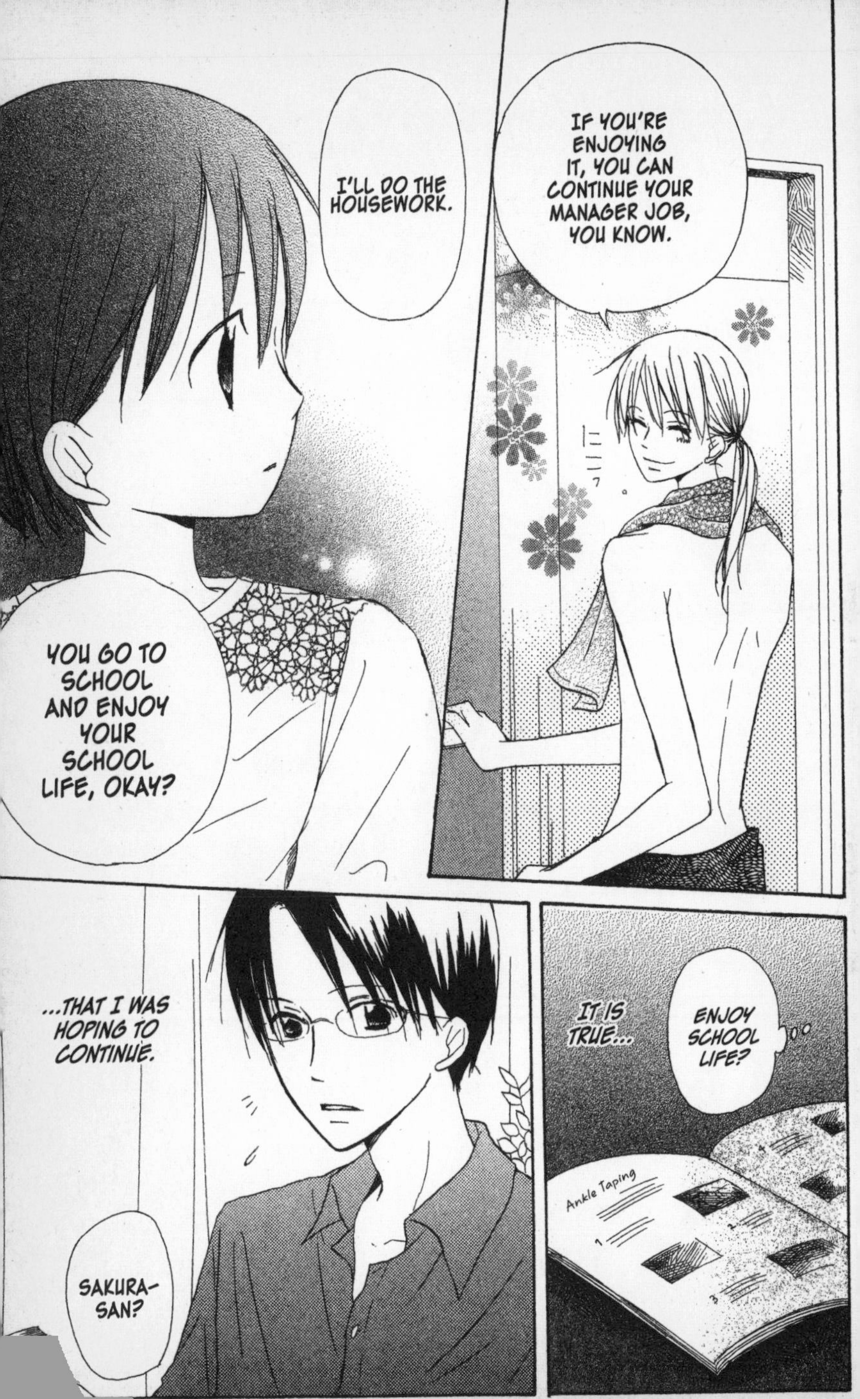
IF YOU'RE ENJOYING IT, YOU CAN CONTINUE YOUR MANAGER JOB, YOU KNOW.
I'LL DO THE HOUSEWORK.
YOU GO TO SCHOOL AND ENJOY YOUR SCHOOL LIFE, OKAY?
ENJOY SCHOOL LIFE?
IT IS TRUE...
Ankle Taping
...THAT I WAS HOPING TO CONTINUE.
SAKURA-SAN?

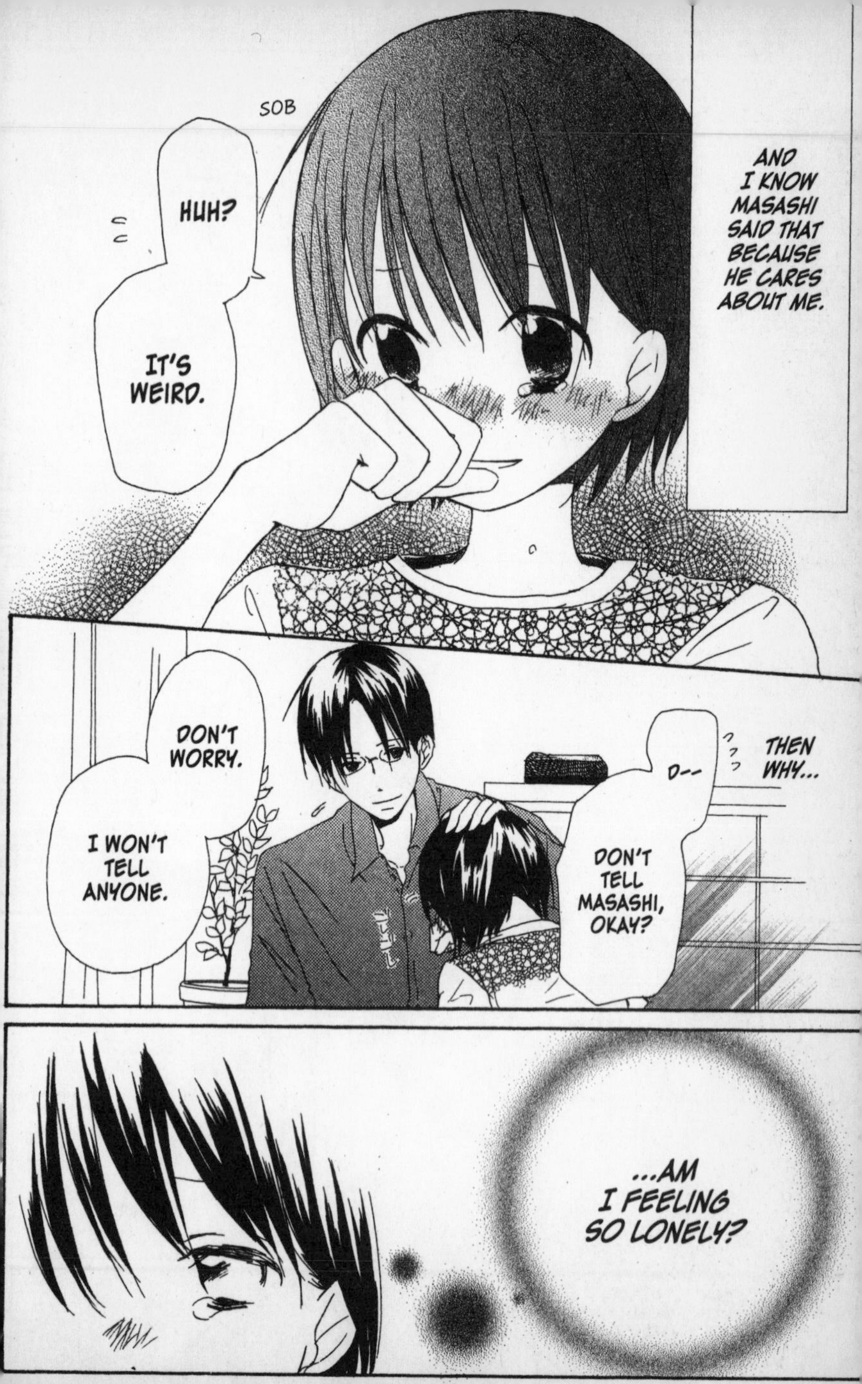
AND I KNOW MASASHI SAID THAT BECAUSE HE CARES ABOUT ME.
SOB
HUH?
IT'S WEIRD.
THEN WHY...
D--
DON'T TELL MASASHI, OKAY?
DON'T WORRY.
I WON'T TELL ANYONE.
...AM I FEELING SO LONELY?

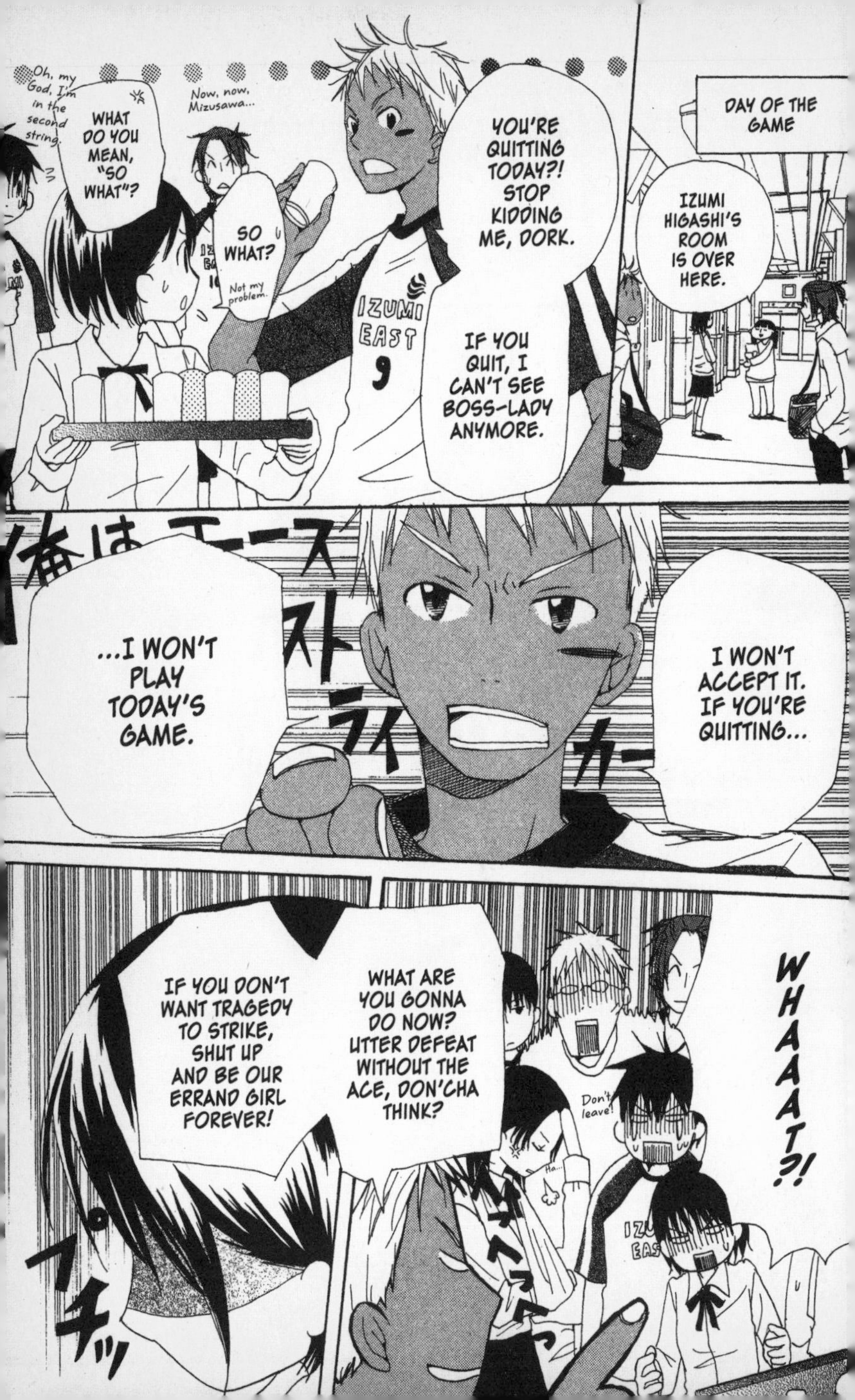
DAY OF THE GAME
IZUMI HIGASHI'S ROOM IS OVER HERE.
YOU'RE QUITTING TODAY?! STOP KIDDING ME, DORK.
IF YOU QUIT, I CAN'T SEE BOSS-LADY ANYMORE.
Now, now, Mizusawa...
SO WHAT?
Not my problem.
WHAT DO YOU MEAN, "SO WHAT"?
Oh, my God, I'm in the second string.
IZUMI EAST 9
I WON'T ACCEPT IT. IF YOU'RE QUITTING...
...I WON'T PLAY TODAY'S GAME.
俺は エース ストライカー
WHAAAT?!
WHAT ARE YOU GONNA DO NOW? UTTER DEFEAT WITHOUT THE ACE, DON'CHA THINK?
IF YOU DON'T WANT TRAGEDY TO STRIKE, SHUT UP AND BE OUR ERRAND GIRL FOREVER!
Don't leave!
Ha...
プチッ

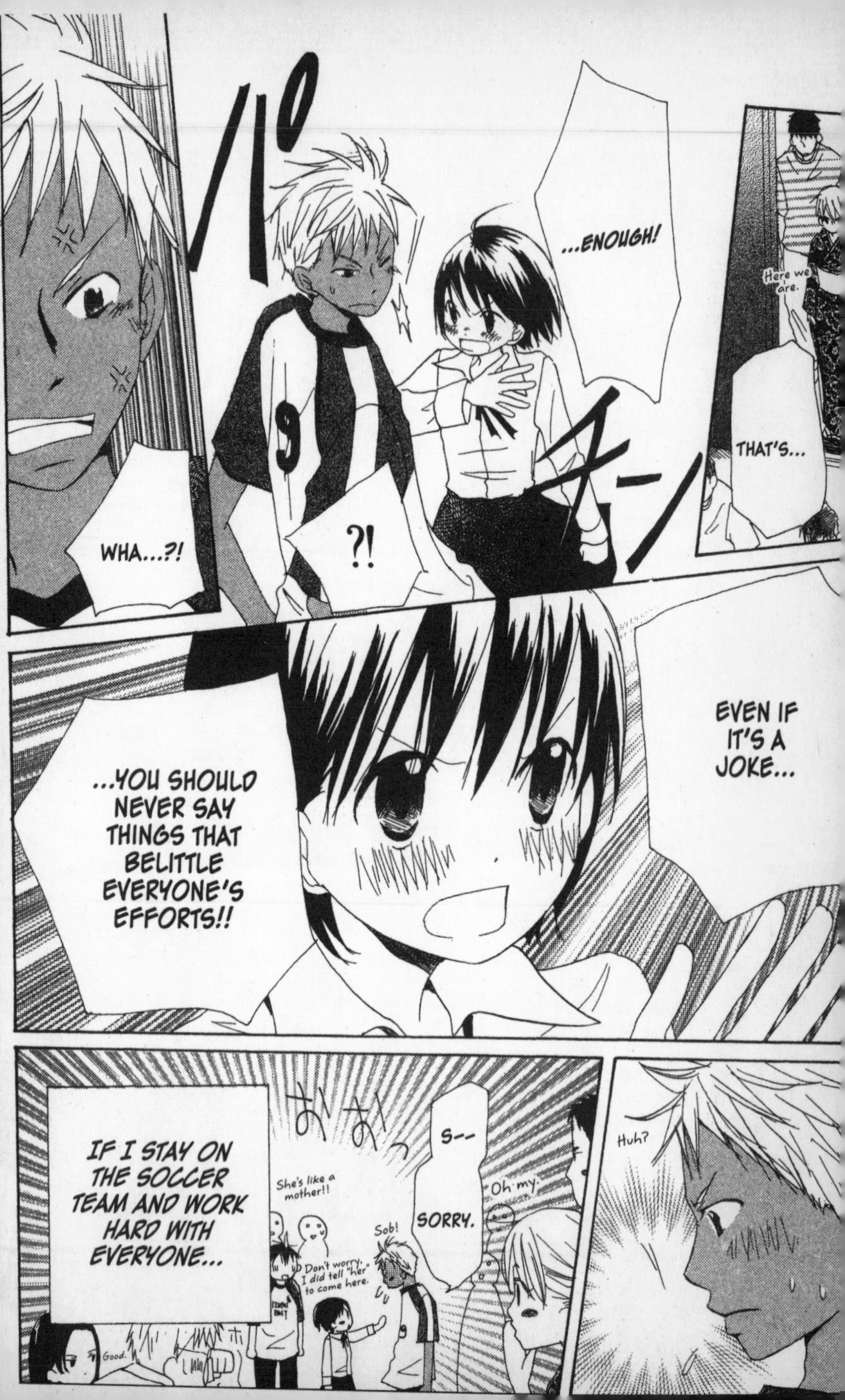
Here we are.
THAT'S...
...ENOUGH!
?!
WHA...?!
EVEN IF IT'S A JOKE...
...YOU SHOULD NEVER SAY THINGS THAT BELITTLE EVERYONE'S EFFORTS!!
Huh?
S--
SORRY.
Oh my.
She's like a mother!!
Sob!
Don't worry, I did tell "her" to come here.
IF I STAY ON THE SOCCER TEAM AND WORK HARD WITH EVERYONE...
Good.

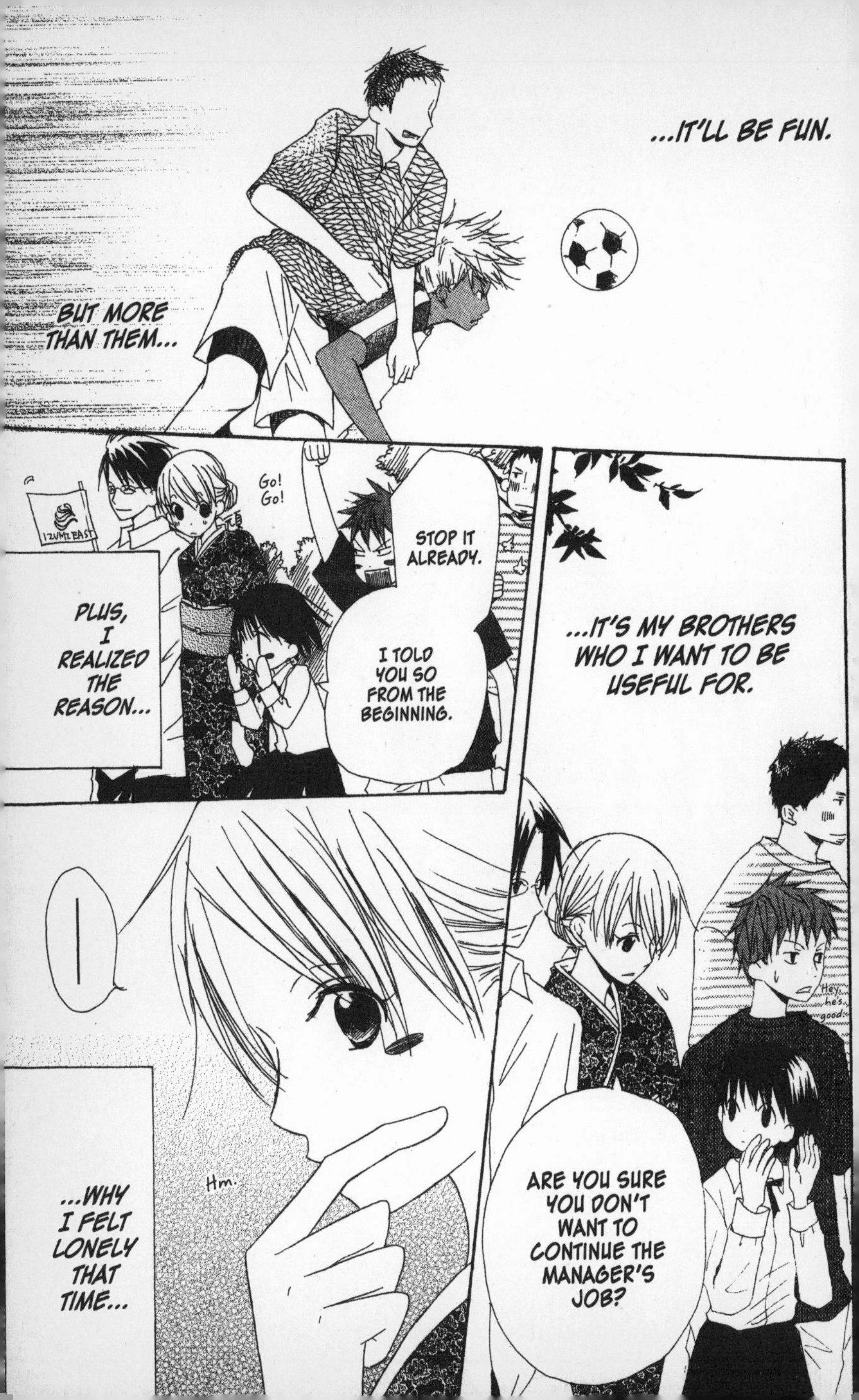
...IT'LL BE FUN.
BUT MORE THAN THEM...
...IT'S MY BROTHERS WHO I WANT TO BE USEFUL FOR.
Hey, he's good.
ARE YOU SURE YOU DON'T WANT TO CONTINUE THE MANAGER'S JOB?
STOP IT ALREADY.
Go! Go!
IZUMI EAST
I TOLD YOU SO FROM THE BEGINNING.
PLUS, I REALIZED THE REASON...
I
Hm.
...WHY I FELT LONELY THAT TIME...

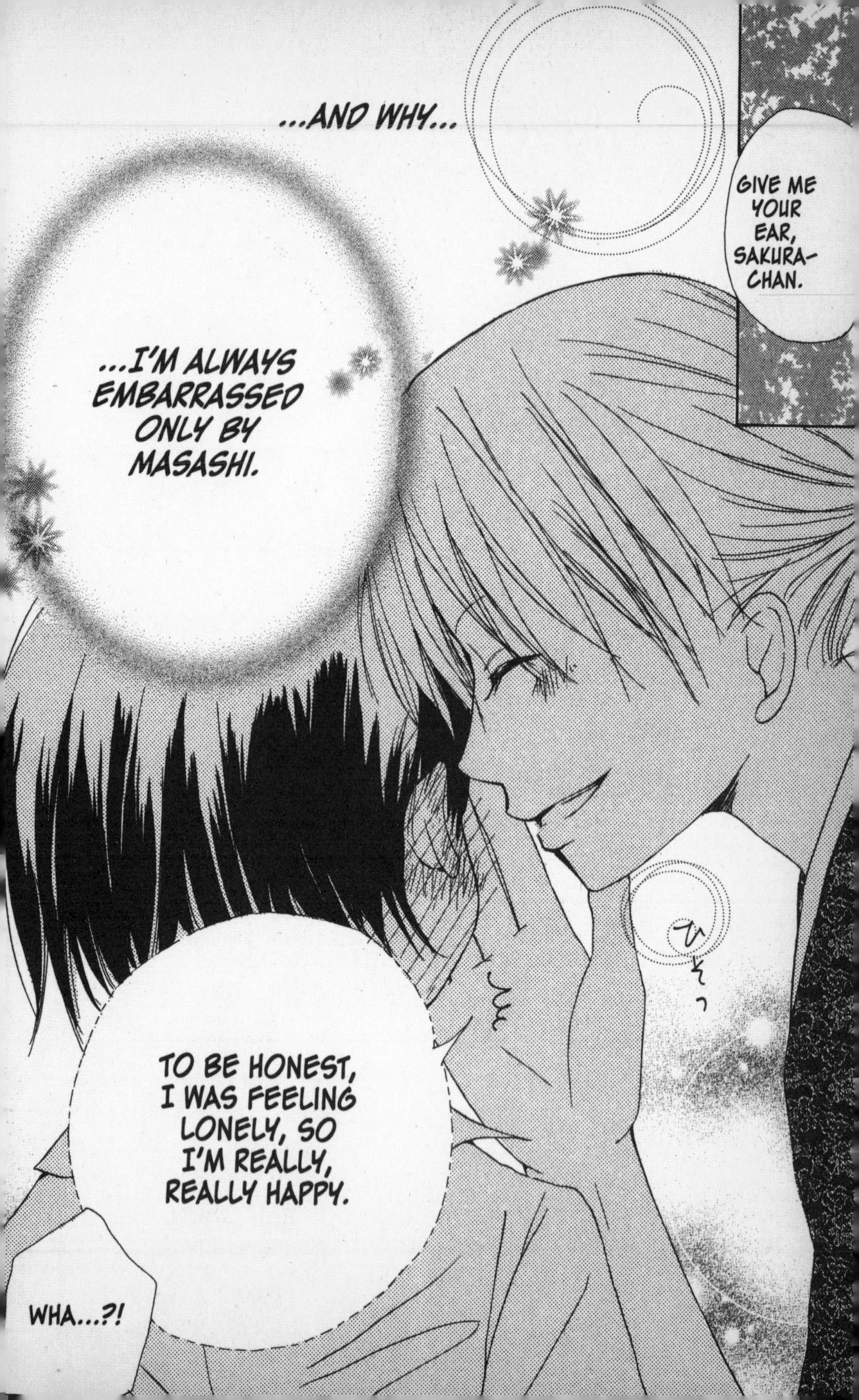
GIVE ME YOUR EAR, SAKURA-CHAN.
...AND WHY...
...I'M ALWAYS EMBARRASSED ONLY BY MASASHI.
TO BE HONEST, I WAS FEELING LONELY, SO I'M REALLY, REALLY HAPPY.
WHA...?!

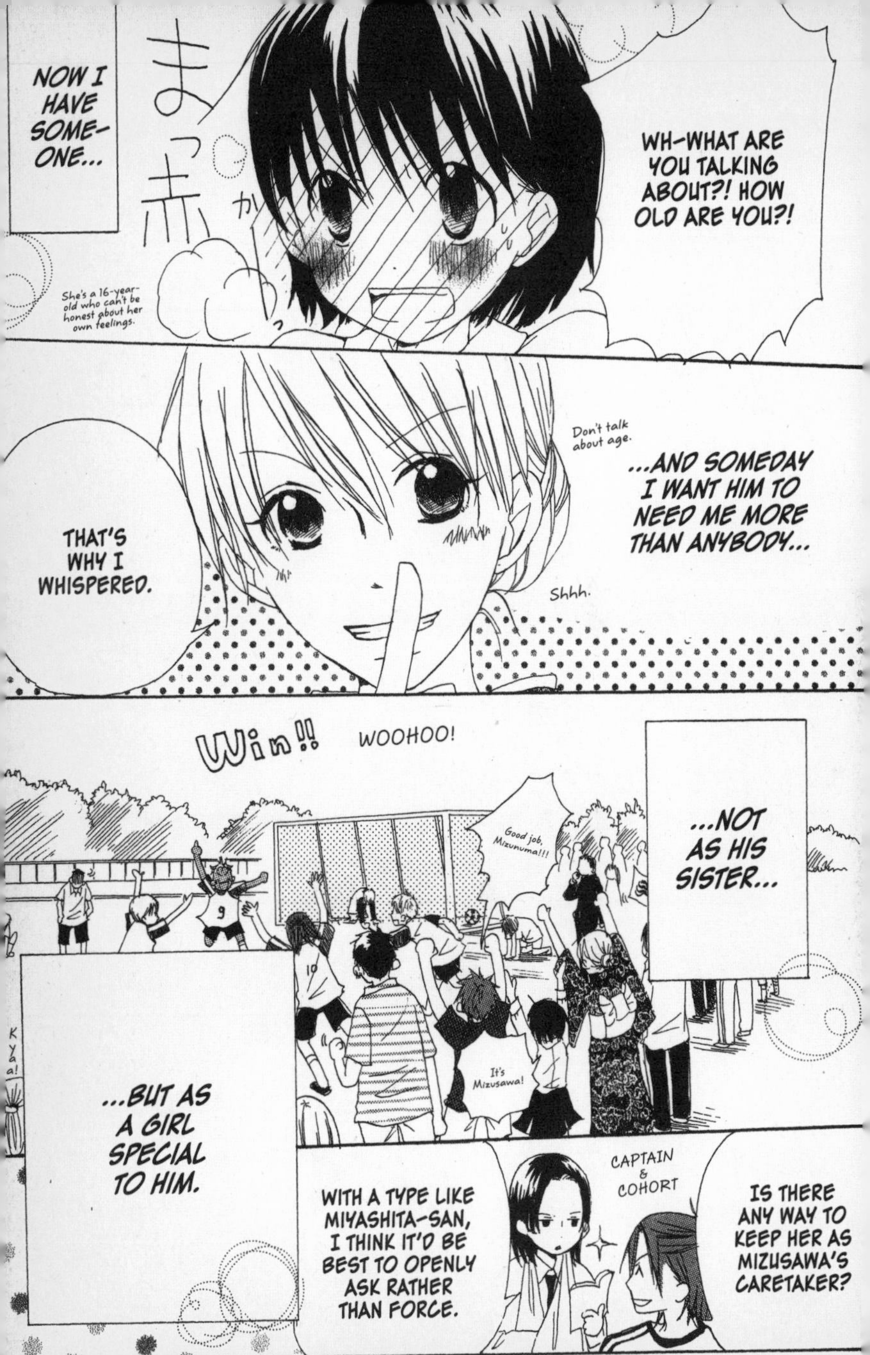
WH-WHAT ARE YOU TALKING ABOUT?! HOW OLD ARE YOU?!
まっ赤
か
NOW I HAVE SOMEONE...
She's a 16-year-old who can't be honest about her own feelings.
Don't talk about age.
...AND SOMEDAY I WANT HIM TO NEED ME MORE THAN ANYBODY...
Shhh.
THAT'S WHY I WHISPERED.
WOOHOO!
Win!!
...NOT AS HIS SISTER...
Good job, Mizunuma!!!
It's Mizusawa!
Kya!
...BUT AS A GIRL SPECIAL TO HIM.
IS THERE ANY WAY TO KEEP HER AS MIZUSAWA'S CARETAKER?
CAPTAIN & COHORT
WITH A TYPE LIKE MIYASHITA-SAN, I THINK IT'D BE BEST TO OPENLY ASK RATHER THAN FORCE.

Me & My Brothers 4 / End

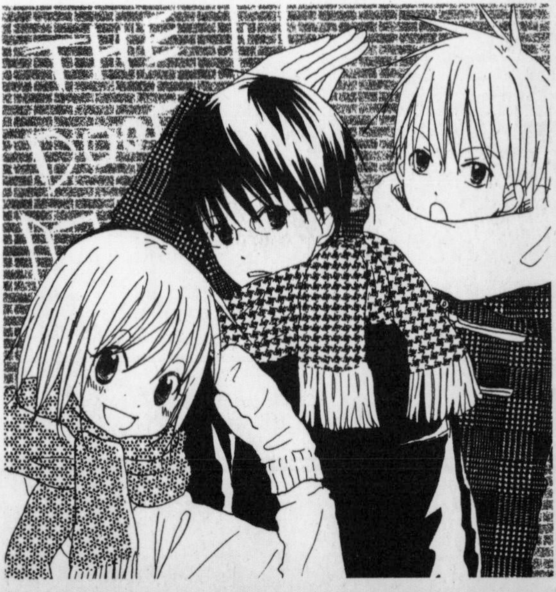
THE

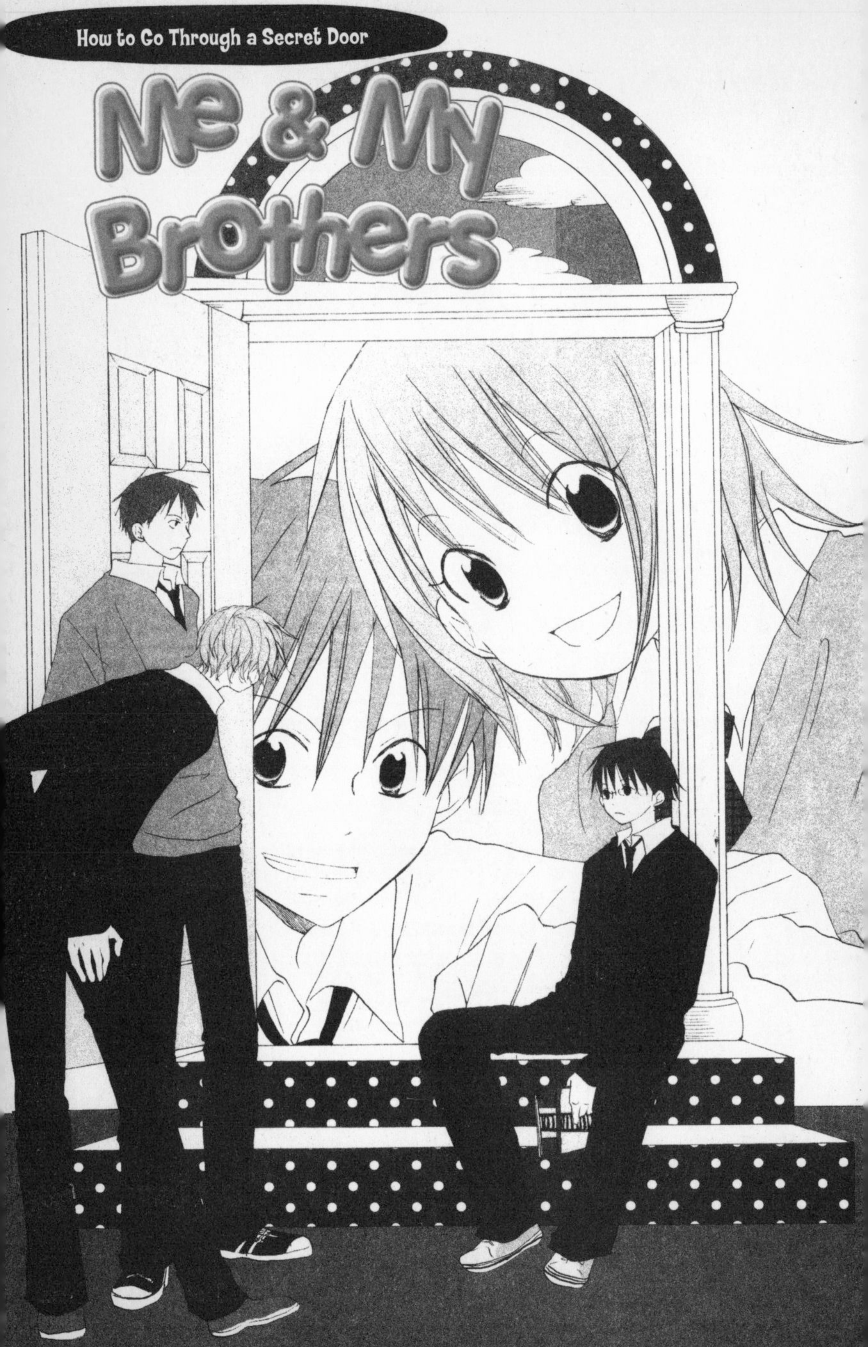
How to Go Through a Secret Door
Me & My Brothers

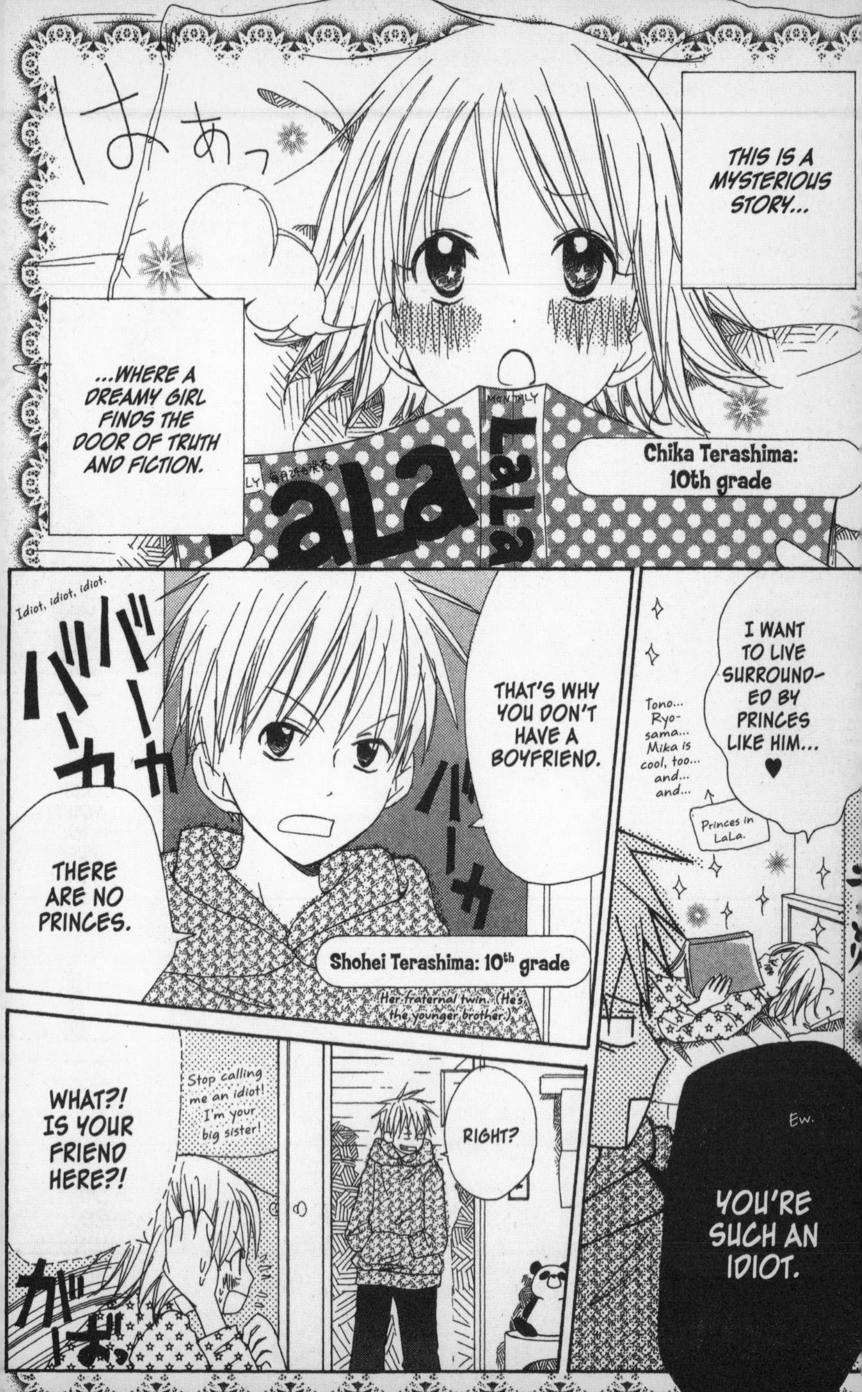
THIS IS A MYSTERIOUS STORY...
はぁあっ
...WHERE A DREAMY GIRL FINDS THE DOOR OF TRUTH AND FICTION.
Chika Terashima: 10th grade
MONTHLY LaLa
I WANT TO LIVE SURROUNDED BY PRINCES LIKE HIM... ♥
Tono... Ryo-sama... Mika is cool, too... and... and...
Princes in LaLa.
THAT'S WHY YOU DON'T HAVE A BOYFRIEND.
バーカ バーカ
Idiot, idiot, idiot.
THERE ARE NO PRINCES.
Shohei Terashima: 10th grade
Her fraternal twin. (He's the younger brother.)
Ew.
YOU'RE SUCH AN IDIOT.
RIGHT?
Stop calling me an idiot! I'm your big sister!
WHAT?! IS YOUR FRIEND HERE?!
がばっ

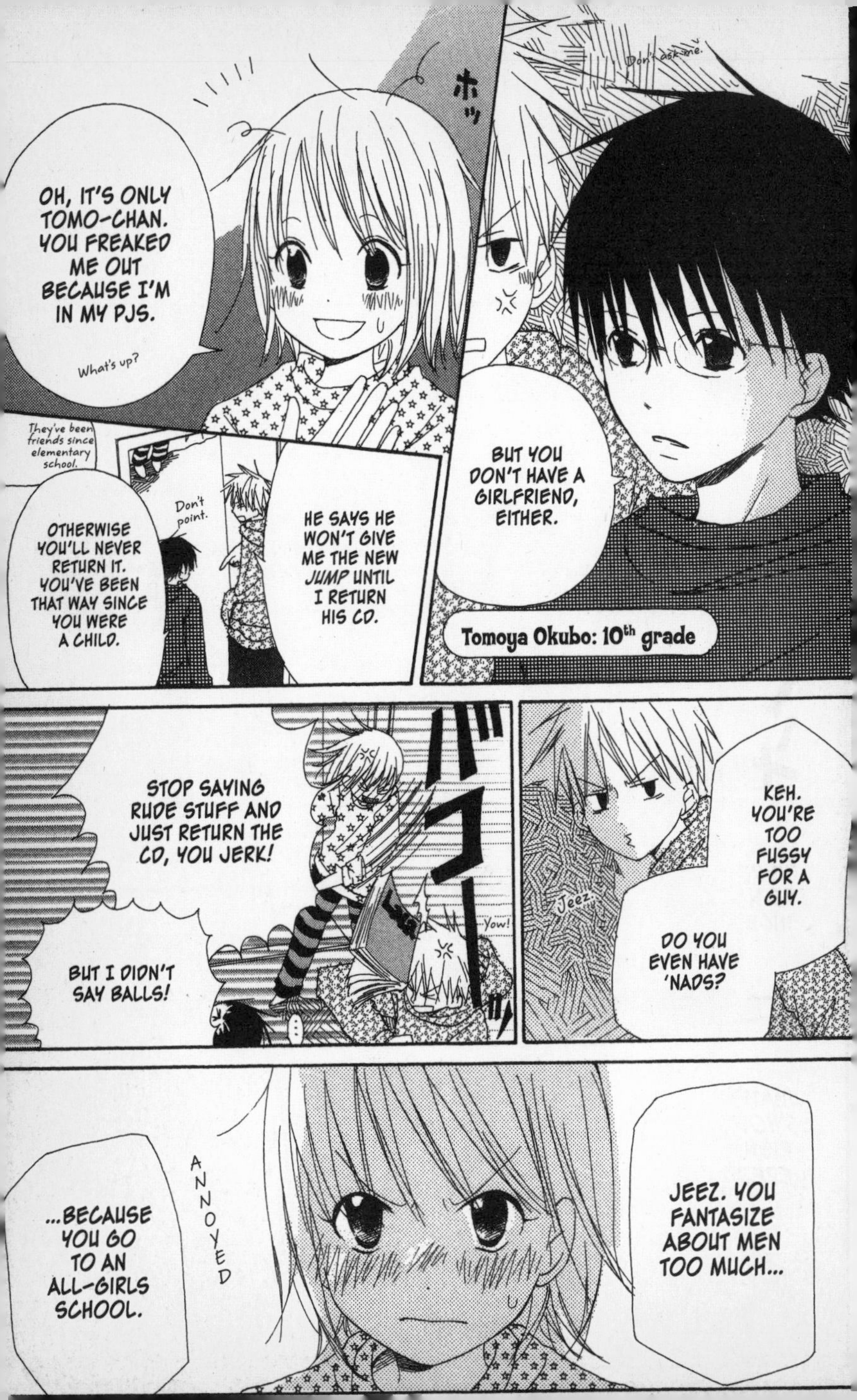
Don't ask me.
BUT YOU DON'T HAVE A GIRLFRIEND, EITHER.
Tomoya Okubo: 10th grade
ホッ
OH, IT'S ONLY TOMO-CHAN. YOU FREAKED ME OUT BECAUSE I'M IN MY PJS.
What's up?
HE SAYS HE WON'T GIVE ME THE NEW *JUMP* UNTIL I RETURN HIS CD.
They've been friends since elementary school.
Don't point.
OTHERWISE YOU'LL NEVER RETURN IT. YOU'VE BEEN THAT WAY SINCE YOU WERE A CHILD.
KEH. YOU'RE TOO FUSSY FOR A GUY.
Jeez.
DO YOU EVEN HAVE 'NADS?
STOP SAYING RUDE STUFF AND JUST RETURN THE CD, YOU JERK!
Yow!
BUT I DIDN'T SAY BALLS!
...
JEEZ. YOU FANTASIZE ABOUT MEN TOO MUCH...
ANNOYED
...BECAUSE YOU GO TO AN ALL-GIRLS SCHOOL.

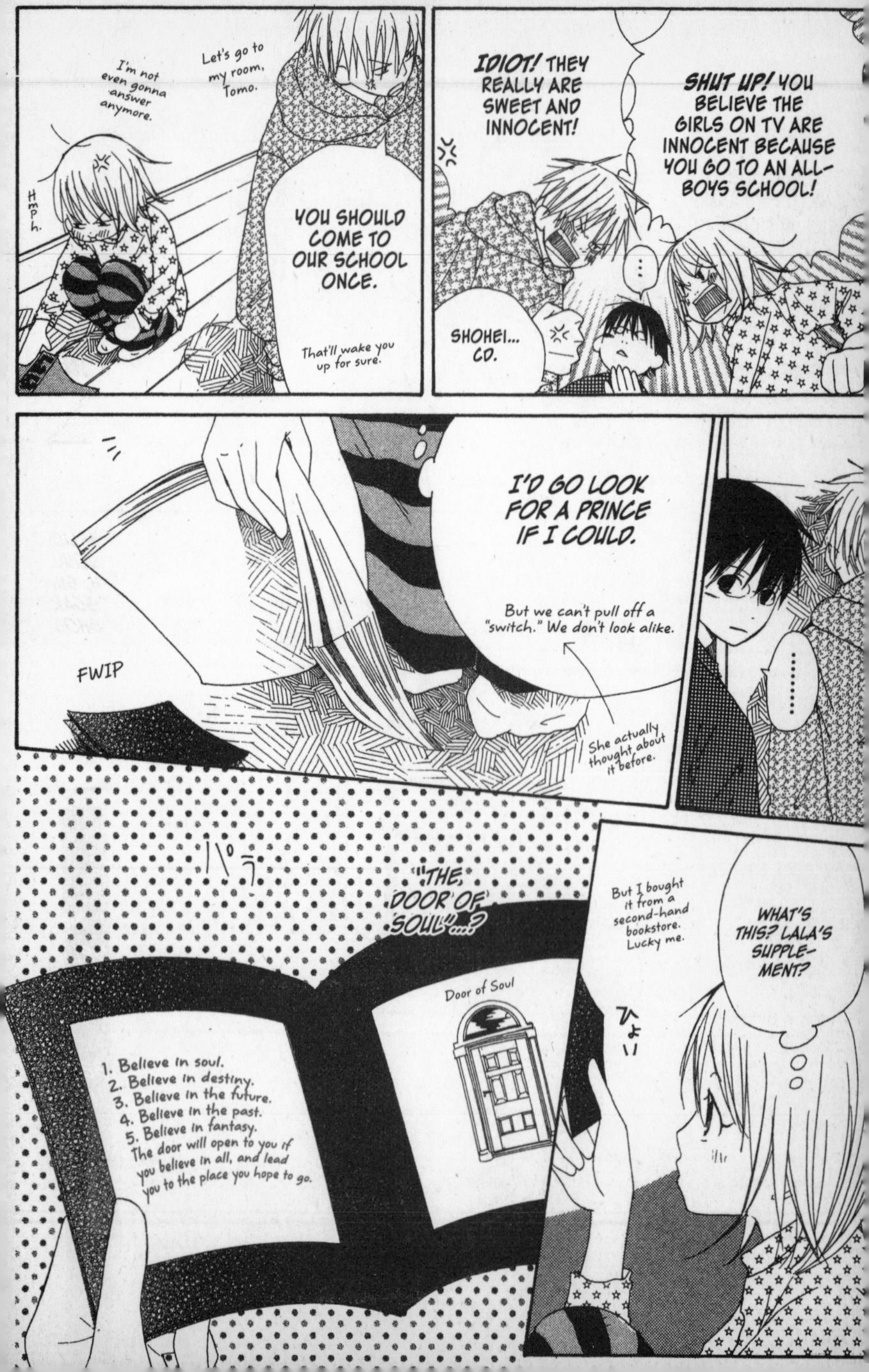
SHUT UP! YOU BELIEVE THE GIRLS ON TV ARE INNOCENT BECAUSE YOU GO TO AN ALL-BOYS SCHOOL!
IDIOT! THEY REALLY ARE SWEET AND INNOCENT!
...
SHOHEI... CO.
Let's go to my room, Tomo.
YOU SHOULD COME TO OUR SCHOOL ONCE.
That'll wake you up for sure.
I'm not even gonna answer anymore.
Hmph.
......
I'D GO LOOK FOR A PRINCE IF I COULD.
But we can't pull off a "switch." We don't look alike.
She actually thought about it before.
FWIP
WHAT'S THIS? LALA'S SUPPLEMENT?
But I bought it from a second-hand bookstore. Lucky me.
ひょい
パラ
"THE DOOR OF SOUL"...?
Door of Soul
1. Believe in soul.
2. Believe in destiny.
3. Believe in the future.
4. Believe in the past.
5. Believe in fantasy.
The door will open to you if you believe in all, and lead you to the place you hope to go.

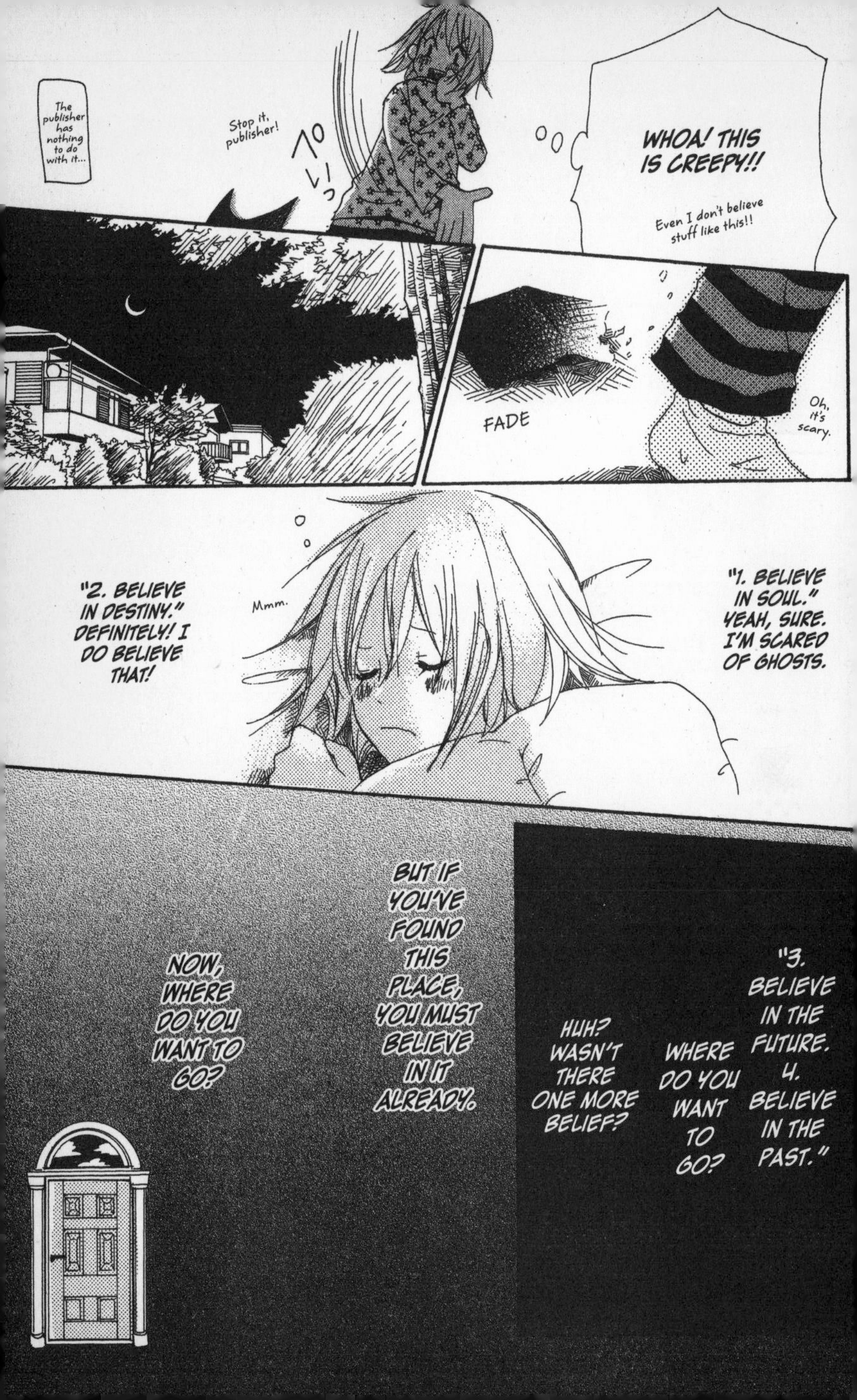
WHOA! THIS IS CREEPY!!
Even I don't believe stuff like this!!
Stop it, publisher!
The publisher has nothing to do with it...
Oh, it's scary.
FADE
"1. BELIEVE IN SOUL." YEAH, SURE. I'M SCARED OF GHOSTS.
Mmm.
"2. BELIEVE IN DESTINY." DEFINITELY! I DO BELIEVE THAT!
"3. BELIEVE IN THE FUTURE. 4. BELIEVE IN THE PAST."
WHERE DO YOU WANT TO GO?
HUH? WASN'T THERE ONE MORE BELIEF?
BUT IF YOU'VE FOUND THIS PLACE, YOU MUST BELIEVE IN IT ALREADY.
NOW, WHERE DO YOU WANT TO GO?

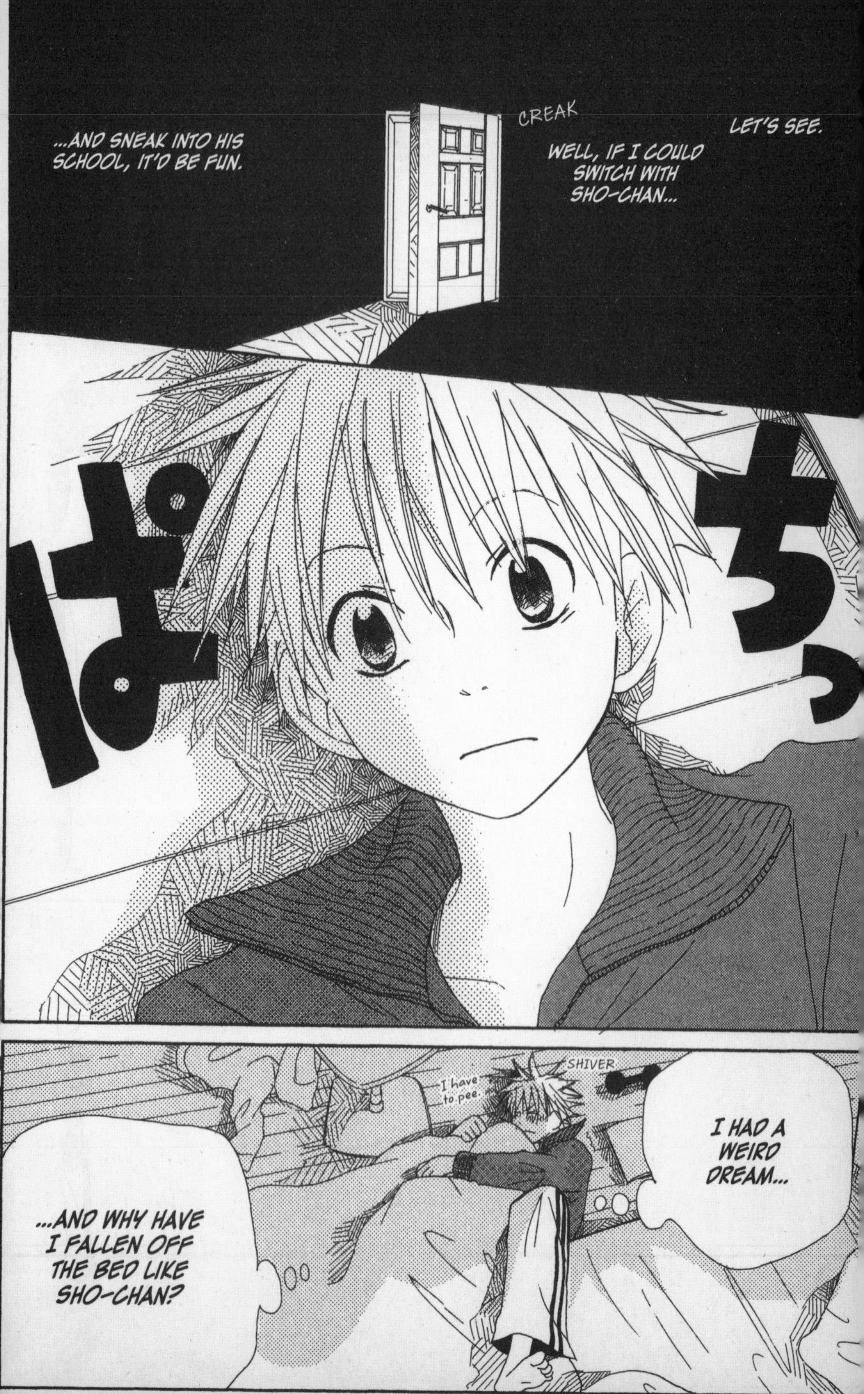
LET'S SEE.
WELL, IF I COULD SWITCH WITH SHO-CHAN...
CREAK
...AND SNEAK INTO HIS SCHOOL, IT'D BE FUN.
ぱちっ
I HAD A WEIRD DREAM...
SHIVER
I have to pee.
...AND WHY HAVE I FALLEN OFF THE BED LIKE SHO-CHAN?

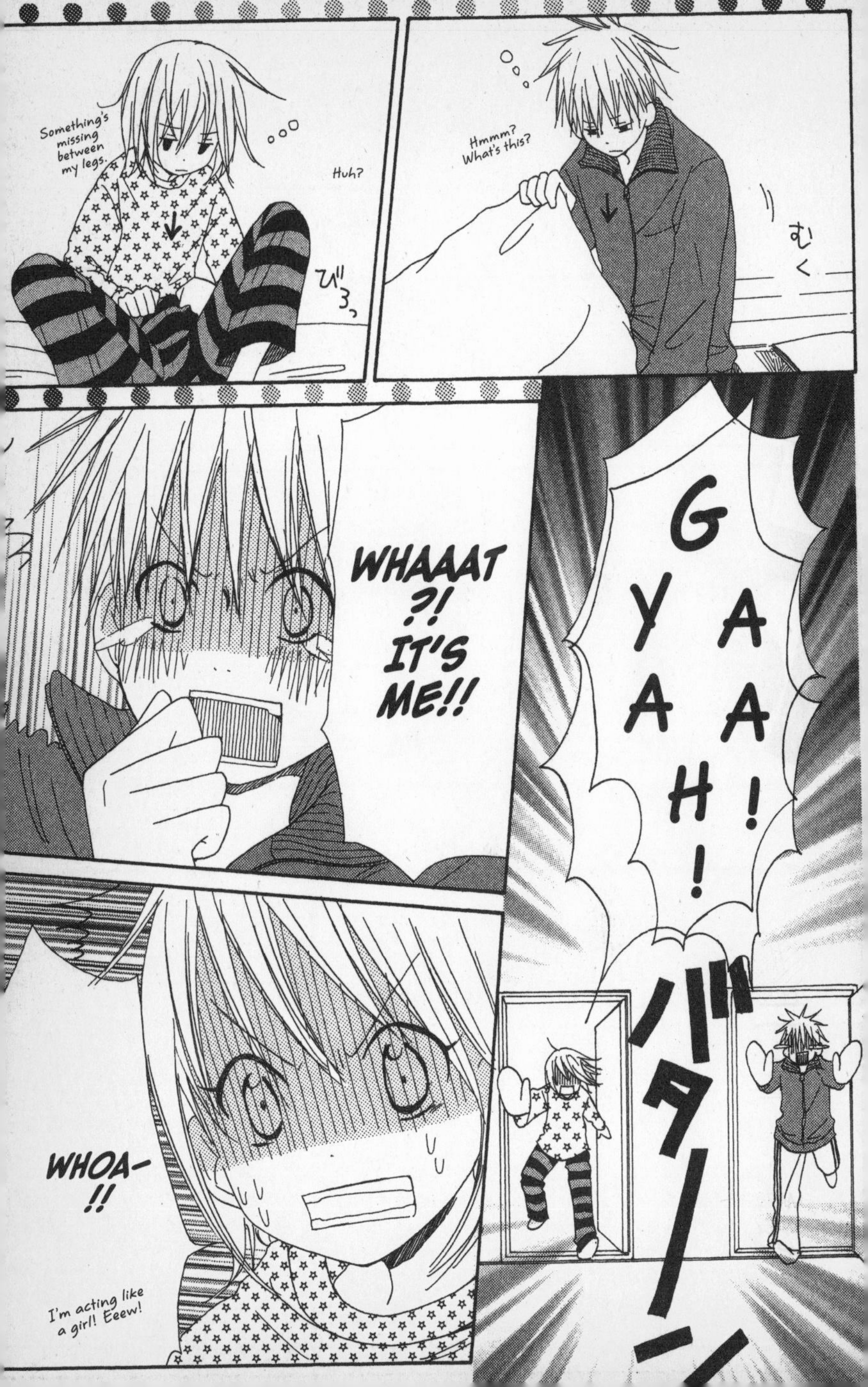
Hmmm? What's this?
むく
Something's missing between my legs.
Huh?
びろっ
GYAAAH!!
バタ—ン
WHAAAT?! IT'S ME!!
WHOA-!!
I'm acting like a girl! Eeew!

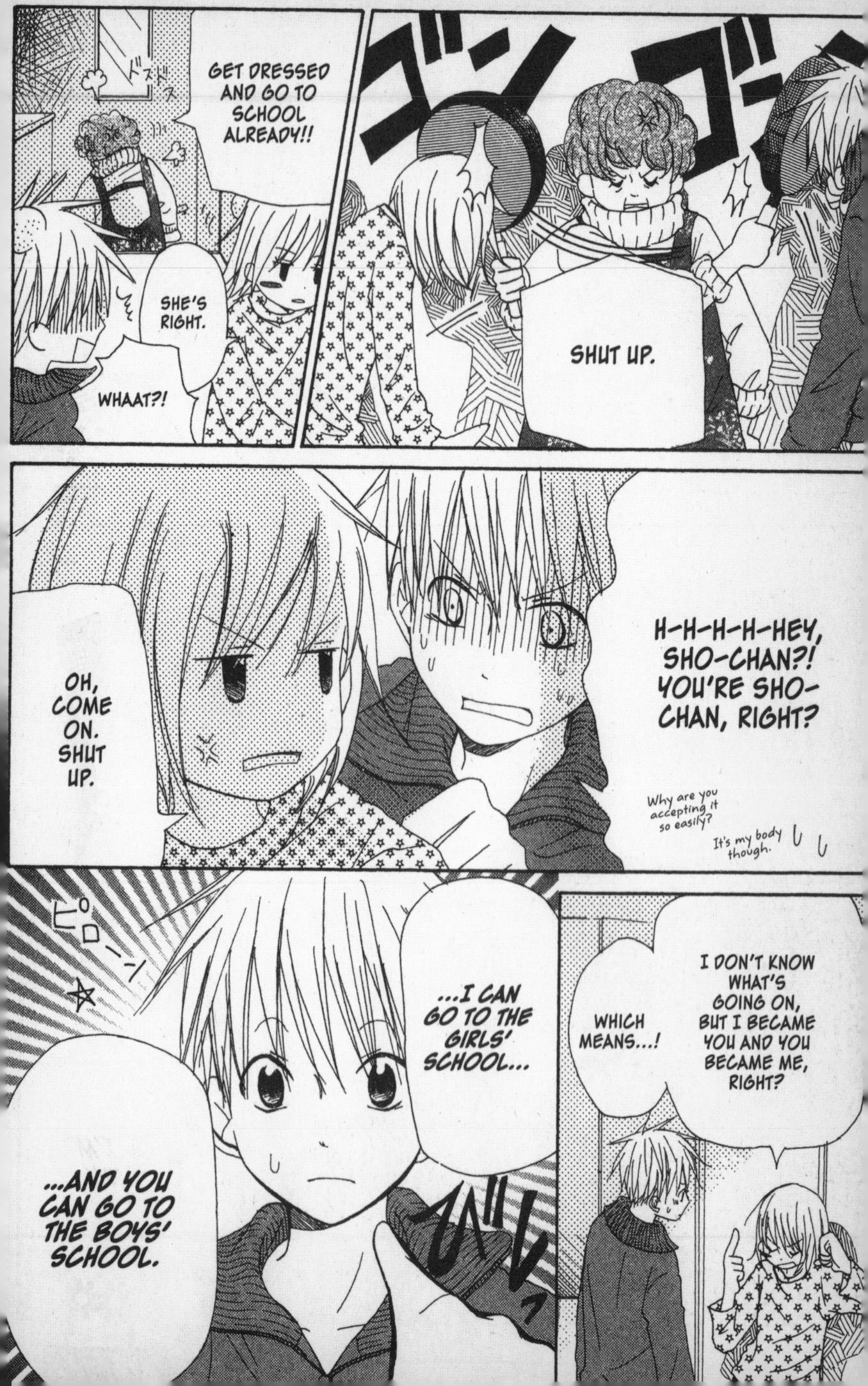
ゴン
ゴン
SHUT UP.
ドスドス
GET DRESSED AND GO TO SCHOOL ALREADY!!
SHE'S RIGHT.
WHAAT?!
H-H-H-H-HEY, SHO-CHAN?! YOU'RE SHO-CHAN, RIGHT?
It's my body though.
Why are you accepting it so easily?
OH, COME ON. SHUT UP.
I DON'T KNOW WHAT'S GOING ON, BUT I BECAME YOU AND YOU BECAME ME, RIGHT?
WHICH MEANS...!
...I CAN GO TO THE GIRLS' SCHOOL...
...AND YOU CAN GO TO THE BOYS' SCHOOL.

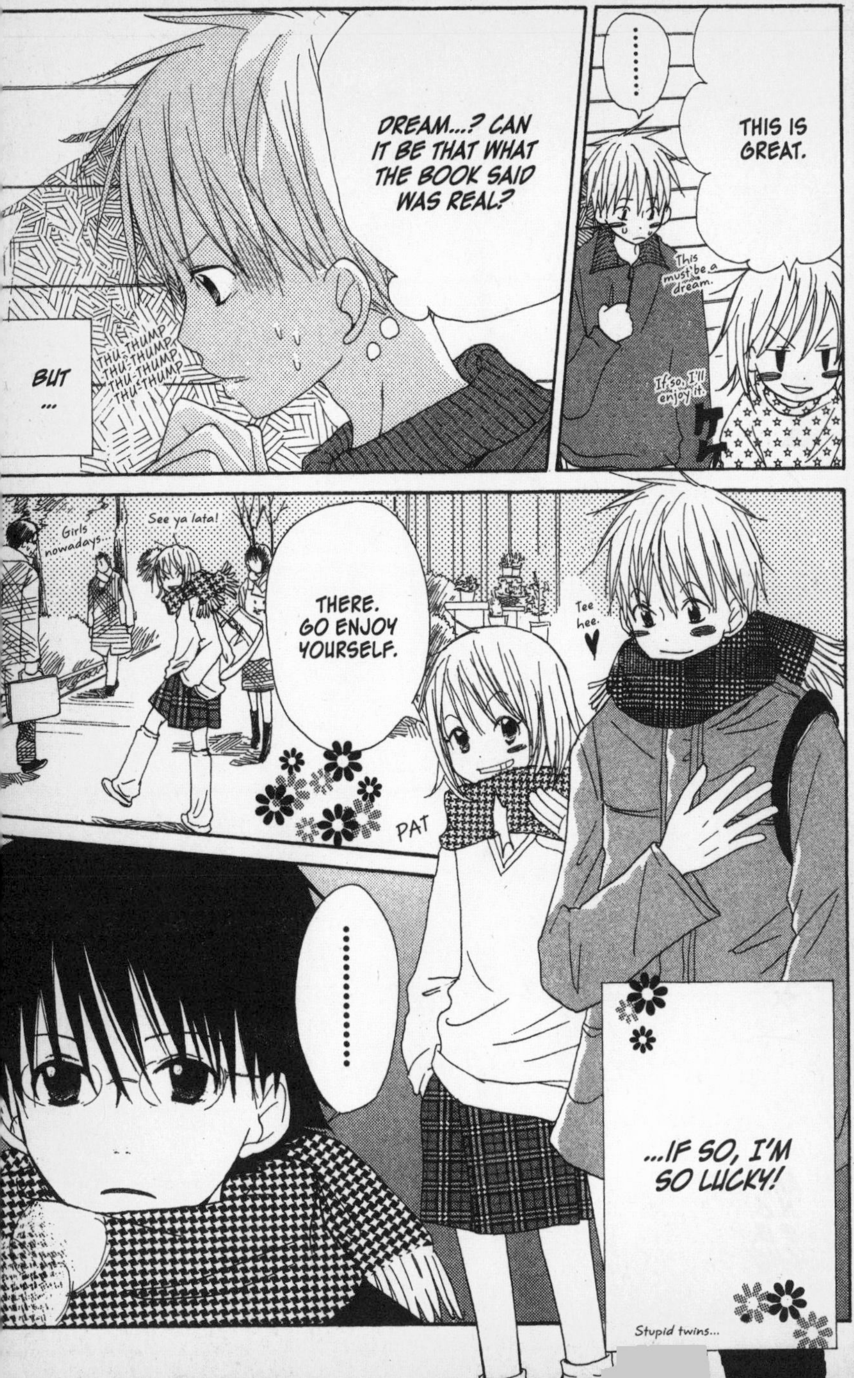
......
THIS IS GREAT.
This must be a dream.
If so, I'll enjoy it.
DREAM...? CAN IT BE THAT WHAT THE BOOK SAID WAS REAL?
THU-THUMP THU-THUMP THU-THUMP THU-THUMP
BUT ...
Tee hee.
THERE. GO ENJOY YOURSELF.
PAT
See ya lata!
Girls nowadays...
...IF SO, I'M SO LUCKY!
Stupid twins...
......

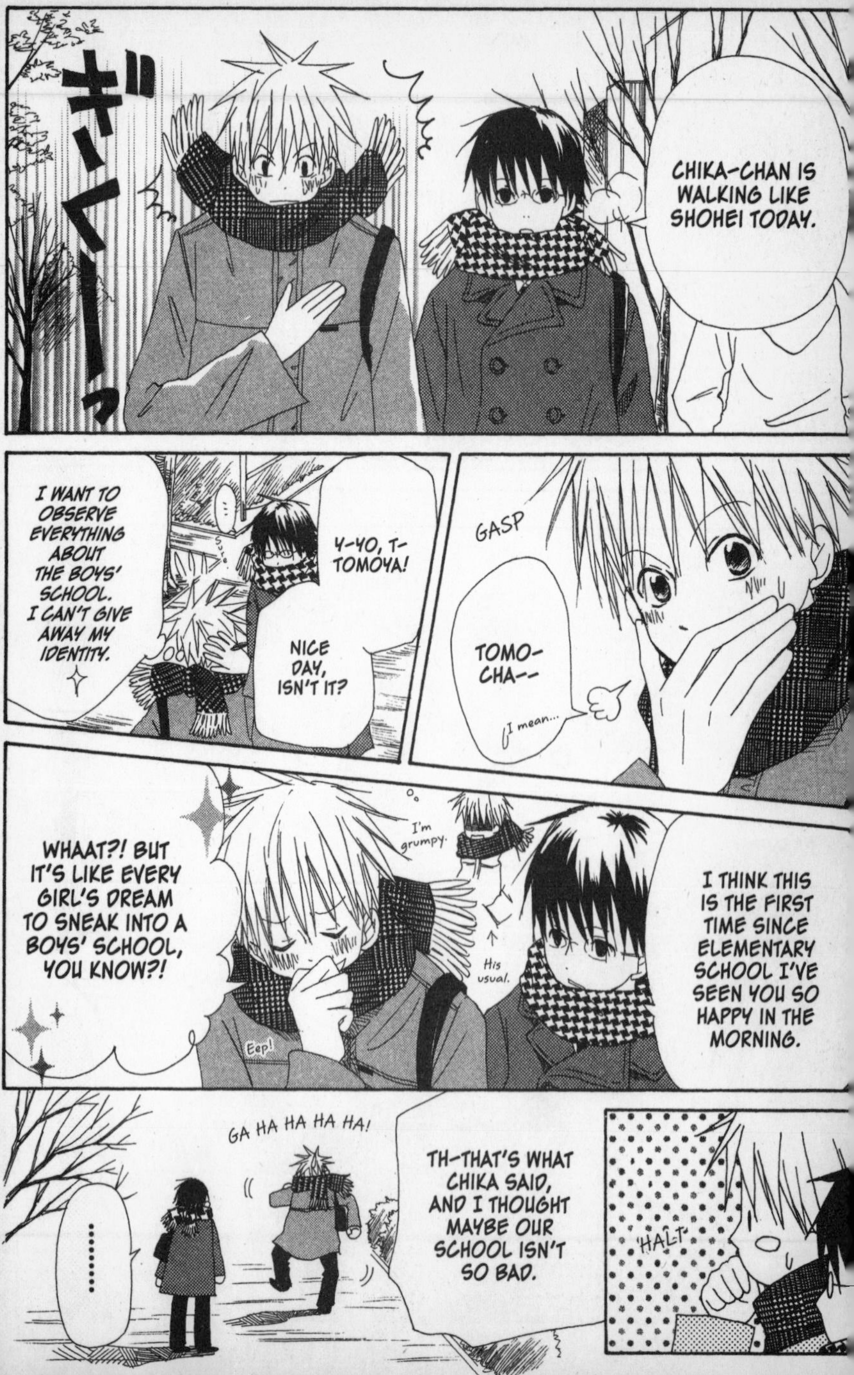
CHIKA-CHAN IS WALKING LIKE SHOHEI TODAY.
GASP
TOMO-CHA--
I mean...
I WANT TO OBSERVE EVERYTHING ABOUT THE BOYS' SCHOOL. I CAN'T GIVE AWAY MY IDENTITY.
...
Sure.
Y-YO, T-TOMOYA!
NICE DAY, ISN'T IT?
I THINK THIS IS THE FIRST TIME SINCE ELEMENTARY SCHOOL I'VE SEEN YOU SO HAPPY IN THE MORNING.
His usual.
I'm grumpy.
WHAAT?! BUT IT'S LIKE EVERY GIRL'S DREAM TO SNEAK INTO A BOYS' SCHOOL, YOU KNOW?!
Eep!
HALT
TH-THAT'S WHAT CHIKA SAID, AND I THOUGHT MAYBE OUR SCHOOL ISN'T SO BAD.
GA HA HA HA HA!
....

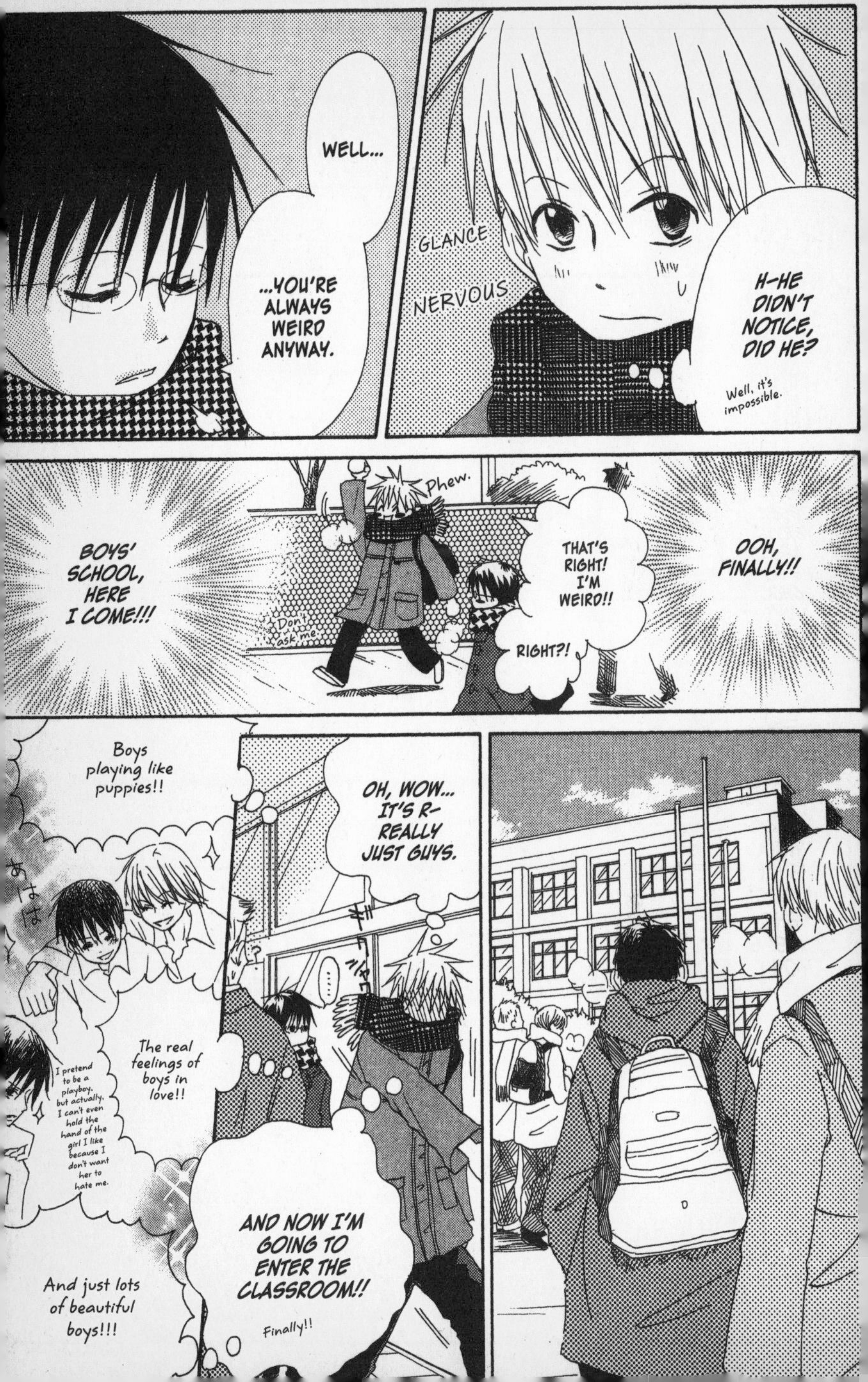
H-HE DIDN'T NOTICE, DID HE?
Well, it's impossible.
GLANCE
NERVOUS
WELL...
...YOU'RE ALWAYS WEIRD ANYWAY.
OOH, FINALLY!!
THAT'S RIGHT! I'M WEIRD!!
RIGHT?!
Phew.
Don't ask me
BOYS' SCHOOL, HERE I COME!!!
OH, WOW... IT'S R-REALLY JUST GUYS.
AND NOW I'M GOING TO ENTER THE CLASSROOM!!
Finally!!
Boys playing like puppies!!
あはは
The real feelings of boys in love!!
I pretend to be a playboy, but actually, I can't even hold the hand of the girl I like because I don't want her to hate me.
And just lots of beautiful boys!!!

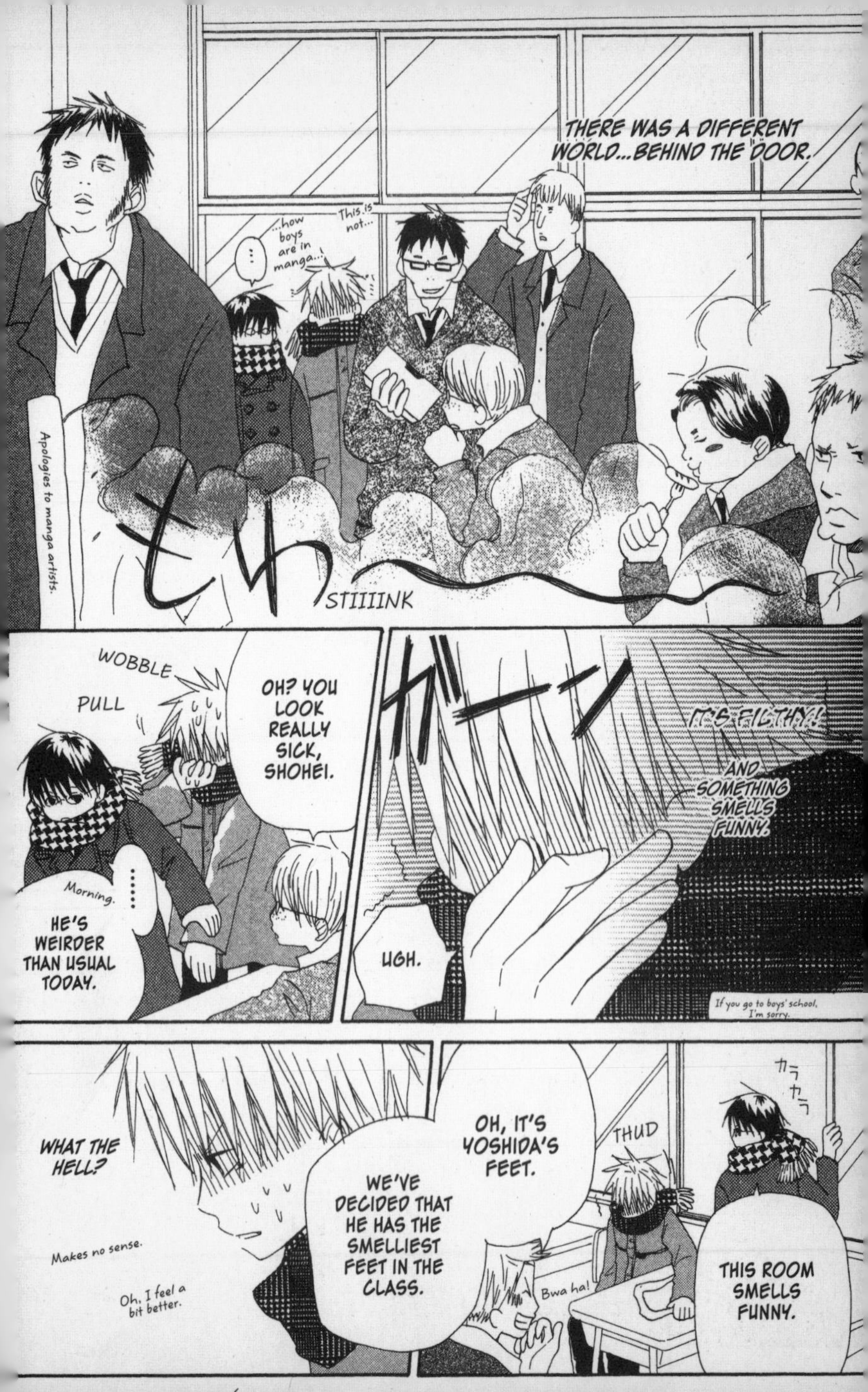
THERE WAS A DIFFERENT WORLD...BEHIND THE DOOR.
This is not...
...how boys are in manga...!
...
Apologies to manga artists.
もわ
STIIIINK
ガーン
IT'S FILTHY!
AND SOMETHING SMELLS FUNNY.
UGH.
If you go to boys' school, I'm sorry.
OH? YOU LOOK REALLY SICK, SHOHEI.
WOBBLE
PULL
......
Morning.
HE'S WEIRDER THAN USUAL TODAY.
カラ カラ
THIS ROOM SMELLS FUNNY.
THUD
OH, IT'S YOSHIDA'S FEET.
WE'VE DECIDED THAT HE HAS THE SMELLIEST FEET IN THE CLASS.
Bwa ha!
WHAT THE HELL?
Makes no sense.
Oh, I feel a bit better.

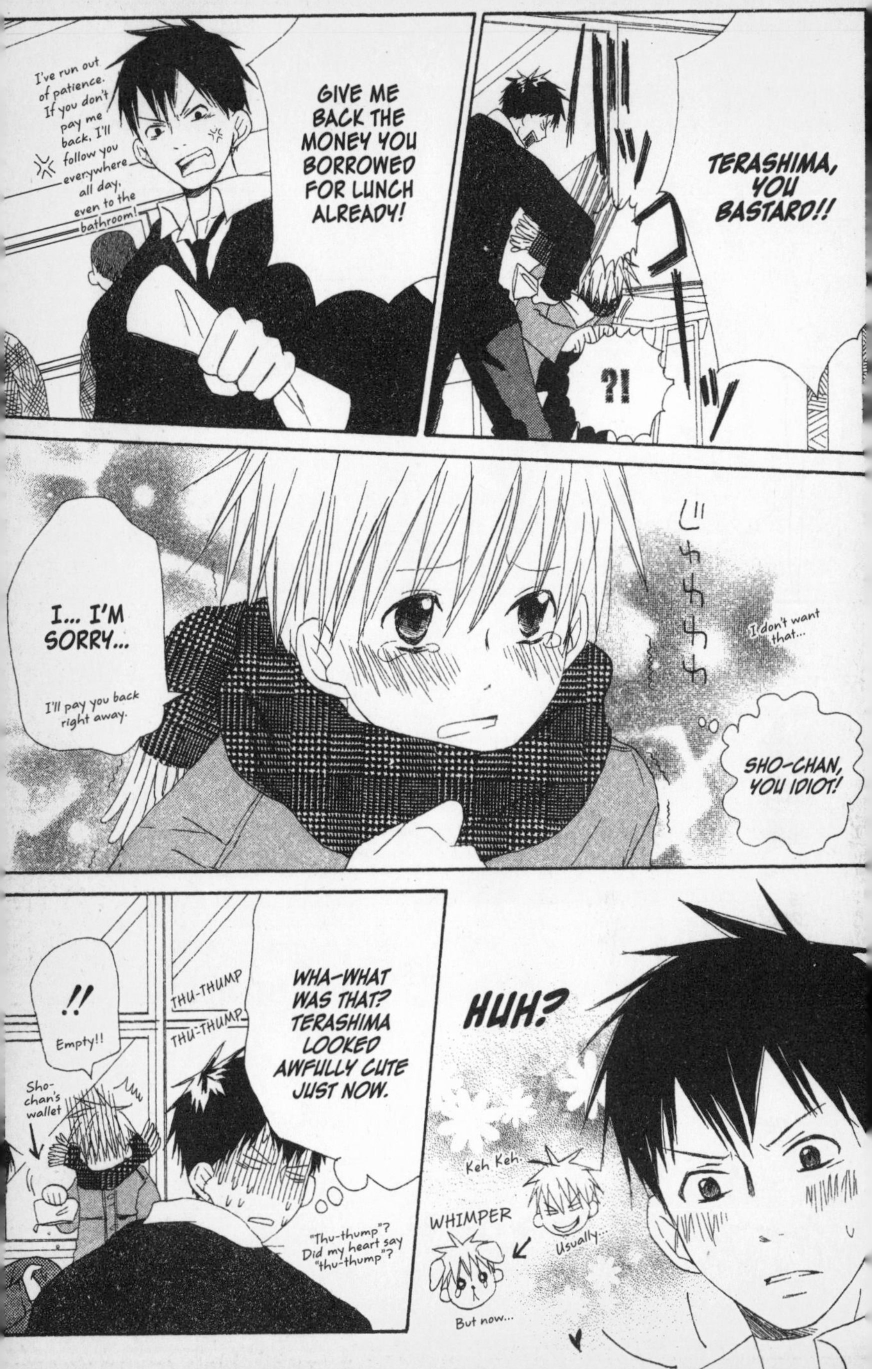
TERASHIMA, YOU BASTARD!!
?!
GIVE ME BACK THE MONEY YOU BORROWED FOR LUNCH ALREADY!
I've run out of patience. If you don't pay me back, I'll follow you everywhere all day, even to the bathroom!
I don't want that...
SHO-CHAN, YOU IDIOT!
I... I'M SORRY...
I'll pay you back right away.
HUH?
Keh Keh.
Usually...
WHIMPER
But now...
WHA-WHAT WAS THAT? TERASHIMA LOOKED AWFULLY CUTE JUST NOW.
THU-THUMP
THU-THUMP
"Thu-thump"? Did my heart say "thu-thump"?
!!
Empty!!
Sho-chan's wallet

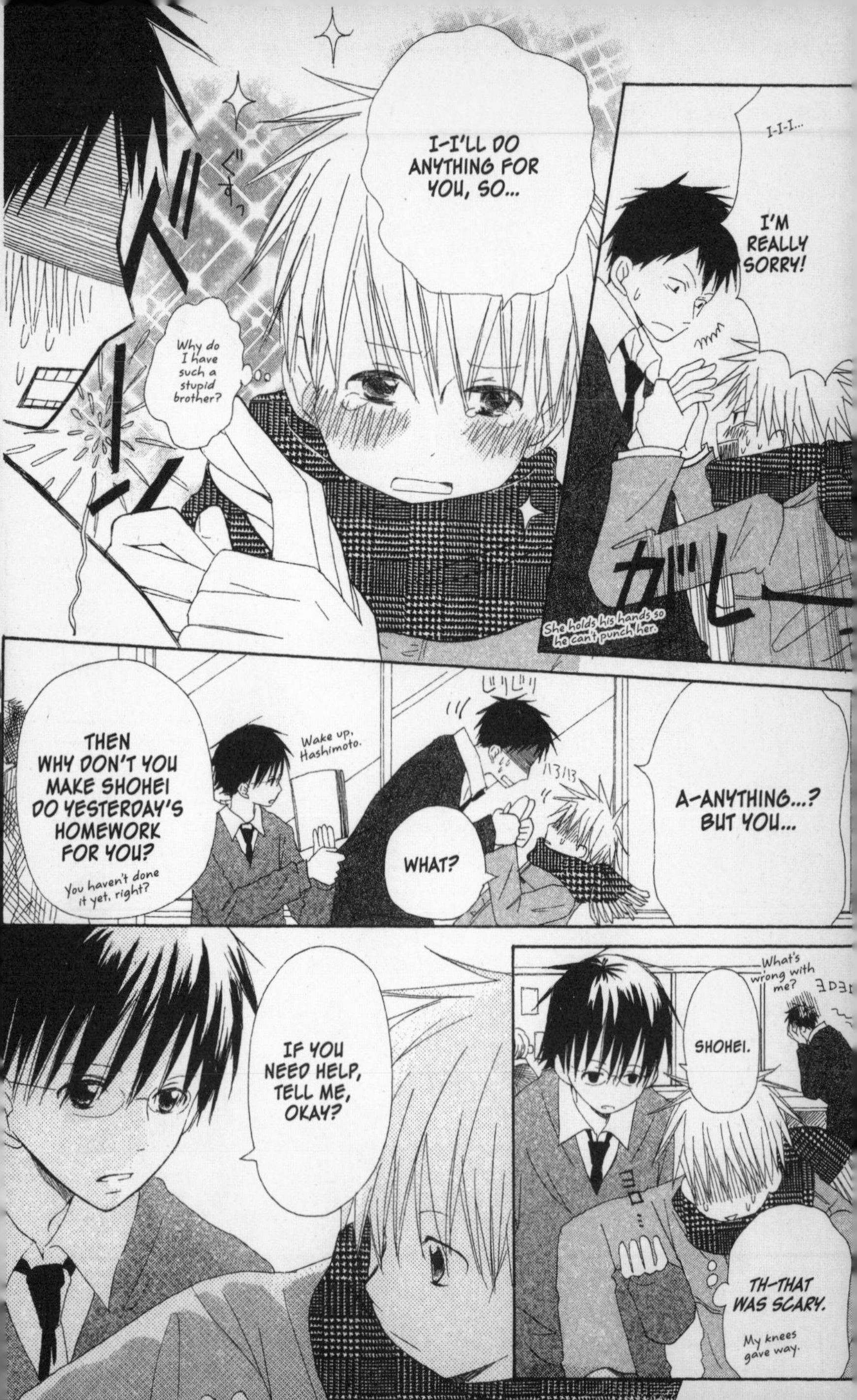

I-I-I...
I'M REALLY SORRY!
She holds his hands so he can't punch her.
I-I'LL DO ANYTHING FOR YOU, SO...
Why do I have such a stupid brother?
A-ANYTHING...? BUT YOU...
WHAT?
Wake up, Hashimoto.
THEN WHY DON'T YOU MAKE SHOHEI DO YESTERDAY'S HOMEWORK FOR YOU?
You haven't done it yet, right?
What's wrong with me?
SHOHEI.
TH-THAT WAS SCARY.
My knees gave way.
IF YOU NEED HELP, TELL ME, OKAY?

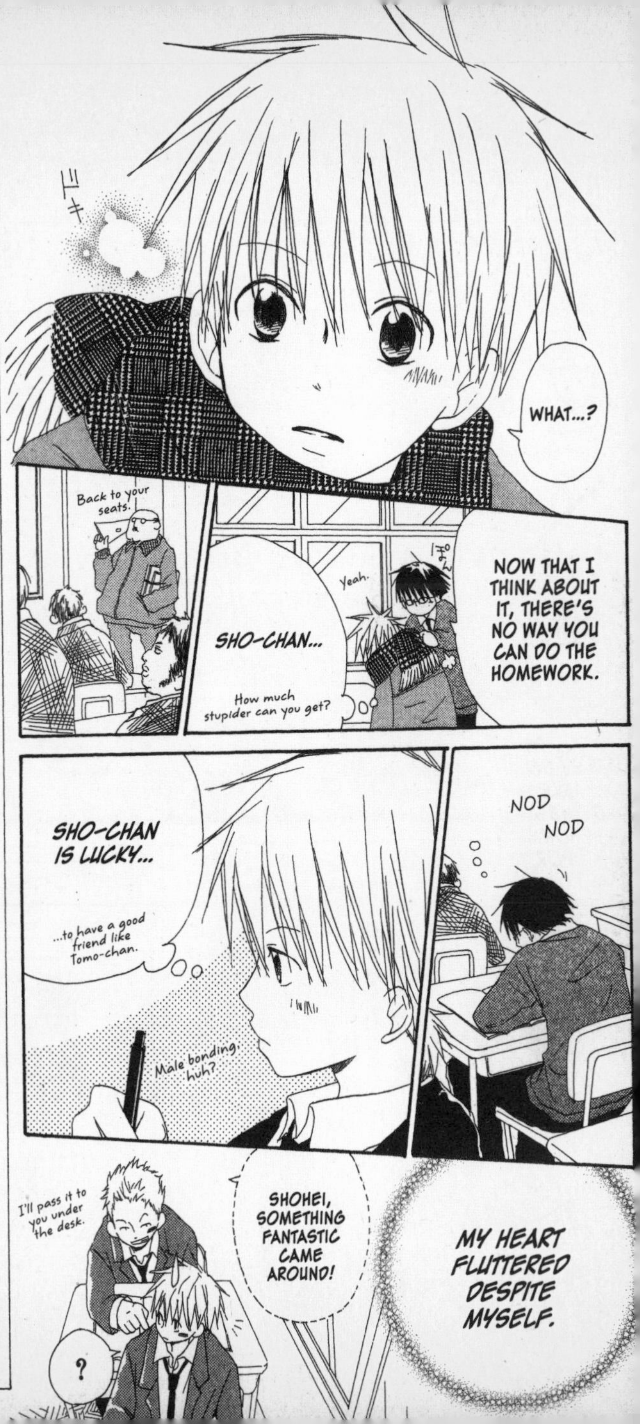
WHAT...?
NOW THAT I THINK ABOUT IT, THERE'S NO WAY YOU CAN DO THE HOMEWORK.
Yeah.
SHO-CHAN...
How much stupider can you get?
Back to your seats.
NOD
NOD
SHO-CHAN IS LUCKY...
...to have a good friend like Tomo-chan.
Male bonding, huh?
MY HEART FLUTTERED DESPITE MYSELF.
SHOHEI, SOMETHING FANTASTIC CAME AROUND!
I'll pass it to you under the desk.
?

☆6☆

This is the last column. My parents liked this short story! (So embarrassing!) They liked it because it's a fantasy like Doraemon. (Seriously, it's embarrassing!!) People who don't usually read manga, like my parents, relatives and friends, buy my manga and read it. It's embarrassing to death but I'm happy to death at the same time. Of course, I most appreciate you fans who picked up this book. Hope to see you again.

Hari Tokeino

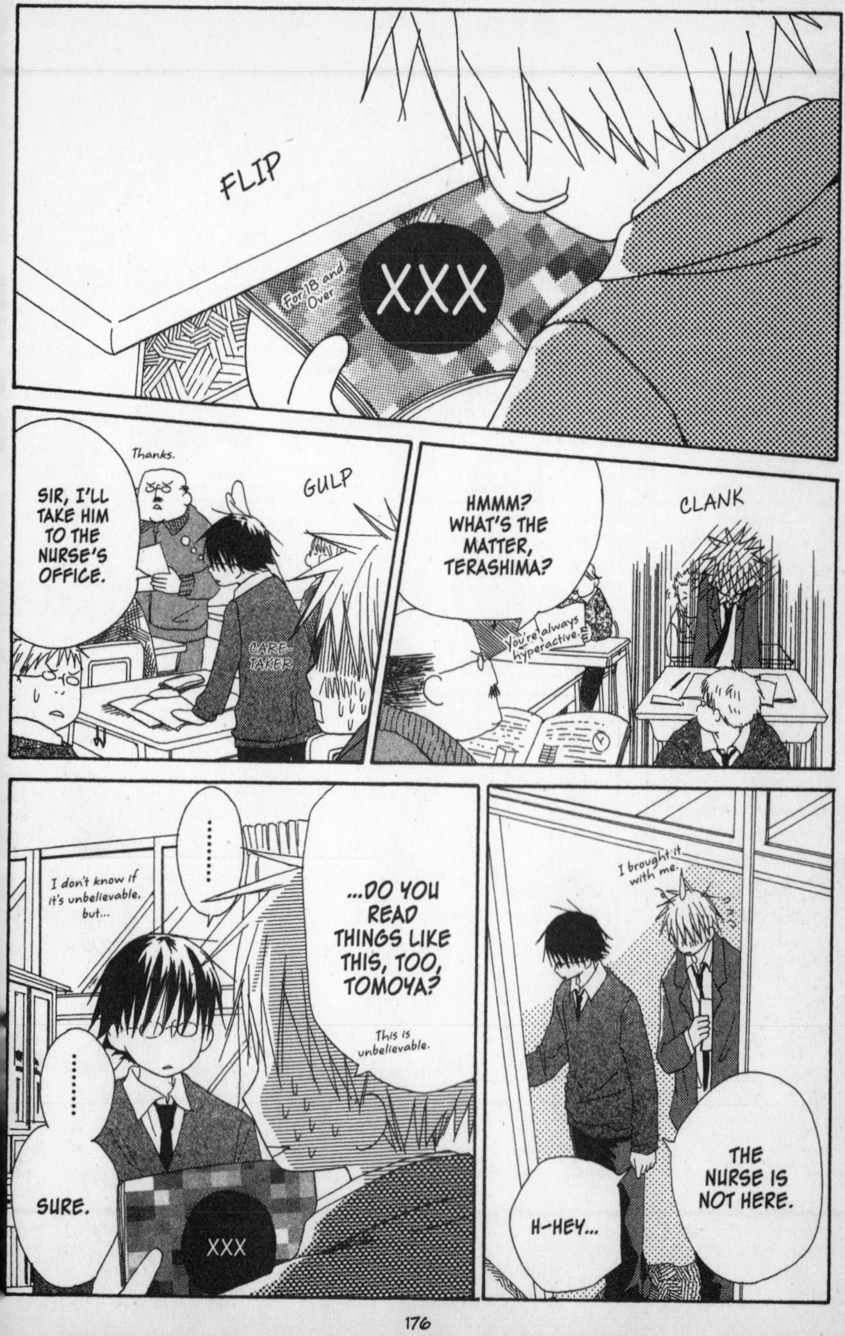
FLIP
For 18 and Over
XXX
CLANK
HMMM? WHAT'S THE MATTER, TERASHIMA?
You're always hyperactive.
GULP
Thanks.
SIR, I'LL TAKE HIM TO THE NURSE'S OFFICE.
CARE-TAKER
I brought it with me.
THE NURSE IS NOT HERE.
H-HEY...
......
...DO YOU READ THINGS LIKE THIS, TOO, TOMOYA?
This is unbelievable.
I don't know if it's unbelievable, but...
......
SURE.
XXX

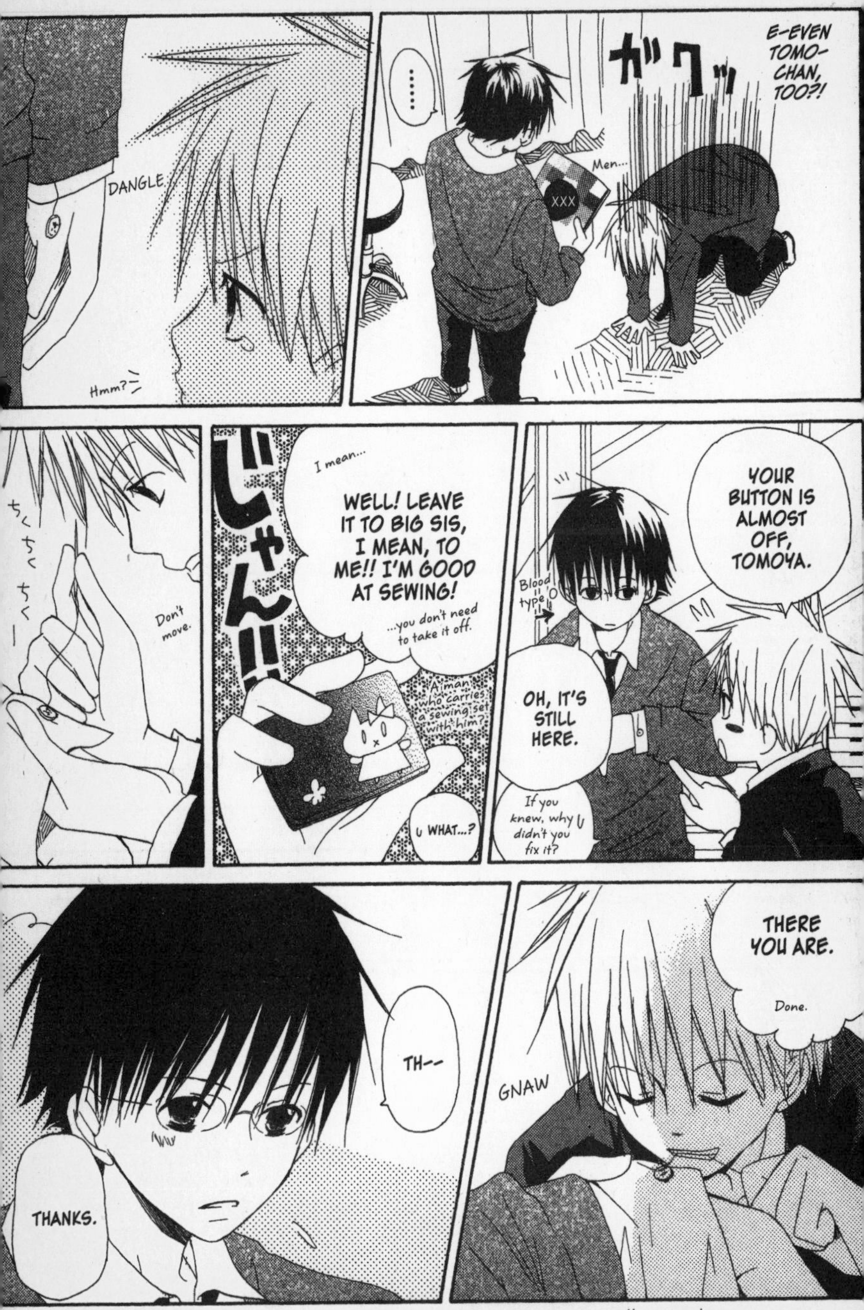
E-EVEN TOMO-CHAN, TOO?!
ガクッ
Men...
......
DANGLE
Hmm?
YOUR BUTTON IS ALMOST OFF, TOMOYA.
Blood type 'O'
OH, IT'S STILL HERE.
If you knew, why didn't you fix it?
じゃん!!
I mean...
WELL! LEAVE IT TO BIG SIS, I MEAN, TO ME!! I'M GOOD AT SEWING!
...you don't need to take it off.
A man who carries a sewing set with him?
WHAT...?
ちくちく ちく
Don't move.
THERE YOU ARE.
Done.
GNAW
TH--
THANKS.

Use scissors!

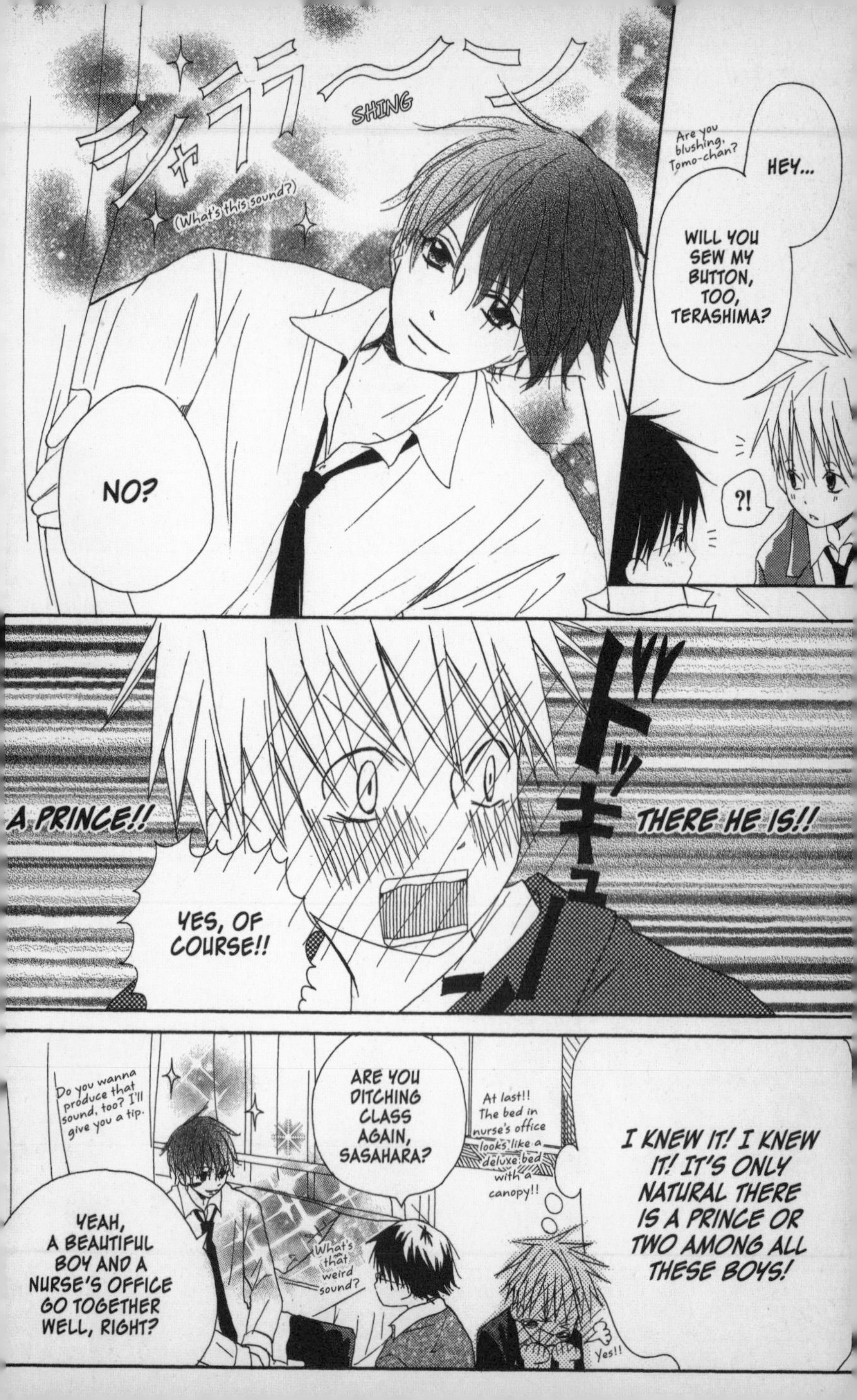
HEY...
WILL YOU SEW MY BUTTON, TOO, TERASHIMA?
Are you blushing, Tomo-chan?
?!
ジャラ〜〜〜ン
SHING
(What's this sound?)
NO?
THERE HE IS!!
ドッキューン
A PRINCE!!
YES, OF COURSE!!
I KNEW IT! I KNEW IT! IT'S ONLY NATURAL THERE IS A PRINCE OR TWO AMONG ALL THESE BOYS!
At last!! The bed in nurse's office looks like a deluxe bed with a canopy!!
Yes!!
ARE YOU DITCHING CLASS AGAIN, SASAHARA?
What's that weird sound?
Do you wanna produce that sound, too? I'll give you a tip.
YEAH, A BEAUTIFUL BOY AND A NURSE'S OFFICE GO TOGETHER WELL, RIGHT?

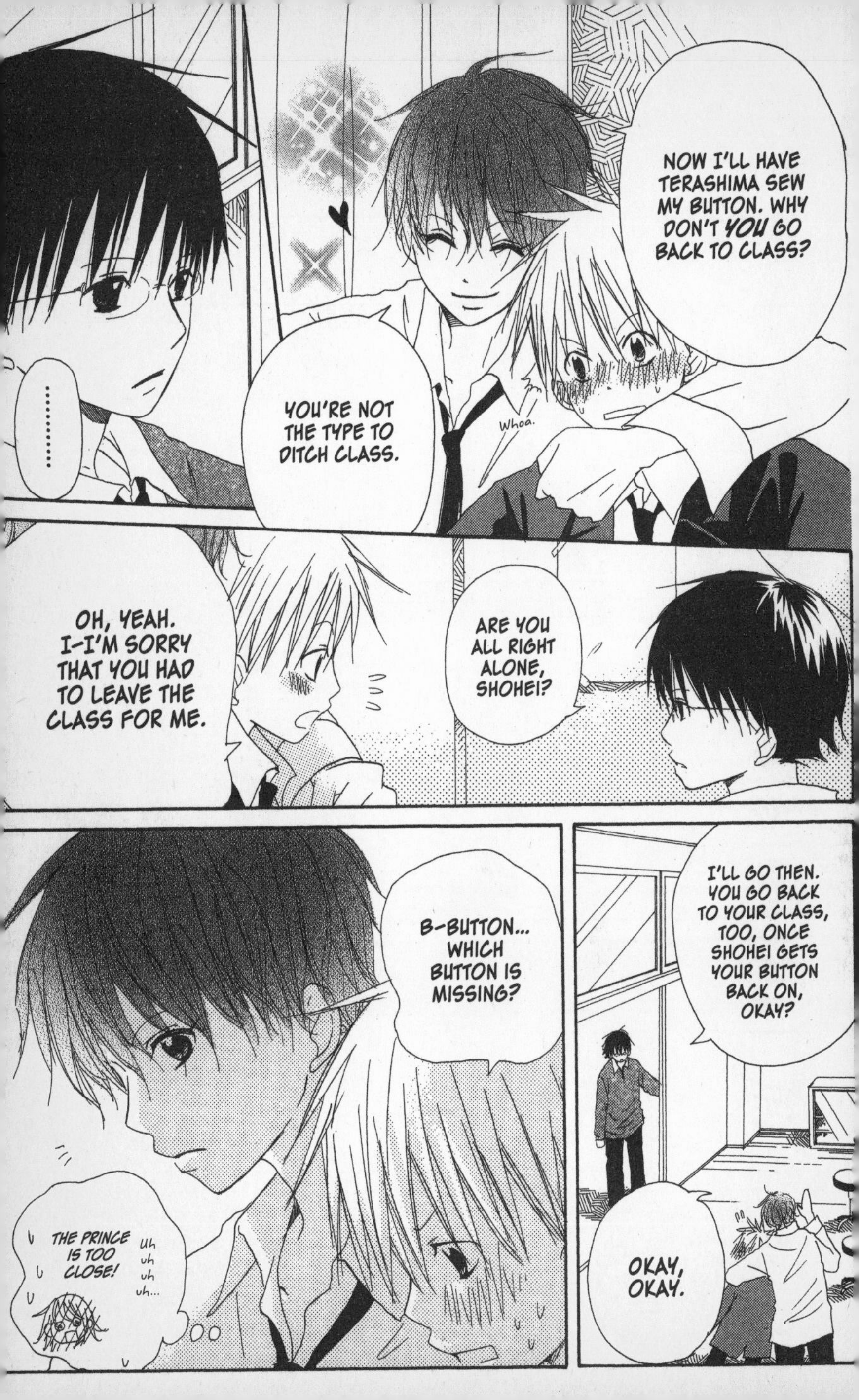
NOW I'LL HAVE TERASHIMA SEW MY BUTTON. WHY DON'T *YOU* GO BACK TO CLASS?
Whoa.
YOU'RE NOT THE TYPE TO DITCH CLASS.
....
ARE YOU ALL RIGHT ALONE, SHOHEI?
OH, YEAH. I-I'M SORRY THAT YOU HAD TO LEAVE THE CLASS FOR ME.
I'LL GO THEN. YOU GO BACK TO YOUR CLASS, TOO, ONCE SHOHEI GETS YOUR BUTTON BACK ON, OKAY?
OKAY, OKAY.
B-BUTTON... WHICH BUTTON IS MISSING?
THE PRINCE IS TOO CLOSE!
uh uh uh uh...

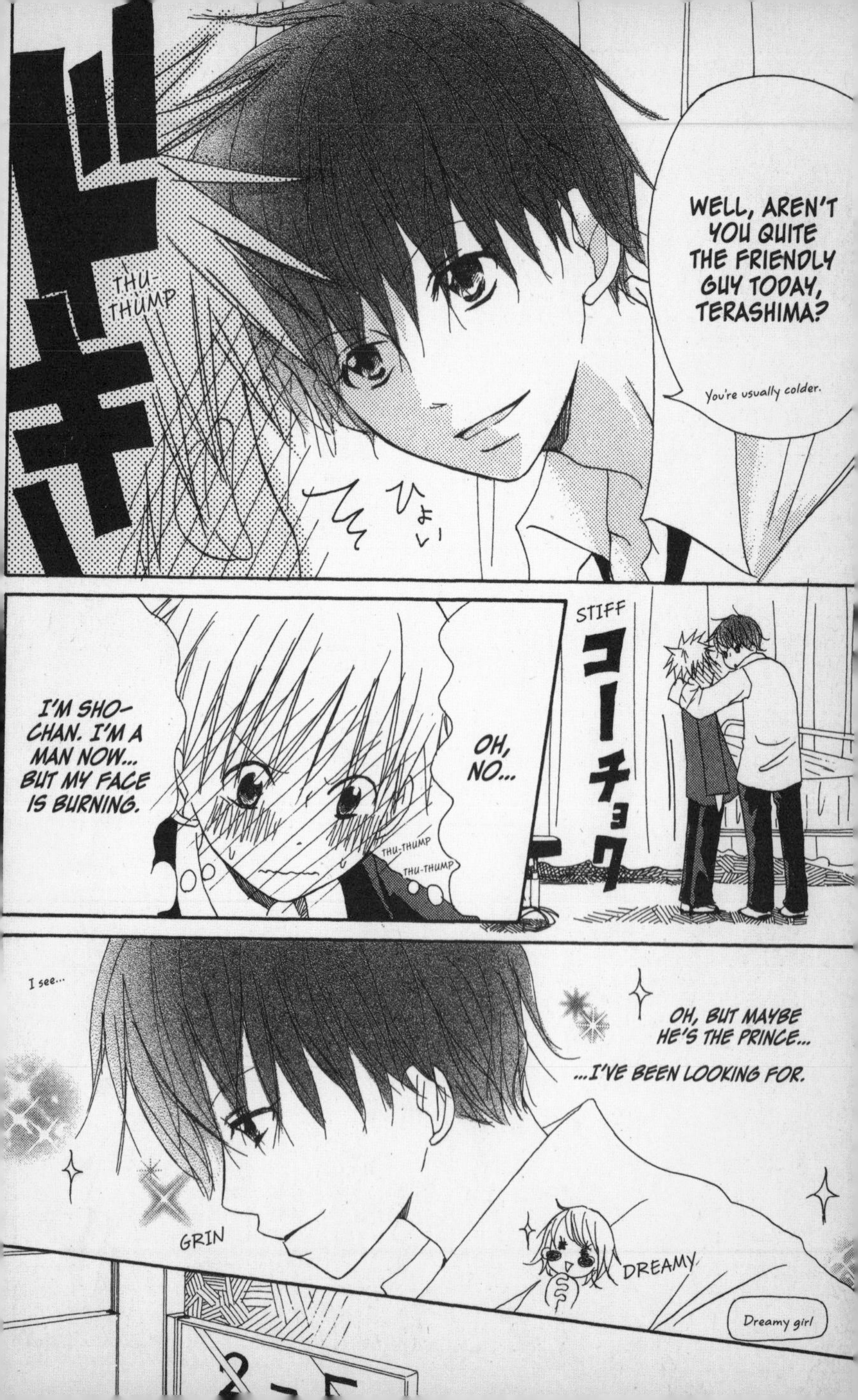
WELL, AREN'T YOU QUITE THE FRIENDLY GUY TODAY, TERASHIMA?
You're usually colder.
ドキッ
THU-THUMP
ひょい
STIFF
コーチョク
OH, NO...
I'M SHO-CHAN. I'M A MAN NOW... BUT MY FACE IS BURNING.
THU-THUMP
THU-THUMP
OH, BUT MAYBE HE'S THE PRINCE...
...I'VE BEEN LOOKING FOR.
I see...
GRIN
DREAMY
Dreamy girl

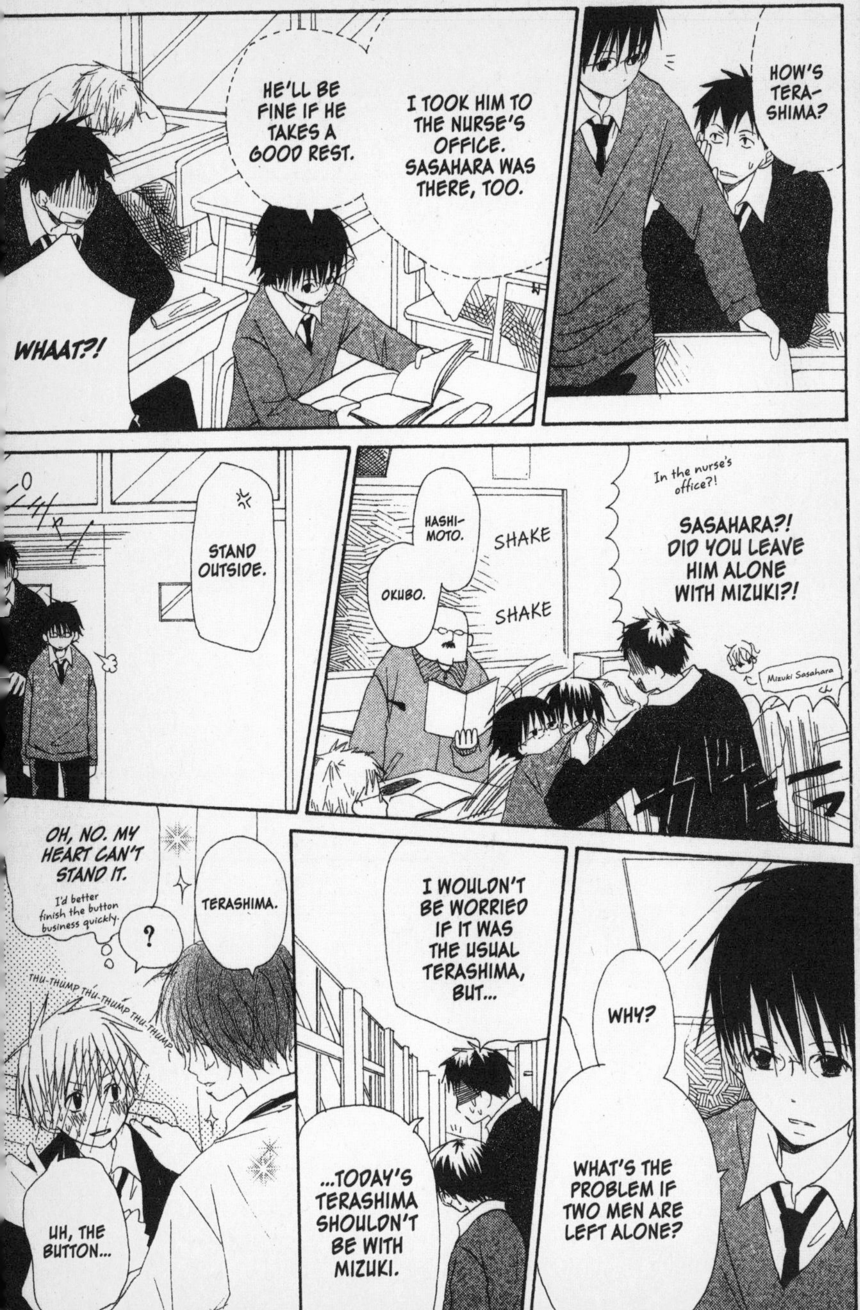
HOW'S TERA-SHIMA?
I TOOK HIM TO THE NURSE'S OFFICE. SASAHARA WAS THERE, TOO.
HE'LL BE FINE IF HE TAKES A GOOD REST.
WHAAT?!
In the nurse's office?!
SASAHARA?! DID YOU LEAVE HIM ALONE WITH MIZUKI?!
Mizuki Sasahara
SHAKE
HASHI-MOTO.
SHAKE
OKUBO.
STAND OUTSIDE.
WHY?
WHAT'S THE PROBLEM IF TWO MEN ARE LEFT ALONE?
I WOULDN'T BE WORRIED IF IT WAS THE USUAL TERASHIMA, BUT...
...TODAY'S TERASHIMA SHOULDN'T BE WITH MIZUKI.
TERASHIMA.
OH, NO. MY HEART CAN'T STAND IT.
I'd better finish the button business quickly.
?
THU-THUMP THU-THUMP THU-THUMP
UH, THE BUTTON...

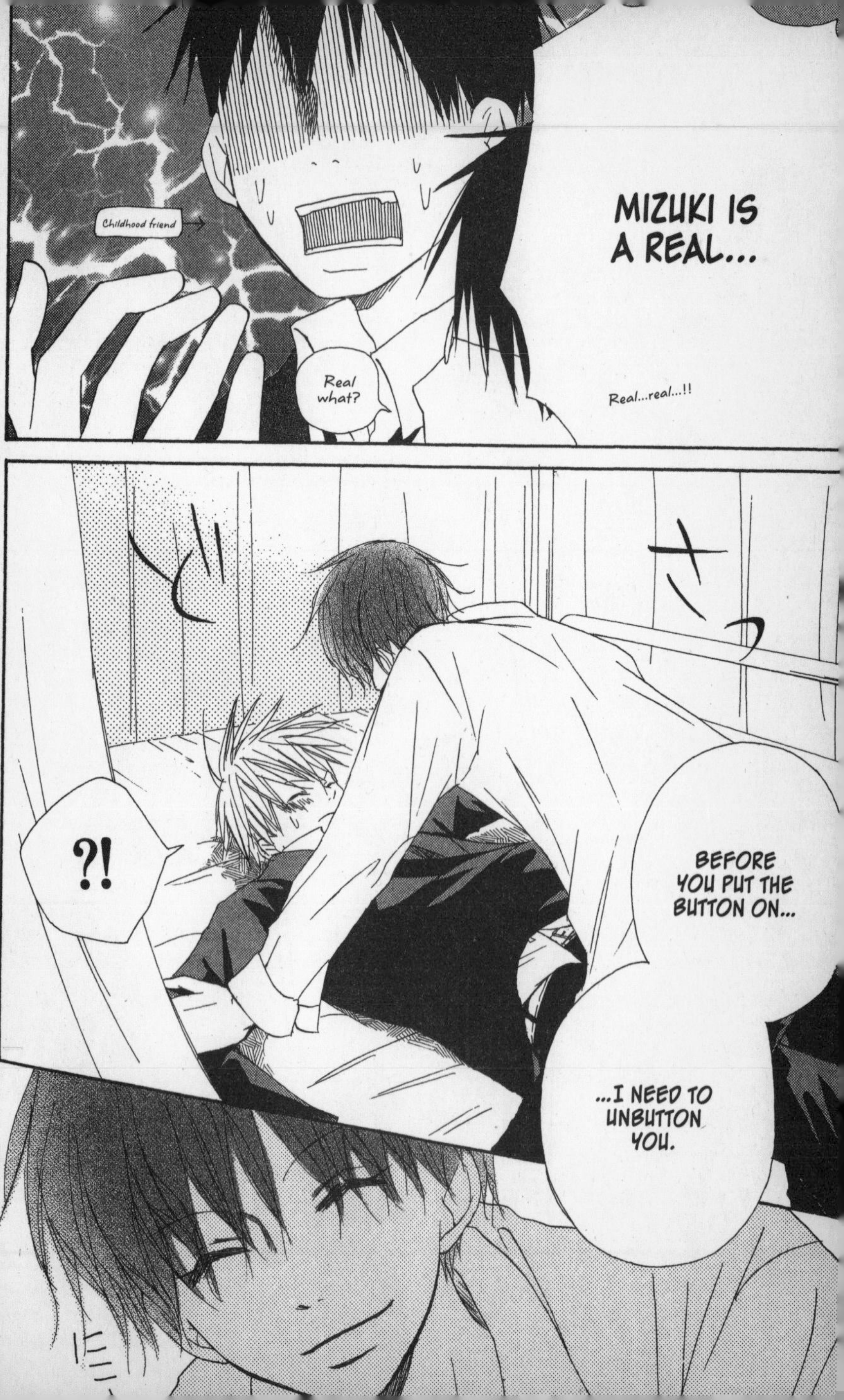

MIZUKI IS A REAL...
Real...real...!!
Real what?
Childhood friend
BEFORE YOU PUT THE BUTTON ON...
?!
...I NEED TO UNBUTTON YOU.

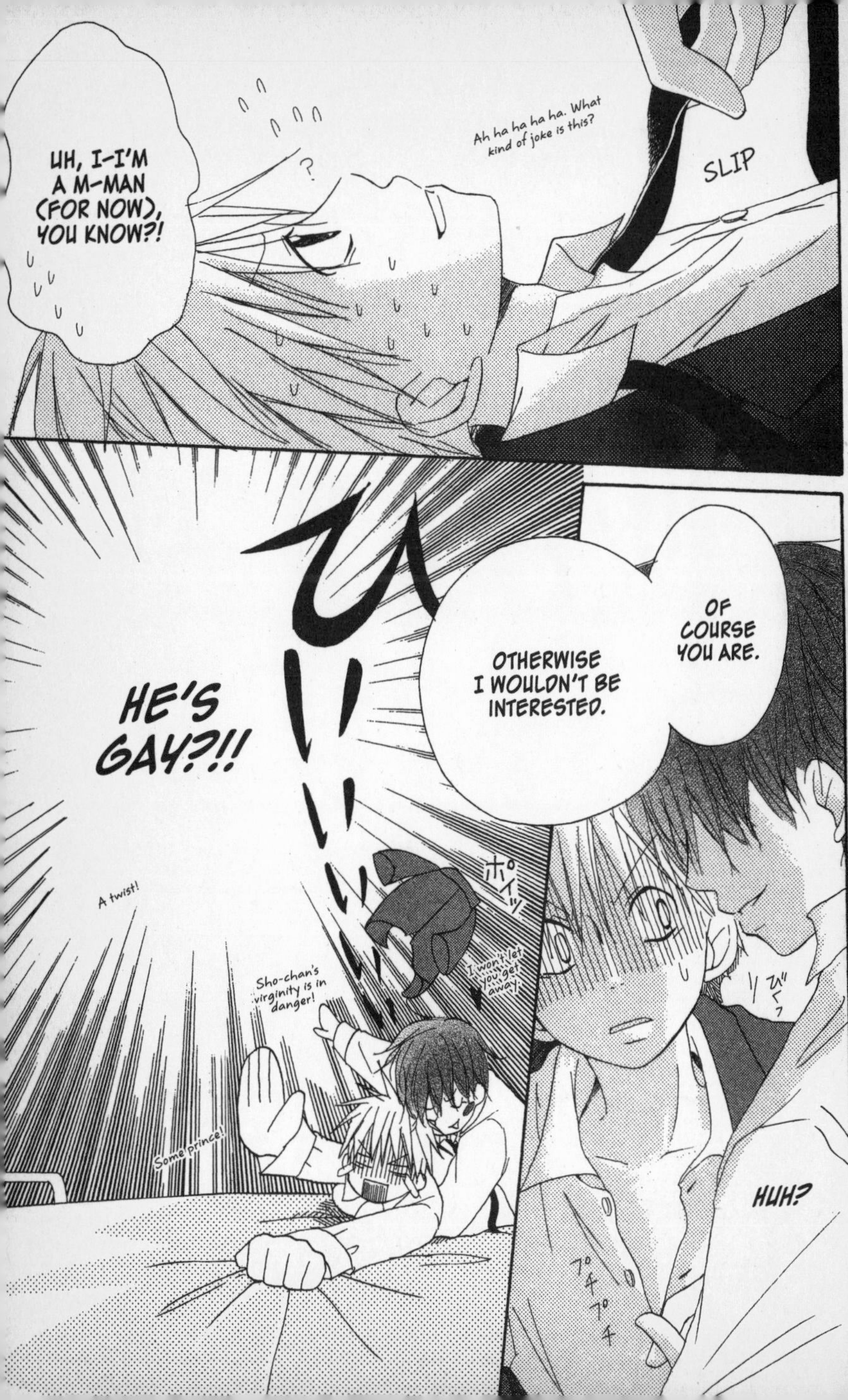
SLIP
Ah ha ha ha ha. What kind of joke is this?
UH, I-I'M A M-MAN (FOR NOW), YOU KNOW?!
OF COURSE YOU ARE.
OTHERWISE I WOULDN'T BE INTERESTED.
びくっ
HUH?
プチプチ
ポイッ
I won't let you get away.
HE'S GAY?!!
A twist!
Sho-chan's virginity is in danger!
Some prince!

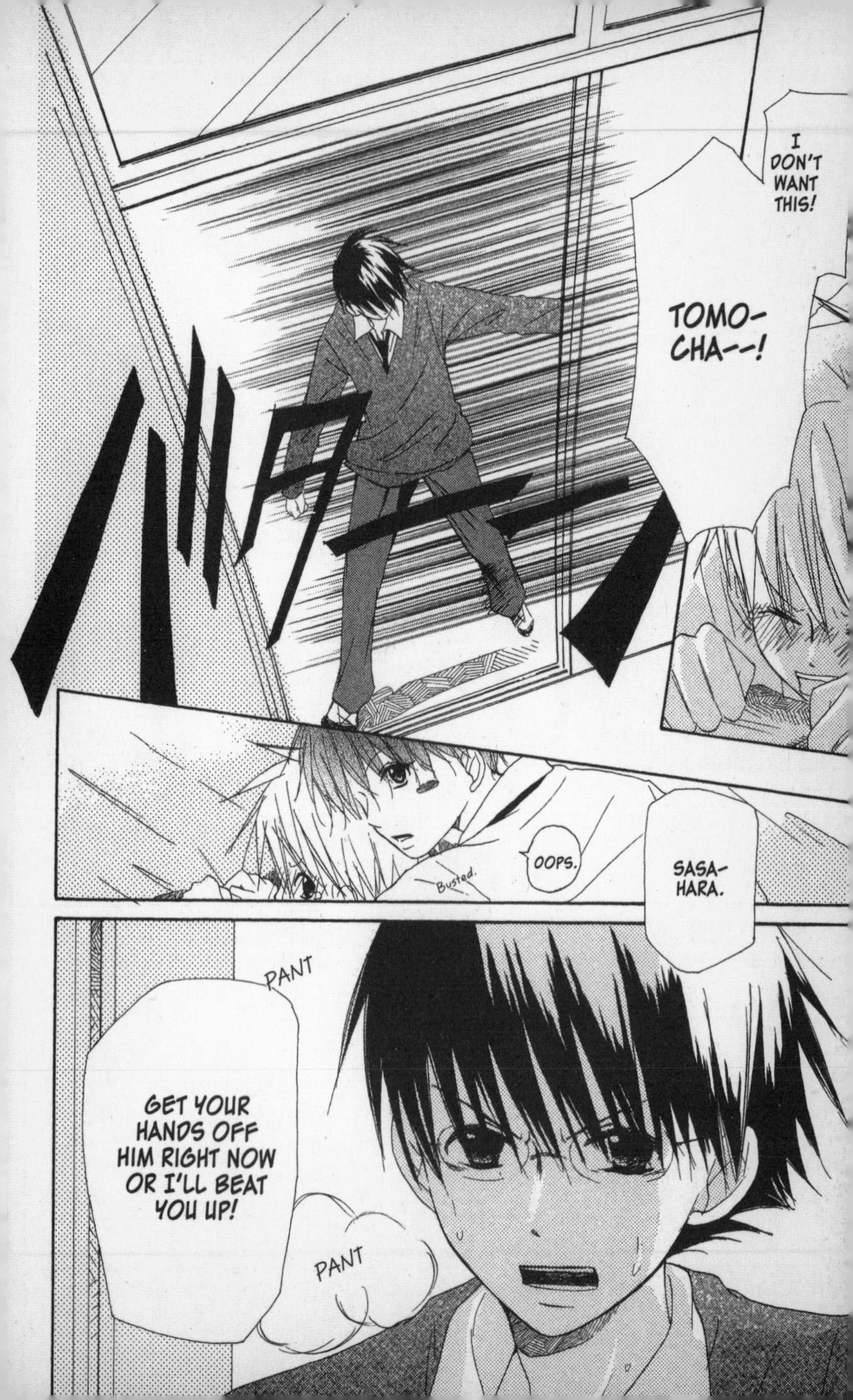
I DON'T WANT THIS!
TOMO-CHA--!
SASA-HARA.
OOPS.
Busted.
PANT
GET YOUR HANDS OFF HIM RIGHT NOW OR I'LL BEAT YOU UP!
PANT

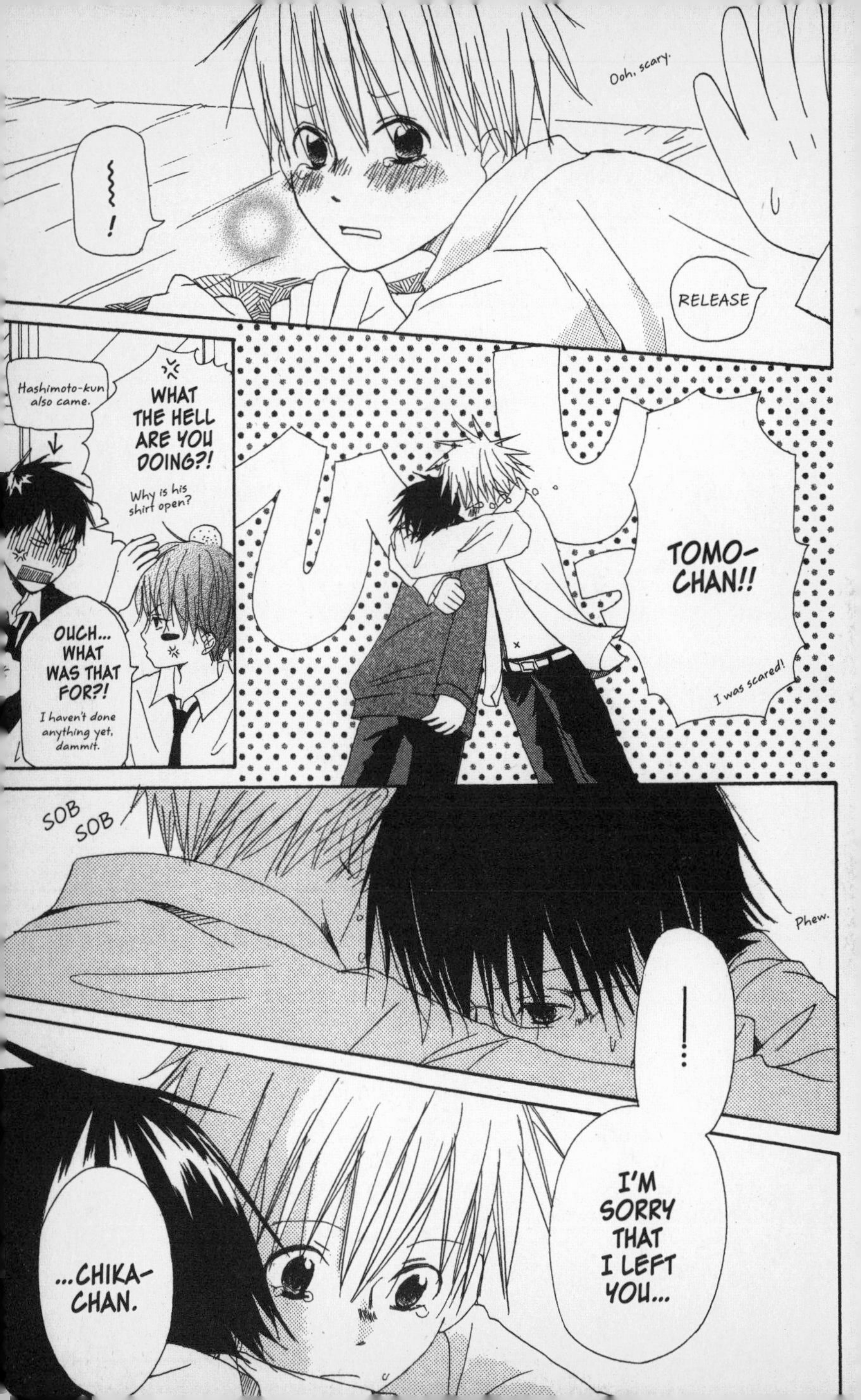
Ooh, scary.
RELEASE
~~~!
TOMO-CHAN!!
I was scared!
WHAT THE HELL ARE YOU DOING?!
Hashimoto-kun also came.
Why is his shirt open?
OUCH... WHAT WAS THAT FOR?!
I haven't done anything yet, dammit.
Phew.
SOB SOB
...!
I'M SORRY THAT I LEFT YOU...
...CHIKA-CHAN.
~~~

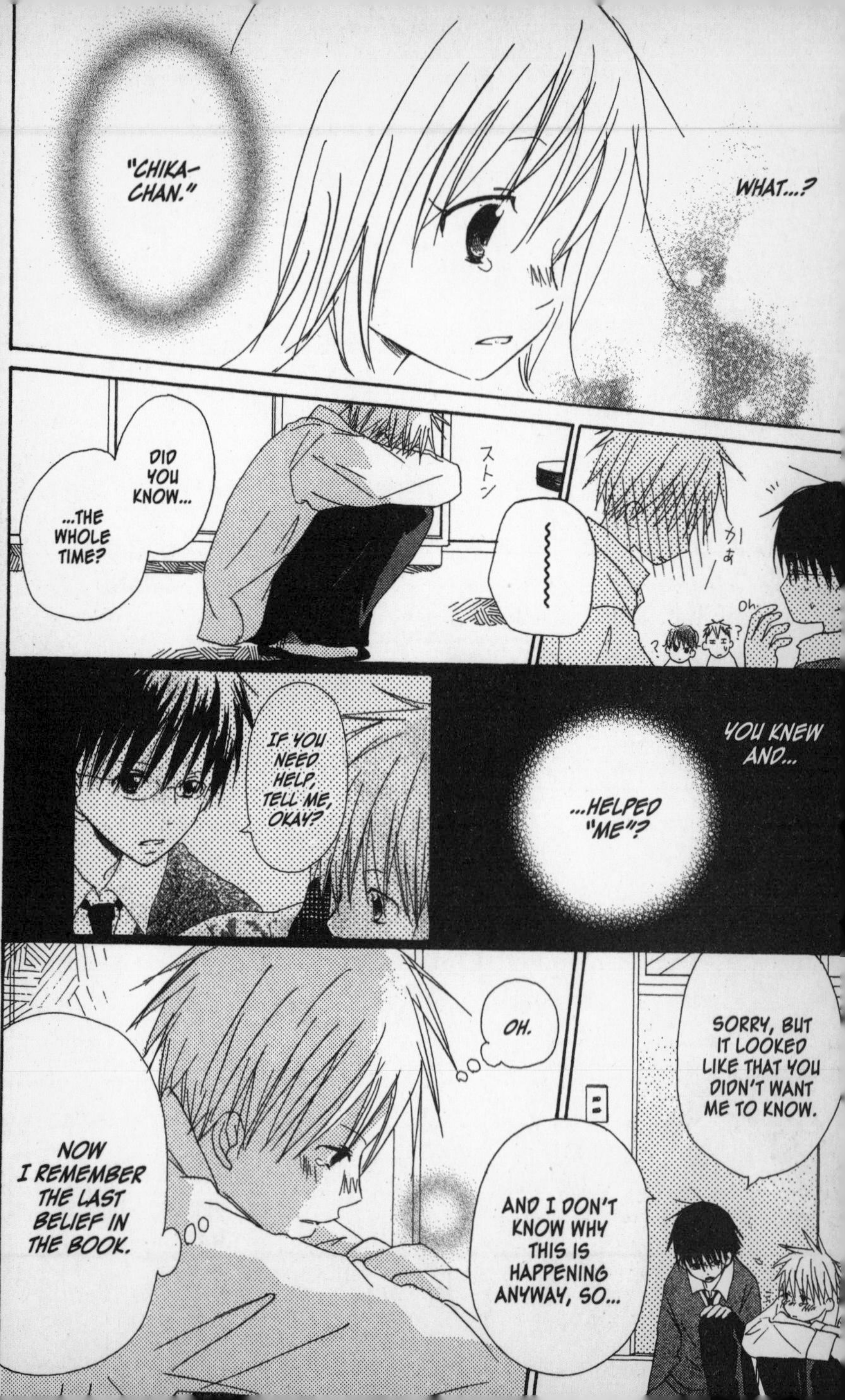
WHAT...?
"CHIKA-CHAN."
Oh.
ストン
DID YOU KNOW...
...THE WHOLE TIME?
YOU KNEW AND...
...HELPED "ME"?
IF YOU NEED HELP, TELL ME, OKAY?
SORRY, BUT IT LOOKED LIKE THAT YOU DIDN'T WANT ME TO KNOW.
AND I DON'T KNOW WHY THIS IS HAPPENING ANYWAY, SO...
OH.
NOW I REMEMBER THE LAST BELIEF IN THE BOOK.

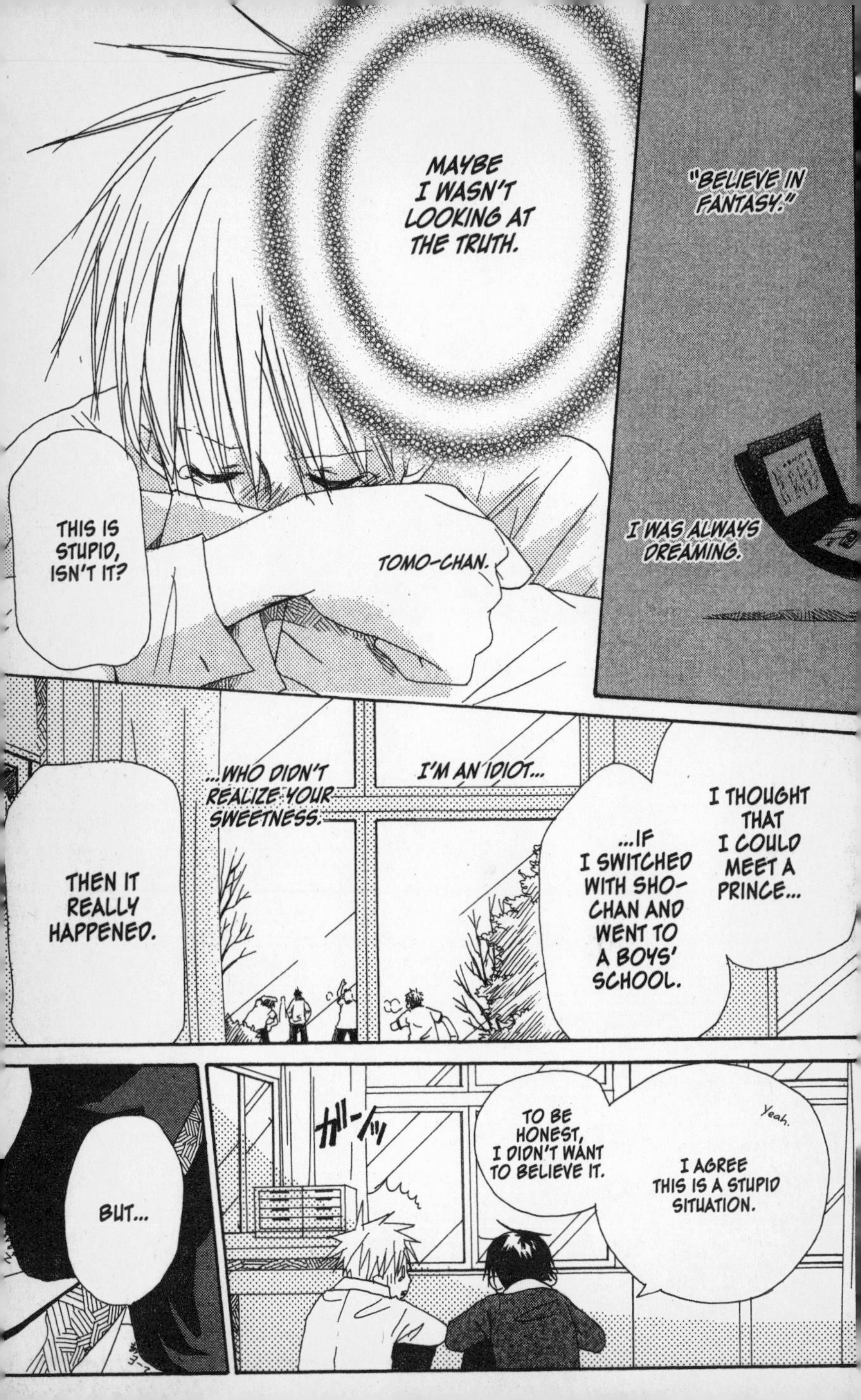
"BELIEVE IN FANTASY."
I WAS ALWAYS DREAMING.
MAYBE I WASN'T LOOKING AT THE TRUTH.
TOMO-CHAN.
THIS IS STUPID, ISN'T IT?
I THOUGHT THAT I COULD MEET A PRINCE...
...IF I SWITCHED WITH SHO-CHAN AND WENT TO A BOYS' SCHOOL.
I'M AN IDIOT...
...WHO DIDN'T REALIZE YOUR SWEETNESS.
THEN IT REALLY HAPPENED.
Yeah.
I AGREE THIS IS A STUPID SITUATION.
TO BE HONEST, I DIDN'T WANT TO BELIEVE IT.
ガーッ
BUT...

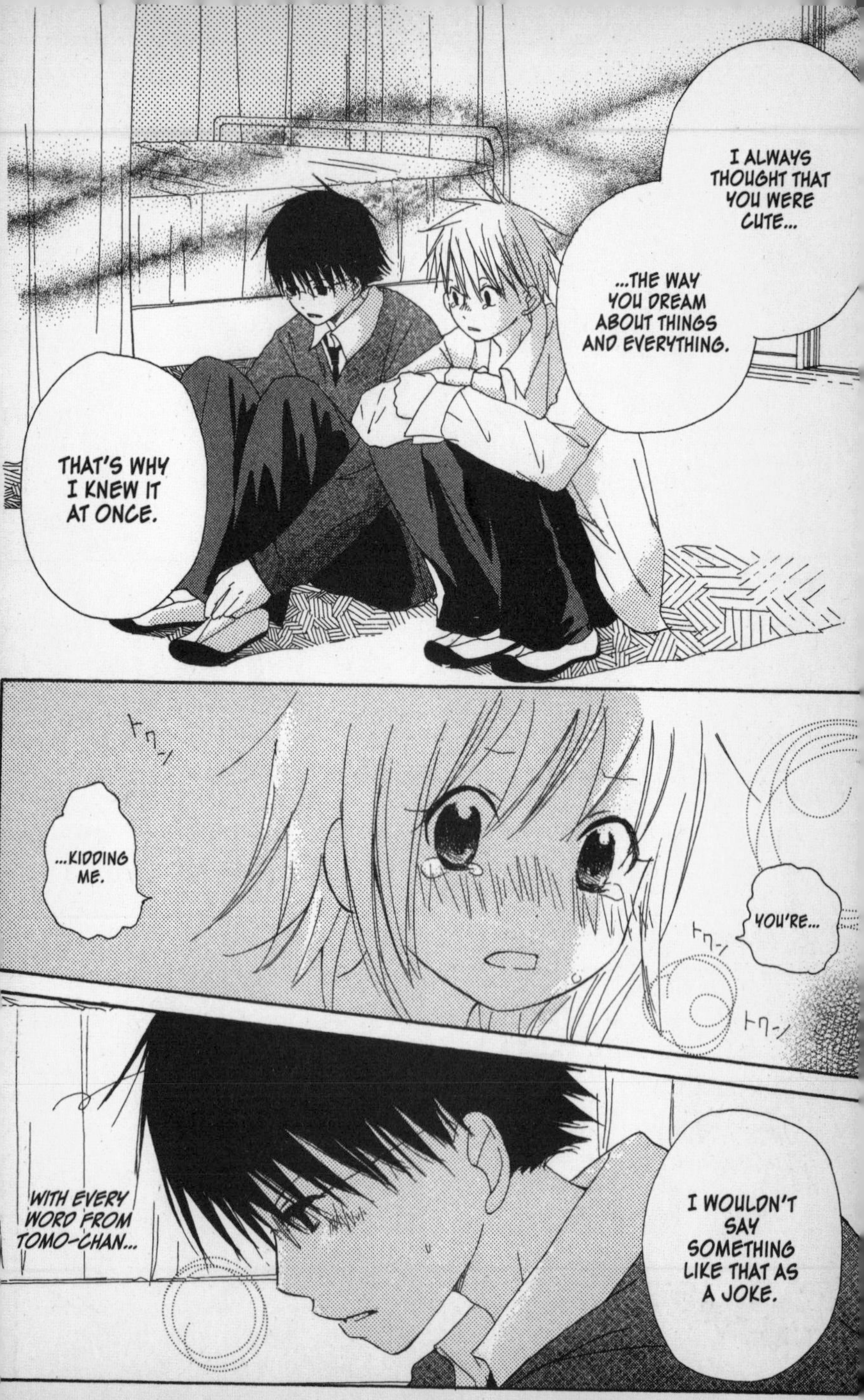
I ALWAYS THOUGHT THAT YOU WERE CUTE...
...THE WAY YOU DREAM ABOUT THINGS AND EVERYTHING.
THAT'S WHY I KNEW IT AT ONCE.
YOU'RE...
...KIDDING ME.
I WOULDN'T SAY SOMETHING LIKE THAT AS A JOKE.
WITH EVERY WORD FROM TOMO-CHAN...

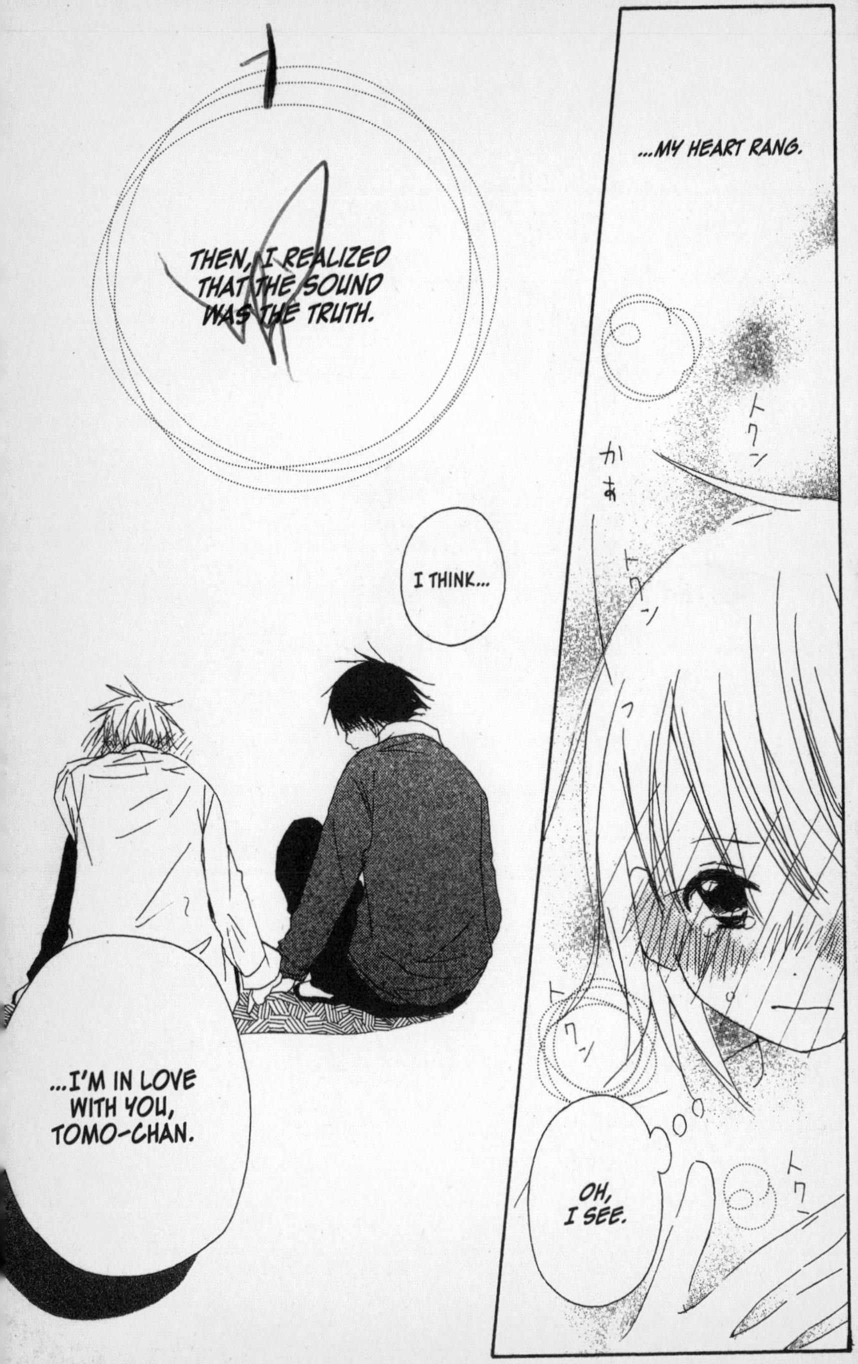
...MY HEART RANG.
トクン
かあ
トクン
トクン
OH, I SEE.
トクン
THEN, I REALIZED THAT THE SOUND WAS THE TRUTH.
I THINK...
...I'M IN LOVE WITH YOU, TOMO-CHAN.

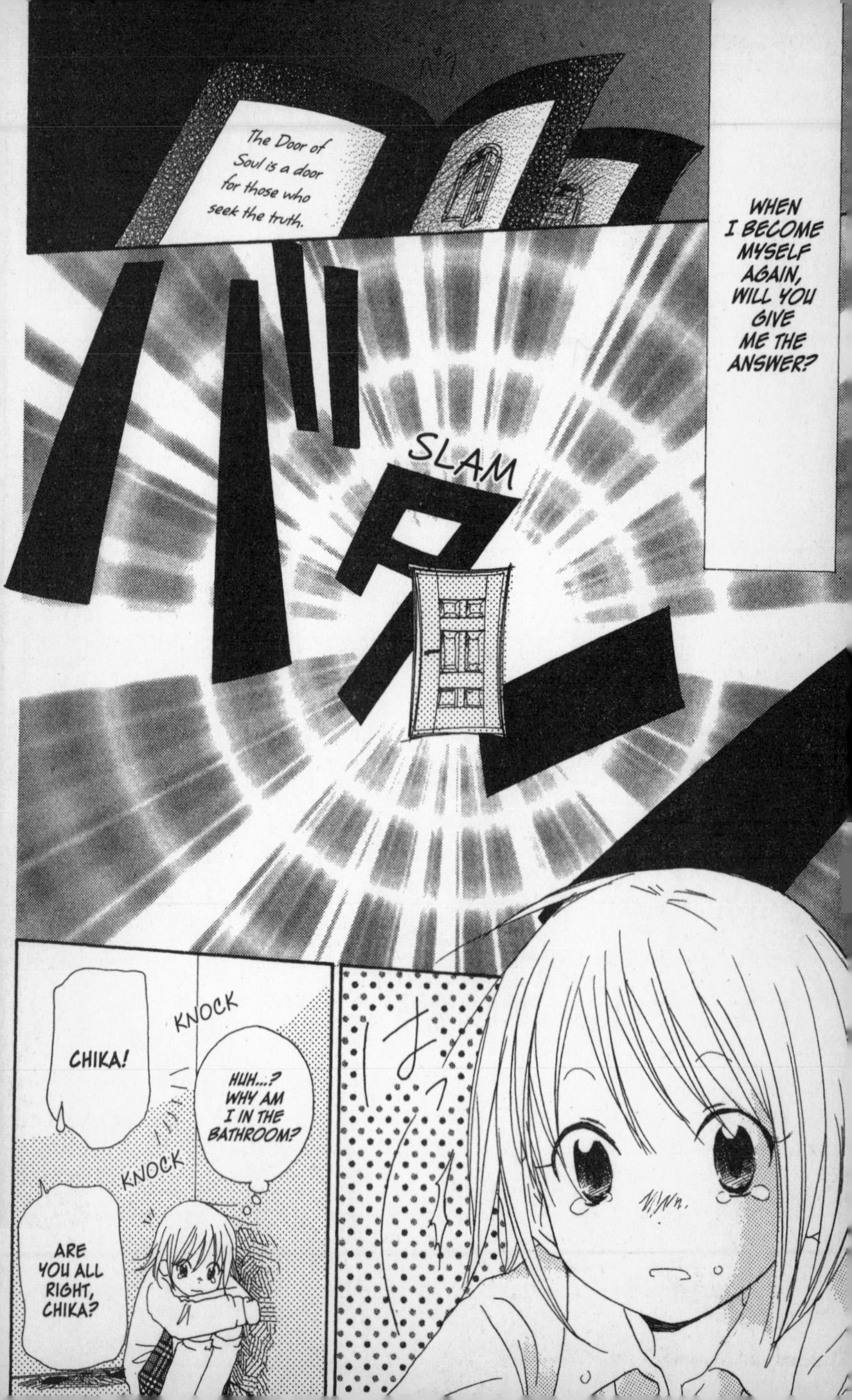
WHEN I BECOME MYSELF AGAIN, WILL YOU GIVE ME THE ANSWER?
The Door of Soul is a door for those who seek the truth.
SLAM
KNOCK
CHIKA!
HUH...? WHY AM I IN THE BATHROOM?
KNOCK
ARE YOU ALL RIGHT, CHIKA?

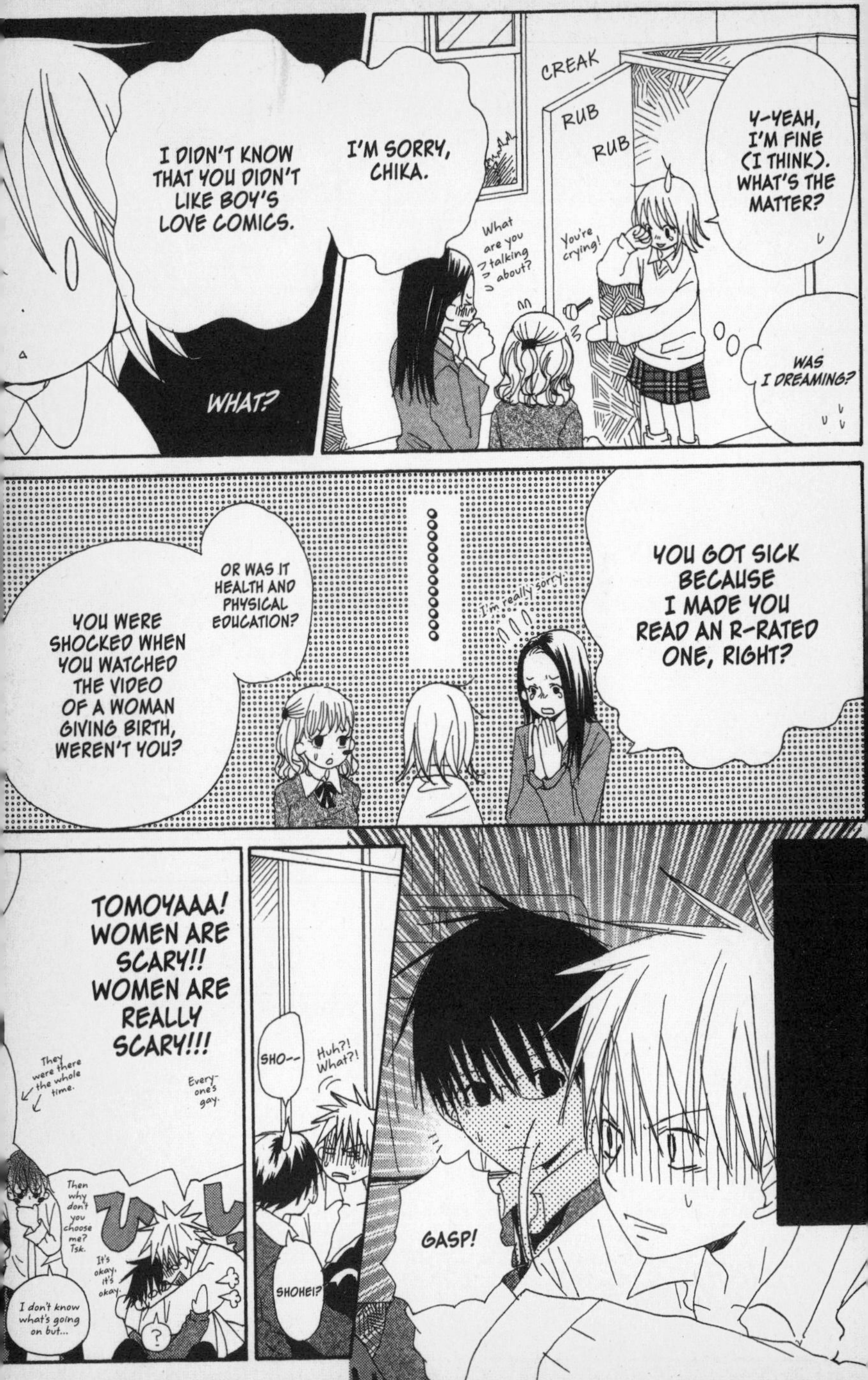
CREAK
RUB
RUB
Y-YEAH, I'M FINE (I THINK). WHAT'S THE MATTER?
You're crying!
What are you talking about?
WAS I DREAMING?
I'M SORRY, CHIKA.
I DIDN'T KNOW THAT YOU DIDN'T LIKE BOY'S LOVE COMICS.
WHAT?
YOU GOT SICK BECAUSE I MADE YOU READ AN R-RATED ONE, RIGHT?
I'm really sorry.
OR WAS IT HEALTH AND PHYSICAL EDUCATION?
YOU WERE SHOCKED WHEN YOU WATCHED THE VIDEO OF A WOMAN GIVING BIRTH, WEREN'T YOU?
GASP!
SHO--
Huh?! What?!
SHOHEI?
TOMOYAAA! WOMEN ARE SCARY!! WOMEN ARE REALLY SCARY!!!
They were there the whole time.
Every-one's gay.
Then why don't you choose me? Tsk.
It's okay, it's okay.
I don't know what's going on but...

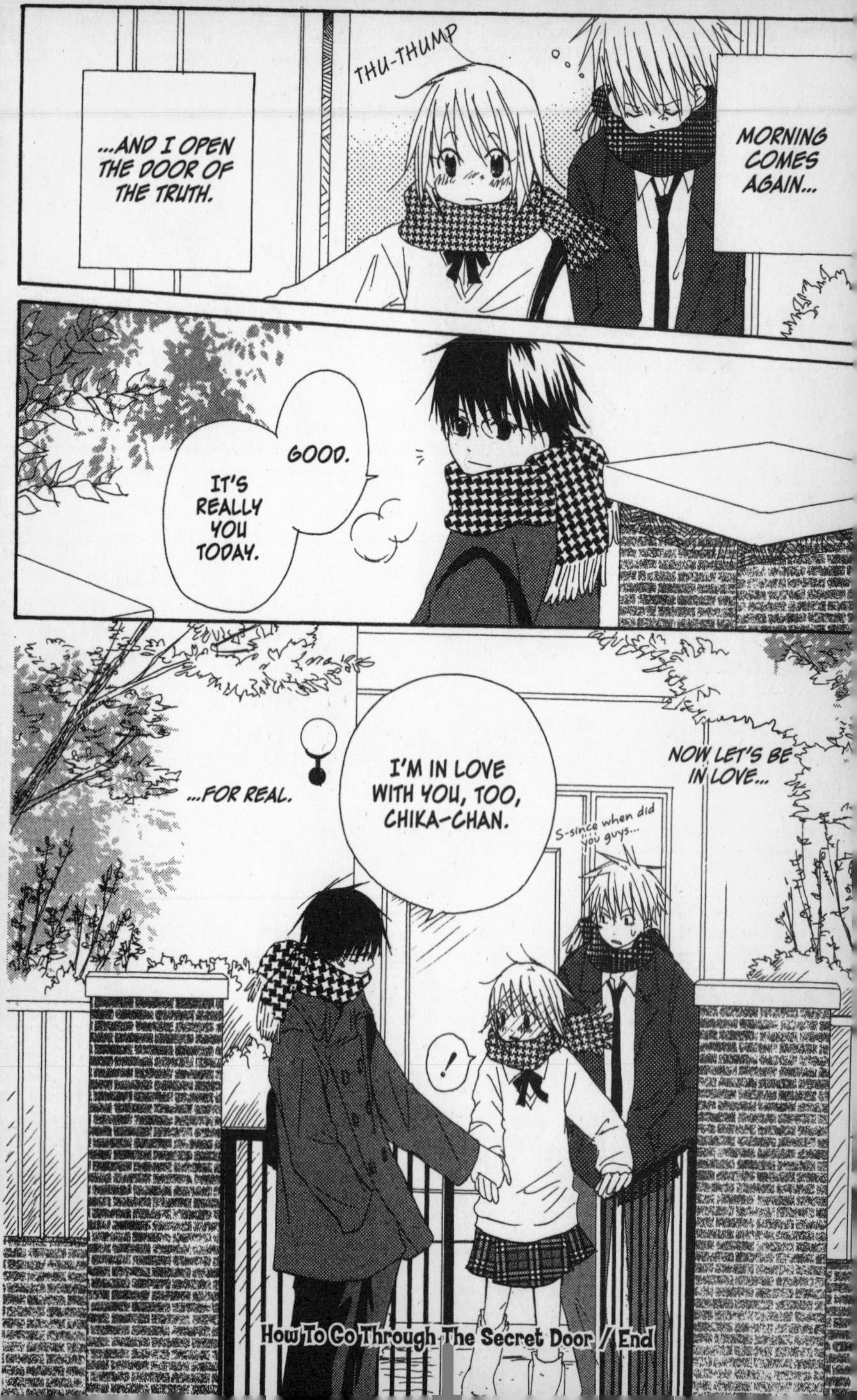
MORNING COMES AGAIN...
THU-THUMP
...AND I OPEN THE DOOR OF THE TRUTH.
GOOD.
IT'S REALLY YOU TODAY.
NOW LET'S BE IN LOVE...
S-since when did you guys...
I'M IN LOVE WITH YOU, TOO, CHIKA-CHAN.
...FOR REAL.
!
How To Go Through The Secret Door // End

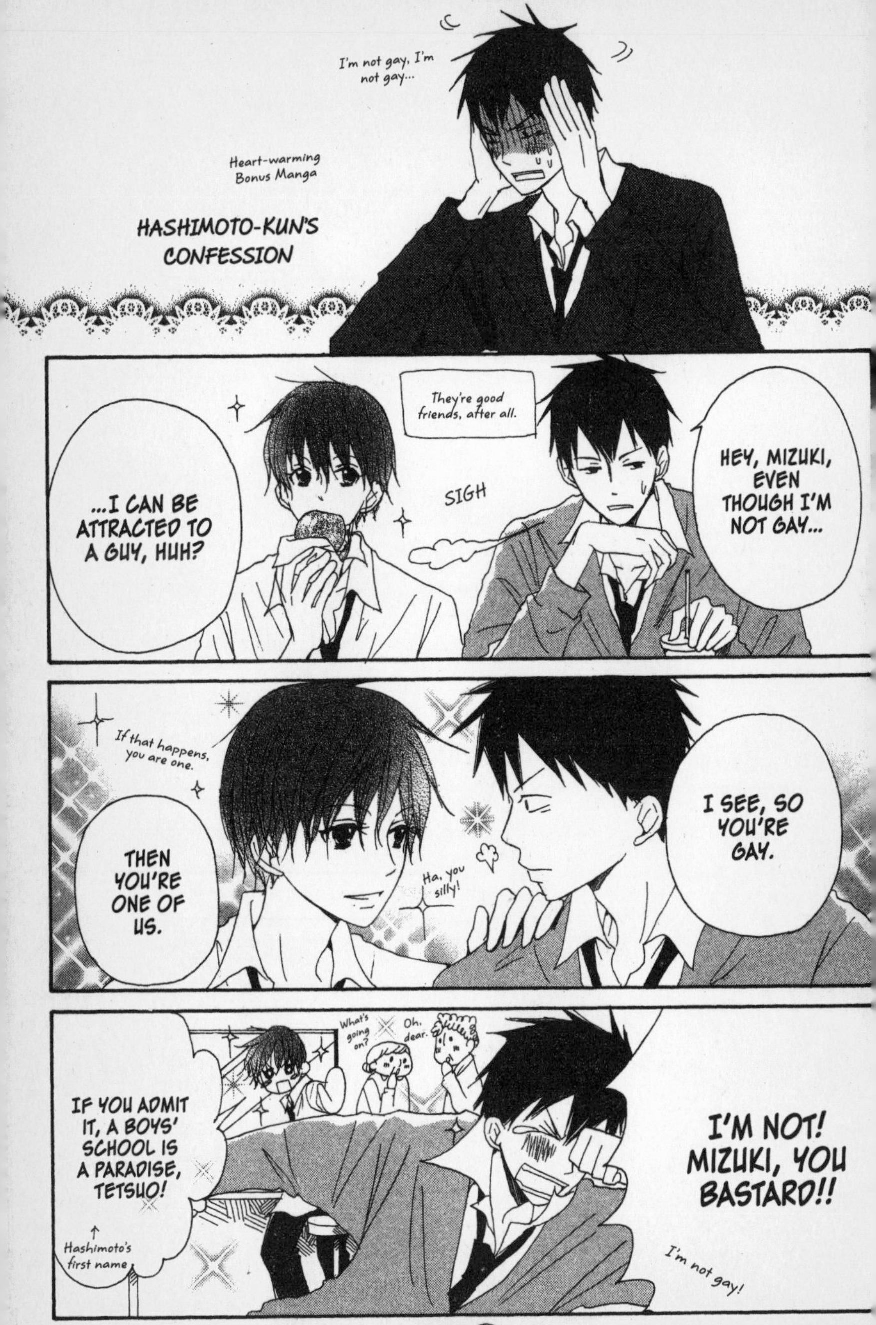
I'm not gay, I'm not gay...
Heart-warming Bonus Manga
HASHIMOTO-KUN'S CONFESSION
HEY, MIZUKI, EVEN THOUGH I'M NOT GAY...
They're good friends, after all.
SIGH
...I CAN BE ATTRACTED TO A GUY, HUH?
I SEE, SO YOU'RE GAY.
Ha, you silly!
If that happens, you are one.
THEN YOU'RE ONE OF US.
I'M NOT! MIZUKI, YOU BASTARD!!
I'm not gay!
Oh, dear.
What's going on?
IF YOU ADMIT IT, A BOYS' SCHOOL IS A PARADISE, TETSUO!
↑ Hashimoto's first name

End

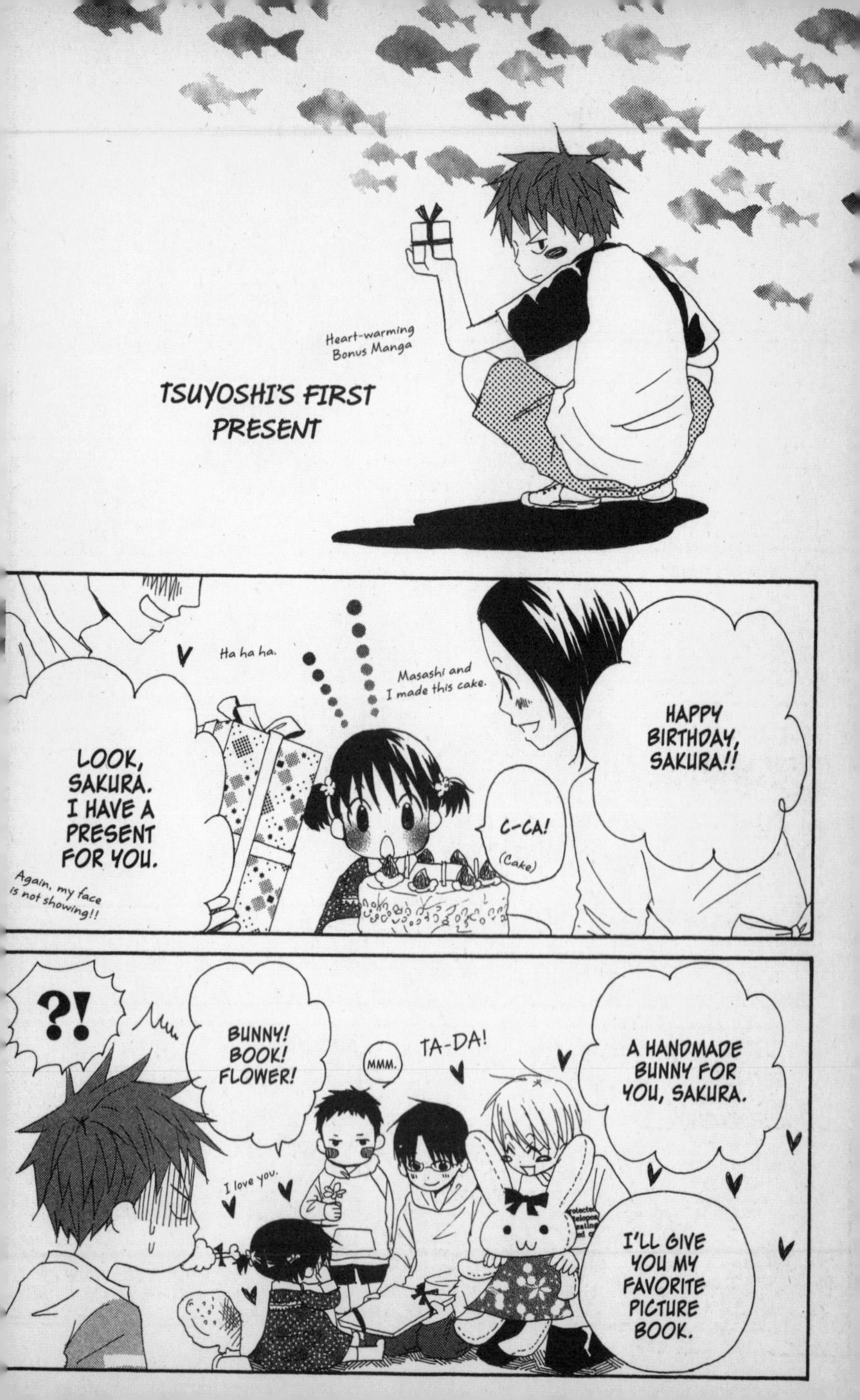
Heart-warming Bonus Manga
TSUYOSHI'S FIRST PRESENT
HAPPY BIRTHDAY, SAKURA!!
Masashi and I made this cake.
C-CA!
(Cake)
Ha ha ha.
LOOK, SAKURA. I HAVE A PRESENT FOR YOU.
Again, my face is not showing!!
A HANDMADE BUNNY FOR YOU, SAKURA.
I'LL GIVE YOU MY FAVORITE PICTURE BOOK.
TA-DA!
MMM.
BUNNY! BOOK! FLOWER!
I love you.
?!

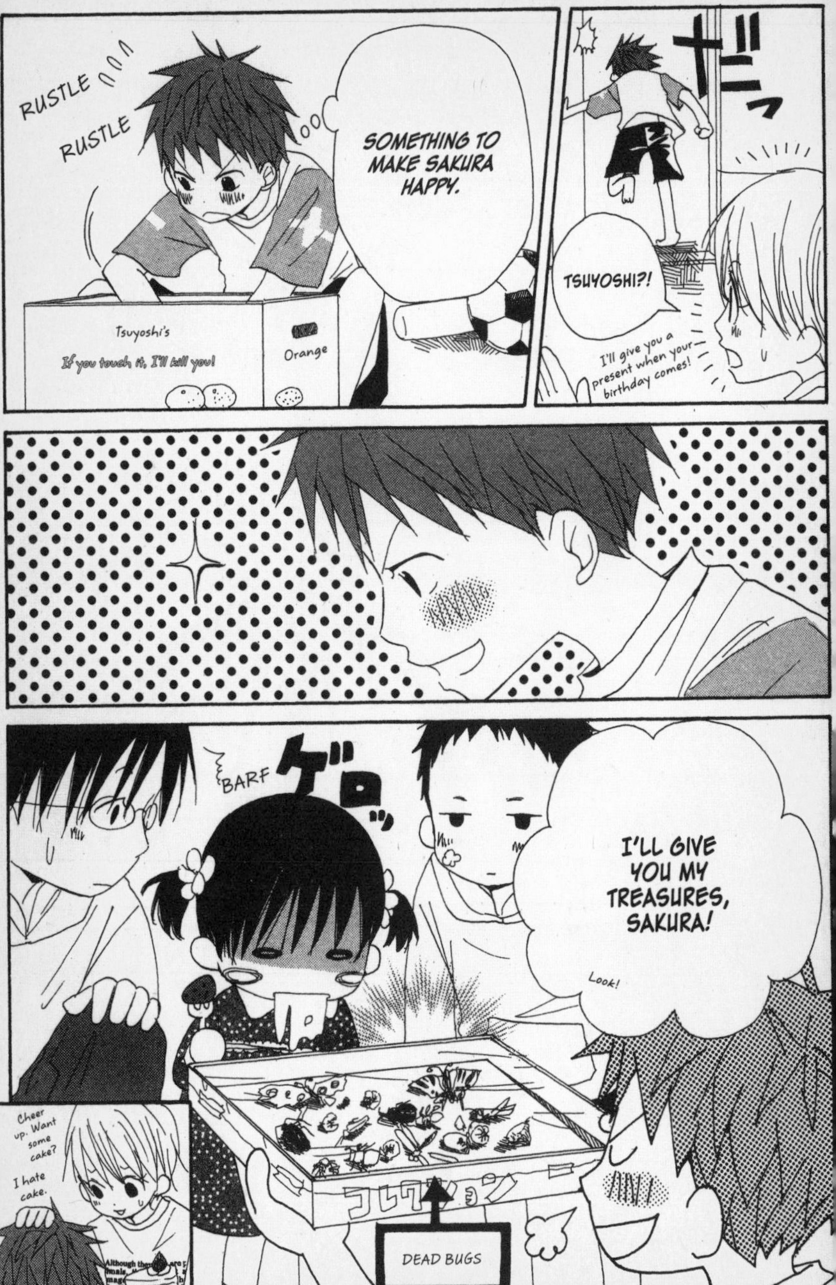
TSUYOSHI?!
I'll give you a present when your birthday comes!
RUSTLE
RUSTLE
SOMETHING TO MAKE SAKURA HAPPY.
Tsuyoshi's
If you touch it, I'll kill you!
Orange
I'LL GIVE YOU MY TREASURES, SAKURA!
Look!
BARF
DEAD BUGS
Cheer up. Want some cake?
I hate cake.

End ⑬

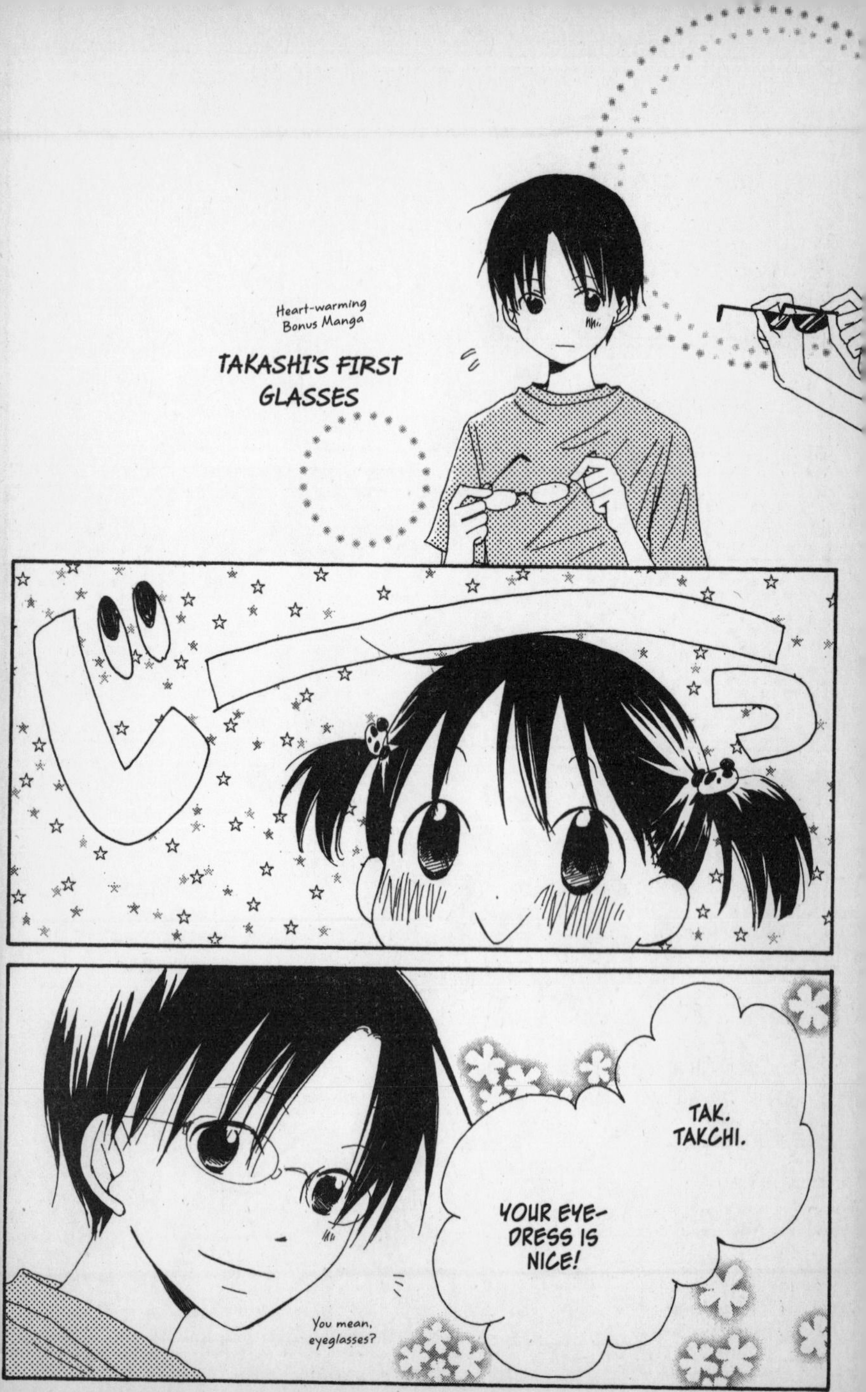
Heart-warming
Bonus Manga
TAKASHI'S FIRST
GLASSES
じーっ
TAK.
TAKCHI.
YOUR EYE-
DRESS IS
NICE!
You mean,
eyeglasses?

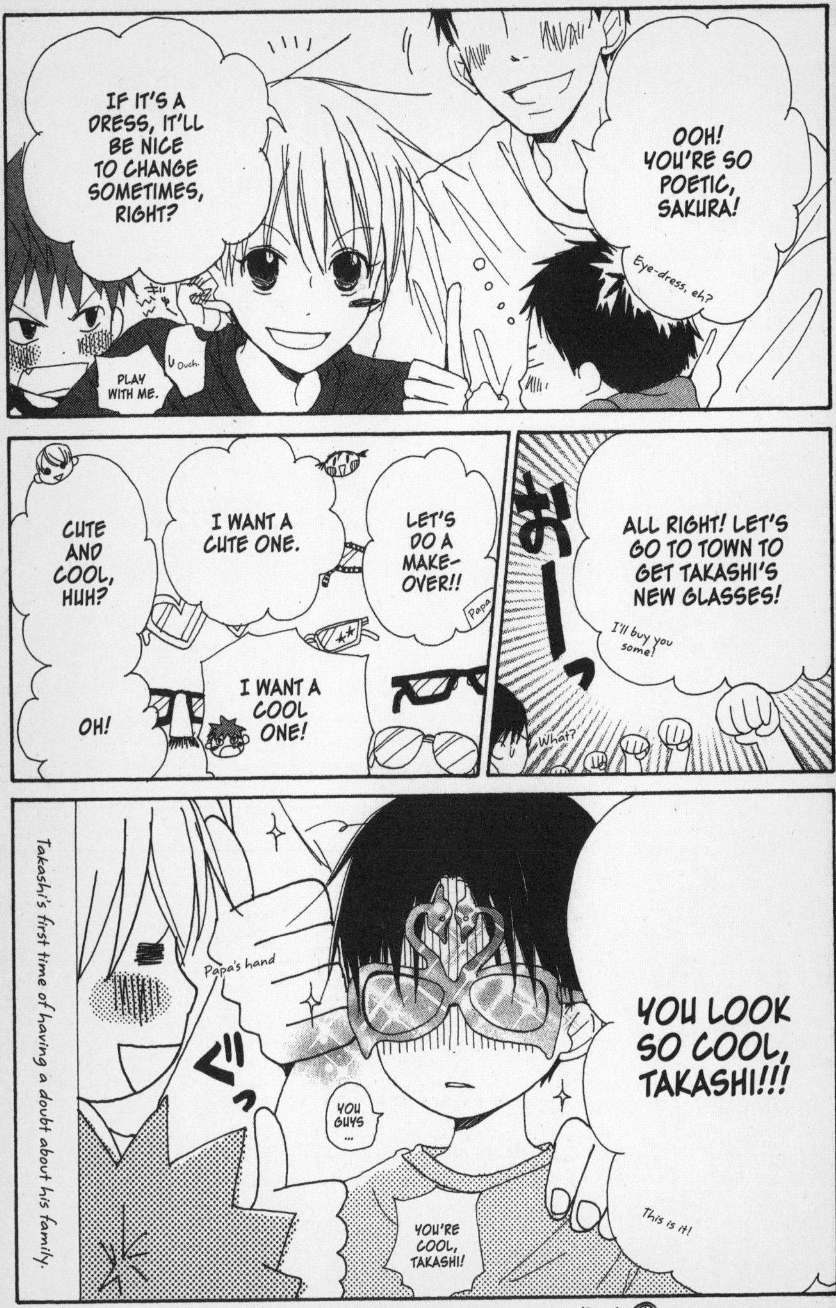
IF IT'S A DRESS, IT'LL BE NICE TO CHANGE SOMETIMES, RIGHT?
OOH! YOU'RE SO POETIC, SAKURA!
Eye-dress, eh?
Ouch.
PLAY WITH ME.
ALL RIGHT! LET'S GO TO TOWN TO GET TAKASHI'S NEW GLASSES!
I'll buy you some!
おーっ
What?
LET'S DO A MAKE-OVER!!
Papa
I WANT A CUTE ONE.
CUTE AND COOL, HUH?
I WANT A COOL ONE!
OH!
YOU LOOK SO COOL, TAKASHI!!!
This is it!
YOU GUYS ...
YOU'RE COOL, TAKASHI!
Papa's hand
ぐっ
Takashi's first time of having a doubt about his family.

The author has these glasses. End

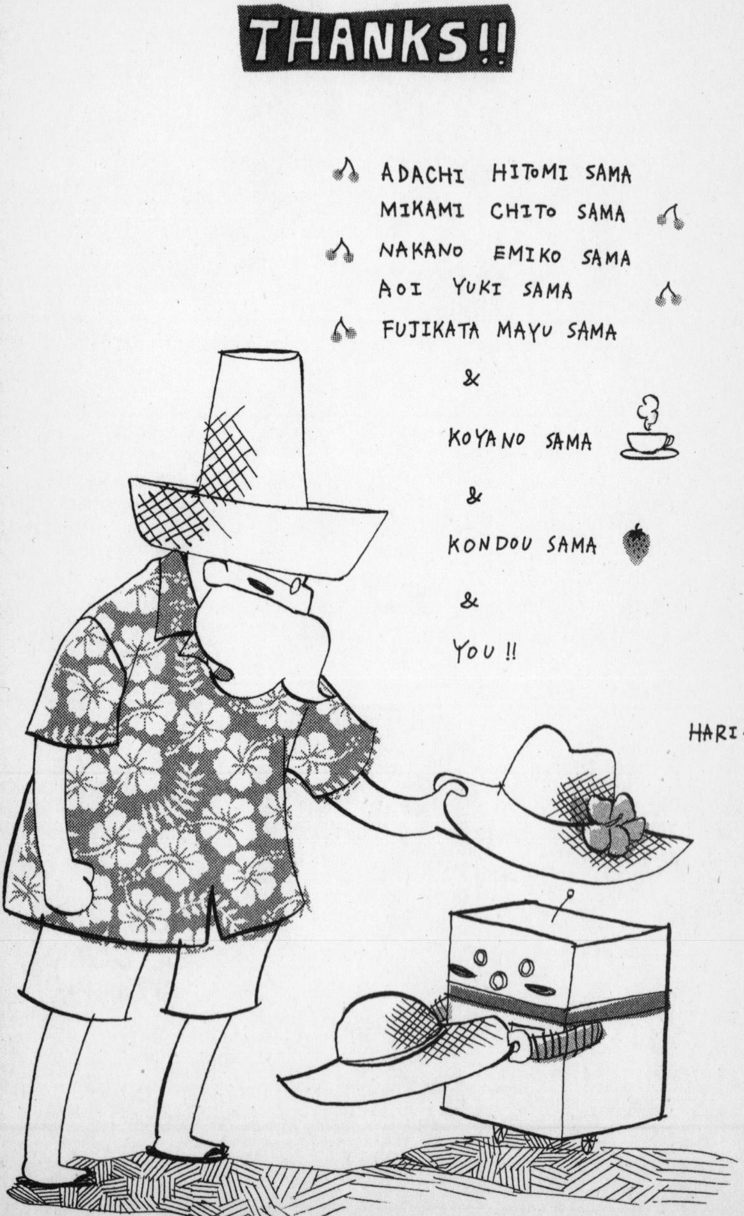
THANKS!!
ADACHI HITOMI SAMA
MIKAMI CHITO SAMA
NAKANO EMIKO SAMA
AOI YUKI SAMA
FUJIKATA MAYU SAMA
&
KOYANO SAMA
&
KONDOU SAMA
&
YOU!!
HARI·

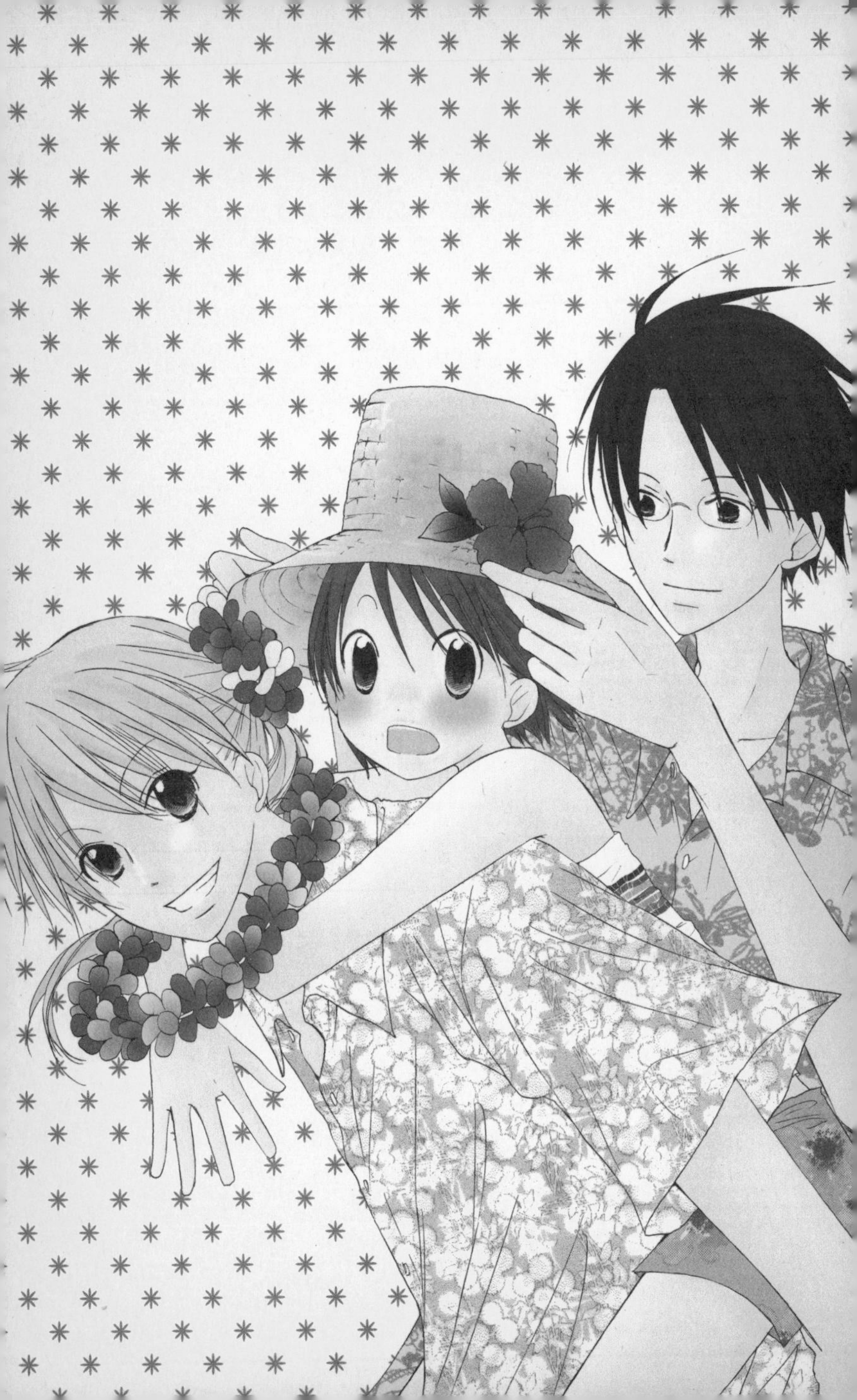

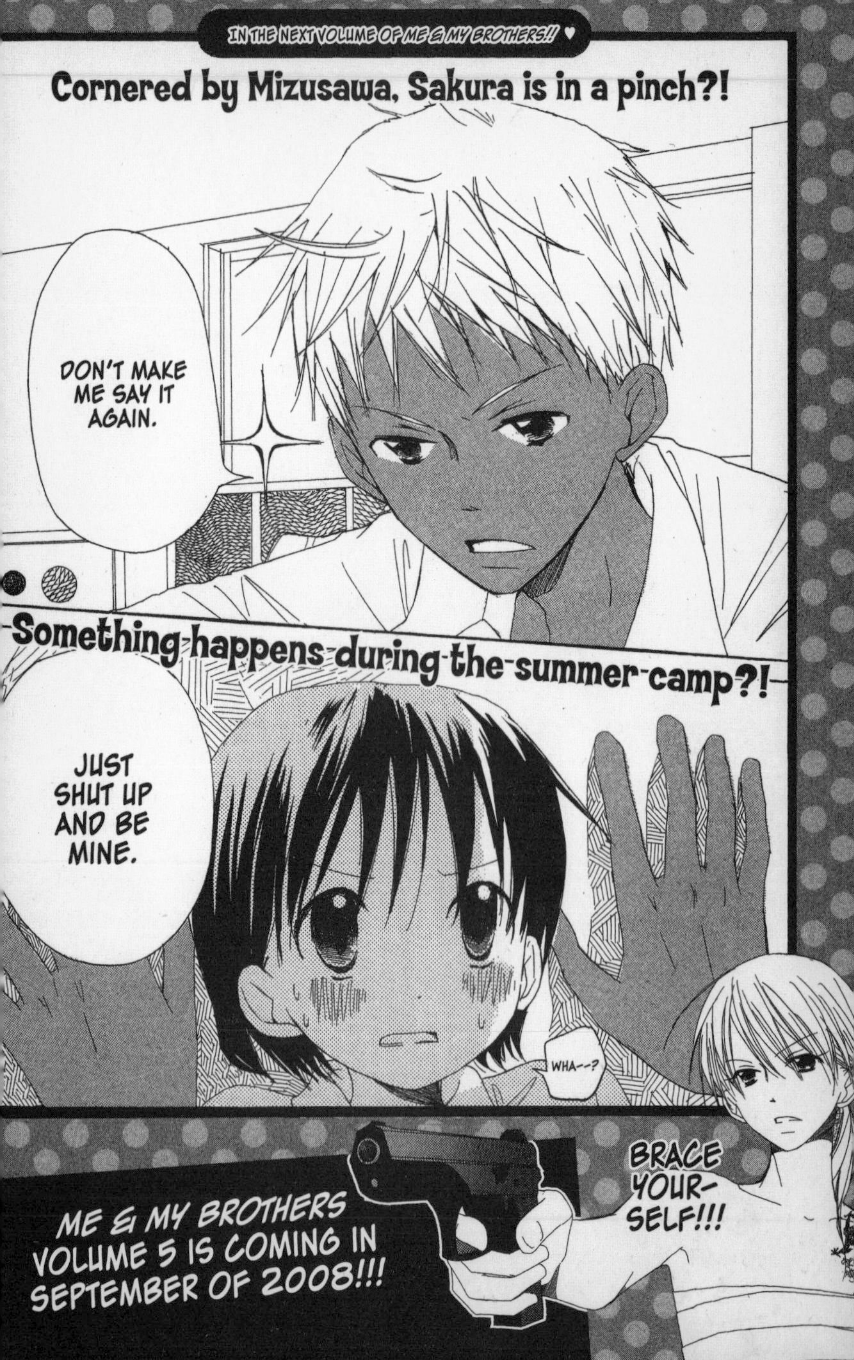
IN THE NEXT VOLUME OF ME & MY BROTHERS!! ♥
Cornered by Mizusawa, Sakura is in a pinch?!
DON'T MAKE ME SAY IT AGAIN.
Something happens during the summer camp?!
JUST SHUT UP AND BE MINE.
WHA--?
BRACE YOUR-SELF!!!
ME & MY BROTHERS VOLUME 5 IS COMING IN SEPTEMBER OF 2008!!!

1
One
2
two
three
3
4
four
5

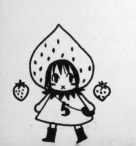

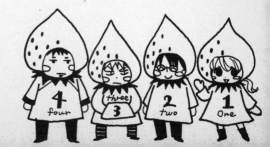

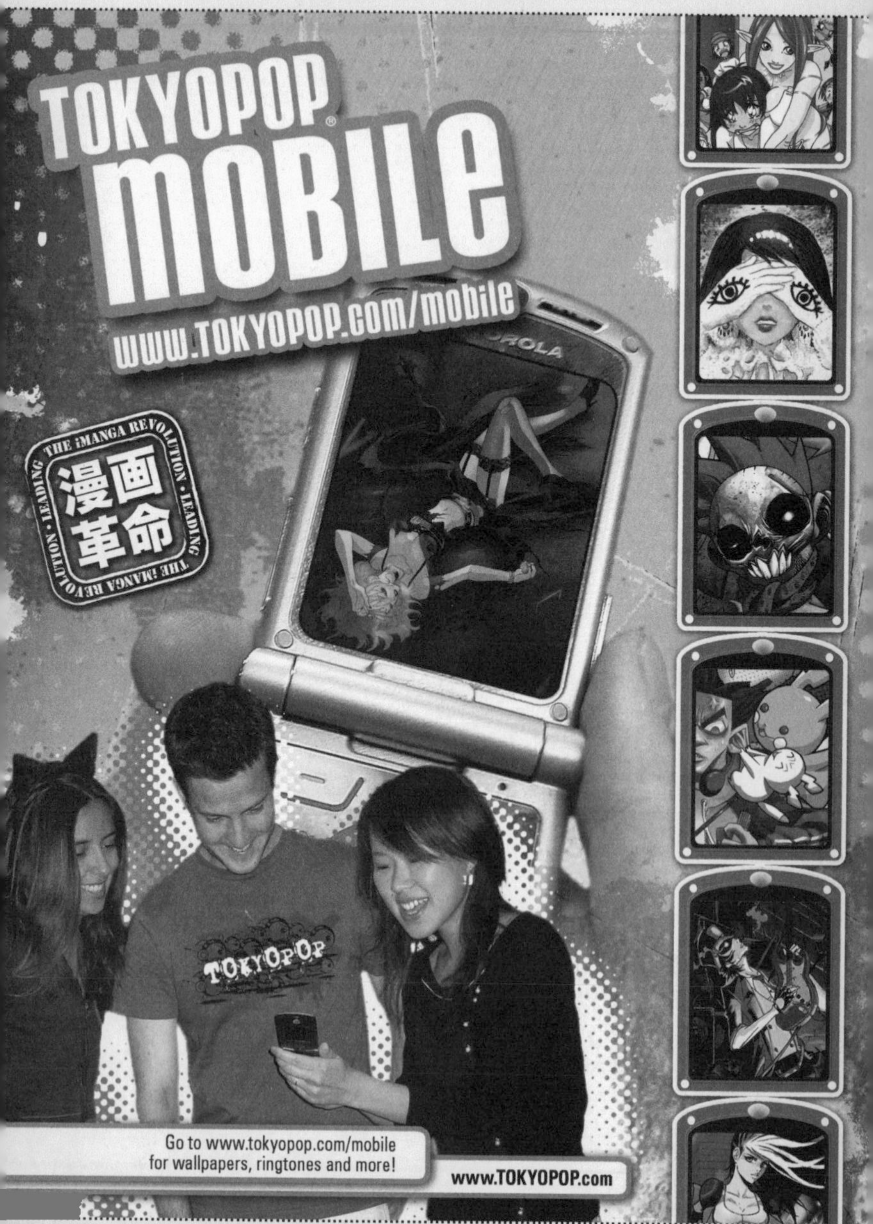
TOKYOPOP®
MOBILE
www.TOKYOPOP.com/mobile
THE iMANGA REVOLUTION · LEADING · THE iMANGA REVOLUTION · LEADING
漫画革命
TOKYOPOP
Go to www.tokyopop.com/mobile
for wallpapers, ringtones and more!
www.TOKYOPOP.com

Fruits Basket™

By Natsuki Takaya

Volume 20

Can Tohru deal with the truth?

After running away from his feelings and everyone he knows, Kyo is back with the truth about his role in the death of Tohru's mother. But how will he react when Tohru says that she still loves him?

Winner of the American Anime Award for Best Manga!

The #1 selling shojo manga in America!

© 1998 Natsuki Takaya / HAKUSENSHA, Inc.

BIZENGHAST

BY M. ALICE LEGROW, NOVEL BY SHAWN THORGERSEN

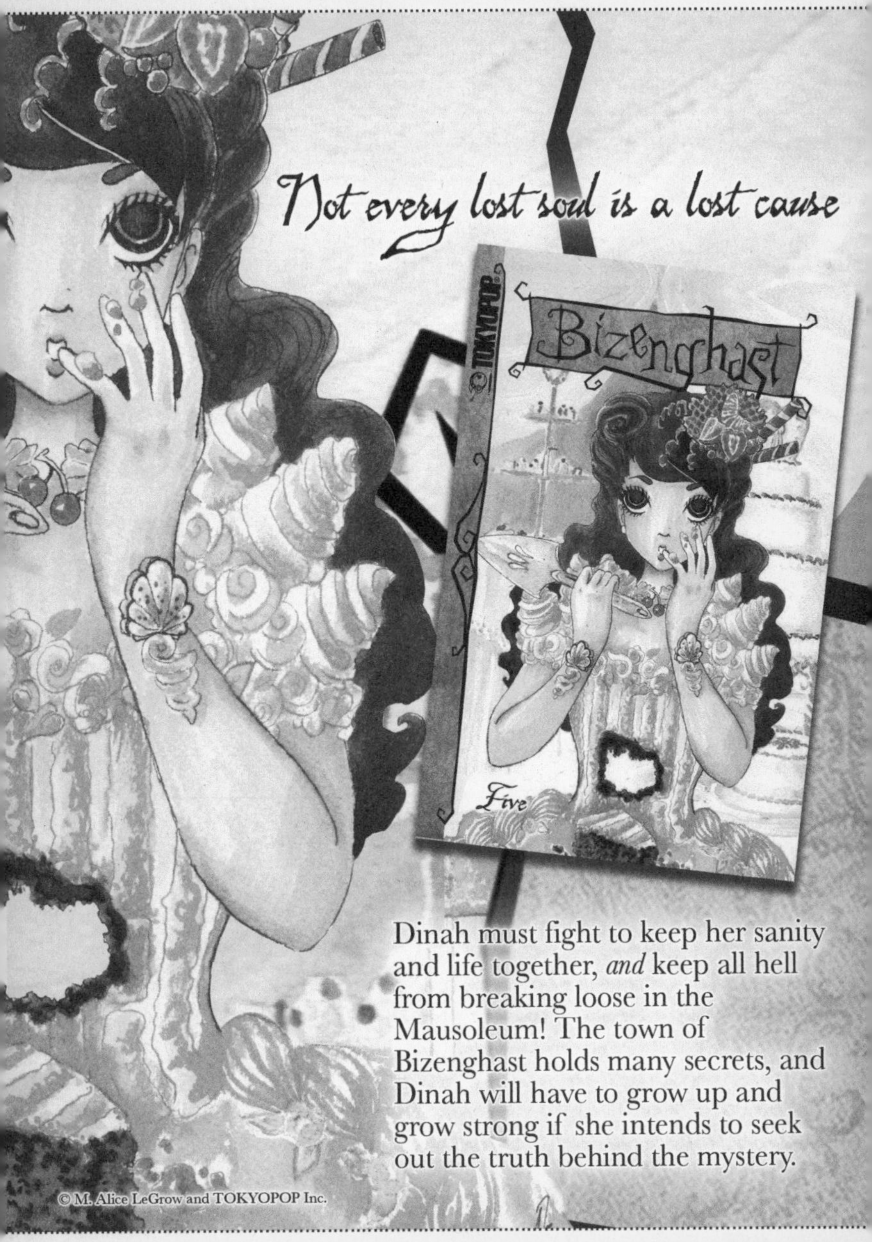
Not every lost soul is a lost cause
TOKYOPOP
Bizenghast
Five
Dinah must fight to keep her sanity and life together, *and* keep all hell from breaking loose in the Mausoleum! The town of Bizenghast holds many secrets, and Dinah will have to grow up and grow strong if she intends to seek out the truth behind the mystery.
© M. Alice LeGrow and TOKYOPOP Inc.

FOR MORE INFORMATION VISIT:

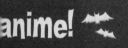

CHIBI VAMPIRE
MANGA BY YUNA KAGESAKI, NOVEL BY TOHRU KAI AND YUNA KAGESAKI

The HILARIOUS adventures of

chibi Vampire™
TOKYOPOP
9
Created By:
Yuna Kagesaki

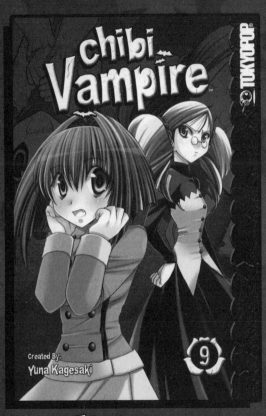

As Karin and Kenta's official first date continues, Anju shows up to keep an eye on the clumsy couple. When Kenta tells Karin how he really feels, will it destroy their relationship? Also, the new girl in town, Yuriya, begins snooping around in search of vampires. Why is she trying to uncover Karin's identity, and what secrets of her own is she hiding?

chibi Vampire™ Inspired the

FOR MORE INFORMATION VISIT:

STOP!

This is the back of the book.
You wouldn't want to spoil a great ending!

This book is printed "manga-style," in the authentic Japanese right-to-left format. Since none of the artwork has been flipped or altered, readers get to experience the story just as the creator intended. You've been asking for it, so TOKYOPOP® delivered: authentic, hot-off-the-press, and far more fun!

DIRECTIONS

If this is your first time reading manga-style, here's a quick guide to help you understand how it works.

It's easy... just start in the top right panel and follow the numbers. Have fun, and look for more 100% authentic manga from TOKYOPOP®!

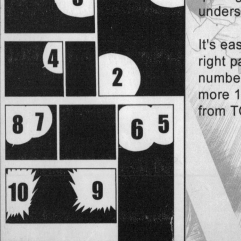